Gallery of Best Cover Letters

A Collection of Quality Cover Letters by Professional Resume Writers

Fourth Edition

David F. Noble, Ph.D.

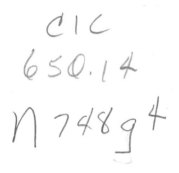

jist Works
America's Career Publisher

Dedication: *In memory of my mother, Christena Brightwell Noble, the letter writer*

Gallery of Best Cover Letters, Fourth Edition
A Collection of Quality Cover Letters by Professional Resume Writers
© 2012 by David F. Noble

Published by JIST Works, an imprint of JIST Publishing
875 Montreal Way
St. Paul, MN 55102
E-mail: info@jist.com

Visit our website at **www.jist.com** for information on JIST, free job search tips, tables of contents, sample pages, and ordering instructions for our many products!

Acquisitions/Development Editor: Heather Stith
Copy Editor: Lori Ryan
Production Editor: Jeanne Clark
Senior Design and Production Specialist: Ryan Hamner
Cover Designer: Alan Evans
Proofreader: Linda Seifert
Indexer: Ginny Noble

Printed in the United States of America
17 16 15 14 13 12   9 8 7 6 5 4 3 2 1

Library of Congress Cataloging-in-Publication data is on file with the Library of Congress.

ISBN 978-1-59357-917-3

Contents

Part 3: Best Resume Tips 351

Best Resume Tips at a Glance................ 352

List of Contributors 385

Occupation Index 393

Introduction

Gallery of Best Cover Letters is a collection of quality cover letters from professional resume writers, each with individual views about cover letter writing. Unlike many cover letter books whose selections "look the same," this book contains cover letters that look different because they are *real* cover letters prepared by different professionals for actual job searchers throughout the country. (Certain information in the cover letters and companion resumes has been fictionalized by the writers to protect, where necessary, each client's privacy.) Even when several cover letters from the same writer appear in the book, most of these letters are different because the writer has customized each letter according to the background information and career goals of the client for whom the related resume was prepared.

In this fourth edition, 111 of the 317 letters are new to give you some of the latest examples of cover letters for contemporary job seekers. If you want to know what kinds of cover letters are helping job searchers find positions in today's job market under current economic conditions, this new edition will give you answers. A number of the captions at the bottom of each cover letter page indicate how a particular applicant was successful in focusing a job search, securing an interview, or eventually getting the targeted job.

Why a Gallery of Best Cover Letters?

One reason is that error-free cover letters are more difficult to write than most people imagine. When you put together a resume, you can work with just phrases, clauses, and lists. The common writing dangers are misspellings, errors with capital letters, wordy phrases, and faulty parallelism (for example, not having certain words in a series or list grammatically parallel). When you write a cover letter, however, you are somewhat obligated to write sentences that hang together in several paragraphs in a meaningful sequence. To write sentences and paragraphs is to enter a minefield of all of the potential errors and stylistic weaknesses that an individual with good communication skills can make. And many people who try to write a cover letter do make such errors.

This *Gallery of Best Cover Letters* shows you, example by example, how to create cover letters that are free of errors and writing weaknesses that could ruin your chances for an interview. By studying the sentences and paragraphs in these letters, you can compare your writing with what you see and find new ways to express what you want to say to win that interview.

Another reason for having a *Gallery of Best Cover Letters* is that many of the cover letters in cover letter books are—there's no other way to say it truthfully—models of bad writing. Often they exhibit not just a stylistic weakness here and there, but grammatical errors that would sabotage your job search if you used those passages verbatim in your own cover letters. To browse through the letters in this book is to walk through a minefield free of mines.

Why Cover Letters by Professional Resume Writers?

Instead of assuming that "one cover letter style fits all," the writers featured in this book believe that a client's past experiences and next job target should determine the type, design, and content of each resume and its related cover letter. The writers interacted with clients to fashion resumes that seemed best for each client's situation at the time and to create one or more cover letters for the job(s) the clients were seeking.

This book features resumes from writers who share several important qualities: good listening skills, a sense of what details are appropriate for a particular resume and its cover letter, and flexibility in selecting and arranging the resume's sections and the cover letter's paragraphs. By "hearing between" a client's statements, the perceptive resume writer can detect what kind of job the client really wants. The writer then chooses the information that will best represent the client for the job being sought. Finally, the writer decides on the best arrangement of the information for that job. With this book, you can learn from these professional writers how to shape and improve your own job search documents. You can create such documents yourself, or, if you want, you can contact a professional writer who, for a fee, might create a custom resume and cover letter for you. See the Appendix, "List of Contributors," for contact information for the professional writers whose works are featured in this book.

Almost all of the writers of the cover letters in this book are members of one or more of three organizations: Career Directors International (CDI), the National Résumé Writers' Association (NRWA), and the Professional Association of Résumé Writers & Career Coaches (PARW/CC). Most of the writers are certified. For example, those who have CPRW certification, for Certified Professional Résumé Writer (again, see the Appendix), received this designation from PARW/CC after they studied specified course materials and demonstrated proficiency in an examination. Those who have NCRW certification, for Nationally Certified Résumé Writer, received this designation from NRWA after a different course of study and a different examination. A few contributors are not currently members of any organization but are past members of one or more professional organizations.

How This Book Is Organized

Part 1, "Best Cover Letter Tips," contains a discussion of some myths about cover letters, plus strategies for writing cover letters and tips for polishing them. Some of the advice offered here applies also to writing resumes.

Part 2 is the Gallery itself, containing 317 cover letters, which are grouped according to 38 occupational categories or levels (for these, see the Table of Contents). Note that the occupational title is usually, but not always, that of the target position the applicant is seeking, not the applicant's current or recent title. In resumes, job titles have to do with the individual's present and past positions. Cover letters, however, are concerned with a target position. You should keep this fundamental difference in mind as you use this book. (If the target position is not stated clearly in a cover letter, the applicant's current or most recent job is used to determine the occupational category of that letter.)

Even though most of the cover letters were written with a target position in mind, you can learn much by reading any or all of them. That is, to get the most from this book about writing cover letters, you should look at all of the cover letters in this collection and not just at those related to your particular profession or position of interest. All of the cover letters form a hunting ground for ideas that may prove useful to you for developing your own cover letters.

In the Gallery, you will notice a few letters displayed in a plain text or e-mail format. This format is appropriate for the electronic submission of letters or resumes. Note that any of the letters in this book can be prepared for electronic transfer. If you intend to apply online for positions, be sure you follow the submission guidelines posted by the employer. If they are not clearly explained, phone or e-mail the company to inquire. You don't want to be disqualified for a job that suits you well because you did not follow the steps for successful submission.

Part 3, "Best Resume Tips," presents some resume-writing strategies, design and layout tips, and resume-writing style tips for making resumes visually impressive. These tips contain references to resumes in an Exhibit of 11 resumes at the end of Part 3. These references are to resumes that illustrate a strategy or a tip, but the references are not exhaustive. If you browse through this Exhibit, you may see other resumes that exhibit the same strategy or tip.

Even though the Exhibit contains only 11 resumes, it offers a range of resumes with features you can use in creating and improving your own resumes. Notice the plural. An important premise of an active job search is that you will not have just one "perfect" resume for all potential employers, but different versions of your resume for different interviews. The Exhibit of resumes, like the Gallery of cover letters, is therefore not a showroom where you say, "I'll take that one." It is a valuable resource of design ideas, expressions, and organizational patterns that can help make your own resume a "best resume" for your next interview.

The List of Contributors contains the names, addresses, phone numbers, and other information of 90 professional resume writers from Australia, Canada, and the United States who contributed cover letters and resumes for this book. The list is arranged alphabetically by country and state. Although most of these resume writers work with local clients, many of the writers work with clients by phone, e-mail, and the Internet.

You can use the Occupation Index to look up cover letters by the job being sought. This index, however, should not replace careful examination of all of the cover letters. Many cover letters for some other occupation may have features that are adaptable to your own occupation. Limiting your search to the Occupation Index may cause you to miss some valuable examples.

Who This Book Is For

Anyone who wants ideas for creating or improving a cover letter can benefit from this book. It is especially useful for active job seekers—those who understand the difference between active and passive job searching. A *passive* job seeker waits until jobs are advertised and then mails copies of the same resume, along with a standard cover letter, to a number of ads. An *active* job seeker believes that both the resume and the cover letter should be modified for a specific job target *after* having talked in person or by phone to a prospective interviewer *before* a job is announced. To schedule such an interview is to penetrate the "hidden job market." Active job seekers can find in the Exhibit's focused resumes a wealth of strategies for targeting a resume for a particular interview. The section "How to Use the Gallery" at the beginning of Part 2 shows you how to use the Gallery for improving your cover letters

What This Book Can Do for You

Besides providing you with a treasury of quality cover letters and companion resumes whose features you can use in your own letters and resumes, this book can help transform your thinking about these job search documents. If you think that there is one "best" way to create a cover letter or resume, this book will help you learn how to design resumes and cover letters that are *best for you* as you try to get an interview with a particular person for a specific job.

Acknowledgments

This fourth edition of *Gallery of Best Cover Letters* was possible because of all the cover letter and resume submissions of the writers featured in this book. For their names, see the List of Contributors at the back of the book. It includes submissions by members of Career Directors International (CDI), the National Resume Writers Association, and the Professional Association of Resume Writers and Career Coaches (PARW/CC).

I also would like to express my thanks to Heather Stith at JIST for her guidance and work on the many details of preparing this fourth edition for publication. Special thanks are directed anew to my wife, Ginny, a former professional editor, who worked at home on necessary tasks for completing this fourth edition, especially the updating of cross-references in Parts 1 and 3.

PART

Best Cover Letter Tips

Best Cover Letter Tips at a Glance

Best Cover Letter Tips

In an active job search, your cover letter and resume should complement one another. Both are tailored to a particular reader you have contacted or to a specific job target. To help you create the "best" cover letters for your resumes, this part of the book debunks some common myths about cover letters and presents tips for polishing the letters you write.

Ten Myths About Cover Letters

The following bold statements are common myths about cover letters. Keep reading to discover the truth about these important job search documents:

1. **Resumes and cover letters are two separate documents that have little relation to each other.** Your resume and cover letter should work together in presenting you effectively to a prospective employer. The cover letter should draw attention to the most important information in the resume, the information you want the reader to be certain to see.

2. **The main purpose of the cover letter is to establish a friendly rapport with the reader.** A resume shows that you *can* do the work required. The main purpose of a cover letter is to express that you *want* to do the work required. But it doesn't hurt to display enthusiasm in your resume and refer to your abilities in your cover letter. The cover letter should demonstrate qualities and worker traits you want the prospective employee to see, such as good communication skills, motivation, clear thinking, good sense, thoughtfulness, interest in others, neatness, and so on.

3. **You can use the same cover letter for each reader of your resume.** Modify your cover letter for each reader so that it sounds fresh rather than canned. Chances are that in an active job search, you have already talked with the person who will interview you. Your cover letter should reflect that conversation and build on it.

4. **In a cover letter, you should mention any negative things about your life experience, work experience, health, or education in order to prepare the reader in advance of an interview.** This is not the purpose of the cover letter. You might bring up these topics in the first or second interview, but only after the interviewer has shown interest in you or offered you a job. Even then, if you feel that you must mention something negative about your past, present it in a positive way, perhaps by saying how that experience has strengthened your resolve to work hard at any new job.

5. **A resume is more important than its cover letter.** In a way, the cover letter can be more important. The cover letter is usually the first document a prospective employer sees. The first impression is often the most important one. If your cover letter has an embarrassing error in it, the chances are good that the reader may not bother to read your resume or may read it with less interest.

6. **An error in a cover letter is not important.** The cost of a cover letter might be as much as a third to a half of a million dollars—even more—if you figure the amount of income and benefits you don't receive over, say, a 10-year period for a job you don't get because of the error that screened you out.

7. **To make certain that your cover letter has no errors, you should proofread it or—better—ask a friend to "proof" it.** Trying to proofread your own cover letter is risky, even if you are good at grammar and writing. Once a document is printed, it has an aura about it that may make it seem better written than it is. For this reason, you are likely to miss typos or other kinds of errors.

   Relying on someone else is risky, too. If your friend is not good at grammar and writing, that person may not see any mistakes, either. Try to find a proofreader, a professional editor, an English teacher, a professional writer, or an experienced administrative assistant who can point out any errors you may have missed.

8. **After someone has proofread your letter, you can make a few changes to it and not have it looked at again.** More errors creep into a document this way than you would think possible. The reason is that such changes are often done hastily, and haste can waste an error-free document. If you make *any* change to a document, ask someone to proofread it a final time just to make sure that you haven't introduced an error during the last stage of composition.

9. **It doesn't take long to write a cover letter.** You should allow plenty of time to write and revise...and revise...a cover letter to get it just right for a particular reader. Most people think that writing is 90 percent of the task of creating a cover letter, and revision is 10 percent. It's really the other way around: Writing is closer to 10 percent of the task, and revision is 90 percent. That is true if you care about the cover letter and want it to work hard for you.

10. **It doesn't take long to print the cover letter.** To get the output of a printer looking just right, you may need to print the letter a number of times. Even if you are submitting your cover letter to an employer as a Word document or PDF file, you should print it out. One reason is that some formatting errors are usually easier to see in the printed letter than on-screen. Also, you never know whether the person receiving the letter may print it out to review it or to pass it on to another employee. In your printed cover letter, watch for extra spaces between words and sentences. Make sure your text is aligned correctly, such as indenting your bullets consistently or lining up all your text flush left. Finally, if you are submitting a hard copy of your cover letter instead of an electronic one, be sure that you leave enough vertical space for your signature between the complimentary close and your typed name.

Tips for Writing Cover Letters

To write well, you need to know why you are writing, the reader(s) to whom you are writing, what you want to say, how you want to organize what you say, and how you want to say it. Similarly, to write a good cover letter, you should clearly know its purpose, audience, content, organization, and style. The following tips, or strategies, should help you consider these aspects of cover letter writing. Consider using some of these strategies to ensure that your letters are impressive, even outstanding—and thus get the attention you deserve.

Purpose Strategies

Never forget that the purpose of a cover letter is to persuade the reader to call you in for an interview and ultimately offer you a specific job. These tips will help you clearly focus your cover letter on this purpose:

- **Make it clear in your letter that you really want this specific job.** See Cover Letters 17, 18, 22, 30, and 191. An employer doesn't want to know that you just want a job. An employer wants to know that you *really* want a particular job. If you display a ho-hum attitude in a letter, the chances are that you will receive a ho-hum response—which usually means rejection.

- **Consider putting a subject line near the beginning of the letter to indicate the position you are seeking.** See Cover Letters 5, 60, 94, 99, 110, 124, 127, 136, 150, 156, 161, 194, 196, 202, 208, 239, 245, 264, 266, 270, 272, 280, 295, 298, 299, and 308.

- **If you are responding to a job that has been posted on an online database, include the reference number, if one has been provided.** See Cover Letter 208.

- **If you are responding to an ad placed in a newspaper, be sure to include the date of the ad.** See Cover Letters 119, 196, and 240.

Audience Strategies

The more you know about the reader of your cover letter, the better you can tailor its content to appeal to that person. Researching the industry, company, and target position through online resources or networking contacts is a great help in this regard. Following these tips also will help you increase your letter's audience appeal:

- **Address the letter to a specific person and use this person's name in the salutation.** Avoid using such general salutations as Dear Sir or Madam, To Whom It May Concern, Dear Administrator, Dear Prospective Employer, or Dear Committee. In an active job search, you should do everything possible to send your cover letter and resume to a particular individual, preferably someone you've already talked with in person or by phone and with whom you have arranged an interview. If you have not been able to make a personal contact, at least do everything possible to find out the name of the person who will read your letter and resume, and then address the letter to that person.

- **If you are replying to an ad without a person's name and have no way to learn it, consider omitting the salutation and varying the subject line.** See Cover Letter 195.

- **If the intended reader of your resume suggested that you send it, or if you have recently spoken with the person, say this in the first sentence of the cover letter.** Indicating that the resume was requested helps to get your resume past any "gatekeeper"—the person who opens the mail and makes preliminary routing decisions—and into the hands of the appropriate reader. See Cover Letters 68, 224, and 232.

- **Similarly, if a third party has suggested that you submit your resume to the reader, mention that at or near the beginning of your cover letter.** See Cover Letters 26, 75, 82, 211, 227, 233, and 238. Even mentioning the third party near the end of the letter may be beneficial. See Cover Letter 104.

■ **Research the prospective company and show in the letter that you know important information about that company.** See Cover Letters 39 and 50. Complimenting the employer in the first sentence is a nice touch in Cover Letter 69.

■ **Toward the end of the cover letter, consider repeating the recipient's name to convey friendliness and to provide a personal touch.** See Cover Letters 59, 66, 197, 251, and 309.

Content Strategies

Knowing what information to include and what to leave out of a cover letter can be tricky. Use the tips in this section to guide you in creating a cover letter that presents you as a top candidate for your target position.

Resume Connections

The cover letter and resume work together to form a complete picture of you as a job candidate. Therefore, the cover letter should not repeat the resume, it should complement it. Keep these tips in mind:

■ **Think of the cover letter as a hook for the resume.** A cover letter is not an end in itself but a means for getting the reader to read the resume. The letter might refer specifically to the most important part of the resume—the part that you want the reader to see for sure. See Cover Letter 38, which contains a boxed sentence referring to examples that are highlighted with borders in the resume. See also Cover Letter 123, which summarizes in a paragraph the candidate's experience with one company and thus echoes the corresponding information in the accompanying resume.

■ **Include important information in your cover letter for which there is no room in the resume.** See Cover Letter 59, which describes the honor of being selected by National Geographic to participate in a summer institute.

Experience and Skills

In the cover letter, it's important to connect your skills and achievements with the requirements of your target position. These tips explain some ways to do just that:

■ **Numbers that quantify accomplishments in dollar amounts or percentages are impressive.** See Cover Letters 1, 21, 37, 95, 101, 158, 189, 202, 204, 234, 262, 270, 271, 277, and 301. Numbers in the opening sentence can be especially eye-catching. See Cover Letter 160.

■ **If you speak two or more languages fluently, say so in your cover letter.** Being bilingual is an important asset in today's job market. See Cover Letters 201, 238, and 288.

■ **When you are short on professional work experience to qualify for a position, consider related voluntary experiences or an internship that may help you qualify.** See Cover Letters 290, 314.

■ **Explain how your real-world experience in an unrelated field has helped qualify you for the current job target.** See Cover Letters 55, 61, 286, and 307. Likewise, if you are returning to a field, explain how your intervening job or additional education is relevant. See Cover Letter 147.

■ **Play down experience that may threaten a prospective employer.** A senior applicant with much experience may have more skills, expertise, and administrative savvy than the hiring employer. Should the employer feel threatened by this disparity, it may be better to tone down some skills and expertise than to display all of one's strengths without restraint.

■ **If you have an impressive success story to tell about your work experience, consider telling the story in your cover letter.** Cover Letter 278 contains a humorous but fictitious story that illustrates the value of the candidate's expertise.

Career Transitions

Most cover letters are written during a work transition of some kind. How this transition affects the content of your cover letter depends on your specific circumstances:

■ **If you were in the military and are now trying to get a civilian job, avoid using military terms that may be unfamiliar to civilians.** Feel free, however, to play up military responsibilities and achievements that a potential employer will understand and appreciate. See Cover Letters 150 and 220.

■ **If you have been downsized and don't want to mention it in your cover letter, consider including the information but "downsizing" its impact by focusing instead on your strengths, abilities, and experiences.** See Cover Letter 170.

■ **If you don't want your present employer to know about your job search, explain clearly the need for confidentiality.** See Cover Letter 230.

■ **Speak positively about a return to the workplace from retirement.** See Cover Letter 294.

Follow-Up Plans

A strong close to your cover letter demonstrates that you are a professional who follows up. Here are some tips on how to word this key part:

■ **At the end of your cover letter, don't make a statement that the reader can use to reject you.** For example, suppose that you close your letter with this statement:

> If you wish to discuss this matter further, please call me at (555) 555-5555.

This statement gives the reader a chance to think, "No, I don't wish to." Here is another example:

> If you know of the right opportunity for me, please call me at (555) 555-5555.

The reader may think, "I don't know of any such opportunity. How would I know what's right for you?" Avoid questions that prompt yes-or-no answers, such as "Do you want to discuss this matter further?" If you ask this kind of question, you give the reader a chance to say no. Instead, make a closing statement that indicates your optimism about receiving a positive response from the reader. Such a statement might begin with one of the following clauses:

> I am confident that...

> I look forward to...

In this way, you invite the reader to say yes to further considering your candidacy for the job.

- **At the end of the letter, consider keeping control of the follow-up by indicating that you will phone later.** See Cover Letters 13, 39, 41, 50, 99, 136, 142, 154, 176, 201, 204, 226, 256, 257, 264, 283, 299, and 300.

- **If you think that calling the prospective employer seems pushy, soften the tone of the statement about calling by asking permission.** See, for example, Cover Letters 74, 258, 267, 268, and 272.

Style Strategies

Unlike a resume, a cover letter uses complete sentences and transitions. The text should flow easily from one idea to the next. The tips in this section will guide you in conveying your ability to communicate well and revealing a bit of your personality.

Language and Tone

The reader of your cover letter will form an impression of your personality based on the words you use. Choose them carefully, using the following tips as a guide:

- **Make each paragraph fresh and free of well-worn expressions commonly found in cover letters.** See, for example, Cover Letters 58, 60, 199, and 244.

- **Do not sound desperate, even a little bit.** The following examples may seem extreme, but avoid using any similar statements in your letter:

    "I'll take anything you have to offer."

    "It makes no difference what kind of job you have."

    "I can start immediately."

    "I am available for employment right away."

    "When's the first paycheck?"

- **It's okay to be enthusiastic in a cover letter.** See Cover Letters 60, 238, and 266.

- **Consider beginning or ending the letter with a quotation that sets the tone and provides insight for understanding your work, character, attitude, outlook, or whatever else you want to convey.** See Cover Letters 7, 21, 22, 55, 65, 87, 90, 254, and 300.

Persuasiveness

The cover letter is a kind of marketing document. In it, you have to sell the reader on the idea that you are the right person for the job. The following tips can help you in this effort:

- **Consider making your cover letter not only informative but also persuasive.** See Cover Letters 19, 27, 58, 191, 267, and 268.

- **Don't let your opening statement or a sentence in your first paragraph give the reader a chance to think "No" and read no further.**

    Example: "I am hoping that you are looking for a new auditor."

The reader can think "I'm not" and stop reading.

    Example: "If you think your auditor should be as good at building teamwork as he is at building reports, we should talk."

The reader can't disagree with this reasoning and will probably read further.

■ **Strive to make your cover letter hard to ignore. Your task is easier, of course, if you are a great catch for any company.** See Cover Letters 27, 121, 199, and 267.

■ **To grab attention, try making your first sentence a bold assertion or question.** See Cover Letters 1, 19, 27, 99, 121, 138, and 267. Cover Letter 291 begins with an excerpt from the mission statement of the Boys & Girls Clubs of America.

■ **Consider using one or more testimonials in a cover letter.** A testimonial is a quotation from a former or current boss, a coworker, or someone else who knows the quality of your work or the strength of your character. Testimonials can be effective in setting your letter or resume apart from other "stock" submissions. If you use testimonials in your cover letters or resumes, be sure to get permission from the sources. See Cover Letters 1, 78, 89, 104, 190, 206, 258, 276, 293, and 300.

Format Strategies

Consider using special fonts, graphics, tables, and bulleted lists in your cover letter to make it stand out. The following tips highlight examples of this type of strategy:

■ **Consider using a combination of bullets and boldfacing to call attention to information you think the reader must see.** See Cover Letters 17, 37, 47, 80, 92, 101, 121, 149, 150, 155, 165, 190, 201, 202, 235, 258, 266, 275, 279, 285, 300, and 308. It's hard to keep your eyes away from information that is bulleted and bold.

■ **For a change, consider putting key points in italic.** See Cover Letters 1, 96, and 237.

■ **Consider using decorative bullets, check marks, or check boxes to draw attention to accomplishments.** See Cover Letters 24, 105, 107, 126, and 132.

■ **To catch the reader's attention, consider inserting a graphic that relates to the job you are seeking or that echoes a graphic appearing in your resume.** See Cover Letters 26, 53, 122, and 178.

Note: If you are submitting your cover letter as an e-mail message, keep the formatting plain. Use standard fonts and avoid graphics to prevent causing any display problems for the reader of your cover letter.

■ **To help the reader see your area of expertise, put a banner at the top of your letter or include information in a column.** See Cover Letters 32, 45, 87, 160, 178, 216, 263, and 298. Think of other ways to make information visually stand out. Cover Letter 243 begins with three words in boldface and italic. Cover Letters 88, 106, 212, and 253 use a box to present quantified achievements.

■ **Consider presenting important information in two corresponding columns: the employer's needs (or requirements) and your qualifications.** See Cover Letters 52, 68, 102, 103, 177, 197, 205, 208, 238, 274, 275, and 287. Compare these with Cover Letter 133.

■ **Try a change in format for a change of pace.** See Cover Letters 45, 46, 110, 178, and 258.

■ **Adjust the margins for a short letter.** If your cover letter is 300 words or longer, use left, right, top, and bottom margins of one inch. If the letter is shorter, you should increase the width of the margins. How much to increase them is a matter of personal taste. One way to take care of the width of the top and bottom margins is to center a shorter letter vertically on the page. A maximum width for a short cover letter of 100 words or fewer might be two-inch left and right margins. You might decrease the width of the left and right margins by two-tenths of an inch for every 50 words you add.

- **If you write your letter with word-processing or desktop-publishing software, use left-alignment to ensure that the lines of text are readable and have fixed spacing between words.** The letter will have a "ragged" look along the right margin, but the words will be evenly spaced horizontally. Be wary of using full justification in an attempt to give a letter a printed look. You can make your letter look worse by giving it some extra-wide spaces between words. Resume writers who are experienced with certain typesetting procedures—such as "kerning," "tracking," and hyphenating words at the end of some lines—can sometimes use full justification effectively for variety in their documents. Note that if you use kerning and tight tracking to fit more words on a line, extra-narrow spaces can look unappealing as well.

- **Create a .txt or .pdf version of your cover letter and resume so that you can customize them as needed and e-mail them in response to online ads or post them to online job databases.** See Cover Letters 3, 40, 123, and 306.

Tips for Polishing Cover Letters

You might spend several days working on your resume, getting it "just right" and free of errors. But if you send it with a cover letter that is written quickly and contains even one conspicuous error, all your good effort may be wasted.

You can prevent this kind of tragedy by polishing your cover letter so that it is free of all errors. The following tips can help you avoid or eliminate common errors in cover letters. By becoming aware of these kinds of errors and knowing how to fix them, you can be more confident about the cover letters you send with your resumes.

Using Pronouns Correctly

Pronouns are a common source of cover letter problems. The following tips provide advice on how to handle such issues:

- **Use *I* and *My* sparingly.** When most of the sentences in a cover letter begin with *I* or *My,* you might appear self-absorbed, self-centered, or egotistical. If the reader is turned off by this kind of impression (even if it is a false one), you could be screened out without ever having an interview. Of course, you need to use these first-person pronouns sometimes, because most of the information you put in your cover letter is personal. But try to avoid using *I* and *My* at the beginnings of sentences and paragraphs.

- **Refer to a business, company, corporation, or organization as *it* rather than *they*.** Members of the Board may be referred to as *they,* but a company is a singular subject that requires a singular verb and pronoun. Note this example:

  New Products, Inc., was established in 2010. It grossed more than $1 million in sales during its first year.

- **If you start a sentence with *This,* be sure that what *This* refers to is clear.** If the reference is not clear, insert a word or phrase to clarify what *This* means. Compare the following:

  > I will e-mail my revised application for the new position to you by noon on Friday. *This* should be acceptable to you.

  > I will e-mail my revised application for the new position to you by noon on Friday. This *method of sending the application* should be acceptable to you.

  A reader of the first example wouldn't know what *This* refers to. Friday? By noon on Friday? The revised application for the new position? The insertion after *This* in the second example, however, tells the reader that *This* refers to the use of e-mail.

- **Use *as follows* after a singular subject.** Literally, *as follows* means *as it follows,* so the phrase is illogical after a plural subject. Compare the following:

Incorrect:	My plans for the day of the interview are as follows:
Fixed:	My plans for the day of the interview are these:
Correct:	My plan for the day of the interview is as follows:
Better:	Here is my plan for the day of the interview:

  In the second set of examples, the improved version avoids a hidden reference problem—the possible association of the silent "it" with *interview.* Whenever you want to use *as follows,* check to see whether the subject that precedes *as follows* is plural. If it is, don't use this phrase.

Using Verb Forms Correctly

The following tips relate to verb usage:

- **Make certain that subjects and verbs agree in number.** Plural subjects require plural forms of verbs. Singular subjects require singular verb forms. Most writers know these things, but problems arise when subject-verb agreement gets tricky. Compare the following:

Incorrect:	My education and experience has prepared me...
Correct:	My education and experience have prepared me...
Incorrect:	Making plans plus scheduling conferences were...
Correct:	Making plans plus scheduling conferences was...

  In the first set, *education* and *experience* are two separate things (you can have one without the other) and therefore require a plural verb. A hasty writer might lump them together and use a singular verb. When you reread what you have written, look out for this kind of improper agreement between a plural subject and a singular verb.

In the second set, *making plans* is the subject. It is singular, so the verb must be singular. The misleading part of this sentence is the phrase *plus scheduling conferences*. It may seem to make the subject plural, but it doesn't. In English, phrases that begin with such words as *plus, together with, in addition to, along with,* and *as well as* usually don't make a singular subject plural.

■ **Whenever possible, use active forms of verbs rather than passive forms.** Compare the following:

Passive:	My report will be sent by my assistant tomorrow.
Active:	My assistant will send my report tomorrow.
Passive:	Your interest is appreciated.
Active:	I appreciate your interest.
Passive:	Your letter was received yesterday.
Active:	I received your letter yesterday.

Sentences with passive verbs are usually longer and clumsier than sentences with active verbs. Passive sentences often leave out the crucial information of who is performing the verb's action. Spot passive verbs by looking for some form of the verb *to be* (such as *be, will be, have been, is, was,* and *were*) used with another verb.

In solving the passive-language problem, you might create another, such as using the pronouns *I* and *My* too frequently (see the first tip in the "Pronouns" section). The task then becomes one of finding some other way to start a sentence while keeping your language active.

■ **Be sure that present and past participles are grammatically parallel in a list.** Present participles are action words that end in *-ing,* such as *creating, testing,* and *implementing.* Past participles are action words that usually end in *-ed,* such as *created, tested,* and *implemented.* These types of words are called *verbals* because they are derived from verbs but are not strong enough to function as verbs in a sentence. When you use a string of verbals, control them by keeping them parallel.

■ **Use split infinitives only when *not* splitting them is misleading or awkward.** An *infinitive* is a verb preceded by the preposition *to,* as in *to create, to test,* and *to implement.* You split an infinitive when you insert an adverb between the preposition and the verb, as in *to quickly create, to repeatedly test,* and *to slowly implement.* About 50 years ago, split infinitives were considered grammatical errors; these days, however, opinion about them has changed. Many grammar handbooks now recommend that you split infinitives to avoid awkward or misleading sentences. Compare the following:

Split infinitive:	I plan to periodically send updated reports on my progress in school.
Misleading:	I plan periodically to send updated reports on my progress in school.
Misleading:	I plan to send periodically updated reports on my progress in school.

The first example is clear enough, but the second and third examples may be misleading. If you are uncomfortable with split infinitives, one solution is to move *periodically* further into the sentence: "I plan to send updated reports periodically on my progress in school."

Most handbooks that allow split infinitives also recommend that they not be split by more than one word, as in *to quickly and easily write.* A gold medal for splitting an infinitive should go to Lowell Schmalz, an Archie Bunker prototype in *The Man Who Knew Coolidge* by Sinclair Lewis. Schmalz, who thought that Coolidge was one of America's greatest presidents, split an infinitive this way: "*to instantly and without the least loss of time or effort find...*"[1]

Using Punctuation Correctly

Refer to the following tips when you need a quick refresher on correct punctuation:

- **Punctuate a compound sentence with a comma.** A compound sentence is one that contains two main clauses (a group of words containing a subject and a verb) joined by one of seven conjunctions (*and, but, or, nor, for, yet,* and *so*). In English, a comma is customarily put before the conjunction if the sentence isn't unusually short. Here is an example of a compound sentence punctuated correctly:

    I plan to arrive at O'Hare at 9:35 a.m. on Thursday, and my trip by cab to your office should take no longer than 40 minutes.

    The comma is important because it signals that a new grammatical subject (*trip,* the subject of the second main clause) is about to be expressed. If you use this kind of comma consistently, the reader will rely on your punctuation and will be on the lookout for the next subject in a compound sentence.

- **Be certain not to put a comma between compound verbs.** When a sentence has two verbs joined by the conjunction *and,* these verbs are called *compound verbs.* Usually, they should not be separated by a comma before the conjunction. Note the following examples:

    I *started* the letter last night *and finished* it this morning.

    I *am sending* my resume separately *and would like* you to keep the information confidential.

    Both examples are simple sentences containing compound verbs. Therefore, no comma appears before *and.* In either case, a comma would send a wrong signal that a new subject in another main clause is coming, but no such subject exists.

Note: In a sentence with a series of three or more verbs, use commas between the verbs. The comma before the last verb is called the *serial comma.* For more information on using the serial comma, see the first tip in the "Punctuation" section in Part 3.

- **Avoid using *as well as* for *and* in a series.** Compare the following:

Incorrect:	Your company is impressive because it has offices in Canada, Mexico, as well as the United States.
Correct:	Your company is impressive because it has offices in Canada and Mexico, as well as in the United States.

[1]Sinclair Lewis, *The Man Who Knew Coolidge* (New York: Books for Libraries Press, 1956), p. 29.

Usually, what is considered exceptional precedes *as well as,* and what is considered customary follows it. Note this example:

> Your company is impressive because its products are innovative as well as affordable.

■ **Put a comma after the year when it appears after the month.** Similarly, put a comma after the state when it appears after the city. Compare the following pairs of examples:

Incorrect:	On January 10, 2012 I was promoted to senior analyst.
Correct:	On January 10, 2012, I was promoted to senior analyst.

Incorrect:	I worked in Springfield, Illinois before moving to Dallas.
Correct:	I worked in Springfield, Illinois, before moving to Dallas.

■ **Put a comma after an opening dependent clause.** A dependent clause is linked and related to the main clause by words such as *who, that, when,* and *if.* Compare the following:

Incorrect:	If you have any questions you may contact me by phone or e-mail.
Correct:	If you have any questions, you may contact me by phone or e-mail.

Actually, many writers of fiction and nonfiction don't use this kind of comma. The comma is useful, though, because it signals where the main clause begins. If you glance at the example with the comma, you can tell where the main clause is without even reading the opening clause. For a step up in clarity and readability, use this comma. It can give the reader a feel for a sentence even before he or she begins reading the words.

■ **Use semicolons when they are needed.** Semicolons are used to separate two main clauses when the second clause starts with a *conjunctive adverb* such as *however, moreover,* or *therefore.* Compare the following:

Incorrect:	Your position in sales looks interesting, however, I would like more information about it.
Correct:	Your position in sales looks interesting; however, I would like more information about it.

The first example is incorrect because the comma before *however* is a *comma splice,* which is a comma that joins two sentences. It's like putting a comma instead of a period at the end of the first sentence and then starting the second sentence. A comma may be a small punctuation mark, but a comma splice is a huge grammatical mistake. What are your chances of getting hired if your cover letter tells your reader that you don't recognize where a sentence ends, especially if a requirement for the job is good communication skills? Yes, you could be screened out because of one little comma!

Another use of the semicolon is to separate items of a series when an item has internal punctuation. Compare these sentences:

Incorrect:	The committee consisted of a manager, three sales-persons, and Beverley, who was hired yesterday.
Correct:	The committee consisted of a manager; three sales-persons; and Beverley, who was hired yesterday.

In the first sentence, commas separate the three items of the series, but visually the comma after Beverley can be confusing. Does it signify another series item to follow? In the revision, semicolons separating the series items make the items plain. There is no way to think that the comma after Beverley precedes another series item to follow.

- **Avoid putting a colon after a verb or preposition to introduce information.** The reason is that the colon interrupts a continuing clause. Compare the following:

Incorrect:	My interests in your company *are:* its reputation, the review of salary after six months, and your personal desire to hire people with disabilities.
Correct:	My interests in your company *are these:* its reputation, the review of salary after six months, and your personal desire to hire people with disabilities.
Correct:	My interests in your company are its reputation, the review of salary after six months, and your personal desire to hire people with disabilities.
Incorrect:	In my interview with you, I would like *to:* learn how your company was started, get your reaction to my updated portfolio, and discuss your department's plans to move to a new building.
Correct:	In my interview with you, I would like to discuss *these issues:* how your company was started, what you think of my updated portfolio, and when your department may move to a new building.
Correct:	In my interview with you, I would like to learn how your company was started, what you think of my updated portfolio, and when your department may move to a new building.

Although some people may say that it is acceptable to put a colon after a verb such as *include* if the list of information is long, it is better to be consistent and avoid colons after verbs altogether.

- **Understand the use of colons.** People often associate colons with semicolons because their names sound alike, but colons and semicolons have nothing to do with each other. Colons are the opposite of dashes. Dashes look backward, whereas colons usually look forward to information about to be delivered. One common use of the colon does look backward, however. Here are two examples:

My experience with computers is limited: I have had only one course in programming, and I don't own a computer.

I must make a decision by Monday: That is the deadline for renewing the lease on my apartment.

In each example, what follows the colon explains what was said before the colon. Using a colon this way in a cover letter can impress a knowledgeable reader who is looking for evidence of writing skills.

■ **Use slashes correctly.** Information about slashes is sometimes hard to find because *slash* often is listed in grammar reference books under a different name, such as *virgule* or *solidus.* If you are unfamiliar with these terms, your hunt for advice on slashes may lead to nothing.

At least know that one important meaning of a slash is *or.* For this reason, you often see a slash in an expression such as ON/OFF. This usage means that a condition or state, such as that of electricity activated by a switch, is either ON *or* OFF but never ON *and* OFF at the same time. This condition may be one in which a change means going from the current state to the opposite (or alternate) state. If the current state is ON and a change occurs, the next state is OFF, and vice versa. With this understanding, you can recognize the logic behind the following examples:

Incorrect:	ON-OFF switch (on and off at the same time!)
Correct:	ON/OFF switch (on or off at any time)
Correct:	his-her clothes (unisex clothes, worn by both sexes)
Correct:	his/her clothes (each sex had different clothes)

Note: Both his-her and his/her are clumsy. Try to find a way to avoid them. One route is to rephrase the sentence so that you use the plural possessive pronoun *their* or the second-person possessive pronoun *your.* (Campers should make their beds before breakfast. Please make your beds before breakfast.) Another way is to rephrase the sentence without possessive pronouns. (Everyone should get dressed before going to breakfast.)

■ **Think twice about using *and/or.*** This stilted expression is commonly misunderstood to mean *two* alternatives, but it literally means *three.* Consider the following example:

If you don't hear from me by Friday, please call and/or e-mail me on Monday.

What is the person at the other end to do? The sentence really states three alternatives: just call, just e-mail, or call *and* e-mail on Monday. For better clarity, use the connectives *and* or *or* whenever possible.

■ **Use punctuation correctly with quotation marks.** A common misconception is that commas and periods should be placed outside closing quotation marks, but the opposite is true. Compare the following:

Incorrect:	Your company certainly has the "leading edge", which means that its razor blades are the best on the market.
Correct:	Your company certainly has the "leading edge," which means that its razor blades are the best on the market.

Incorrect:	In the engineering department, my classmates referred to me as "the girl guru". I was the youngest expert in programming languages on campus.
Correct:	In the engineering department, my classmates referred to me as "the girl guru." I was the youngest expert in programming languages on campus.

Note this exception: Unlike commas and periods, colons and semicolons go *outside* double quotation marks.

Using Words Correctly

Poor word choice in a cover letter can keep you from getting called in for an interview. These tips can help you choose your words wisely:

- **Avoid using lofty language in your cover letter.** A real turn-off in a cover letter is the use of elevated diction (high-sounding words and phrases) as an attempt to seem important. Note the following examples, along with their straight-talk translations:

Elevated:	My background has afforded me experience in...
Better:	In my previous jobs, I...

Elevated:	Prior to that term of employment...
Better:	Before I worked at...

Elevated:	I am someone with a results-driven profit orientation.
Better:	I want to make your company more profitable.

Elevated:	I hope to utilize my qualifications...
Better:	I want to use my skills...

In letter writing, the shortest distance between the writer and the reader is the most direct idea.

- **Check your sentences for excessive use of compounds joined by *and*.** A cheap way to make your letters longer is to join words with *and* and to do this repeatedly. Note the following wordy sentence:

  Because of my background and preparation for work and advancement with your company and new enterprise, I have a concern and commitment to implement and put into effect my skills and abilities for new solutions and achievements above and beyond your dreams and expectations. (44 words)

Just one inflated sentence like that would drive a reader to say, "No way!" The writer of the inflated sentence has said only this:

  Because of my background and skills, I want to contribute to your new venture. (14 words)

If you eliminate the wordiness caused by this common writing weakness, an employer is more likely to read your letter completely.

- **Avoid using abstract nouns excessively.** Look again at the inflated sentence in the preceding tip, but this time with the abstract nouns in italic:

  > Because of my *background* and *preparation* for *work* and *advancement* with your *company* and new *enterprise,* I have a *concern* and *commitment* to implement and put into *effect* my skills and *abilities* for new *solutions* and *achievements* above and beyond your *dreams* and *expectations.*

  Try picturing in your mind any of the words in italic. You can't because they are *abstract nouns,* which means that they are ideas and not images of things you can see, taste, hear, smell, or touch. One certain way to turn off the reader is to load your cover letter with abstract nouns. The following sentence, containing some images, has a better chance of capturing the reader's attention:

  > Having created seven multimedia tutorials with my digital camcorder and HP Pavilion Media Center PC, I now want to create some breakthrough adult-learning packages so that your company, New Century Instructional Technologies, Inc., will exceed $50,000,000 in contracts by 2012.

  Compare this sentence with the one loaded with abstract nouns. The one with images is obviously the better attention-grabber.

- **Avoid wordy expressions in your cover letters.** Note the following examples in the first column and their shorter alternatives in the second column:

at the location of	at
for the reason that	because
in a short time	soon
in a timely manner	on time
in spite of everything to the contrary	nevertheless
in the event of	if
in proximity to	near
now and then	occasionally
on a daily basis	daily
on a regular basis	regularly
on account of	because
one day from now	tomorrow
would you be so kind as to	please

  Trim the fat wherever you can, and your reader will appreciate the leanness of your cover letter.

2
P·A·R·T

The Gallery of Best Cover Letters

The Gallery at a Glance

How to Use the Gallery

You can learn much from the Gallery just by browsing through it. To make the best use of this resource, however, read the following suggestions before you begin.

- **Look at the cover letters in the category that contains your field, related fields, or target occupation.** Use the Occupation Index to help you find cover letters for certain fields. Notice what kinds of cover letters other people have used to find similar jobs. Always remember, though, that your cover letter should not be "canned." It should not look just like someone else's cover letter, but should reflect your own background, unique experiences, knowledge, areas of expertise, skills, motivation, and goals.

- **Use the Gallery primarily as an "idea book."** Even if you don't find a cover letter for your specific position or job target, be sure to look at all the letters for ideas you can borrow or adapt. You may be able to find portions of a letter (the right word, a phrase, a strong sentence, maybe even a well-worded paragraph) that you can use in your own letter but modify with information that applies to your own situation or target field.

- **Compare some of the beginning paragraphs of the letters.** Notice which ones capture your attention almost immediately. In your comparison, examine paragraph length, sentence length, clarity of thought, and the kinds of words that grab your attention. Are some statements better than others from your point of view? Do some paragraphs fit your situation better than others?

- **Compare some of the closing paragraphs of the letters.** What trends do you notice? What differences? What endings are more effective than others? What are the different ways to say thank you? What are the best ways to ask for an interview? How are follow-up plans expressed? Which closing paragraphs seem to match your situation best? Continue to note differences in length, the kinds of words and phrases used, and the effectiveness of the content. Jot down any ideas that might be true for you.

- **Compare the middle paragraphs across the letters of the Gallery.** See how the person introduces herself or himself. Look for a paragraph that seems to be a short profile of an individual. Notice paragraphs devoted to experience, areas of expertise, qualifications, or skills. How does the person express motivation, enthusiasm, or interest in the target position? Which letters use bullets? Which letters seem more convincing than others? How are they more persuasive? Which letters have a better chance of securing an interview?

  As you review the middle paragraphs, notice which words and phrases seem to be more convincing than other typical words or phrases. Look for words that you might use to put a certain "spin" on your own cover letter as you pitch it toward a particular interviewer or job target.

■ **Note how the information in different letters is organized.** For example, the first paragraph of a letter might indicate the person's job goal, the second paragraph might say something about the person's background, the third paragraph might indicate qualifications, and the last paragraph might express interest in an interview. This letter would then have a Goal-Background-Qualifications-Interview format. If you review the letters in the Gallery this way, you will soon detect some common cover letter formats. The purpose of doing this is to discover which formats are more effective than others—all so that you can make your cover letter the most effective letter it can be.

By developing a sense of cover letter organization, you will know better how to select and emphasize the most important information about yourself for the job you want to get.

■ **Compare the cover letters for their visual impact.** Look for horizontal and vertical lines, borders, boxes, bullets, white space, and graphics. Which cover letters have more visual impact at first glance, and which ones make no initial impression? Do some of the letters seem more inviting to read than others? Which ones are less appealing because they have too much information, or too little? Which ones seem to have the right balance of information and white space? If visual impact is important, you will want to send a letter through the regular mail on fine paper or as an e-mail file attachment that can be read in Microsoft Word—or as a PDF—and printed without losing your letter's formatting. If sending a letter online quickly is more important than the letter's appearance, you may want to send your letter as a text (.txt) file with a minimum of formatting, or copy and paste it directly into an e-mail message.

After comparing the visual design features, choose the design ideas that might improve your own cover letter. Be selective here and don't try to work every design possibility into your letter. Generally, "less is more" in cover letter writing, especially when you integrate design features with content.

Questions for Cover Letters

Use the Gallery of cover letters as a reference whenever you need to write a cover letter for your resume. As you examine the Gallery, consider the following questions:

1. **Does the writer show a genuine interest in the reader?** One way to tell is to count the number of times the pronouns *you* and *your* appear in the letter. Then count the number of times the pronouns *I, me,* and *my* occur in the letter. Although this method is simplistic, it nevertheless helps you see where the writer's interests lie. When you write a cover letter, make your first paragraph *you*-centered rather than *I*-centered.

2. **Where does the cover letter mention the resume specifically?** A main purpose of a cover letter is to call attention to the resume. If the letter fails to mention the resume, the letter has not fulfilled its purpose. Besides mentioning the resume, the cover letter might direct the reader's attention to one or more parts of the resume, increasing the chances that the reader will see the most important part(s). It is not a good idea, however, to put a lot of resume facts in the cover letter. Let each document do its own job. The job of the cover letter is to point to the resume.

3. **Where and how does the letter express interest in an interview?** The immediate purpose of a cover letter is to call attention to the resume, but the *ultimate* purpose of both the cover letter and the resume is to help you get an interview with the person who can hire you. If the letter doesn't display your interest in getting an interview, the letter has not fulfilled its ultimate purpose.

4. **How decisive is the person's language?** This question is closely related to the preceding question. Is interest in an interview expressed directly or indirectly? Does the person specifically request an interview on a date when the writer will be in the reader's vicinity, or does the person only hint at a desire to "meet" the reader some day? Some of the letters in this book are more proactive and assertive than others in asking for an interview. When you write your own cover letters, be sure to be direct and convincing in expressing your interest for an interview.

5. **How does the person display self-confidence?** As you look through the Gallery, notice the cover letters in which the phrase "I am confident that..." (or a similar expression) appears. Self-confidence is a sign of management ability and essential job-worthiness. Many of the letters display self-confidence or self-assertiveness in various ways.

6. **Does the letter indicate whether the person is a team player?** From an employer's point of view, an employee who is self-assertive but not a team player can spell T-R-O-U-B-L-E. As you look at the cover letters in the Gallery, notice how they mention the word *team*.

7. **How does the letter make the person stand out?** Do some letters present the person more vividly than other letters? If so, what does the trick? The middle paragraphs or the opening and closing paragraphs? The paragraphs or the bulleted lists? Use what you learn here to help you write effective cover letters.

8. **How familiar is the person with the reader?** In a passive job search, the reader will most likely be a total stranger. In an active job search, the chances are good that the writer will have had at least one conversation with the reader by phone or in person. In that case, the letter can refer to any previous communication.

After you have examined the cover letters in the Gallery, you will be better able to write an attention-getting letter–one that leads the reader to your resume and to scheduling an interview with you.

Important Notes About the Gallery

The following Gallery contains sample cover letters that were prepared by professional resume writers to accompany resumes. (Some representative resumes are included in Part 3 of this book.) Names, addresses, dates, company names, and other facts have been changed to ensure the confidentiality of the original sender and receiver of the letter. For each letter, however, the essential substance of the original remains intact.

Note: Omitting an address or salutation in a cover letter is another way of protecting a client's privacy. For this reason, some of the letters in this book include generic salutations such as "Dear Hiring Manager." In an actual letter, such a salutation should be replaced with the name of an individual who works at the company to which you are applying.

The 317 cover letters and 11 resumes in this book represent 93 unique styles of writing–the exact number of professional resume writers who contributed to this book. For this reason, you may notice a number of differences in capitalization. To showcase important details, many of the writers prefer to capitalize job titles and other key terms that usually appear in lowercase. Furthermore, the use of jargon may vary considerably—again, reflecting the choices of individual writers and thus making each letter and resume truly "one of a kind."

Variations in the use (or nonuse) of hyphens may be noticeable. With the proliferation of industry jargon, hyphens seem like moving targets, and "rules" of hyphenation vary considerably from one handbook to another. In computer-related fields, some terms are evolving faster than the species. Electronic mail comes in many varieties: email, e-mail, Email, and E-Mail. But the computer world is not the only one that has variety: both healthcare and health care appear in the cover letters and companion resumes in this book.

Although an attempt has been made to reduce some of the inconsistencies in capitalization and hyphenation, differences are still evident. Keep in mind that the consistent use of capitalization and hyphenation within a cover letter or resume is more important than adherence to any set of external conventions.

Note: In some of the comments below the cover letters, the views of the resume writers themselves appear in quotation marks.

MARK FISHER, MBA, CPA

555-555-5555
jmf@email.com
5555 Kraft Lane, Knoxville, TN 55555

February 4, 20XX

Barry Fox, President
National Bank
5555 George Street
Lincoln, NE 55555

Dear Mr. Fox:

"Your hard work positions our organization well for 20XX."

General Manager

"During his tenure, Mark demonstrated a strong ability to drive for results for his team."

Director,
Consumer Ops

When was the last time you hired a **Senior Management Executive** who was able to hit the ground running and *generate expense reductions quickly?* Please allow me to introduce myself. As a Certified Public Accountant with extensive financial and auditing experience, I approach every situation from the perspective of operational efficiency.

Producing results requires leadership. Achieving fast results demands a new perspective, an ability to embrace and implement change, and buy-in from everyone involved. Results-driven highlights include

- Listening to front-line employees and responding to their concerns and suggestions. *Recommended that senior management eliminate customer online disconnect ability, yielding a $5 million annual savings.*

- Developing the incentive plan for sales reps that *drove market penetration to 35% on customer loyalty product sales.*

- Being *hand selected* by senior management for the Capstone Leadership Program, *a privilege afforded to the top 5 to 10%* of employees.

Controlling costs and reducing expenses are critical to an organization's profitability and viability. If you are looking for a results-driven leader holding a CPA and MBA who can *produce positive results quickly,* perhaps we should meet to discuss your needs and how I might help. I will call you next week and look forward to speaking with you.

Sincerely,

Mark Fisher

Enclosure

Certified Public Accountant. *Cindy Kraft, Valrico, Florida*

The first paragraph introduces the applicant, the second indicates bulleted achievements quantified in dollars and percentages, and the third proposes a meeting. Two testimonials sell the applicant.

PAUL KEENE, CPA, CMA

October 24, 20XX

Hiring Agent, Title
Company Name
Address

Dear Hiring Agent:

As an accomplished financial professional with a solid background in both GAAP and managerial accounting, as well as experience as a controller, I believe I offer expertise that would be of benefit to your company. With a proven record in building solid financial infrastructures, improving accounting and reporting procedures, and providing sound financial analysis, I would like to explore the possibility of putting my talents to work for you.

As you can see from my enclosed resume, I was brought into my current position to integrate and upgrade the financial operations of four affiliated companies. For this challenging task, I successfully introduced a new financial reporting system, brought the books of all four companies into compliance with GAAP standards, instituted new procedures that standardized and improved operational reporting, and established new systems that simplified asset accounting. In addition, as a certified management accountant trained to use the EVA™ metric system, I am frequently called upon to provide the expert financial analysis that drives successful corporate decision making.

Equally skilled in closing the financial books and conducting analysis of financial results, I consider myself a team player willing and able to tackle any challenge in the financial arena. However, my true passion lies in cost analysis and the identification of cost-saving opportunities. Related to this, I pride myself on my ability to develop clear, cohesive financial reports that provide the basis and justification for change and improvement initiatives. Knowledgeable and forward thinking, I have proven to be a respected and valued financial leader in the past. With a record of success behind me, I am confident that I will be an asset to you as well.

I will be relocating to your area shortly and hope to find a rewarding position that provides the same diverse, fast-paced challenge that I currently enjoy. Therefore, I would be pleased to have the opportunity to meet with you to discuss your needs and how I might be able to meet them. I will contact you shortly to arrange an interview. I look forward to speaking with you soon.

Thank you for your consideration.

Sincerely,

Paul Keene, CPA, CMA

Enclosure

5 SIDNEY ROAD   •   BRIARCLIFF, NEW YORK 10001   •   (333) 333-3333
pkeene@aol.com

2

Controller. *Carol A. Altomare, Three Bridges, New Jersey*

A cover letter for a resume should direct attention to the resume. The second paragraph mentions the resume and directs the reader's eyes to it and the notable accounting achievements it contains.

Re: Senior Tax Consultant

I have

~ 10+ years of tax and consulting experience working with industry leaders Penney Waterhouse, Delloise & Tooshe, and Motorcola.

~ Level 3 CGA, a Master's degree in Accountancy, and a Master's degree in Taxation.

~ Strong technical tax skills that include transfer pricing, corporate tax, sales and use tax, customs duties, excise taxes, VAT, tax research, international tax legislation, and tax reviews for contingent liabilities.

~ Gained a reputation for client service, commitment, knowledge, and creativity.

In my most recent position as Senior Associate with Penney Waterhouse, I specialized in transfer pricing issues and planning for corporate clients both in Canada and the U.S. In addition to demonstrating the strong tax research and analysis skills required of the position, I demonstrated the critical ability to understand and gain familiarity with the financial systems of large corporate clients - a skill necessary for completing the financial analyses for complex transfer pricing reports.

Throughout my career, I have developed the ability to thoroughly understand a company's business and industry, analyze data, identify material tax issues, and provide sound recommendations to the simplest and most complex tax issues.

I would welcome the chance to meet in person to learn more of this position and to see if my expertise meets your needs. Please feel free to review my attached resume and contact me at (555) 666-2222 to arrange an interview.

Thank you for your consideration.

Sincerely,
Julia Gaither

3

Senior Tax Consultant. *Ross Macpherson, Whitby, Ontario, Canada*

This cover letter is in .txt (text) format for e-mailing. The letter begins with bullets so that the first 10 to 15 lines in the reader's e-mail window capture attention and display the applicant's qualifications.

William DeCoons, CPA

555 Seneca Ave., Waldwick, NJ 55555, (555) 555-5555 x555, wdecoons@aol.com

December 14, 20xx

Mr. Robert B. Mishkoff
Mishkoff/Work Executive Search, Inc.
555 Madison Ave., Ste. 400
New York, NY 10022

Dear Mr. Mishkoff,

As an active partner in a CPA accounting firm who has developed the firm's consulting business, I am seeking to focus <u>all</u> my energies into management consulting.

My background includes 18 years of experience in accounting, auditing, finance and consulting. I am skilled in performing diverse financial analysis and developing business plans for various public- and private-sector enterprises and high-income individuals.

For each challenge, I have exceeded expectations and produced excellent results. Most notably, I

- Developed a business plan for a client that would expand his business while protecting his assets.
- Developed a consulting niche with municipal clientele that will net more than $100,000 in annual fees.
- Prepared a "Full Accounting of a Trust" by utilizing accounting software that would provide the format required by the New York State courts.
- Grew my private practice to more than $110,000 in revenues.

My goal is to join a progressive management consulting firm where I can help create value through innovative financing. I think and act "outside the box," and a company that values profitable problem solving will value me, for that is what I do best.

I prefer to stay in the metropolitan New York City area and anticipate an annual compensation package in excess of $100,000.

I look forward to speaking with you regarding any current search assignments appropriate for a candidate with my qualifications. Thank you in advance for your consideration.

Sincerely,

William DeCoons, CPA

Enclosure

4

Certified Public Accountant. *Igor Shpudejko, Mahwah, New Jersey*

This CPA wanted to transition to full-time management consulting. After doing some consulting, he discovered that he liked to find problems and fix them. The letter is addressed to a recruiter, who requires salary expectations.

Brooke Cummings

0000 Rock Cove • Parker, CO 80134
555.555.5555 • brooke@earthlink.com

November 7, 20XX

Janis Dodge
Senior Vice President—Chief Financial Officer
New Era Mortgage Corporation
12345 Beverly Boulevard, Suite 100
Los Angeles, CA 92612

Re: Vice President—Controller

Dear Ms. Dodge,

Accounting can be a powerful resource to an organization. It is up to the controller to educate the organization on how to effectively use accounting resources to improve productivity and profitability.

I was delighted when Jane Doe informed me of the Vice President—Controller position at New Era Mortgage Corporation. I am currently the Controller at Colorado Funding, a mortgage lender in Lone Star, CO. My financial management expertise, leadership skills, and extensive experiences are an excellent fit with your position, and I am very interested in relocating to the area to be closer to family and friends.

As a top performer with 20+ years of experience in accounting, I have the knowledge and expertise it takes to bring about positive change. My enclosed resume highlights my contributions and accomplishments in the areas of general accounting, financial statements, audits, cash management, budgeting, profit performance, strategic planning, and regulatory compliance. I take great pride in my work and my abilities. I have made great strides in being recognized as a key player on the management team. My accomplishments will speak for themselves.

My success is due to a passion for quality and excellence, tenacity, and a willingness to confront and conquer tough challenges. I have exceptional organizational skills and a keen eye for detail. My strengths lie in building quality financial processes that meet and exceed expectations. I believe gaining a thorough understanding of all aspects of the business is required to financially guide the organization.

You will find that I am very skilled at developing sound action plans, as well as administering and following through on those plans. I strive to build and maintain a principle-centered environment that preserves the organization's core values while stimulating growth and profitability.

I am eager to begin contributing to the bottom line of New Era Mortgage Corporation. I welcome the opportunity to explore my potential with you.

Thank you for your consideration; I look forward to speaking with you soon.

Sincerely,

Brooke Cummings

Enclosure: Resume

5

Vice President–Controller. *Roberta F. Gamza, Louisville, Colorado*

This letter names the source of a referral. The reference to the resume summarizes the applicant's areas of accomplishments, and the letter shows strongly that she can do the job and wants it.

Laura Weston

000 Cyprus Avenue
Birmingham, AL 55555

lauraweston000@xxx.com
Cellular: (555) 555-5555

October 2, 20XX

Cynthia Barton, CPA
Bailey, Watson & Cooper
PO Box 0000
Birmingham, AL 55555

RE: Staff Accountant Position

Dear Ms. Barton:

Your staff accountant position interests me greatly, but my situation is a little different from that of the typical accounting graduate. I was already a young businesswoman with a bachelor's degree in economics and logistics when the downturn in the commercial property sector motivated me to reevaluate my career goals. It is often said that accounting is the language of business, and I decided that I wanted to become fluent in that language, so I enrolled at Birmingham University. This fall I will graduate with an accounting degree.

Currently, I am directing property sales and acquisitions and evaluating real estate investments full–time, working as a graduate assistant at BU, and maintaining a 3.4 GPA in my senior–level accounting courses. In addition to a proven work ethic, I offer you and your clients a perspective on business that can be earned only in a real–world environment. As someone who has driven the bottom line and grown successful business relationships, I can help you build rapport and trust with your clients.

The enclosed résumé describes my experience, education, and accomplishments. After reviewing it, I hope you agree with me that someone with both an accounting degree and a few years in the business world would be a great asset to Bailey, Watson & Cooper.

I hope you will call to arrange a mutually agreeable time that we can meet to discuss my future contributions to your firm. Thank you for your time, and I look forward to talking with you.

Sincerely,

Laura Weston

Enclosure

6

Staff Accountant. *Alexia Scott, Montgomery, Alabama*

After the economy dealt this businesswoman's industry a bad blow, she used this letter to get an internship with a CPA firm. That internship led eventually to a job with a Big Four accounting firm.

KATY SNOW
000 East Street • Charlottetown, NC 20000
(555) 555-5555

January 19, 20xx

Mr. James Cathcart
Speedway Enterprises
5555 Racing Boulevard, Suite 555
Charlottetown, NC 55555

Dear Mr. Cathcart:

It is a long way we've come from those early race cars run in 1948 to the dynamic cars we have today, from the first NASCAR race in Daytona to the intricately engineered tracks of the present. Truly the exciting history of NASCAR is even more eventful today.

Those early days have disappeared, like the physician who made house calls, but they will never be forgotten. And neither will I forget my early years growing up in California, where my mother worked for an exhaust manifold manufacturer, Edelbrock, and my husband raced motorcycles. We attended NASCAR races at Riverside and Ontario Speedways in the late 1970s.

Over the years, though, I built not race cars, but a career in accounting and finance, moving across the country (no longer by motorcycle but by car), eventually settling in Charlottetown in 1995. During this period I assumed responsible positions as a controller, operations manager, or finance manager, with wide-ranging challenges, from accounting and finance to operations, information and systems integration, and human resources.

With each opportunity came new challenges. With each advancement and move, I went through the same experience—a desire to grow and build value within each organization I joined. Along the way, I became even more enchanted with NASCAR events, frequently traveling on weekends to races in Charlotte, Bristol, Martinsville, and Atlanta. And two years ago, I took "NASCAR 101" (my name) at Central Community College to learn more about racing, its advertising and promotion strategies, and pre- and post-race driver activities. I even toured Lowe's Motor Speedway. The class, presented by NASCAR TV commentator Tony Raines, was enlightening, engaging, and exhilarating.

Over the last few years, I've been preparing myself for the next step: to apply these skills to an organization within the NASCAR industry. My children are grown, and, with fewer familial obligations, my life has changed. Now I would like to join a winning NASCAR team. During this period of change, I view my situation much as Napoleon did when asked how he intended to combat seemingly insurmountable circumstances. His reply: "Circumstances? . . . I *make* circumstances."

If you are interested and have a need for someone with my skills, a desire to work hard, and enthusiasm for NASCAR, then give me the green flag. To quote William D. Smith, Vice President of the Jewel Tea Company back in 1948 (and it still makes sense today): "Take your job seriously—but don't take yourself too seriously. Believe that HOW you work is more important than WHERE you work [unless it's NASCAR] . . . To keep young you must play and you must have fun; make your job and your life a game—and play the game to win."

If you need a capable, devoted, and hardworking professional, I may be able to help. Can we talk? I will call to explore the possibility of an in-person meeting.

Sincerely,

Katy Snow

7

Controller. *Doug Morrison, Charlotte, North Carolina*

Having always worked in accounting and finance, this applicant wanted to combine her skills with her avocation—being an avid, lifelong NASCAR fan—and change her work environment completely.

BARBARA JONES

55 Cherokee Lane, Matawan, NJ 00000 ♦ Home (555) 555-5555 ♦ Cell (555) 555-5555 ♦ BJones@xxx.com

SENIOR ACCOUNTANT

Meticulous Work Ethic • Adaptable Across Corporate Environments • Professional & Disciplined Approach

February 15, 2012

Mr. David Jenkins
Controller
Harbor Electronics
555 Waterview Way
Parsippany, NJ 55555

Dear Mr. Jenkins:

Allow me to put the breadth of my accounting knowledge to work for you. With my demonstrated business acumen and strong understanding of financial statement analysis, revenue recognition, and expense management, I have the expertise and knowledge necessary for your posted position of **Senior Accountant.** My résumé is enclosed for your consideration.

Highlights of my special projects experience include the following:

- **Created More Effective Filing Systems**—Worked with CFO to facilitate identification of unpaid invoices, increase efficiency of paying vendors, and eliminate need for miscellaneous files by realigning filing system by fiscal year and paid date rather than vendor name.

- **Achieved Greater Accuracy with New Procedures**—Established policy of requiring W-9s for vendors and independent consultants before issuing first payment, and filing them alphabetically by name in a separate binder rather than merging them in with paid vendor files.

- **Trusted to Facilitate Bankruptcy and Acquisition Proceedings**—Across multiple situations, chosen by senior management to assist with bankruptcy proceedings, the sale of assets, and the transition and transfer of knowledge post-acquisition.

Although I hold my present employer in the highest esteem, my position is seasonal, and I am open to exploring a new full-time opportunity that could most benefit from my mix of strong technical skills and effective communication skills. I am confident that my strengths would make an immediate and lasting contribution within your organization and would welcome an interview at your earliest convenience.

I will call your office next week to follow up.

Sincerely,

Barbara Jones

Enclosure: Résumé

8

Senior Accountant. *Laurie Berenson, Franklin Lakes, New Jersey*

The applicant had two part-time seasonal jobs in small accounting departments and wanted the stability of one full-time position. Her breadth of experience is cast as a benefit to a future employer.

CONFIDENTIAL

Kristen Sheff, CPA

0000 Teal Lake Drive Houston, Texas 00000

✉ ksheffcpa@xxx.com ☎ 555.555.5555 (home) – 555.555.4444 (cell)

Tuesday, XX September, 20XX

Ms. Joanne Carlson
CFO
Topline, Inc.
00 Madison Parkway
Suite 000
Houston, Texas 00000

Dear Ms. Carlson:

If you could "design" the best Senior Accountant for Topline, would the following capabilities meet your toughest specifications?

- ❑ An accounting specialist with the heart of an entrepreneur, but the eye of an auditor, to balance liability with ROI,

- ❑ A senior team player so fluent in the "language" of every internal and external customer that she can deliver powerful solutions they use almost intuitively, and

- ❑ A productivity multiplier who can balance exacting accuracy, solid compliance, and profitability — even under the toughest conditions.

You have just read the *Reader's Digest* version of my résumé. You'll find all the details starting on the next page.

That document may not look like others you've reviewed. I thought you deserved to see seven profit-building capabilities I want to put at Topline's disposal at once. Backing them up are seven contributions made to one of America's leading accounting firms supporting a Fortune 100 client.

It's my natural preference for serving customers — especially internal customers — that drives the suggestion that follows. Because words on paper can't replace people speaking with people, I would like to hear about Topline's unique senior accounting needs in your own words. May I call in a few days to arrange a time to do that?

Sincerely,

Kristen Sheff, CPA

Encl.: Résumé

CONFIDENTIAL

9

Senior Accountant. *Don Orlando, Montgomery, Alabama*

This former consultant for a major firm was concerned about downsizing. The target was an accounting position in a smaller market where there are more opportunities for accountants.

Margaret V. Baxter

000 Anoka Drive
Waterford, Michigan 55555

555-555-5555
mbaxter@network.net

March 15, 20xx

Dear Practice Manager:

My previous five-year-long position as a Medical Receptionist/Biller was the best job of my life! I enjoyed the patients and my coworkers. I loved the challenges it presented and that each day was different. My most recent job took me away from the medical field, and I have really missed it. That's why I am contacting you—to learn about employment opportunities for an experienced, effective, and, most important, motivated receptionist/biller/administrative support provider. My resume describes my experience.

When you review my resume, I hope you will notice that, although I have been working with engineers and automobiles instead of patients and charts, the same skills are important. For example, in my current position I must be highly accurate when working with vehicle part numbers. That isn't much different from coding patient charts with the precise ICD-9 numbers. Among my responsibilities is keeping track of vehicles, keys, and projects. That ability to multitask is equally valuable in a medical office. Also, people are people, and I believe I possess strong communication and interpersonal skills.

Bottom line, I am eager to get back into the medical field to share my enthusiasm and commitment to patients. I am confident that I would be an enhancement to your practice. I am prepared to work hard to get back up to speed with the billing side of the office as quickly as I can. I will give you a call to arrange an interview. Thank you for your time and attention.

Sincerely,

Margaret V. Baxter

Enclosure

10

Medical Receptionist/Biller. *Janet L. Beckstrom, Flint, Michigan*

This applicant wanted to move from a position that was too analytical and had little interaction with people and to return to a position in a field she truly enjoyed (medical office administration).

Katherine Sullivan
555 County Lane, Newton, MA 05050

505-555-0505   ksullivan@xyz.com

March 5, 20XX

William Lodge
Dexter & Lodge Recruiters
555 Commonwealth Ave.
Boston, MA 05550

Dear Mr. Lodge,

For 15 years I have been providing administrative support to senior managers and busy departments. With a corporate reorganization pending, I am currently looking for an opportunity to apply my skills in a new setting. Perhaps one of your clients is looking for the experience and expertise I have to offer.

As the enclosed resume indicates, I thrive in a high-pressure environment and welcome the challenge of performing multiple tasks. My background includes introducing a wide variety of procedures that improve office efficiency and free managers to attend to other tasks. Given a high degree of autonomy, I have made key purchasing recommendations and decisions; coordinated a wide variety of conferences, meetings, and special events; and performed day-to-day administrative functions. In particular, I have developed a high level of expertise with a variety of software applications, most notably creating PowerPoint presentations, and have been called upon by secretaries and managers for computer training and technical assistance. My dedication, hard work, and excellent performance throughout my career are a source of pride for me, and they have been recognized over the years through numerous promotions and achievement/excellence awards.

I am very interested in talking with you about the contribution I can make in a new position. You can reach me at 505-555-0505. I look forward to hearing from you. Thank you for your consideration.

Sincerely,

Katherine Sullivan

Enclosure

11

Administrative Assistant. *Wendy Gelberg, Needham, Massachusetts*

This letter, sent to a recruiter, plays up the applicant's value in a role that often does not have quantifiable results. The writer calls attention to background, efficiency, and scope of operations.

GIMMIE A. SAMPLE
234 Typist Street
Somewhere, IL 60654
555-232-3241
admin@adminit23.com

Dear Hiring Manager:

I would like to join your team in a position where I may utilize my customer service skills, and I'm attaching my resume for your review. Specifically, I would like to expand my experience in sales support, reception, customer service, and personnel administration.

✓ My most recent positions at Tectura, the Signature Group, and Dominick's required extensive customer communications and problem-solving skills, and I've been recognized for my ability to expedite inquiries tactfully, promptly, and accurately.

✓ I am very dependable and self-motivated, and have proven my ability to bring out these qualities in the people I supervise. I'm also very time sensitive, efficient, and quality minded, and this helps me work well with all types of customers.

These are among the skills I can now bring to your company. I am available for an interview and will contact you next week to set up a convenient time.

Thank you for your time and consideration.

Sincerely,

Gimmie A. Sample

Enclosure

12

Administrative Assistant. *Steven Provenzano, Streamwood, Illinois*

The first paragraph indicates interest in a position, and the two statements show that the person has the skills to be effective in that position. The second paragraph looks for an interview.

AMANDA PIERCE

55555 Road 19
Hollings, NC 00000

Cell: 555.555.5555
amanda245@msn.com

Date

Hiring Manager
Company
Address
City, State ZIP

Re: [Job Title] advertised [where and when]

Dear [person or title],

As a hardworking individual with excellent administration and communication skills, I would like to explore the possibility of putting my skills and experience to work for you as a [job title]. Highlights of my background and abilities include the following:

- Extensive experience in providing efficient office support in a variety of environments.

- Proven ability to implement new processes in order to realize increased efficiency and cost savings.

- Expertise with written and verbal communications, including relating well to a wide range of people and writing contracts, letters, and minutes.

- Excellent ability to coordinate small and large special events and meetings, as well as organize travel arrangements.

The accompanying resume will provide you with additional details of my accomplishments and skills. I would welcome the opportunity to meet with you and learn how I can make a positive contribution to your company. I will call next week to inquire about the possibility of a meeting.

Thank you for your time and consideration.

Sincerely,

Amanda Pierce

13

Administrative Assistant. *Michele Angello, Aurora, Colorado*

The applicant was applying to many job postings, so the writer created a letter template that could be personalized for each job. The bullets highlight administrative abilities crucial to employers.

MARSHA NEWBERG

1212 Lake Lane – Minneapolis, MN 88888
999.888.7777 (C) – marsha.newberg@tfl.net

ADMINISTRATIVE ASSISTANT ~ PROJECT MANAGER

December 12, 20XX

John Brown
CEO
ABC Corporation
1122 9th Street
Madison, WI 99999

Dear Mr. Brown:

As an effective administrative assistant / project manager, I can identify problems and provide solutions. I also have the unique ability to translate concept into accomplishment as well as possess the vision to capture opportunities that will contribute to the long-term profitability of an organization.

Throughout my career, I have leveraged my leadership, planning, organizational, and financial skills to streamline processes, optimize efficiencies, reduce costs, and increase customer satisfaction. As my resume demonstrates, I have

- Improved project processes through identification of best practices and the creation of resolutions. Increased productivity by maximizing organizational skills and capabilities. Been an integral part in the seamless integration of two organizations by unifying processes and procedures—as Executive Assistant to the Chairman.

- Saved 50% in man-hours by designing more efficient office forms—as Executive Assistant to the Chairman.

- Expedited the merger of the company as Lead Support Administrator for one of 16 integration teams—as Executive Secretary to the Division VP.

- Consistently met deadlines and budget goals and was an essential player in the formulation of training manuals, materials, and presentations—as Administrative Assistant.

My success is due, in part, to an inherent ability to communicate effectively with others. It has enabled me to motivate and lead cross-functional teams. Likewise, it also has assisted me in the mentoring and retention of exceptional personnel committed to professional excellence.

Due to the relocation of my husband's position, I am seeking new career challenges and look forward to the opportunity to discuss your needs and my potential contributions. I will contact you by e-mail in a few days to set up a time we can meet.

Sincerely,

Marsha Newberg

Enclosure

14

Administrative Assistant. *Sally McIntosh, St. Louis, Missouri*

This letter for a high-level administrative assistant includes a bulleted list of accomplishments mentioned in the resume. A spouse's relocation is the occasion for her job change.

Susan E. Williams

0000 Indianwood Road
Clarkston, Michigan 55555

555-555-3333
sueew@network.net

[Date]

[Name]
[Company]
[Address]
[City, State ZIP]

Dear Director of Employment:

A BBA degree, 20+ years of experience in the banking industry, and a background in administrative support—that's what I have to offer your organization. After a rewarding career at Michigan National Bank, I find myself in the position of seeking new career opportunities. My resume is enclosed for your review.

My career at the bank encompassed diverse areas that required skills valuable to any industry. For example:

- ❖ Thorough understanding of administrative/office operations
- ❖ Event-planning and management experience
- ❖ Customer-focused attitude
- ❖ Attention to detail and strong organizational skills
- ❖ Ability to oversee multiple responsibilities simultaneously
- ❖ Computer fluency

In combination with my financial responsibilities, I took a personal interest in every client. There were cases that necessitated my intervention to arbitrate differences between feuding beneficiaries. Sometimes I was called upon to schedule doctor appointments or arrange for home repair on a client's behalf. But serving the client (or the client's estate, as the case may be) was always my top priority.

Thank you for taking the time to review my credentials. I hope you feel a personal meeting would be beneficial; I am available at your convenience. If you have any questions—or when you are ready to schedule an interview—please give me a call at 555-555-3333.

Sincerely,

Susan E. Williams

Enclosure

15

Administrative Assistant. *Janet L. Beckstrom, Flint, Michigan*

This applicant was downsized by a bank after 30 years. The writer prepared this general cover letter. The applicant was hired as an administrative assistant for a large medical center.

Sydney Murray
214-555-1111
1234 Festival Lake Dr.
Houston, TX 55555
bbsydney@xxx.com

October 10, 20XX

Mr. Hatcher, Human Resources Director
Crazy Little Shoe Company
4321 Lake View Ave.
Houston, TX 55555

RE: Executive Assistant to the VP of Design

Dear Mr. Hatcher,

Who is the ultimate Executive Assistant?

You need strong organizational skills and attention to detail. You need your Executive Assistant to always be a step ahead and juggle multiple tasks at once. You need your Executive Assistant to be proactive in eliminating speed bumps and "cool in a crisis" when they do arise. Who encompasses all these skills in career *and* personal endeavors? Sydney Murray, pleased to meet you.

I have not only provided outstanding support and organization to my past employer—for the last four years, I also have been a stay-at-home mom. Whether I'm organizing and coordinating hectic schedules for my family or serving as the primary liaison for upper-level management in a corporation, I bring the same outstanding dedication and superior support skills needed to accomplish tasks big and small.

Because a résumé can neither fully detail all of my skills and accomplishments, nor predict my potential to your organization, I welcome the opportunity to meet and discuss the merging of my talent and experience with your company's needs.

Thank you for your time and attention.

Sincerely,

Sydney Murray

16

Executive Assistant. *Devon Benish, San Antonio, Texas*

The applicant was out of the workforce for four years as a stay-at-home mom. The letter so impressed the hiring manager that he kept open a position so that the applicant could be interviewed.

PURDEEP MEHTA

000 Elizabeth Street
Augusta, Ontario A1A 1A1
555-555-5555

February 17, 20xx

Joseph Camarra
Director of Administration
Fieldway Automotive Partners
440 Torris Boulevard
Augusta, Ontario
B2C 3D4

Dear Mr. Camarra,

I understand you are looking for a "Girl Friday"—someone to take control of the critical administrative and customer service functions at your location in Pinehurst, Ontario. If you're looking for a motivated and hardworking professional with an above-average performance record, outstanding interpersonal skills, and a "get it done" attitude, I think you've found the best person for the job.

Over the past few years, while working for Group Six Security, I have routinely met with your company's representatives. From this contact, I have gained an understanding of the work that you do and an appreciation for your need for strong administrative support. In my current role with TGO Consulting, I do just that: managing all critical administration for the company and supporting the activities of 30 consultants and project managers.

I invite you to review my attached resume, which details the skills and experience I offer. Highlights include

✓ **Strong communications and interpersonal skills**—personable and friendly, with the ability to work well with colleagues, superiors, clients, and vendors

✓ **Extensive administrative and office support skills**—includes invoices, billing, scheduling, A/P and A/R, file management, and data entry

✓ **Outstanding customer service**—award-winning performance providing friendly and effective customer service in both corporate and retail environments

✓ **Self-motivated and hardworking**—personally love challenges, extremely quick learner, and motivated to exceed expectations

I believe that my strong skills and solid work ethic would make a significant contribution to your team, and I would welcome the opportunity to meet in person to discuss this position and why I believe I am the strongest candidate you will see.

Thank you for your consideration. I will contact you soon to arrange a personal interview.

Sincerely,

Purdeep Mehta
Encl.

17

Administrative Support Position. *Ross Macpherson, Whitby, Ontario, Canada*

The applicant had heard about an unposted job through contacts in the industry. This cover letter was a bid for that position. Bullets point to her skills and traits. The entire letter displays confidence.

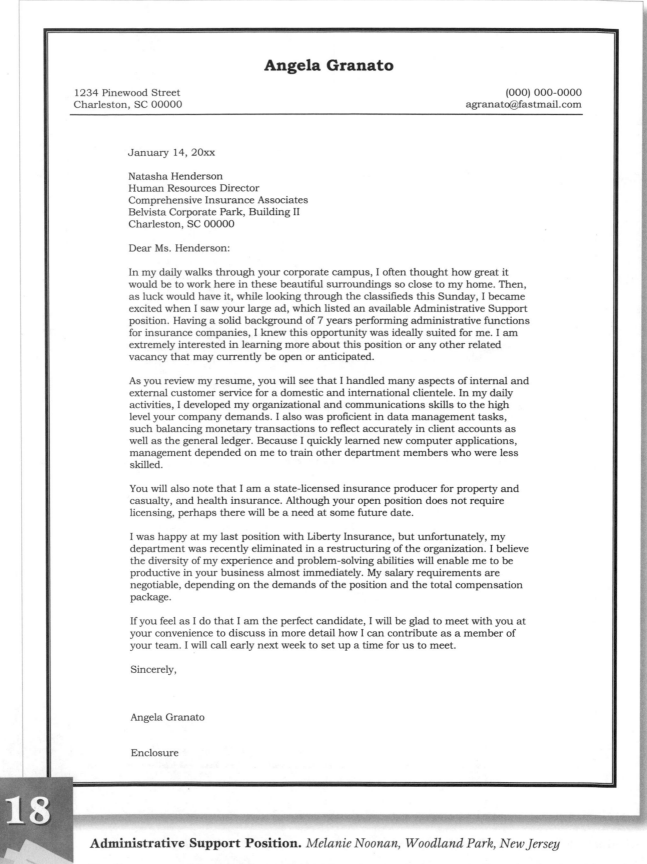

Angela Granato

1234 Pinewood Street
Charleston, SC 00000

(000) 000-0000
agranato@fastmail.com

January 14, 20xx

Natasha Henderson
Human Resources Director
Comprehensive Insurance Associates
Belvista Corporate Park, Building II
Charleston, SC 00000

Dear Ms. Henderson:

In my daily walks through your corporate campus, I often thought how great it would be to work here in these beautiful surroundings so close to my home. Then, as luck would have it, while looking through the classifieds this Sunday, I became excited when I saw your large ad, which listed an available Administrative Support position. Having a solid background of 7 years performing administrative functions for insurance companies, I knew this opportunity was ideally suited for me. I am extremely interested in learning more about this position or any other related vacancy that may currently be open or anticipated.

As you review my resume, you will see that I handled many aspects of internal and external customer service for a domestic and international clientele. In my daily activities, I developed my organizational and communications skills to the high level your company demands. I also was proficient in data management tasks, such balancing monetary transactions to reflect accurately in client accounts as well as the general ledger. Because I quickly learned new computer applications, management depended on me to train other department members who were less skilled.

You will also note that I am a state-licensed insurance producer for property and casualty, and health insurance. Although your open position does not require licensing, perhaps there will be a need at some future date.

I was happy at my last position with Liberty Insurance, but unfortunately, my department was recently eliminated in a restructuring of the organization. I believe the diversity of my experience and problem-solving abilities will enable me to be productive in your business almost immediately. My salary requirements are negotiable, depending on the demands of the position and the total compensation package.

If you feel as I do that I am the perfect candidate, I will be glad to meet with you at your convenience to discuss in more detail how I can contribute as a member of your team. I will call early next week to set up a time for us to meet.

Sincerely,

Angela Granato

Enclosure

18

Administrative Support Position. *Melanie Noonan, Woodland Park, New Jersey*

The first paragraph makes known the applicant's extreme interest in the advertised position. The letter then indicates her experience, licensing, and reason for applying. See the corresponding Resume 1 in Part 3.

One Concentric Circle
Nobleton, Virginia 12345
June 1, 20xx

Dear Hiring Manager:

How does one make an office run smoothly, like a well-oiled machine?

- By understanding its components and their interrelationships, for example, the different kinds of equipment necessary to run a modern office, how they are used, and how they interact and interface.

- By understanding not only the machinery, but the people who use it. By understanding how they feel about the technology they use. By understanding the conditions under which they use the machinery best.

I have been making things run smoothly at Brite Industries for more than ten years. I understand machines, and I like machines. But it's my understanding of people that has made possible the kinds of success documented in the attached resume, detailing my progressively responsible administrative career at Brite and elsewhere. Many listen. I listen and acknowledge. It's one thing to be heard, but another to know you're being heard. I think, and then determine better and faster ways of doing things. When something goes wrong, I discover the misunderstanding that caused the problem and clarify it.

This is how I saved $100,000 and increased productivity 40% at Brite. This is how I upgraded five positions, significantly improving morale. This is how I anticipated a question from our president, ensuring it was answered *before* it was asked. This is how I recommended, for an incident center, a new location that was subsequently approved by management, saving both time and money. This is how I significantly reduced absenteeism through informal and formal counseling to departmental staff.

And this is how I can help you. Please take a look at the attached document. I am confident that, on reviewing it, you will agree I have the potential to become a worthy member of your team. Kindly phone or e-mail me to set a convenient time to meet, so that we could discuss how I might best serve your organization.

Sincerely yours,

Anna Marie Di Magenta

P.S. Please call me at (777) 654-3210 or e-mail me at dimagenta@aol.com.

19

Office Equipment Support Position. *Howard Earle Halpern, Toronto, Ontario, Canada*

Cover letters that resemble other cover letters can be boring. This letter is different in *offering* the reader original ideas to be helpful in the selection process, instead of *asking* for something.

BRENDA BELLOWS

000 Morris Street • Bronx, NY 00000
Brenda456@mail.com

Home: (555) 555-5555   Mobile: (555) 655-5555

November 13, 20xx

[Name]
[Title]
[Employer]
[Address]
[City, State ZIP]

Dear [Mr. or Ms. Name]:

A high-performing marketing organization staffed with individuals demonstrating a successful track record is an essential part of your company's continued growth.

I believe you will agree that my qualifications, highlighted in the enclosed resume, confirm that I have the creativity, marketing savvy and management experience that can contribute to your company's success.

Specifically, what do I offer?

- Fashion, beauty, fragrance and cosmetics industry background
- Developing marketing programs, promotions and events
- Coordinating national print and broadcast advertising
- Leading the creation and production of marketing materials
- Nurturing strategic partnerships with clients and trade publications
- Managing and delivering multiple projects/budgets in deadline-driven environments

Examples of my accomplishments:

- Restructured entire co-op advertising program at Estée Lauder, improving budget controls, tracking system and forecasting.
- Orchestrated successful marketing programs for an outdoor advertising association, including the annual award show and gallery that increased participation 50% each year.
- Initiated sales/marketing tool that contributed to new business development at a start-up media company.
- Saved more than $100,000 just in production/tagging costs through effective negotiation skills.

I welcome the opportunity to meet with you and discuss the value I would add to your team as a Marketing Coordinator. May I call next week to set an appointment?

Sincerely,

Brenda Bellows

20

Marketing Coordinator. *Louise Garver, Broad Brook, Connecticut*

With print, broadcast, and outdoor advertising experience, this applicant wanted to move to the next level in marketing. This letter enabled her to win interviews that led to an excellent offer.

Chase Williams

SENIOR-LEVEL MARKETING EXECUTIVE

ADVERTISING · BRANDING · PUBLIC RELATIONS

[Insert Date]

[Insert Contact Name]
[Insert Contact Title]
[Insert Company Name]
[Insert Contact Address]
[Insert Contact Address]

An entrepreneur at heart, I get the job done. "There is always a better way" is my mantra and the force that drives me to consistently achieve seemingly impossible results and ROI.

Dear [Insert Contact Name]:

As a seasoned senior-level marketing professional with client-side, agency, and consulting experience, as well as a background building a spectrum of major organic and natural brands—including Tom's of Maine, Burt's Bees, and Nature's Bounty—I can help [Insert Company Name] meet the rapid challenges in today's marketplace.

With a thorough understanding of marketing, business, and global trends, coupled with a deep knowledge of consumer wants, needs, and buying behaviors, I will leverage the strengths of your organization. I know how to drive spirited strategy development and implementation, construct solid organizational and product-line plans, optimize the use of funds, and keep the business and tech sides on the same page. I typically get it right the first time, no matter the challenge!

You will find me to be a low-risk hire who will deliver needed ROI. I determine ways to execute campaigns correctly without compromising their effectiveness due to internal constraints, and I use all technology (internal and external) to the company's advantage. Significant accomplishments predictive of contributions I can make to [Insert Company Name] include

- Successful launch of a new Green Mountain brand, seamlessly and without disruption to other core businesses.

- Reduction of acquisition costs by up to 75% in key segments—35% on average—through remarketing targeted to nonpurchasing Green Mountain prospects.

- Launch of Hannaford's most successful new North American product in 25+ years.

- Leadership of a group that delivered a 42% year-over-year increase in fee revenues for Stonyfield, Inc.

Strategy is hard-wired into my thinking—I play chess three to five moves out and plot a marketing or business plan the same way. Everywhere I have worked I have anticipated and solved likely problems before they happened. I am known to quickly learn from mistakes and redirect energies. A strong team player, I play to win the prize for the company. I operate as an agent to deliver change and lead by example.

Marketing today is not as simple as it used to be. Time to market is crucial, and it is no longer acceptable to progress at a comfortable pace with internal capabilities when these resources are lacking. I maximize profitability of customer segments through the entire customer life cycle to grow ROI and sustain competitive strength. As an entrepreneurial and strategic leader, I squeeze the most possible out of internal expertise and capabilities and then supplement and draw on external solutions as needed to buttress internal capabilities.

[Insert Contact Name], I'd like to discuss with you my ability to 1) continue to cost-effectively drive leads that convert into customers in the increasingly complex organics space, 2) overcome the infrastructure weaknesses specific to growing companies, 3) build a brand while reducing customer acquisition costs, and 4) use segmentation and modeling to maximize ROI. May we schedule a meeting?

Sincerely,

Chase Williams

4573 Cliff Drive, Denver, CO 55555 ▪ 000-000-0000 ▪ organicmktng@aol.com

21

Senior Marketing Executive. *Deb Dib, Medford, New York*

Resumes for senior executives with much experience are often longer and more detailed. The same is true for their cover letters. The bulleted items list notable, quantified achievements.

Williamina Rasmussen

"I have always believed that writing advertisements is the second most profitable form of writing. The first, of course, is ransom notes." ~ Philip Dusenberry

May 14, 20XX

Bill Smith, Advertising Director
The Daily Times Newspaper
123 City Street Northwest
Somewhere, Montana 55555

Dear Mr. Smith:

I read of your "immediate opening for a bubbly advertising writer" … I'm available, immediately! My passion is copywriting and developing advertising campaigns that earn customers' trust. *The Daily Times* has the potential to reach a community of 50,000 people, which translates into 50,000 potential readers and customers. In our current economy, many of your customers believe marketing should be the first thing they cut from their budgets. I would love an opportunity to prove them wrong. Unique, appealing advertising has a large impact on sales, so advertising clearly should be one thing they keep.

The eleventh hour is a good time for me; the pressure of a deadline throws the creative switch "on" in my brain, and my pen responds by writing clever ad copy, captivating word phrases and catchy titles. My creativity, imagination and communication skills were polished at The University of Montana as a print journalism major working in the advertising department of the student newspaper. I am a word-savvy writer with a quirky sense of humor who completed her bachelor's degree this week and is ready to write!

As a member of your team, I will demonstrate an uncompromising focus on being creative and efficient and making the customers and products I represent irresistible to consumers. To show you I am not all talk, I have included an ad I created for a bed and breakfast where I worked last summer. Please allow this new college graduate to share in a personal interview her enthusiasm and willingness to learn. I am confident I will prove to be an excellent hire.

Respectfully,

Williamina Rasmussen

Enclosures: résumé and advertisement

555 Main Street | Somewhere, Montana | 406.555.5555 | wrasmussen@xxx.com

22

Advertising Writer. *Cheryl Minnick, Missoula, Montana*

The local newspaper posted an ad for a "bubbly advertising writer," and this letter was written to convey the applicant's witty writing style and quirky sense of humor without being over the top.

Heeru Singh

555 Clyde Street ▪ Forest Hills, NY ▪ C: XXX-555-5555 ▪ hsingh@xxx.com
LinkedIn: http://www.linkedin.com/xx/xxxxxxxx ▪ Twitter: @xxx

October 7, 20XX

YYYYY XXXX, SVP Digital
Digisocial
555 Church Street
New York, NY 55555

Dear Ms. XXXX:

Building and scaling digital media advertising campaigns is my expertise and my passion. My diverse experience in marketing, business development, ad operations, and software engineering has been leveraged to help top European brands in multiple verticals gain a foothold in the U.S. market and achieve double-digit revenue growth. I have solid analytical skills and strong direct-response experience and can utilize Web analytics systems, data provider intelligence, and optimization tools to create technically sound and robust digital platforms that get my clients recognized. As VP of Media for Mash Interactive, I have

♦ Created the digital advertising campaign that rocketed a cosmetics client to the top beauty merchant on PayQuick.

♦ Identified the media strategy for a public service announcement video that exceeded all performance measurement goals exponentially and achieved standing as *Most Viewed PSA Video* on YouTube.

♦ Introduced innovative online engagement models that built community, increased page views, and significantly curbed bounce rate for a new beauty product with no previous online exposure in a U.S. market.

In addition to my digital agency experience, I have ad operations and technology back-end experience on the digital publishing side. I launched the MailMeItNow advertising department and created the vision to monetize 100% of their ad space. Earlier at OpsAll, I created the ad operations infrastructure and partnered with top digital publishers including AOL and Yahoo!. My digital media experience began at TechZ.com where I optimized ad campaigns and troubleshot technical issues.

Excited by the prospect of an opportunity with your company and impressed by the strength of your brand, I would welcome the chance to meet with you to discuss my qualifications in more detail. I am confident that I can deliver results similar to those described above for your organization and look forward to a personal interview.

Sincerely,

Heeru Singh

Attachment

Digital Advertising Campaign Developer. *Barbara Safani, New York, New York*

This applicant was looking for a position to make use of exceptional digital media skills. Three bulleted items call attention to noteworthy achievements. Excitement is evident throughout.

Andrew Adams, M.P.A.
55 S. Tetley Highway, State Street, Georgia 55555
andrewwebmaster@xxx.com
555-555-5555

NEW BUSINESS DEVELOPMENT
"Good business is good, when it's good for all concerned."

October 4, 20XX

Steven Jobbers
Principal
The Association of Graphic Administrators
5 West DSL Street
Digital Stream, Florida 55555

RE: Advertising/Sponsorships Manager position

Dear Mr. Jobbers:

During recent discussions with Peter Lowe and Randy Owen, former executive directors of the Super Highway Marketing Group (SHMG), I was intrigued when they suggested I apply for the above-referenced position. My extensive background leading teams in selling print/digital advertising, sponsorships, and exhibit space for associations seems to be an ideal match for this opportunity.

Complementing my ability to directly add to the bottom line by creating customized media bundles for association trade shows is my proven experience as a sales manager. Throughout my career I have led high-performing teams, served as a trainer and educator, and gained a reputation as a leader capable of bringing out the best in each representative. My track record has included

 ➢ **Increasing the number of client accounts 33% by leveraging network, growing relationships, and providing customized solutions.** (Digital Interactive Association)
 ➢ **Achieving 47% additional revenue for association clients by advising 50 chapters on sales best practices.** (The Center for Internet Users)
 ➢ **Adding 20% more partners in highly competitive market.** (Internet Cafe Center of Industry)

After working with the SHMG while at Digital Interactive Association, I am excited by the possibility of working with another respected association. I would like to meet with you to further discuss your needs and how my qualifications could fulfill them. I will call next week to follow up, but if you would like to contact me earlier, I can be reached at the telephone number and e-mail address listed above. Thank you for your time and consideration.

Sincerely,

Andrew Adams, M.P.A.

Enclosure: resume

24

Advertising/Sponsorships Manager. *Charlotte Weeks, Chicago, Illinois*

This applicant had contacts who knew the hiring manager. The writer addressed this connection in the first paragraph and tailored the rest of the letter to fit the job ad as closely as possible.

National Golf Members Association

February 23, 20xx

Dear Human Resources Representative:

I am submitting my resume in consideration for your ***Advertising Account Services*** position. Please review my qualifications, as I believe my background complements your company's needs. My attached resume quantifies my account management accomplishments, results, and ability to exceed all job performance metrics. I am targeted toward the National Golf Members Association out of personal interest, as I played golf in college and follow all aspects of the game. I am a member of your organization, and I have been impressed with your growth and new expansion into the international market.

I am a quality-driven professional with a ***bachelor's degree in business administration*** and a proven track record of success in building client relationships. My work experiences testify to my ability to prioritize and organize while delivering desired results on time and under budget. The knowledge, skills, and abilities of this position are a solid match for my experience. My work is analytical and requires creativity and quick decision-making and problem-solving skills. Daily I am presented with diverse points of view, and I build consensus and make decisions concerning them. I work with deadlines, so I understand the concept of urgency. I am extremely self-motivated because I have worked under commission most of my career.

I have ongoing projects to manage and new projects that must meet deadlines, so multitasking and prioritizing are inherent parts of my work. Attention to detail and recognizing inaccuracies are the foundation of my work and the key to maintaining profit margins in my position. I work with Excel daily and enjoy learning new operation systems and business processes. I can work either independently or as part of a team. I have outstanding communication skills, proven teamwork skills, and the freedom to produce during flexible hours. I can offer excellent employer references and job performance evaluations.

Please feel free to contact me at your convenience, and thank you for your consideration.

Sincerely,

Doug King

25

Advertising Account Services Position. *Sharon McCormick, Durham, North Carolina*

This person did not have experience managing accounts in the golf industry, but a resume quantifying achievements and this enthusiastic letter secured an interview.

Melissa O'Brien
XXXX Manchester Court • Valley Center, KS 55555
flygirl@xxx.com • 555-555-0000

Mr. John Ward, Contract Recruiter
Avicor Aviation Inc.
XX NW Bethany Blvd., Suite XXX
Beaverton, OR 55555

Dear Mr. Ward:

Recently I had the opportunity to talk with Monica Montgomery, a flight attendant with your organization. She urged me to share my resume with you in consideration of possible employment. Monica and I worked together in the past, and she is familiar with my level of professionalism, dedication to providing exceptional customer service, and comprehensive understanding of corporate aviation. Please review my resume, which is attached.

As you can see, I have been a corporate flight attendant for 10 years, including a stint as a Chief Flight Attendant with Deere & Company. My resume specifies the aircraft on which I have flown as well as the training I've completed, which is on par with your commitment to safety. I am very experienced traveling abroad and easily relate to diverse cultures and environments.

I expect you are also interested in my intangible skills, as in how I serve my passengers. My track record speaks for itself: I am frequently requested by customers for repeat flights. They know that I will do whatever it takes to make them comfortable and meet their needs, sometimes even recognizing what they want before they do! My interaction with passengers is professional and in keeping with executive expectations.

My extensive industry experience and intuitive personal skills prepare me to seamlessly become a valued member of your flight attendant team. I am eager to begin a conversation about how my background meshes with Avicor's high standards, so I hope you will contact me. Thank you for your time and consideration.

Sincerely,

Melissa O'Brien

Attachment

26

Flight Attendant. *Janet L. Beckstrom, Flint, Michigan*

This letter begins by mentioning the name of the person who recommended the applicant and continues by describing the applicant as a consummate professional with years of experience working as a flight attendant for private companies. This letter and its accompanying resume (see Resume 2 in Part 3) resulted in an interview.

Ready to relocate to the Clovis area

Charles Henry Kraft

0000 Sledgeway Street — Anchorage, Alaska 55555
☎ 907.555.5555 (Cell) — apmaster@whiz.att.net

Thursday, February 26, 20xx

Mr. Joe North
Director of Maintenance
TopLine Airlines, Inc.
555 Northridge Parkway
Suite 555
Clovis, New Mexico 55555

Dear Mr. North:

I want to make it easy for TopLine Airlines to add me to your team as your newest aircraft maintenance supervisor.

As a first step, I thought you deserved to see more than the usual tired lists of jobs held and training completed. In their place you'll find a half dozen examples of maintenance teams motivated, productivity boosted, liability reduced — in short, problems solved. And, while a resume format tailored to your needs is good at documenting results, it cannot tell you *how* I contribute to our leadership's peace of mind.

Therefore, as you read, I hope the following ideas stand out:

☐ I am only as good as the last job I signed off — conditions in the remote parts of Alaska leave little room for maintenance errors.

☐ I am only as good as my last quarter's MX statistics. If I don't spot and correct trends, we'll lose time and money.

☐ I am only as good as the teams I attract, recruit, train, and retain. Our labor market is among the tightest in the nation.

I'm employed now and my company likes my work. However, I want to relocate to be closer to my family. That's why I am testing the waters with this confidential application.

When it comes to something as important as finding TopLine Airlines' next aircraft maintenance supervisor, words on paper are no substitute for people speaking with people. So let me suggest a next step. I'd like to get on your calendar in a few days so that we can explore how I might serve your special maintenance needs. I will call to set up a time to meet.

Sincerely,

Charles Henry Kraft

Encl.: Resume

27

Aircraft Maintenance Supervisor. *Don Orlando, Montgomery, Alabama*

This writer is a master at avoiding clichés and whatever else is trite, timeworn, and customary. Study this and his other cover letters in this book for his fresh ideas.

Dean Roland, Jr.
5555 Coyote Pike
Cheyenne, WY 55555
(555) 555-0000 // deanjr@xxx.xxx

August 24, 20XX

TransAmerica Airlines
5555 Blue Sky Highway
Fort Worth, TX 55555

Reference Code XXXX – Airframe and Powerplant Mechanic

Good morning ladies and gentlemen,

While exploring employment opportunities for aircraft mechanics with TransAmerica Airlines' facilities at DFW Airport in Texas, I learned of the above-referenced requisition that interests me very much. I am enclosing my resume for your consideration. I believe that you will find that my experience and education provide an excellent foundation on which to build a mutually rewarding relationship.

My qualifications include a current FAA Airframe and Powerplant License and an Associate of Science in Aviation Maintenance Technology from Embry-Riddle Aeronautical University to be awarded in May 20XX. Until I was honorably discharged in 2005, I served in the U.S. Air Force as a Journeyman Jet Engine Mechanic where I inspected, maintained, and repaired jet engines on Boeing E-3 (AWACS) aircraft. In my current position as an Overhaul Mechanic at RAA of Wyoming, Inc., I have developed considerable experience working on Boeing 707 engines. Prior to this position, I served as a Passenger Seat Technician for Best Airflight Services, performing installations on Boeing 727, 737, and 757 aircraft.

The successful performance of my duties can be attributed to my strong visual acuity, manual dexterity, and commitment to careful checking of details to support reliability of testing equipment as well as quality verification of parts and systems produced. My skills have been extensively utilized in tool and gauge calibration and applications such as complex machine housings, gears, torque shafts, and soldering/plating operations, which demand extreme precision.

My international experience and daily interaction with coworkers, military personnel, executives, and the general public have given me the ability to communicate effectively with persons from all age, educational, ethnic, and socioeconomic groups. I project a professional image, have a high work ethic, work well under pressure, and can contribute to a team effort as well as work independently. I also bring a high energy level and enthusiasm to my daily endeavors and am always looking for better ways to improve productivity, enhance flight safety, and meet performance goals.

Because of relocation of operations at RAA, I am now seeking a challenging opportunity where I can apply my extensive background and experience to the benefit of TransAmerica Airlines. I would welcome a chance to speak with you and discuss in further detail my qualifications and your needs. If the above-referenced vacancy has already been filled, please keep my application on file should a similar opportunity present itself in the near future.

Sincerely,

Dean Roland, Jr.

Enclosure

28

Aviation Mechanic. *Melanie Noonan, Woodland Park, New Jersey*

The potential employer gave preferential treatment to ex-military personnel. The letter makes clear that the applicant is an Air Force veteran with a background in maintaining jet engines.

KAREN L. DUNLOP *Expert at Promoting 100% Client Satisfaction & Loyalty*

5555 K Place ◆ McKinney, TX 55555 ◆ (555) 555-5555 ◆ karendunlop@xxx.com
http://www.linkedin.com/x/xxxxx

July 9, 20XX

Mr. Kenneth Fouchard
VP Client Relations
Teleomm International
555 Industry Way
Frisco, TX 00000

Dear Mr. Fouchard:

Would you like to significantly maximize your revenue in this challenging economy and improve your workflow processes?

As a *Client Relations Management / Key Account Management Expert*, I've generated $80K in new revenue within a 6-month period.

My accomplishments include

- **Saving a top-dollar client account** and successfully salvaging the client relationship by getting to the root cause of the client's problems and resolving them promptly.
- **Achieving 98% client-retention ratings** by building sustainable relationships with key clients.
- **Increasing profitability 25%** by collaborating with IT design team to construct a relationship-profitability application.

If you would like to benefit from these qualifications and achieve results like these, then let's schedule a time to talk. I am most interested in a *Client Relations Management / Case Management position* where I can optimize my client relations management expertise to assist your company in maximizing ROI.

Sincerely,

Karen L. Dunlop

Enclosure

29

Client Relations Manager. *Leeza Byers, Marietta, Georgia*

This applicant wanted to move from sales to the next level of leadership positions. The letter positions her as an expert in turning around business units by improving processes. See Resume 4 in Part 3.

Willing to relocate to the New York City area

Donald M. Butler
Post Office Box 0000 Burlington, Vermont 00000
db2011@xxx.net • 555.555.5555

Wednesday, 28 February 20XX

Martin Hammond
Google Ideas
00 Ninth Avenue
4th Floor
New York, New York 00000

Dear Mr. Hammond:

As soon as I saw the announcement for a Google Ideas Principal, Business Operations and Strategy, I made submitting this application my first priority.

I've complied with the on-line application process, but I just couldn't let it end there. I thought the position called for what's driven me, precisely and powerfully, most of my professional life.

In applying for this position, I challenged myself to rise above the traditional format to give you what I though you needed. That's why the document you are about to read is different from most résumés.

Because advocacy must rest on value, I wanted you to see five capabilities I would love to offer you at once. Supporting those assertions are nine selected proofs of performance. As you read, I hope you'll see Google Ideas' approach to integrating structure, innovation, culture and value reflected strongly.

I am happy where I am. My clients value the innovative, cooperative solutions I've built with them for nearly a decade. But I crave to be part of the "think *and do* tank" culture described in the announcement.

If this were a traditional letter, here is where courtesy would dictate that I ask you to contact me. My passion won't allow that. It drives me to hear about Google Ideas' unique needs in your own words. May I get on your calendar briefly in the next few days for that purpose?

Sincerely,

Donald M. Butler

Encl.: Résumé

30

Principal, Corporate Think Tank. *Don Orlando, Montgomery, Alabama*

Evident in this letter are traits of both the applicant and the professional writer of the letter: a tendency to rise above traditional formats, plus a respect for innovative solutions and value.

Will consider relocation

Martin M. Bristow

125 West 00th Street New York, NY 00000

✉ martinbristow@xx.com ☎ 555.555.5555 (cell) — 555.555.7777 (home)

Thursday, XX September, 20XX

Mr. John R. Hodges
CEO
Arista Services, Inc.
000 West 00th Street
Suite 000
New York, New York 00000

Dear Mr. Hodges:

If your organization is driven primarily by quarterly bottom-line numbers, please don't read any further.

But if Arista Services is dedicated, as I suspect it is, to long-term, enduring growth and profit, we should explore overcoming any obstacles between your vision and the market share you deserve. I think I can help as your newest COO.

What I do isn't magic. I find, integrate, and synergize the wisdom and drive of people who know their part of industry better than anyone else. Certainly, my team and I get outstanding results. But if the truth be known, I lead because it's fun for me, my team, and our customers.

My success has continued as I have helped lead PE and VC organizations. But I much prefer guiding companies to enduring growth for their own sake, not to position them for takeovers. And I know I would be happiest closer to daily operations as a COO.

You'll find all the details in my résumé. It probably doesn't look like others you've seen; I tailored it for busy executives who want real answers. That's why my pledge of value—four powerful capabilities I want to put at Arista Services' disposal—are right at the top. And just below are seven transferable proofs of performance.

If you like what you read, I want to hear about your unique operational needs in your own words. May I get on your schedule in the next few days for that purpose?

Sincerely,

Martin M. Bristow

Encl.: Résumé

31

Chief Operating Officer. *Don Orlando, Montgomery, Alabama*

This highly experienced CEO wanted a less stressful position as a COO in a different industry that still provided the excitement of working in operations. A main task of this cover letter was to show his transferable skills.

Tom J. Jones

5 Exeter Road ● Las Vegas, NV 55555 ● Home: (555) 555-5555 cell: (555) 555-1776 ● Thomas@xxx.com

DYNAMIC OPERATIONS EXECUTIVE

September 27, 20XX

Laura Bell
Human Resources Manager
TNT Corp
55 Swan Road
Las Vegas, NV 55555

Opportunity: **Chief Operating Officer**

Dear Ms. Bell,

Turning visions and strategic plans into thriving operations has been the focal point of my career as a distinguished operations executive. As the attached résumé illustrates, my leadership performance, visionary approach, and passion for maximizing human talent have enabled me to lead organizations to high levels of success. I am confident that you will find my qualifications to be a precise fit for your organization.

With a background that encompasses various business sectors (banking, retail, logistics, and manufacturing), I offer proven, ongoing bottom-line results. My résumé shows the trend in increased profitability, revenue generation, and staff productivity throughout my career. I consistently exceed corporate objectives through my trademark ability to engage contributors in operations by being a

- **Resourceful Problem Solver** who combines technical knowledge and business acumen to deliver results.
    - Improved on-time delivery by 54% in a custom-engineered metal fabrication shop.

- **Effective, Customer-Focused Communicator** with a proactive approach.
    - Reduced plant expansion costs by 14% ($5M) through supply chain partnerships.

- **Innovative Leader** adept at planning, streamlining, delegating, driving productivity, and enhancing profitability.
    - Lowered fuel costs by $1M and energy costs by $2M through equipment optimization and conservation.

This synopsis of my professional achievements is but a sample of the quality and caliber of my performance; the enclosed documentation includes more detail. My professional mandate is to drive key business metrics to sustain improved profitability, and incorporate engagement and accountability across all business functions to improve the entire organization.

TNT Corp has a reputation for innovation and demonstrates a clear commitment to growth—both in your mission statement and annual reports. For this reason, I look forward to meeting with you to discuss further the details of joining such a prominent organization. I will follow up next week with a phone call to arrange a meeting at your convenience to discuss our mutual interests and the assets that I will bring to this role.

Regards,

Tom Jones

Enclosure: Résumé

32

Chief Operating Officer. *Tanya Sinclair, Pickering, Ontario, Canada*

Bulleted items indicate three of the applicant's key traits and three accomplishments. The last paragraph shows that he read the company's mission statement and annual reports.

FINN JOHANSEN, CMA, ICD.D

000 Park City Blvd. • Easton, OR 00000
Phone: (000) 000-0000 • E-mail: fjohansen@xxx.com

December 30, 20XX

Mr. Joe Smith
Chief Operating Officer
EFG Corporation
0000 Springfield Blvd.
Heber City, CT 00000

Dear Mr. Smith:

My interest in exploring a new challenge has motivated my writing to you. The enclosed resume briefly describes my expertise at **designing, developing and leading operations for recreation and event sports venues**. In today's economic climate, an essential ingredient for success is a combination of a proven record of surpassing clients' expectations while exceeding ROI for shareholders. I am confident that my solid reputation for building sustainable, profit-generating venues would make me a positive candidate for the **Chief Operating Officer position with ABC International.**

Selected achievements include

- Being an industry expert on LEED Certification programs with respect to multiuse venues and sports arenas. Interviewed/quoted regularly in reputable publications, such as *New York Times, Wall Street Journal, USA Today, The Connecticut Post,* and *LEED Operating Management.*
- Receiving international recognition for revitalizing the Center for Athletic Excellence in Albany, NY, which is recognized as the *"#1 Sports Training Complex for Olympic Athletes in the World."*
- Pioneering a user-driven functional design and detailed specifications for design-build construction, which led to projects being completed on time and on budget. Implemented the design for large, multiuse development projects in the U.S., South America, and Europe.
- Earning a master's degree in Economics from Cornell University and an undergraduate degree in Economics and Commerce from the Royal Military College in the UK. Also earned Certified Management Accountant (CMA) credentials and Director Accreditation (ICD.D.) by the Institute of Corporate Directors.

I am adept at handling difficult situations and consider adversity an opportunity—not a challenge. I would very much like to speak with you directly to discuss ABC International and how our association could be mutually beneficial. I can be reached at the above phone number or by e-mail and welcome the opportunity to talk with you in person.

Thank you in advance for your time and consideration.

Sincerely,

Finn Johansen, CMA, ICD.D

33

Chief Operating Officer. *Donna Allen, Heber City, Utah*

Boldfacing in the first paragraph and italic in two of the bulleted items help to direct a reader's attention to important information. Two other bulleted items point to international experience. See Resume 5 in Part 3.

JOE BROWN, R.PH, MBA

555 Manilow Drive, Chicago, IL 55555 | 555-555-5555 | jbrownmba55@xxxxx.com

[Date]

[Hiring Manager]
[Title]
[Company Name]
[Address]
[City, State ZIP]

[Dear Hiring Manager]:

As an executive leader in biotechnology and pharmaceuticals, I have been instrumental in developing business strategies and operational programs that achieve global results. Now in pursuit of new opportunities, I would be pleased to apply my strong leadership skills in organizational management, sales, and marketing as a [Title] with [Company Name].

Since 2007, I have contributed as President and CEO to the growth and strategic direction of XYZ Therapeutics, a start-up biotechnology firm that develops TB compounds. I played a key role in raising VC and expanding the company, which is now valued at over $280M. Prior to XYZ, I served as EVP in a general manager role for the U.S. Metabolic and Endocrinology Division of DEF Laboratories. While at DEF, I grew endocrinology revenues by $38M with minimal resources.

My early career experience includes extensive sales and marketing management. I am particularly proud of my success at ABC Sciences as Senior Director of Global Marketing. While there, I successfully positioned the TB medication Viroxin (Tabodir DF) to become an all-time, top-selling product, which catapulted ABC to new heights.

Additional highlights include the following:

- In 2011 CHIBiz.com recognized me as one of Chicago's top 30 most influential people in healthcare. Additionally, I earned a core member award from BIOCHI.
- I took the metabolic and endocrinology division of DEF Laboratories to new heights with sales of $160M. Initially the third poorest performing group, we became #1 under my direction.
- While at Majo Pharma, I initiated and led a $100M philanthropic TB campaign, collaborating effectively with the U.S. government, World Bank, and UN.
- I am active on numerous advisory boards and have been invited to speak at multiple learning institutions over the years. In 2001 I was honored with a Hero Award from the International Association of Physicians in Tuberculosis Care for my contributions.

My résumé is enclosed to provide you with a more comprehensive understanding of the depth and breadth of my experience. My operational expertise, innovative strategy development, and commitment to excellence have consistently led to outstanding business achievements. I would like to explore my background and qualifications with you in a personal interview. Please feel free to contact me at the number above to arrange a time to speak.

Sincerely,

Joe Brown, R. PH, MBA

Enclosure:

34

Chief Executive Officer. *Debra Wheatman, Parlin, New Jersey*

The first paragraph expresses the applicant's interest in an unspecified position, and the next three paragraphs make clear his current and past experience, plus distinctive career highlights.

Russell C. Burns

0000 Terrace Curve, Grapevine, Virginia 00000
✉ rcburns@xxx.com ☎ 555.555.5555 (cell) — 817.555.7777 (home)

Thursday, XX August 20XX

Ms. Clementine Whitcomb
Health for America
Chair, Board of Directors
000 X Street, NW
Suite 000
Washington, DC 00000

Dear Mr. Whitcomb:

As soon as I learned Health for America was searching for its newest CEO and President, I made tailoring this package my first priority. I am driven by missions I believe in. And Health for America's mission aligns with my lifelong passions.

I, too, look for passionate people when I hire. But passion itself isn't enough. Like you, I must consider the return on investment each hiring decision offers. That's why I thought you deserved more than the usual résumé. I've focused mine on the kind of return I know you demand. I replaced the standard "objective statement" with my pledge of value—capabilities Health for America will see me perform on the job right from the start.

In place of traits, responsibilities, and assertions that so often populate a "Summary of Qualifications," you'll see seven examples of problems solved—illustrations of my pledges in action.

As you read, I hope these central ideas stand out:

- ❏ I am happiest transforming organizations into the entities they've always wanted to be.

- ❏ I find great personal satisfaction guiding individuals and teams to achieve results they didn't think possible by aligning their personal goals with our organization's vision. Toward that end, I am expanding my professional development program to ensure my currency in federal issues and the decision makers who champion them.

- ❏ I love to share an organization's pride that comes from the regard, credibility, and trust their stakeholders, constituents, partners, and legislators hold them in.

In the end, however, words on paper can never substitute for people speaking with people. Therefore I would like to explore how I might better meet Health for America's needs. May I call in few days to arrange time for that purpose?

Sincerely,

Russell C. Burns

Encl.: Résumé

Chief Executive Officer. *Don Orlando, Montgomery, Alabama*

This successful CEO of a nonprofit organization in the Midwest wanted to move closer to his home in the DC area. He used this letter to apply to organizations having a lobbying function.

Russell C. Burns

0000 Terrace Curve, Grapevine, Virginia 00000
✉ rcburns@xxx.com ☎ 555.555.5555 (cell) — 817.555.7777 (home)

Thursday, XX August 20XX

Dr. Suzanne Konigsburgh
Chair, Board of Directors
American Optometric Association
0000 Carter Boulevard
Suite 000
Rockville, Maryland 00000

Dear Dr. Konigsburgh:

If the press of daily business sometimes interferes with bringing your board's vision to life, I would like to explore serving AOA as your next President and CEO. My goal is simple: I want you and your board free to concentrate on the strategic thinking that makes the American Optometric Association an engine moving healthcare to new levels of respect and service.

I would thrive translating your board's ideas into smoothly running, transparent operations. I would do that simply by working hard in these roles:

- ❑ As a champion who would infuse your model of success into the thinking of every staff member, every "customer," every partner organization,
- ❑ As a thought leader who would build, defend, and grow an irresistible, nimble brand, and
- ❑ As an executive with an entrepreneur's passion for quality and an auditor's eye for return on investment.

You've just seen the "movie trailer" version of my résumé. The proof of performance is in the next pages. That document might not look like other résumés you have seen. Four growth-building capabilities are right at the top of the first page, and they're backed up with five selected results. As you read, I hope a central thought stands out: I led my nonprofit organization to perform the best it ever has…without the resources so common in the private sector.

I enjoy my work as the CEO of the National Consortium of Health Care Professionals. But I want to put my energy and talent at the disposal of an organization that offers even greater responsibilities and opportunities.

When it comes to something as important as AOA's mission, words on paper are no substitute for people speaking with people. Therefore, I would like to hear about your needs in your own words. May I get on your calendar in the coming week to hear your views on that subject?

Sincerely,

Russell C. Burns

Encl.: Résumé

36

Chief Executive Officer. *Don Orlando, Montgomery, Alabama*

This letter is a version of the preceding cover letter and was used to apply to organizations without a lobbying arm. The applicant emphasizes high performance and growth.

TOM CARTER

555 Maple Drive   555-555-5555
Pittsburgh, PA 55555   tcarter@aol.com

August 30, 20xx

Mr. James Ryan
Cooper and Associates
5555 Peachtree Lane
Atlanta, GA 55555

Dear Mr. Ryan:

A fresh perspective, new strategies, and an objective viewpoint are just a few of the distinguishing characteristics I can bring to your company. As an executive, my focus has always been on growth and improving the company's bottom-line performance through progressive, customer-driven strategies. I welcome the opportunity to do the same at your company.

No business can progress and grow without leadership. In the final analysis, leadership and effective management are the only real advantages one organization has over another, especially in today's competitive marketplace. As both a career training and development executive with Fortune 500 companies and a leader/manager of small businesses focusing on delivering training and professional education, here is a snapshot of recent accomplishments:

- **Turnaround experience**—transitioned underperforming company with $40 million in revenue and 4% profit to $70 million and 13% profit within 18 months.

- **Successful P&L experience**—range of $1 million to $70 million.

- **Challenging environments**—manage successfully in a very complex international environment, as a service provider to the federal government, as President and CEO of the largest subsidiary of a publicly traded company.

- **New program development and execution**—direct market research; course design; delivery infrastructure; product positioning; marketing; sales; and finally profitable, recurring revenue streams.

- **Strategic partnerships and business alliances**—initiate, negotiate, and implement domestic and international alliances that benefit all parties.

As you review the enclosed resume, I am confident you will determine that my background and management skills match or exceed those required by your company. I would be delighted to meet with you to expand on my achievements and discuss how I can apply my strengths to positively impact your company's bottom line. I will call to schedule a meeting. Thank you for your time and professional consideration.

Sincerely,

Tom Carter

Enclosure: resume

37

Training and Development Executive. *Jane Roqueplot, West Middlesex, Pennsylvania*

Bullets and boldface highlight accomplishments to meet the job description of a prospective position. The second paragraph presents the applicant's views on company competitiveness.

JOHN HARMAN
1111 Greenberry Court
Montgomery, Alabama 00000
jharman2@capitol.net
☏ [334] 555-5555 (Home) — [334] 555-6666 (Cell)

Friday, January 20, 20xx

Ms. Sandy Reisman
Industrial Training Program Developer & Technical Writer
Alabama Industrial Development Training
One Technology Court
Montgomery, Alabama 00000

Dear Ms. Reisman:

As soon as I saw your announcement for a Training Program Developer and Technical Writer, I thought my experience in manufacturing in Alabama might make me a perfect match for you. Said another way, I wish I had the benefit of AIDT-trained employees in my plants. Thinking about AIDT's immediate future, I wanted to meet your needs, our employers' needs, and the needs of people seeking to enter the workforce. I have covered the details in the attached resume.

My resume documents function, performance, and results—not just lists of job titles and responsibilities. There are 15 examples of payoffs I've gotten for employers just like the ones AIDT serves. The six training examples are highlighted with borders. As you read, I hope this central idea stands out: All my job titles have a manufacturing aspect. However, I was always evaluated on how well I recruited, trained, and retained my workforce. I was measured on productivity. Even so, there is essential information no resume can transmit well.

I think of myself as a trainer with a subject matter expert's point of view. That has always been necessary because my bosses didn't grade my work based on lesson plans, test question ease indexes, or strict compliance with standardized terminology in writing objectives and samples of behavior. They demanded what your customers demand: increased productivity, reduced costs, and lowered liability. So I did much more than skills training. For me, skills without a solid work ethic didn't count for much. All my "students" got both the skills and attitude to underwrite their success in the workplace.

I know you'll soon make a decision about whom to interview. Nevertheless, I would like to hear about AIDT's "needs analysis" in your own words. If I am fortunate enough to be hired, that's the best way I know to be productive right from the start. I will call in a few days to explore opportunities for a meeting.

Sincerely,

John Harman

Encl.: Resume

38

Training Program Developer and Technical Writer. *Don Orlando, Montgomery, Alabama*

To make this letter different from the average letter, the writer placed "CONFIDENTIAL" in a header and a footer, used a phone graphic, and put a border around the sentence about borders.

Nancy T. Ditillio

000 Raven's Way ▪ Martinsburg, WV 21775 ▪ 555-000-0732 ▪ nditillio@hotmail.com

October 4, 20xx

AB&C Group
Robert Vance, Human Resources
One Executive Way
Ranson, WV 25438

Dear Mr. Vance:

Finding and retaining good employees are reported to be two of the biggest challenges faced today by businesses large and small. Retention data suggests that employees target and remain faithful to companies that are committed to their personal and professional development.

A recent visit to the AB&C Group Web site confirmed for me that yours is a company dedicated to employee development and training. Your acknowledgement in the *Wall Street Journal,* the Ranson Learning Center, and the Elaine Looney Achievement Center are testimonies to your commitment. I share in that commitment and have a proven record of achievement to that end. For these reasons, it is with great interest and enthusiasm that I am submitting my resume for consideration in filling your current opening for a **Director of Corporate Training.**

With more than 18 years in the education, employment, and training arena, I am confident I have much to offer:

> ▶ **Experience designing, developing, and delivering training.** I have written curricula covering everything from life skills and career management to computer software applications and the Internet. I have trained college students, corporate professionals, customer service representatives, professional peers, and factory workers, to name a few.

> ▶ **A proven record of delivering projects on time,** best exemplified by my experience in successfully writing and coordinating the submission of numerous federal grants.

> ▶ **Strong platform skills** and ongoing recognition as a high-energy, entertaining, and motivational trainer and workshop facilitator.

> ▶ **Supervisory and leadership experience,** whether serving on a board of directors for a community organization or coaching and mentoring individuals to define and take charge of their own success.

> ▶ **Creativity** and an innate ability to identify areas in need of improvement and the vision to develop and implement successful action plans.

Since this correspondence can only provide you with a brief overview of my skills and accomplishments, I would welcome the opportunity to talk with you about AB&C Group and your vision for developing your corporate training programs. I will phone early next week to follow up on this correspondence and explore the possibility of scheduling some time with you. I look forward to talking with you then.

Sincerely,

Nancy T. Ditillio

39

Director of Corporate Training. *Norine Dagliano, Hagerstown, Maryland*

This letter was a response to a newspaper ad. Bulleted items incorporate both the actual requirements listed in the ad and the candidate's experience that matches each requirement.

From: marck@aol.com
To: director@primosalons.com
Subject: Trainer/Manager Position

Could you use a high-energy, creative salon professional
who appreciates the vital link between well-trained,
motivated personnel and increased company profits? If so,
I would enjoy speaking with you to discuss how my skills
and experience might strengthen your organization.

With more than 20 years in the cosmetology industry, I
recently made a short-term move from "behind the chair"
to a training and management position at Hair Club for
Men. As has always been my nature, I met this new challenge
head-on. I am proud to say that, through expert training
and motivational team building, my contributions have proven
instrumental in positioning the Falls Church, Virginia, center
as a leader in the corporation for sales and service.

I discovered that I not only love personnel training but also
am good at it! My current manager credits me with being
"an integral part of changing the way the HCM seasoned
stylist thinks when it comes to what is best for the client."

I feel I have taken advantage of all that my current position
has to offer and am ready to push my career to the next level
as a full-time Trainer or Manager. I am very open to a
geographic move and amenable to travel.

My resume is pasted below. I have also attached, for your
convenience, a copy in Word 2010 format. This will provide you
with some additional information about my background.

Please phone or email me at the address or numbers listed
below. I look forward to talking with you!

Sincerely,
Marianne M. Clark
0000 Berkeley Lane
Frederick, MD 21701
marck@aol.com
301.555.5555 (home)
301.000.0000 (cell)

40

Trainer/Manager. *Norine Dagliano, Hagerstown, Maryland*

The candidate e-mailed this cover letter with a resume to different hiring managers in her industry.

AEVAH B. JONES

0000 Summers Court • Anywhere, Michigan 55555 • (555) 222-2222
aevah@email.com

December 8, 20xx

Tomas Smith, Director
ABC Incorporated
555 Main Street
Anywhere, Michigan 55555

Dear Mr. Smith,

As a successful and established recruiting professional, I bring more than eight years of experience and knowledge in locating highly qualified candidates pursuing mid-management to executive-level positions for various employers in diverse industries. I have the drive for developing business relationships and enjoy working one-on-one with employers and candidates. I find networking is key to professional and personal growth.

Through my efforts and success as a recruiter, I have received two prestigious awards from my last employer and have built a reputation for providing genuine leadership and working effectively with others. My talents and expertise in creative sourcing, networking, interviewing techniques and presentations have allowed me to make significant contributions to my employers, as noted in my resume.

Because I have been very successful in recruiting and enjoy the everyday challenges of my profession, I have decided to launch my career as an independent recruiter. I would appreciate the opportunity to speak with you personally to provide more details on my background and the expertise I can offer your firm.

Your time and consideration in reviewing my credentials are appreciated. I will contact you next week to see if we can schedule a day that we can meet to answer any questions you may have regarding my qualifications. I look forward to speaking with you soon.

Sincerely,

Aevah Jones

Enclosure

41

Independent Recruiter. *Maria E. Hebda, Trenton, Michigan*

The letter indicates in four paragraphs the applicant's experience and motivation, awards and areas of expertise, new direction and interest in an interview, and plans for following up the letter.

Greta Beninski CRSP, CPRW, CPCC
555-555-9999
gretab@xxxxxxxx.com
55555 Hill Country Drive
San Antonio, Texas 55555

May 19, 20XX

Edward Johnson, Director of Staffing Operations
Future Staff Direct Placement
000 NW Loop 0000
San Antonio, TX 55555

RE: Corporate Recruiter II

Dear Mr. Johnson:

I am a second-generation career matchmaker. I was trained by my mother, a Top Ten CPRW and multipublished author on career services. Since then, I have personally connected more than 75% of my clients with their current employer. I specialize not only in procedure but also in people. My specialty? Knowing that everyone is different and that stellar results are always in details and nuances.

Being triply certified—Certified Recruiting and Staffing Professional, Certified Professional Career Coach, and Certified Professional Resume Writer—I build a comprehensive knowledge of *all* functions in a field through independent research, previous experience, and a strong presence in several HR, recruiter, and job coaching groups. I formulate ideas about improving professionalism, eliminating confusion, shortening job searches, and giving all clients a superior experience.

I am available at your convenience for a personal meeting to further discuss how my skills and experience meet your company's needs.

Hire someone as committed to excellence in pairing talent and need as you are. Hire me.

Thank you for your time and consideration.

Sincerely,

Greta Beninski

42

Corporate Recruiter. *Devon Benish, San Antonio, Texas*

This applicant wanted to show that she had done all the things that a successful recruiter does and with strong skills had innovated a new, streamlined, and more profitable way to do them.

JOHN S. WILKENS

5 Holly Street
Raleigh, North Carolina 55555
Email: JSW@xxx.com

Home: (000) 555-0000
Cell: (000) 555-0500

Date:

Southern Transportation Limited
000 E. Wilmington Court
Raleigh, North Carolina 55555

Dear Mr. Johnston

During my research for corporations that are excelling in the 21st Century, I was pleased to find your posting for a Corporate Recruiter/Trainer on the Southern Transportation Limited website. As I am seeking to change my career direction from law enforcement to the broader aspects of corporate recruiting, training, safety and corporate security, I feel that I possess the qualifications to be an excellent candidate for the Corporate Recruiter/Trainer position.

The requirements specified for this position—sourcing, recruiting, interviewing, reviewing, facilitating training and establishing productive professional relationships—are in direct correlation to the responsibilities and duties I have been performing in my decorated law enforcement career for more than 15 years. In addition, I have recently completed the Safety-First Comprehensive Driving Course with the Defensive Driving Institute that would benefit the travel requirements of this position. As I make my transition, I would welcome the opportunity to be part of a corporation that has safety, customer focus, innovation, integrity and teamwork at the forefront of core values, along with being a Fortune 500 company.

Entrusted with great responsibility during my vast and diversified career, I have consistently demonstrated strong leadership, management and exceptional organizational skills. My time as a Deputy Sheriff and Special Investigator afforded me the opportunity to fully hone and successfully execute my sourcing procedures while developing creative interviewing skills. As the Team Leader of Special Circumstance Crimes, I was ultimately responsible and hands-on with training, motivating, counseling and developing personnel.

My attached resume further details my former law enforcement experience, leadership responsibilities and achievements. I would appreciate the opportunity to discuss with you how I might contribute to the continued success of one of the premier transportation companies in the world—***Southern Transportation Limited.***

I appreciate your consideration and look forward to hearing from you in the near future.

Sincerely,

John S. Wilkens

Enclosure

43

Corporate Recruiter/Trainer. *Kara Varner, Hampton, Virginia*

The individual, in law enforcement for 25 years, wanted to become a corporate recruiter/trainer. The writer researched the company and focused on relevant skills and values.

James Howard

0000 Tracer Downs ◆ Perry, GA 00000 ◆ jhoward@xyzmail.com ◆ 000-000-0000

[Date]

Mr. (Ms.) _____
[Company]
[Address 1]
[Address 2]

Dear Mr. _____

[Insert 2-line paragraph about how you heard of the position and why you are applying for it. For example: "If the information in the *Times Courier* is still accurate, you are currently seeking to fill the position of Customer Service Manager. This letter is to introduce myself as a candidate for just such a position."]

I am an experienced and highly qualified management professional. My areas of expertise lie in operations management, facilities management, transportation and embarkation, inventory and logistics, purchasing and procurement, personnel and human resources, materials management, public and motivational speaking, written and oral communications, information gathering, data analysis, team coordination, and budget administration. I accepted my current position with the Air Logistics Center at Robins AFB, GA, in an attempt to gain meaningful employment within the infrastructure of civil service. Because opportunities for advancement from this position are quite limited, I am seeking a position within the community at large where my wealth of knowledge and expertise can be fully utilized to the benefit of both my employer and myself.

The enclosed resume briefly outlines my experience and accomplishments. If my qualifications appear to meet your current needs, I would be happy to discuss my background in a meeting with you. I will contact you next week to explore the possibility of an interview.

Sincerely,

James Howard

Enclosure

44

Customer Service Manager. *Lea J. Clark, Macon, Georgia*

This letter, based on a template, is in progress. Some information is not yet supplied. The first paragraph still has directions for the paragraph. In effect, you are looking over the writer's shoulder.

Alena Avery

55 Long Avenue, Youngstown, OH 55555
Telephone: 555.555.5555 — Email: aavery@xxx.com

Success Insights™
Personal Style DISC report

Responsible

Open-Minded

Balanced Judgment

Tactful & Logical

Positive Achievements

Secretary of McMahon House
Council
20XX–20XX

Phi Eta Sigma
Inducted 20XX

Emerging Leaders
20XX–20XX

Awards/Scholarships

BRITE Scholarship

MARC Scholarship

Dean's List

President's List

Professional Development

LeaderShape 20XX

The LEADERSHAPE INSTITUTE®
challenges participants to *lead
with integrity*™ while working
toward a vision grounded in
their deepest values.

Dear Hiring Authority:

Coupled with great enthusiasm and a desire to contribute to your organization's goals, I am submitting my resume, which displays my achievements, work experience, and key behaviors that will support your team objectives.

You will find that my personal traits, strengths, and characteristics are a great complement to your **customer service, help desk** or **service-oriented** needs. My evaluations, peers, and superiors describe me as being dependable, analytical, systematic, and compliant.

My positive activities prove my ambition to succeed as part of a team, uphold company missions, complete team tasks, and hold myself accountable. I have and will always **strive for quality results.**

Please contact me to further discuss existing or future employment opportunities.

Sincerely,

Alena Avery

Enclosure: resume

View and/or print my resume:
www.resumespotlight.com/aavery

45

Customer Service Help Desk Worker. *Jane Roqueplot, West Middlesex, Pennsylvania*

This person had a "trial and error" education with a limited work history. The letter emphasizes in a side column her key worker traits, positive accomplishments, and awards.

SUSAN ALLEN

Call Me: **(000) 000-0000**
Write to Me: **susanallen000@xxx.com**
Connect with Me: **LinkedIn.com/xx/xxxx**

COVER LETTER

SUSAN ALLEN

Dear Mr. Smith,

My upcoming relocation to the Denver area in September has motivated this letter to you. I am interested in exploring career opportunities with ABC Corporation. Review of my attached resume will demonstrate my **customer service success**, **marketing achievements** and **creative approach to challenges**. In each of my past employment positions, I have gained valuable experience that would help me to quickly become a contributing member of ABC Corporation's Customer Service Team.

I possess excellent communication skills, am adept at planning and organizing, and can work well under pressure. My ability to assess existing operations and identify ways to streamline efficiencies, as well as enhance technical marketing and administrative functions (especially Search Engine Optimization [SEO] and online presence), has played a strong role in helping my past employers expand market presence and meet financial objectives.

Once you have had an opportunity to review the enclosed resume, I would appreciate the chance to speak with you directly. I can be reached at the above phone number, by e-mail, or on LinkedIn if you use the QR code above. Thank you in advance for your time and consideration. I look forward to hearing from you.

Sincerely,

Susan Allen

Enclosure

Customer Service — Marketing — Social Networking Specialist

46

Social Networking Specialist. *Donna Allen, Heber City, Utah*

Without reading one word of the letter, the reader is apt to understand that the applicant is technically savvy, in touch with today's marketing and social network climate, and creative.

— LYNN MATHEWS —

5 Spring Road • Riverside, Pennsylvania • (555) 555-5555 • lynnmat@aol.com

[Date]

[Name]
[Title]
[Company]
[Address]

Dear _____:

Perhaps your graphics department needs a professional with demonstrated creativity and technical skills along with a strong desire to continue learning and to succeed. If so, the qualifications I can offer to your department include the following:

- **Design/illustration experience.** Earned a Bachelor's degree in Illustration from the University of Hartford and acquired extensive training in illustration and design/graphics, utilizing computer software programs such as Adobe Illustrator, Photoshop, and InDesign with a Macintosh system.

- **Award-winning talent.** Recipient of several awards/honors for my artistic talent and academic achievements: the Faith Ferguson Art Award, first place winner in the Honors Art class, and membership in the National Art Honor Society. Many of my illustrations were selected and displayed in the Senior Illustration Show.

- **Technical skills.** Proficient in using various media, including oils, acrylics, gouache, scratchboard, pen and ink, cut paper, color pencils, watercolors, image processing, and etching. Credited for my innovative approach, a great eye for color, excellent technique, and an ability to generate clever ideas.

In both educational and employment settings, I have proven myself to be a dependable, hardworking individual who is always prepared, well organized, and able to manage multiple projects/assignments. I take great pride in the quality of my work, never having missed a single deadline. Additionally, I possess excellent interpersonal skills, am team-oriented, and am willing to "go the extra mile" as needed.

I would welcome a conversation to discuss the contributions I can make to your department, even if you do not have a position available now. I am eager to begin a career in my chosen profession and look forward to speaking with you soon. Thank you for your consideration of my qualifications.

Very truly yours,

Lynn Mathews

Enclosure

47

Graphic Designer. *Louise Garver, Broad Brook, Connecticut*

The applicant was a recent college graduate in the field of art. Bullets point to strong experience, talent, and skills. She secured a position as a graphic designer at a consumer products company.

JENNIFER GEORGE

78 Holland Brook Road • Mooresville, NJ 22222 • (333) 333-3333 • jngrge@earthlink.net

January 10, 20xx

[Hiring Agent, Title]
[Company Name]
[Address]

Dear Hiring Manager:

Your posting for a [position title] caught my attention as it seems an ideal match for my experience and talents. As an accomplished graphic designer with a broad range of industry experience, I believe I am someone who will be an asset to your company. With strong creative instincts and a proven record in producing visual designs and written copy that sell products, I would like to explore the possibility of putting my skills and experience to work for you.

As you can see from my enclosed resume, my career encompasses roles in marketing, advertising, sales, and management. An award-winning graphic designer, I am also well-versed in managing all aspects of client projects to successful completion. Key to my success, the depth of my creative talents is fully matched by a disciplined focus on achieving outstanding results. Therefore, I am someone who consistently delivers top-quality projects no matter what the challenge.

Among my other strengths, I have solid sales instincts and have been successful in cultivating long-term relationships with key clients. With a strong customer focus, I often earn the repeat business of clients. Persuasive, self-confident, and effective, I have proven to be a respected and valued employee in the past. With a record of success behind me, I am confident that I will be an asset to you as well.

I would be pleased to have the opportunity to discuss future employment and look forward to speaking with you. I will contact you to set a mutually convenient time.

Thank you for your consideration.

Sincerely,

Jennifer George

Enclosure

48

Graphic Designer. *Carol A. Altomare, Three Bridges, New Jersey*

This letter is for an applicant who had both creative and administrative/relationship management skills. Each of the first three paragraphs shows that she is a designer with extra talent.

SAMUEL LAFITTE

555555 Rio Grande
Valencia, California 91355
Email: lafitte@earthlink.net

Voice mail: 555-555-5555
Residence: 000-000-0000

January 13, 20xx

Goldcrest Graphics, Inc.
25517 16th Street
Santa Clarita, California 91321

Ensuring Quality Control requires an experienced staff with the expertise to analyze an independent contractor's or employee's ability to do the job correctly for the best price. I possess an innate ability to assess employees' work, equipment, and quality standards. My commitment is to quality while remaining price conscious.

Earlier this year, as a Senior Graphic Designer for Adexa, I acted as liaison for the director, writer, and printers and edited the full project. Through my supervision of others, I was able to develop a cohesive unit that worked toward a common goal. My management skills led to **greater efficiency** and **cost reduction** while easily meeting deadlines.

Others have pointed out my unparalleled imagination, which allows me to properly evaluate designs, whether for catalogs, Web sites, or software. My diverse background encompasses

- Work for the Los Angeles County Arts Commission
- Murals for Transamerica Insurance, Inc., toy stores, restaurants
- Character design and model creation for a television pilot
- Animation, direction, and production of a short claymation film
- Logo creation

Additional strengths include

- Capability to handle many tasks at one time and meet every deadline, even when those deadlines occur hourly
- Motivation and desire to complete all projects in a timely manner
- Ability to remain respectful, patient, and level-headed under pressure

Artists are famous for being perfectionists, and it is a reputation that is well earned. Although I design on a Mac, I also use a real-world, hands-on approach to business and am confident I can make a significant contribution to Goldcrest Graphics. I can serve both your creative and post-production needs. I am available for any shift, for contract work, for travel, on any basis—you name it. I have no ego, only a desire to do my job to perfection and an ability to use technical skills with creativity to achieve an artistic end.

Eager to hear your ideas, I would appreciate a moment of your time. Could you spare a few minutes to discuss this with me in person? I will call next week to set a time for a personal interview.

Sincerely,

Samuel Lafitte

Enclosure

49

Senior Graphic Designer. *Myriam-Rose Kohn, Valencia, California*

Short paragraphs make a long letter easier to read. Bullets introduced by one or two sentences help to break up a page of short paragraphs. Both techniques are used effectively in this cover letter.

215 Crestview Avenue
Indianapolis, IN 46220
555.555.5555
PhOstbg@earthlink.com

November 15, 20xx

Mr. Douglas Shuck
Human Resources Manager
WTW Architects
609 Candlewood Street
Pittsburgh, PA 15212-5801

Dear Mr. Shuck:

Each architect holds his/her own unique paradigm. It has **always** been my dream to be an architect. As an elementary student, I remember drawing projects from my own perspective—viewing the world through different eyes than those of my classmates. Because I enjoy my work and know that success and fulfillment stem directly from working in one's passion, I submit my resume and portfolio to you for consideration.

My resume clearly shows that I have a variety of qualifying skills and abilities. Briefly, they include the following:

(1) A Bachelor of Arts School of Architecture degree from Miami University with a respectable GPA achieved through hard work and attention to detail,

(2) A strong background in computer-oriented design as evidenced by keen realistic imaging and detail-oriented visualization to provide innovative, practical design solutions while utilizing a consistent application of the fundamentals, and

(3) A sincere desire to apply these artistic and technical skills in a creative, fulfilling position in a firm such as yours.

I recently saw on the cover of *Buildings* magazine that WTW Architects was awarded "Best New Construction" for the Hetzel Union Building/Paul Robeson Cultural Center at Pennsylvania State University. The article caught my attention because I visited Penn State with my cousin in the spring and saw the "HUB." The building's oval interior commands a unique presence through the use of natural light and open spaces—a concept developed and perfected by Frank Lloyd Wright. One of your senior principals, Paul Williams, stated in the article, "The circle is symbolic of mankind—a symbol of civilization; a symbol of the town, the village, and the individual." The influence of Frank Lloyd Wright's design and expression is clearly evident through your firm's architecture—the same design and expression woven throughout my portfolio.

As you can see from my portfolio, I take pride in my work, too. It would be an honor to be a contributing member of your team and to work hard toward achieving WTW's goals and objectives. Because "proven skills" are best explained in person, I welcome the opportunity to introduce myself in an interview to discuss the value I offer WTW Architects. I will follow up with a phone call the week of November 21. Thank you for reviewing my portfolio, and I look forward to our meeting.

Sincerely,

Phillip Ostberg
Enclosures

50

Architect. *Sharon Williams, Louisville, Kentucky*

The writer used the AIDA style of business writing for persuasive sales letters, where Attention, Interest, Desire, and Action paragraphs sell the product—in this instance, the candidate.

Susan D. Chambers

100 Windy Way
Madison, CT 00000
(800) 555-1212
schambers@email.com

[Date]

[Mr./Ms. _____]
[Company]
[Address 1]
[Address 2]

Dear Hiring Professional,

As a qualified educator with a strong background in Special and Early Childhood education, I am writing to introduce myself as a candidate for the position of Special Education Administrator that was advertised in the *Daily News* on September 7, 20XX.

I am a skilled and qualified professional with extensive experience in Special Education and Early Childhood Education Administration. I have exceptional skills as an educator, as well as the ability to analyze, coordinate, and implement special-needs and early-childhood curriculum based on the individual needs of the classroom and the child.

My background includes managing personnel and administrating activities related to maintaining federal grants. Based on previous successes in the educational field, and recognition by state and local agencies as an expert in my field, I believe I would be an immediate asset to your organization's management team.

The enclosed resume briefly outlines my experience and accomplishments. If it appears that my qualifications meet your current needs, I would be happy to further discuss my background in a meeting with you. Please feel free to contact me at the above telephone number or e-mail address.

Sincerely,

Susan D. Chambers

Enclosure

51

Special Education Administrator. *Lea J. Clark, Macon, Georgia*

A cover letter concentrating on experience wasn't working. The writer wrote this letter to high-light accomplishments and administrative abilities. The applicant got four interviews within a few weeks.

Wendy R. McClean

0000 Potter Street
Saginaw, MI 55555

555-555-5555

February 19, 20xx

Discovery Center
Attention: Search Committee
9874 E. Maple Road
Troy, MI 48084

Dear Search Committee Members:

I was excited to read your advertisement in the *Oakland Press* for Director of the Discovery Center. It seems as if the ad could have been written for me! Most of my adult life has been spent working with or for children, culminating in an Associate degree in Early Childhood Education. I am enclosing my resume for your review.

As I said, I match the qualifications you are seeking. Let me elaborate:

Your Requirements	*My Qualifications*
♥ CDA	♥ I have applied for my CDA and expect approval soon.
♥ At least 12 credits in child development, child psychology, or early childhood education	♥ I recently earned an Associate degree with High Honors in Early Childhood Education.
♥ Strong leadership skills	♥ In addition to operating my own day care center for four years, I have been instrumental in planning and implementing several fund-raising events for the Easter Seals Society.

When you take a look at my resume, you will see that my quest to improve my knowledge hasn't stopped in the classroom. I regularly attend conferences, professional association activities and continuing education opportunities so that I can remain current in the field. The fact that I worked full-time (operating my own day care center) while attending college exemplifies my motivation and commitment.

In conclusion, I am confident I have the training and experience to excel in this position. I hope you will contact me to arrange an interview at your convenience. Thank you for your time and consideration.

Sincerely,

Wendy R. McClean

Enclosure

52

Child Care Center Director. *Janet L. Beckstrom, Flint, Michigan*

The applicant had just earned her associate degree and wanted to head a child care center. The Your Requirements…My Qualifications scheme calls attention to the applicant's relevant credentials.

SHANNON GROVE

555 Pinegrove Avenue, Los Angeles, CA 55555 ● (555) 555-5555 ● shannon.grove@xx.com

April 2, 20XX

Clara Smith, M.Ed.
Director, Student Support Services
Middlebury Elementary School
5555 Chance Avenue
Los Angeles, CA 55555

Dear Ms. Smith:

I am writing to express my considerable interest in the ***Elementary School Special Needs Teacher*** position announced by Middlebury Elementary School at SimplyHired.com. Having completed my bachelor's degree in elementary education, mild / moderate disability K-12, and severe and profound disabilities, I believe I am a strong fit for the role.

As I begin my teaching journey, I am excited to learn about the role because of its connection to my education and practical experience. To that end, I offer differentiated instruction experience across a spectrum of disability specializations including:

- ADD / ADHD
- Emotional Disturbances
- Autism
- Oppositional Defiant Disorder
- General Anxiety Disorder
- Down Syndrome
- Learning Disabilities
- Cerebral Palsy
- Physical and Intellectual Disabilities
- Vision Impairments

I also can adapt materials to the needs of diverse learners and have a strong understanding of technology, enabling me to create a tapestry of interactive slide show and data management teaching tools.

My résumé is enclosed for your review, and I hope you will agree that it makes sense for us to meet. You will find me proactive and able to motivate students, using positive reinforcement, individualized praise, and token economy principles.

Please reach me any time at shannon.grove@xx.com or 555-555-5555 (cell). I look forward to meeting you soon.

Sincerely,

Shannon Grove

Encl: Résumé

53

Elementary School Special Needs Teacher. *Jared Redick, San Francisco, California*

Specializations are bulleted so that the letter can be easily customized for each new position announcement. The first paragraph shows the announcement source for easy tracking by the hirer.

ELIZABETH BENNET

555 Lincoln Avenue ▪ Pemberley, Massachusetts ▪ 555.555.5000 ▪ ebennet@xxx.com

October 21, 20XX

Mr. William Frank
Principal
Pemberley Primary School
00 Washington Street
Pemberley, Massachusetts 55555

Dear Mr. Frank:

There is no greater reward for a teacher than seeing the light in a child's eyes when she finally grasps a difficult concept. **Igniting a love of learning in students with learning disabilities and other special needs requires a teacher with the skills, dedication, and flexibility to adapt to challenging circumstances.** As my enclosed resume demonstrates, going the extra mile to advocate for my students has been a hallmark of my 6-year career as a special education teacher.

I was fortunate enough to complete my 1st through 12th grade education in Pemberley, where I encountered many dedicated teachers determined to help me succeed. This experience provided me with the foundation I needed to achieve my goals, and also sparked my desire to give back to the community by seeking a teaching opportunity within the school system that gave me so much. I will be relocating to the area next month.

Among the qualities and accomplishments I can deliver are a

- **Solutions-oriented approach:** Initiated collaborative efforts among teachers, administrators, parents, and social workers to resolve bullying situations, nutritional issues, and other extracurricular circumstances affecting student performance.

- **Commitment to diversity and innovation:** Challenged to overcome language barriers and apathy toward learning in low-SES, multicultural, urban setting; engaged students in lessons by recruiting relatable guest speakers and incorporating music and hands-on lessons.

- **Expertise in assessment and differentiated instruction:** Skilled in assessing needs of students with Asperger's, autism, and other learning differences; introduced individualized teaching strategies for preschoolers through high school-age students that improved academic and social adjustment.

I believe strongly in the philosophy that every child can learn—and when I received a "thank you" e-mail not long ago from a former student who progressed before my eyes from disengaged student with failing grades to college honor student, it was a wonderful reminder of why I do what I do every day. I am confident that I can make similar contributions in Pemberley and am eager for the opportunity to meet with you to discuss any openings that you anticipate in the near future. Thank you for your time and consideration.

Sincerely,

Elizabeth Bennet

Enclosure: Resume

54

Special Education Teacher. *Jennifer Fishberg, Highland Park, New Jersey*

The applicant did not have a history of long-term positions, so the writer turned the number of short-term positions into a strength by playing up the applicant's flexibility in adapting to new circumstances.

Susan Wiley

Permanent Address:
1111 Clinton Avenue
Houston, TX 00000
(281) 000-0000

swiley2222@msn.com
cell: (000) 000-0000

Current Address:
2102 Indiana Street #222
Lubbock, TX 00000
(806) 000-0000

January 30, 20xx

Jan Pearson, Principal
Hart Elementary School
2323 Middleton Street
Houston, TX 00000

"One hundred years from now it will not matter what my bank account was, the sort of house I lived in, or the kind of car I drove, but the world may be different because I was important in the life of a child."
—Anonymous

Dear Mrs. Pearson:

I love the preceding quote! Although it may be seen as too "sentimental" by some, I truly believe that being able to make a positive difference in children's lives is a worthwhile endeavor—and the *true* reward in life. I am excited about the opportunity to launch my teaching career and influence student growth, and I am certain that my enthusiasm and ability to motivate would be a welcome addition to your faculty.

My educational experiences have convinced me that being a teacher is a wonderful career choice. While taking upper-level courses in secondary education and completing observation hours at local junior high and high schools, I studied educational theory and, more importantly, realized the value of consistent discipline enforcement, student-centered learning, and classroom/lesson organization, among many other educator functions. Through my Cum Laude G.P.A. and performance on major grade projects, I demonstrated a strong background knowledge in these areas, and although theory does not always translate into practice, I am confident that my knowledge will transfer effectively in an educational setting.

I have had two very different, yet interesting experiences in my employment history that indirectly prepared me for some of the challenges I will face as an educator. As a server at The Olive Garden restaurant, I was recognized by management for providing excellent, prompt service in an environment that could best be described as fast-paced and highly stressful. As an intern reporter for the *Moore County News Press*, I developed a keen appreciation for the richness and value of small-town living through firsthand observations and interviewing local residents for human-interest stories. Although both experiences are quite different from working day-to-day in an educational setting, I do feel that these positions prepared me for handling difficult situations and relating to diverse individuals on a one-to-one basis.

My resume is enclosed to provide details about my background and qualifications. If permissible, I will contact you to follow up on this letter of inquiry, or you may contact me at the number of my current residence. I look forward to meeting with you and discussing how I can contribute to the success of your school.

In addition, I have a particular interest in sponsoring extracurricular activities and would like to discuss with you how I could contribute to your school in this regard.

Thank you for your time and consideration.

Sincerely,

Susan Wiley

Enclosure

55

Entry-Level Teacher. *Daniel J. Dorotik, Jr., Lubbock, Texas*

The anonymous quotation amounts to the applicant's philosophy of teaching and enables her to express in the first paragraph her excitement and enthusiasm at the beginning of her teaching career.

Julia Scully

20 Angela Street ♦ Colonie, NY 00000 ♦ (555) 555-5555 ♦ sclly@sage.edu

[Date]

[Hiring Agent Name]
[Title]
[School Name]
[Address]
[City, State ZIP]

Dear Mr. / Ms. _____:

As a dedicated, highly knowledgeable Teacher with certification to teach pre-Kindergarten through grade 6, I believe my skills and talents can make an immediate and long-term contribution to [name of school].

During my intensive teaching assignments with Russell Sage College, I have enjoyed teaching elementary and preschool students in a variety of jobs and educational settings. I am skilled at developing and implementing stimulating lesson plans, administering and evaluating standardized tests, writing profiles, and conducting parent-teacher conferences. I am a team player capable of working well and building strong rapport with students, professionals, parents, and staff members. My educational background includes a Bachelor's degree in Elementary Education with a minor in Psychology from Russell Sage College. My proven ability to help children achieve their highest levels through positive motivation will be an asset to your team.

The accompanying resume provides further details of my accomplishments and what I have to offer. I believe it would be mutually beneficial for us to meet and discuss your current or anticipated teaching positions. I will call next week to inquire about such a meeting.

Thank you for your time and consideration.

Sincerely,

Julia Scully

Enc. resume

56

Pre-Kindergarten Teacher. *John Femia, Altamont, New York*

This letter is for a recent graduate. The opening paragraph indicates her occupational goal, the middle paragraph sells the candidate, and the third paragraph looks for an interview.

LORRAINE SIMMONS

899 Forest Lane   (555) 555-5555
Southland, PA 00000   lorsim@aol.com

[Date]

[Name]
[Company]
[Address]
[City, State ZIP]

Dear [Name]:

My interest in contributing to your school system as an elementary teacher has prompted me to forward my resume for your consideration. With several years of service in different grade levels and all curriculum areas, my qualifications are a match for the position.

Specifically, I offer the following:

Education	◆ Master of Arts in Teaching from the College of Our Lady of the Elms.
Experience	◆ I have 8 years of experience in elementary school environments, including the past 5 years as a classroom teacher instructing fourth-grade students. ◆ I have taught diverse student populations representing various cultural and socioeconomic backgrounds as well as different emotional/learning needs. ◆ My experience includes curriculum design and using a variety of creative teaching techniques to engage students with different learning styles and needs.
Leadership	◆ Extensive planning, program development, organizational and coordination skills combine with leadership strengths, including serving on a committee to develop and implement a performance-evaluation program for the faculty.
Philosophy and Attributes	◆ A skilled and dedicated teacher, I have excellent classroom-management, conflict-resolution, communication and interpersonal abilities. ◆ Monitoring, evaluating and actualizing teaching practices to facilitate the academic, social and personal needs of all learners are among my strengths.

If you are seeking a teaching professional who can stimulate elementary students' interests and focus their intensity and curiosity, then I may be the candidate you need. I enjoy challenges, and I work diligently and cooperatively to achieve common goals. Equally important, I am committed to the students, parents and community whom I serve. In addition, I strive to build effective relationships in my interactions with other educators and administrators.

I appreciate your serious consideration and will call in the near future to arrange a meeting to discuss the position further.

Sincerely,

Lorraine Simmons

57

Elementary Teacher. *Louise Garver, Broad Brook, Connecticut*

This letter helped the applicant secure an elementary teaching position. Bulleted items are clustered according to four criteria as bold side headings, making the items easier to comprehend.

Jennie S. Donaldson

000 Sheridan Place • Saginaw, MI 48601 • 555-555-5555 • jennied@comcast.net

[Date]

[Name]
[Company]
[Address]
[City, State ZIP]

Dear Administrator:

The education field is in a predicament right now, isn't it? Many districts are faced with a need for teachers but may not have the funds to hire experienced educators, especially those with advanced degrees. I am one of those "seasoned" teachers, and I would like to explain why I believe my experience is valuable to your district.

This is my eleventh year of teaching at the early elementary level. Over time I have learned what works and what doesn't, what motivates children and what turns them off. Since I know what to expect from students at the beginning of each year, we can get right down to the business of learning. Given the importance of standardized test scores such as MEAP, it is important to start covering relevant material as soon and as often as possible. I don't have to teach by trial and error—I've been there, done that.

My ability to earn the trust and respect of my students is a key point as well. Getting parents involved in their children's education is important, too. My classroom is high energy and creative, and I'm not afraid to try new techniques. Completing a master's degree in teaching and curriculum has certainly helped round out *my* education.

I hope you'll give me an opportunity for an interview so that I can give you additional information about my teaching style, capabilities, and enthusiasm for the job. I'll contact you next week to explore a convenient time to meet. Thank you for your time and attention.

Sincerely,

Jennie S. Donaldson

Enclosure

58

Elementary Teacher. *Janet L. Beckstrom, Flint, Michigan*

Many teacher layoffs had created a huge applicant pool. Districts were hiring less-experienced teachers for less money. This letter explains why this experienced elementary teacher is "worth it."

CHRISTINE L. BERNARDO
000 ATTAWA ROAD
NEW VISTA, NM 88888

March 22, 20xx

Dr. Stephanie Stasos, Assistant Superintendent
Human Resources Department
New Vista Public Schools
New Vista, NM 88888

Dear Dr. Stasos:

Recently, my neighbor, who teaches at New Vista High School, informed me that there may be several elementary and middle school teaching positions available for the coming school year. Since my last correspondence with you, I have received my middle school endorsement, in addition to my certification to teach in elementary grades. I am now certified to teach social studies at the middle school level through grade eight.

May I add that I feel quite honored to have been chosen from among more than 200 applicants to participate—along with mainly seasoned teachers—in a fully paid summer institute sponsored by the National Geographic Society. I am confident that this unique experience will add much interest to my own classes in project development and general class discussions.

As a substitute teacher in the New Vista schools this past year, I found administrators, supervisors, and faculty exceptionally helpful and pleasant. Such welcoming support from them is particularly assuring to entry-level teachers like me. I felt like one of the family!

Thank you, Dr. Stasos, for taking time from your busy schedule to see me last spring, and I look forward to another meeting with you soon to discuss in more depth my goals and long-range ambitions in the teaching profession. I would appreciate your scheduling me for a formal interview as I apply for a teaching position in the New Vista Public School District.

Sincerely,

Christine L. Bernardo

Enclosures: resume; employment application packet

---

(555) 555-5555   ◊   Cell: (000) 000-0000   ◊   chrsbrnrdo@earthlink.com

59

Middle School Teacher. *Edward Turilli, Bonita Springs, Florida*

Networking breaks the ice in the first paragraph. The applicant strengthens her candidacy by informing the superintendent of her recent accomplishments and complimenting his school system.

Ethan Breines

86 Pinegrove Avenue, Mapleshade, NJ 55555

555-555-5555 (h) | 000-000-0000 (c) | etbreines@tru.net

January 5, 20xx

Jillian Holmes
Superintendent of Schools
Mapleshade School District
76-23 Third Street
Mapleshade, NJ 55555

RE: Middle school or high school Social Studies teaching position.

Dear Ms. Holmes:

Recent deep school-budget cuts mean that there are many candidates for a very limited number of positions in the Mapleshade School District. Why should you hire me?

Here's the difference I believe I bring to Mapleshade's students—dedication, motivation, and fun. I can make students work hard, I can make them laugh, and I can make them want to come to class. And I'll do it with all students, not just the top of the class.

But that's not the whole picture. I am absolutely committed to helping students see the world as a whole, not as a town in New Jersey. I want them to know that they are important to this country and to the world—that as citizens they have an obligation to be informed, to make considered choices, to vote, and to participate in the democratic process. I want them to be excited about the past and about how the lessons of the past impact the future.

I want them to love to come to Social Studies class and to groan if they have a substitute teacher because I make Social Studies the best part of their school day. I want them to love to learn, to be excited about what every class brings, to be inspired critical thinkers and writers, and to do well on tests so they will have a better future. I want them to see me walking the halls, chatting with students, attending school events, and coaching sports. I want them to know that I care enough to be there off-hours.

Maybe that's how all new teachers think, but I am sincere and believe I can make it happen—or at least I can try, and never give up. In fact I know it can happen because I've had teachers like that—and that is why I'm writing you today.

Thank you very much for your attention; I look forward to meeting with you and the school board.

Sincerely,

Ethan Breines

Enclosure

60

Social Studies Teacher. *Deb Dib, Medford, New York*

The question at the end of the first paragraph hooks the reader for the next paragraph. The repetition of "I can make" and "I want them" keeps interest in the middle three paragraphs.

Donald R. Jones

206 Hawkins Lane • Columbus, Ohio 43200 • 614.456.0000 • drjones@juno.com

April 17, 20xx

Mr. Scott Trobough
Superintendent
Columbus City Schools
1234 Morse Road
Columbus, Ohio 43200

Dear Mr. Trobough:

After a successful career in government, I recently fulfilled a lifelong desire to become an educator at the secondary level. I have completed my education and licensure requirements and am excited to begin my teaching career. This letter is sent to inquire about possible teaching opportunities within the Columbus City Schools. The enclosed resume will provide detailed information regarding my background and experience in support of my candidacy.

To briefly highlight my qualifications, I offer you the following:

- Social Studies Comprehensive Certification (7–12) complemented by a Bachelor of Arts degree in Political Science

- Successful classroom teaching experience as a substitute and student teacher in diverse classroom settings—experienced in developing and implementing integrated lesson plans for cooperative learning

- More than 10 years of professional involvement in government at the local, state and federal levels providing invaluable insight and knowledge to bring into the classroom

In short, I bring a unique combination of education and "real world" experience not often found in today's classroom teachers. I believe the time I spent in government can only enhance my social studies teaching. Should you have a teaching position available, I would appreciate being considered a serious candidate. You should also know that I would be interested in serving as an advisor for extracurricular clubs and/or activities. Feel free to contact me to set up an interview or to answer any questions you may have regarding my background and experience.

Thank you for your time and consideration. I look forward to hearing from you.

Sincerely,

Donald R. Jones

Enclosure

61

Social Studies Teacher. *Melissa L. Kasler, Athens, Ohio*

The applicant was transitioning from government employment to teaching. Because of his background in real-world government and politics, he wanted to be a social studies teacher.

MICHAEL STACK

000 Lexington Drive / Albany, NY 00000 / (555) 555-5555 / stackm@email.com

February 10, 20xx

Dr. Taylor Raine Coleman
Putnam Valley Central School District
111 Peekskill Hollow Road
Putnam Valley, NY 10579

Dear Dr. Coleman:

Please accept this letter and enclosed resume for the social studies position that is currently available within your district. As an experienced social studies teacher, I offer vast classroom exposure, a great deal of energy, and a commitment to the students.

Over the course of my career, I have taught both middle-school and high-school students in a variety of subjects, including U.S. History and Global History. Two years ago, my wife and I relocated to the Mohawk Valley from Albany, NY. Currently, I teach 8th-grade social studies in Herkimer Central School District. Prior to this, I taught for 14 years at Schenectady Central School District.

As a professional educator, my efforts extend beyond academics. I work hard at instilling a sense of school pride, building community awareness, and motivating students to set higher standards. In addition to general education, my teaching experience encompasses inclusion classes. With all my students, I take the time to connect with each one, demonstrating genuine sensitivity when working with those who have special needs. Through an ongoing process of planning, delivering, reflecting, and refining lessons, I am consistently successful at balancing individual needs with the NYS Standards & Assessments. I also have a proven record of success (98% passing rate) with the 8th-Grade Social Studies Assessment.

Most significant to my teaching ability is my enthusiasm for the material and appropriate sense of humor. Through these, I am able to engage students and facilitate the learning process. Daily lessons include classroom discussion of current events while activities focus on creating and using information for knowledge and understanding. I also highlight the modes of communication within the community and integrate technology and media into lessons. Whatever the topic, my goal is to emphasize the fact that knowledge and access to information are essential to responsible citizenship and participation in a democracy.

Thank you in advance for your time. I look forward to speaking with you to further discuss my qualifications and will call to schedule an appropriate time.

Sincerely,

Michael Stack

Enclosure

62

Social Studies Teacher. *Kristin M. Coleman, Poughkeepsie, New York*

In this well-designed letter, the last sentence of the first paragraph indicates the key topics of the second, third, and fourth paragraphs, respectively. The letter gives the impression that the applicant has an orderly mind.

LINUS JEFFERSON

555 Cedarwood Circle ▪ Portland, ME 55555 ▪ 555.555.5555 ▪ ljefferson@xx.com

January 19, 20XX

Lake Placid High School
000 School Street
Lake Placid, MI 55555
Attn: Superintendent Russell

Dear Ms. Russell:

It is with great enthusiasm that I submit this application for the middle school science teacher position. I am excited about the opportunity to leverage my diverse background in education, strengths in classroom management, and creativity in teaching science to enhance the student learning experience and achievement at Lake Placid High. My passion for teaching, ability to establish rapport with students and parents, and success in challenging educational environments would be a genuine benefit to your organization.

For the past nine years, I have demonstrated excellence as an educator in various settings. My background includes teaching science, math, and other subjects to middle and high school students. I have taught special education and science, including geology, biology, cell biology, and evolution, continually improving instruction to meet student needs.

I have engaged students in learning and increased achievement on state biology and math assessments. When resources have been scarce, I have created effective curriculum and activities with available texts, online resources, computer simulations, and limited lab supplies. My ability to connect with students, build an encouraging learning atmosphere, and differentiate instruction to meet diverse needs has improved learning outcomes for students at all levels.

My strengths include encouraging open communication with parents, students, and administrators. I have developed and implemented surveys to gather feedback from parents and students, building better relationships and continuously improving teaching methods. My willingness to involve students and parents in the learning process has been critical in decreasing negative classroom behaviors.

The enclosed résumé details my experience and education. I would welcome the opportunity to interview with you to discuss further how my background could be a fit for your institution. In the next few days, I will follow up with you to confirm receipt of my information and determine next steps.

Thank you in advance for your time and consideration.

Sincerely,

Linus Jefferson

63

Middle School Science Teacher. *Marie Zimenoff, Fort Collins, Colorado*

The applicant was returning from the military and wanted to get back into teaching. The writer leveraged the applicant's diverse background. Interviews came quickly, and then, a dream job.

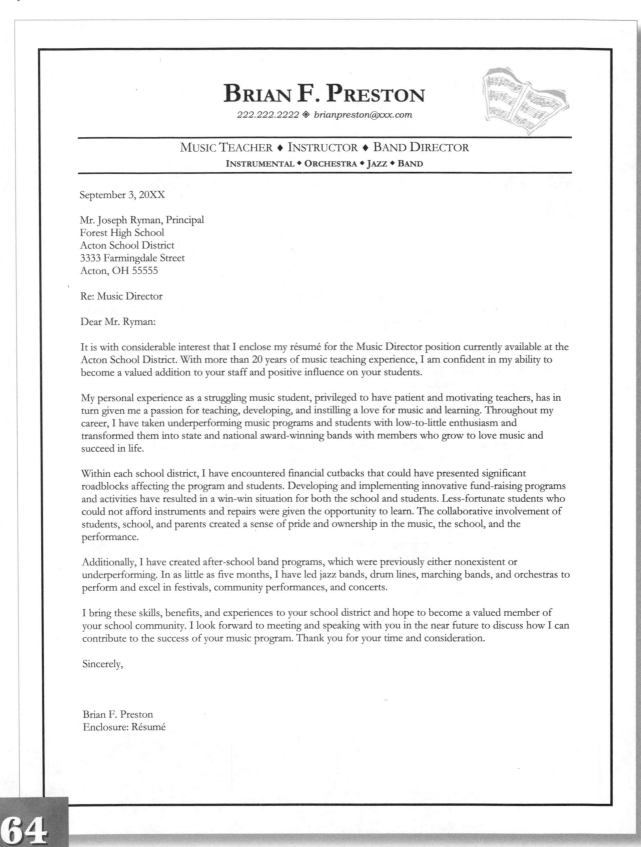

BRIAN F. PRESTON

222.222.2222 ◈ *brianpreston@xxx.com*

MUSIC TEACHER ◆ INSTRUCTOR ◆ BAND DIRECTOR
INSTRUMENTAL ◆ ORCHESTRA ◆ JAZZ ◆ BAND

September 3, 20XX

Mr. Joseph Ryman, Principal
Forest High School
Acton School District
3333 Farmingdale Street
Acton, OH 55555

Re: Music Director

Dear Mr. Ryman:

It is with considerable interest that I enclose my résumé for the Music Director position currently available at the Acton School District. With more than 20 years of music teaching experience, I am confident in my ability to become a valued addition to your staff and positive influence on your students.

My personal experience as a struggling music student, privileged to have patient and motivating teachers, has in turn given me a passion for teaching, developing, and instilling a love for music and learning. Throughout my career, I have taken underperforming music programs and students with low-to-little enthusiasm and transformed them into state and national award-winning bands with members who grow to love music and succeed in life.

Within each school district, I have encountered financial cutbacks that could have presented significant roadblocks affecting the program and students. Developing and implementing innovative fund-raising programs and activities have resulted in a win-win situation for both the school and students. Less-fortunate students who could not afford instruments and repairs were given the opportunity to learn. The collaborative involvement of students, school, and parents created a sense of pride and ownership in the music, the school, and the performance.

Additionally, I have created after-school band programs, which were previously either nonexistent or underperforming. In as little as five months, I have led jazz bands, drum lines, marching bands, and orchestras to perform and excel in festivals, community performances, and concerts.

I bring these skills, benefits, and experiences to your school district and hope to become a valued member of your school community. I look forward to meeting and speaking with you in the near future to discuss how I can contribute to the success of your music program. Thank you for your time and consideration.

Sincerely,

Brian F. Preston
Enclosure: Résumé

64

Music Director. *Jasmine Marchong, Farmington, Michigan*

By highlighting this music teacher's passion for teaching, value in creating award-winning bands, and ability to raise funds, this letter helped to generate numerous interviews.

Wanda Ortiz

2 Fir Lane   (555) 555-5555
Smithtown, NY 11787   w_ortiz@aol.com

There is no more beautiful life than that of a student.
~ F. Albrecht

During my years as a bilingual educator, I have developed a keen understanding of the importance of student assimilation and respect for their native upbringing. These key principles make teaching bilingual students a rewarding and challenging career path.

As an educator, I wear many different hats: those of teacher, motivator, and leader. I am confident in my ability to create a "love of learning" environment for bilingual students that will enrich their academic growth.

I adhere to new procedures and commissioner regulations for LEP and have hands-on knowledge of the following academic standards: Language for Information and Understanding, Language for Literacy Response and Expression, Language for Critical Analysis and Evaluation, and Language for Social Interaction.

If your school district is looking for an enthusiastic and engaging educator who enjoys building brighter futures, I would love to speak with you. I will contact you next week to set up a personal interview.

Sincerely,

Wanda Ortiz

Enclosure

65

Bilingual Educator. *Linda Matias, Long Island, New York*

The applicant was going to use the cover letter at a teachers' job fair. Therefore, she could not personalize each letter. Instead of a salutation, the writer put first an inspirational quotation.

JAMES L. HAMMARLUND
63 Bay Vista Street, Westerly, WA 00000
(555) 333-4444
jlhamm@aol.com

February 22, 20xx

Dr. Frank Kessler, Superintendent
Westerly School District
788 Whitman Road
Westerly, WA 00000

Dear Dr. Kessler:

Please accept this letter in response to your advertisements in *The Westerly Weekly Press*, February 20, 20xx, and *The Westerly Sunday Journal*, February 22, 20xx, for a Physical Education / Health teacher at Westerly High School. I have enclosed my resume and a completed application for employment.

As a Washington State–certified, experienced, and successful teacher of Physical Education / Health and an athletic coach for nine years, I have consistently demonstrated my ability to motivate and handle youngsters, both in the classroom and on the playing field. Equally important, I possess a sincere caring for teenagers and extend myself to help ensure their success.

My strengths as a teacher include patience, dedication, and a strong sense of organization. Although I enjoy working within a rather structured curriculum, I am quite able to adapt to most working environments. Finally, of utmost importance to me is that my students receive physical education instruction of the highest quality. I strive to inculcate integrity in all that they do as students and future citizens and leaders of our city and country.

Thank you, Dr. Kessler, for considering my application for employment in the Westerly School District. I look forward to meeting with you to reveal and discuss my objectives during professional development. May I call next week to set up an appointment to meet?

Sincerely,

James L. Hammarlund

Enclosures: resume / application

66

Physical Education/Health Teacher. *Edward Turilli, Bonita Springs, Florida*

This physical education teacher makes the point that he teaches the whole student instead of promoting only the student's physical well-being. This approach makes him appear unique.

Arthur Hampton, **M.Ed.**

1111 Parker Street   Home: 222-999-5555
Brunswick, New Jersey 07777   ahteach@aol.com   Office: 222-777-6600

January 16, 20xx

Worthington Area School District
ATT: James Drury, Superintendent
14 Atherton Street
Worthington, New Jersey 06666

Dear Superintendent Drury:

Allow me to introduce myself.

For the past 19 years I have been involved in the educational leadership of two highly respected private schools. Two of my key responsibilities have been to introduce competitive and demanding instructional programs and to hire and develop the appropriate staff to meet those challenges. I'm happy to say that I have been successful in both areas, as reflected in the enclosed resume. Best of all, I have enjoyed making learning an exciting and enjoyable process for the students!

I am at a point in my professional career where I am ready for a new challenge. Key areas where I can make a contribution to your district are the following:

- Planning and developing curriculum
- Achieving accreditation
- Building teamwork and cohesive work groups
- Setting goals and high academic standards
- Managing budgets and fund-raising activities

It would be my pleasure to meet with you to discuss the ways in which I can make an immediate and positive impact on your fine district.

Thank you for your consideration and professional courtesy in reviewing my resume. I will call you soon to explore the possibility of an interview.

Sincerely,

Arthur Hampton

Enclosure

67

Administrative Position. *Karen Conway, Bend, Oregon*

At a pivotal point in his long career, this educational leader wanted an administrative position in which he could further apply his leadership skills. Bullets point to his possible key contributions.

YVETTE SEITLIN

555 Andrews Road, Apt. 4   Pasadena, California 91030   555-555-5555   YvetteS@history.tulane.edu

March 6, 20xx

Mr. James Goldberg
Cataloguing Operations Manager
Survivors of the Shoah Visual History Foundation
P.O. Box 3129
Los Angeles, California 90078-3168

Dear Mr. Goldberg:

It was a pleasure meeting you on Friday. I would like to join the Survivors of the Shoah Visual History Foundation project. My position at UCLA ends in December, and I am eager to win one of the research positions you mentioned at the tour's end. My experience in historical research, teaching, publishing and study qualify me for the position.

Your Needs	My Qualifications
M.A. degree in history	♦ Ph.D. Candidate in History, Tulane University, expected in 20xx. Coursework focused on war and nationalism in the United States and in modern Europe.
	♦ Doctoral research focuses on civilians who faced enemy soldiers during the Civil War, much like the Holocaust survivors themselves.
	♦ M.A. in History, plus B.A. in History and English.
Superior research skills	♦ Doctoral research has taken me to more than 15 archives in 9 states. In addition, I have used countless other published, online and microfilm sources.
	♦ Awarded national and university funds to conduct research in field of study.
Ability to prioritize many tasks under deadline while displaying excellent attention to detail	♦ Selected as a research assistant for 2 noted professional historians. Completed many tasks while balancing my own coursework.
	♦ Conducted independent research for thesis, dissertation, conference presentations and research assistant projects.
	♦ Met all self- and institution-imposed deadlines for all research, coursework and publications.

68

Historical Researcher. *Gail Frank, Tampa, Florida*

The applicant found out about a "hidden" job by taking a tour of the Shoah Foundation. The tour-giver mentioned open research positions for which the applicant was a perfect fit. This letter highlights her interest in the position. She was so confident in her ability that she included a set

YVETTE SEITLIN PAGE 2

Your Needs	My Qualifications
Strong interpersonal skills and excellent communication ability	◆ Taught as an adjunct instructor at UCLA for an upper-level history course.
	◆ Taught as a Teaching Assistant for an undergraduate history course at the University of Cincinnati.
	◆ Successfully presented 2 papers at History conferences with 2 more papers proposed for 20xx.
	◆ Copy edited 2 books, one of which was a historical atlas with geographical terminology.
	◆ B.A. degree in both History and English demanded ability to write well.
Team player willing to make a commitment to the foundation	◆ Strong, lifelong interest in Holocaust and its causes and significance. Belief in importance of this project.
	◆ Jewish ancestry makes this project even more significant to me.
	◆ Demonstrated ability to make long-term commitment to research and writing through achievement of thesis and pending dissertation.
Computer skills	◆ Strong skills in Microsoft Word and Excel, the Internet and database programs.

My resume/CV provides further details of my accomplishments. I have also attached a sheet of my references for your convenience. I will contact you next week to arrange a meeting so that we may discuss the foundation's needs in greater detail.

Sincerely,

Yvette Seitlin

Enclosures

cc: Professor T. Smythe, Tulane University
    Professor G. Ryder, Tulane University
    Professor A. Roberts, UCLA

of references. Although this is not usually done, she wanted to provide all of the needed information right away (and she alerted her references to possible inquiries about her).

MICHAEL R. KELLEY

4567 Ridgeway Avenue • Lewiston, KY 44444 • 606.123.4567 • mrk@aol.com

July 22, 20xx

Ms. Nancy Spires
Human Resources
Kenyon College
1234 Meadowbrook Avenue
Racine, Ohio 45771

Dear Ms. Spires:

First off, belated congratulations to everyone at Kenyon College for being listed in the *Kaplan/Newsweek* "How to Get into College" issue as one of the year's "hottest colleges." To that end, it would be an honor for me to join the Kenyon staff as the Head Men's Basketball Coach and strive to uphold the high standards of your institution. Please accept the enclosed resume as my sincere interest in this position.

With 18 years of coaching (14 of those at the collegiate level), extensive experience in Division III athletics and broad knowledge of the North Coast Athletic Conference, I have much to offer as the Head Coach of the Kenyon Lords.

In addition, my background as a Division III player and coach have greatly helped shape my coaching and administration philosophies regarding intercollegiate athletics. Those philosophies begin and end with academics and the true meaning of being a student-athlete.

I am eager to discuss with you my background and the position of Head Men's Basketball Coach. Feel free to contact me if you have any questions concerning my resume and references. I look forward to the opportunity of meeting with you to discuss my candidacy and will contact you soon to set an appointment. Thank you for your time and consideration.

Sincerely,

Michael R. Kelley

Enclosure

69

Head Men's Basketball Coach. *Melissa L. Kasler, Athens, Ohio*

This coach wanted to convey his knowledge of the school/athletic program to which he was applying. To set a positive tone, the writer first congratulates the college on a recent achievement.

JOAN SMITH

6 Honeyberry Court • Frankston • VIC 3333
Phone: (613) 000 0000 (W) • (613) 000 1111 (H) • email: j.smith@hotmail.com

Date

Mr. De Kretzer
Head Dean
Melbourne University—Deakin Campus
65-150 Richmond Road
Melbourne, VIC 3000

Dear Mr. De Kretzer:

With the pending conferral of my Doctor of Philosophy, I am seeking a position as **Researcher / Educator** with your university and believe my academic accomplishments, extensive research and teaching expertise would certainly be transferable to this role.

My enclosed resume demonstrates my

☑ Distinguished record in teaching and technical innovation achieved through conceptualisation, development and implementation of flexible delivery style learning techniques. I have lectured to several campuses simultaneously through ISL (Distance) Education and through self-developed Online Course Web pages, and I am proficient in the operation of numerous popular software applications.

☑ Expertise in applying sophisticated quantative and qualitative research methodologies demonstrated in working towards successful completion of Ph.D.; numerous self-researched/published writings; continued professional development and conference attendance; and extensive research assistant work, utilising SPSS and NVivo.

☑ Exceptional interpersonal, communication and presentation skills. Able to build and maintain strategic relationships with students and colleagues from diverse backgrounds. Recognised as a positive role model, teacher, lecturer, tutor and mentor.

☑ Facilitation of proactive classroom environments, encouraging active student participation to further enhance learning outcomes. Committed to holistic student development and learning experiences.

☑ Visionary, goal-driven work ethic, combined with solid team collaboration competencies and individual strengths utilising sound follow-through and detail orientation to plan and achieve projects from concept to successful conclusion.

Given the combination of these competencies, I am confident that I have developed a professional resourcefulness and personal diversity that will enable me to become a productive member of your faculty. Your consideration of my qualifications and academic and professional accomplishments will be appreciated.

Sincerely,

Joan Smith

Enclosure

70

Researcher/Educator. *Annemarie Cross, Hallam, Victoria, Australia*

This applicant was nearing the completion of her Ph.D. She had gained extensive experience throughout her short career. This letter sums up her experience and what she has to offer.

PATRICIA GREEN

444 Circle Drive • Brentwood, NY 55555 • (555) 444-2222 • Trainer@ITclass.net

[Date]

[Name]
[Company]
[City, State ZIP]

Dear [Name]:

Perhaps your organization is seeking to recruit a talented instructor to teach the complexities of advanced networking infrastructures to broad student populations. If this is the case, then please find the accompanying resume, highlighting my career as an MCSE instructor, Systems Administrator, and Consultant, for your review and consideration for a position teaching advanced MCSE curriculums/Windows with your facility.

Currently, I maintain tenure as an MCSE instructor with InfoTech Training Solutions, a leading provider of high-end networking certifications in Microsoft, Novell, and Cisco; and as an innovator of the industry's first Hands-on–Technical Training Lab (HOTT™). In this capacity, I continue to effectively teach classes throughout InfoTech's headquarters and university-based satellite locations. I oversee the instruction of other trainers as part of the organization's Train-the-Trainer program, which I initiated, developed, and continue to implement.

My ability to teach curricula based on both theory and realistic business models not only has prepared students for today's competitive workplace, but also has resulted in an unprecedented 100% student passing rate on A+, MCP, and all MCSE core exams. I am confident that my verifiable track record, coupled with my personal and professional dedication to quality teaching, would greatly benefit your organization.

Although the accompanying resume illustrates my background well, I feel that a personal interview would better demonstrate my knowledge and abilities. Therefore, I would appreciate an opportunity to meet with you for an in-depth interview to discuss the possible merging of my strengths with your organization's training objectives. Thank you for your review and consideration. You will hear from me soon regarding the possibility of an interview.

Sincerely,

Patricia Green

Enclosure

71

MCSE Instructor. *Ann Baehr, East Islip, New York*

The first paragraph is a probe to learn of any interest in an instructor, and the second indicates the applicant's current position and areas of expertise. The third attests to her effectiveness.

RICHARD BOULDER

55 Forest Drive • Dayton, OH 00000

Home: 555-555-5555 • Mobile: 555-555-5555 • boulderr5005@hotmail.com

[Date]

[Person's Name]
[Title]
[Company Name]
[Street Address]
[Town, State, ZIP]

Dear [Person's Name]

As a Senior Software Engineer, I would bring to your organization more than ten years of experience in software design and development within the telecommunications and defense-related industries and expertise in all phases of the software development life cycle. In addition, I have substantial experience analyzing, troubleshooting, and resolving complex software issues. Further highlights of my background include

- An extensive background developing and debugging software systems and solutions in C, C++, Perl, and Java in UNIX, Linux, and Windows environments.
- Proficiency as technical lead or individual contributor on cross-functional product development teams challenged with ensuring on-time, on-budget, and on-target results.
- A Bachelor of Science Degree in Electrical Engineering with a concentration in VLSI design and microwave engineering.

For the past ten years I have provided engineering expertise for multiuser telecommunications systems at Cummings Networks, where I have been called upon to investigate and resolve complex software issues, troubleshoot and repair bugs, design new functionality and software enhancements, and deliver technical product training to peers and field engineers. I've earned a sound reputation as THE person to call on when critical customer acceptance issues have eluded resolution by others.

If your organization is seeking a dependable, results-driven team player with a solid-performance track record and outstanding technical capabilities, you need look no further. The accomplishments noted within the accompanying resume will illustrate the valuable contributions I can make to your team. I would be very interested in learning more about your open position and discussing my qualifications more fully. I will take the initiative to contact you next week to see if we can arrange for a mutually convenient meeting.

Thank you for your time and consideration. I look forward to speaking with you.

Sincerely,

Richard Boulder

72

Senior Software Engineer. *Jeanne Knight, Tyngsboro, Massachusetts*

The applicant wanted to move from product support to software development. The writer highlighted experience in software design and development. He got an immediate interview.

RYAN G. SMITH

555-555-5555
ryansmith@email.com

0000 Snowfall Drive
Colorado Springs, CO 80903

March 30, 20xx

Mr. Robert Johnson
Lockheed Martin Corporation
6801 Rockledge Drive
Bethesda, MD 20817-1877

Dear Mr. Johnson:

➢ More than 13 years of professional experience in engineering sophisticated avionic systems, with a Bachelor of Science in Mechanical and Manufacturing Technology;

➢ Keen analytical and problem-solving skills;

➢ Proven ability to deliver quantifiable cost savings, whether leading the project, working independently, or operating as part of a cross-functional team;

➢ Experience in authoring ISO, process control writings, and training syllabi, as well as delivering the associated training; and

➢ A verifiable record of improving workflow and manufacturing processes that positively impact budgetary goals.

I would like to bring my expertise and experience as a **process engineer** to Lockheed Martin. My technical knowledge, drive, determination, and solid communication skills will allow me to make an immediate contribution to your organization.

Thank you for your consideration. I look forward to speaking with you and will call you next week to set up an interview.

Sincerely,

Ryan G. Smith
Enclosure

73

Process Engineer. *Cindy Kraft, Valrico, Florida*

Creating a simple vertical line and positioning the letter in the second "column" can make a letter stand out from a host of other letters. Starting the letter with bulleted items also is unique.

Benito Hoover
maintenance reliability engineer

90 Carleton Drive
Macon, Georgia 00000
000.000.0000 — bh1@smartx.net

Thursday, June 17, 20xx

Mr. Charles W. Moran
Crest, Inc.
2130 Interstate Parkway
Suite 400
Atlanta, Georgia 00000

Dear Mr. Moran:

If you think Crest's maintenance reliability engineer should go beyond the important functions of asset protection and regulatory compliance, we should explore adding me to your team.

To start, you'll find five solid, profit-building capabilities I can offer your company on the next pages. Backing them up are a half dozen examples of problems solved, thousands of dollars saved, durable measures taken to ensure compliance, and new corporate standards set to boost productivity.

I am employed by one of the largest companies in the world. I love what I do and GE has promoted me four times in the last seven years. And, although there are always contributions to be made, the challenges I handle every day aren't as interesting as I would like them to be. Hence, I'm testing the waters with this confidential application.

I thrive when I can help management uncover and fix the problems so that firms like Crest get all the benefits of maintenance reliability. So let me suggest a next step: May I call in a few days to explore your special requirements? I'll do my best to make that time very well spent.

Sincerely,

Benito Hoover

Encl.: Resume

74

Maintenance Reliability Engineer. *Don Orlando, Montgomery, Alabama*

Too often in the past, this applicant found jobs that turned out to be far below his abilities. This letter was designed to position the applicant as a key advisor to the management team.

EVERETT C. DANIELS

505 Trevor Lane • Dover, DE 50005
505.500.0505 • evcdan5@aol.com

December 16, 20xx

Mr. Jacob B. Smythe
Unit Director
Department of Transportation
State of Delaware
Dover, DE 50005

Dear Mr. Smythe:

Donald Hurley suggested it could prove valuable for us to talk. I am presently exploring
opportunities toward which my extensive background managing successful civil, environmental,
and heavy construction projects would be an asset. Specifically, I am interested in being
considered as a candidate for the position of Senior Project Manager.

As my background demonstrates, I have had the opportunity to leverage business development
opportunities for each of my employer companies through well-executed expansion into related
industries. I have broad expertise in all aspects of civil, engineering, and heavy construction and
a proven ability to effectively manage a profitable operation. My background is complemented
by a degree in Surveying/Civil Engineering as well as a very high level of customer service
orientation. My projects are consistently characterized by the professional manner in which
objectives are achieved—and all parties are satisfied, even when working through sometimes
extensive change order processes.

My managers describe me as a self-motivated, ambitious, and hardworking team player with a
strong sense of working collaboratively. My track record of performance in all areas reflects my
ability to learn quickly and competently, and I always give 110% to any job I undertake. I have a
reputation for doing whatever it takes to give exceptional quality and value. I am able to
effectively team with individuals at all levels—from superintendents and general contractors,
project owners, and municipal leaders to laborers and tradesmen in the field … skills that will
prove invaluable to the DOT.

In addition to these strengths, I have key skills in the area of business development and
management and possess expert relationship management skills. I am known for my tact and
diplomacy and an ability to effectively troubleshoot and successfully resolve any situation. I look
forward to meeting with you to discuss the DOT's hiring needs for a Senior Project Manager and
how I might contribute to your operations. I will contact you next week to set an appointment.

Sincerely,

Everett C. Daniels

75

Senior Project Manager. *Jan Melnik, Durham, Connecticut*

The applicant used a mutual contact to seek an opportunity with the state DOT. The writer highlighted a background in civil and environmental engineering and heavy construction.

BILL RASMUSSEN

555 Northwest Montana Street | Butte, MT 55555 | Cell Phone: 406.555.5555 | Email: brasmussen@xxx.com

June 1, 20XX

ABC Group, Inc.
John Doe, President
PO Box 55555
Missoula, MT 55555

Dear Mr. Doe:

While earning my civil engineering degree, I kept a keen eye on ABC Group, recognizing the firm's reputation for integrity, excellent design solutions, and passion for engineering established over a distinguished 35-year history. I always hoped to begin my career with a firm like yours, which recognizes that engineers build neighborhoods and communities, not just streets and bridges. As a recent graduate, I am interested in expanding my engineering skills at ABC, a firm that provides challenging projects and can drive and nurture my future in civil engineering.

I am a hard-working young man with a passion for engineering showcased through my service as president of the student chapter of the International Society of Civil Engineers and passing the FE exam one month prior to my graduation with honors from Montana Tech. As a summer 20XX intern with Bridge Engineering Diagnostics in St. Louis, Missouri, I gained experience working with the DOT and many construction companies on structural load testing services for bridges in various parts of the country. Not one to sit idle, I am currently working on obtaining EI certification for the State of Montana and am interested in growing my passion for transportation and bridge construction and developing my interest in construction services, as well as municipal water and sewer.

After reviewing my résumé, if you have a place in your firm for a young professional with high standards of engineering excellence and solid communication skills, I would be honored to talk with you about joining your team of professional engineers, surveyors, practiced land-use planners, and CAD technicians. I would welcome an opportunity to convey, in person, the value I will bring to ABC Group and may be reached via cell at 406-555-5555 or email at brasmussen@xxx.com. Thank you for your strongest consideration.

Sincerely,

Bill Rasmussen

Enclosure: résumé

76

Entry-Level Civil Engineer. *Cheryl Minnick, Missoula, Montana*

This cold-call letter was for a recent college graduate seeking an entry-level civil engineering position with a high-profile engineering firm in his state with no posted job openings.

CHRISTOPHER CASHTON One Concentric Circle • Suite 000 • Toronto M5M 5M5
BSc, PEng

September 1, 20XX

Mr. Hy Ringo Thorty
Director of Engineering
Galactic Enterprises, Inc.
555 Milky Way, 5th Floor
Toronto, ON M5M 5M5

Dear Mr. Thorty:

I want to be your next **Systems Engineer.**

As the attached resume indicates, I have had more than 12 years of progressively responsible related employment.

I demonstrated the ability to work efficiently as *Systems Engineer/Coordinator* at Universal Electronics, Inc., where I installed 15 television distribution systems in only three months. Normally, it takes two-and-a-half days to install such a system in an open area. I can do it in under five hours. I am efficient because I am well organized.

If I had to name one characteristic that I believe makes me a good employee, it would be flexibility. This quality helped me greatly as a supervisor at Universal. I got along well with staff because I paid attention to them. I made a point of finding out the strengths of each employee. I motivated them by showing confidence in them when I knew they had the capacity to do a particular task well.

I gave them leeway, so that they would have a sense of ownership in their work. When they proved themselves worthy, I gave them more leeway. I also maximized my own productivity by delegating liberally.

My flexibility was instrumental in enabling me to work well on teams. I observed that people typically withheld information, motivated by a competitive spirit. I made a point of sharing information with my colleagues. In so doing, I was able to help them do their job better, and this was appreciated. I recognize individual differences. I understand there is more than one way of doing something well and, by avoiding a judgmental attitude, engender good will not only among those I supervise, but also peers.

Please have a look at the attached resume. I am confident that, on reviewing it, you will agree I have the potential to become a worthy member of your team. I will phone to set a convenient time to meet, so that we can discuss how I might best serve Galactic Enterprises.

Yours truly,

Christopher Cashton

P.S. I can be reached at (555) 000-0000.

Attachment: resume

77

Systems Engineer. *Howard Earle Halpern, Toronto, Ontario, Canada*

The letter explains how the applicant worked efficiently, elaborates on his supervisory style, highlights attributes recruiters typically seek, and shows how he is a flexible team player.

Kerri Mulligan

5555 W 55th Ave. | Bozeman, MT 55555
555.555.5555 | kmulligan@xxx.com

August 8, 20XX

Steven Rally, Program Leader
National Forest Service
5555 Pine Ridge Pkwy.
Livingston, MT 55555
555.555.7777 phone
555.555.8888 fax
steven_rally@xxx.gov

Re: **Community Planning Intern Opportunity**

Dear Mr. Rally:

As an environmental planning graduate student with a solid background in environmental science, I believe that I have much to offer the National Forest Service's Conservation Legacy Program as your next Community Planning Intern.

For three summers during my environmental management undergraduate studies, I gained direct experience working with local, state, and federal organizations and government agencies. I compiled data, conducted desktop and in-field research, and prepared reports, first for a land-surveying services firm and later for the Ohio Department of Environmental Management (ODEM). Now that I have settled into Montana and established myself as a strong student within my graduate program, I am eager to apply my newly acquired and constantly developing environmental planning skills. The Community Planning Intern position excites me because of the program's focus on cooperative conservation and recreation planning initiatives, and, because I am able to schedule my graduate studies around my employer's needs, I will gladly commit however much time is necessary to advancing the initiatives of the National Forest Service.

My attached résumé contains additional information on my experience and skills. I would appreciate the opportunity to meet with you in person and will follow up with you early next week to answer any preliminary questions you may have.

Your time and consideration are most appreciated.

Sincerely,

Kerri Mulligan

Kerri Mulligan

"I have worked closely with student summer interns throughout my employment with ODEM since 20XX and can honestly say Ms. Mulligan is **the most impressive student I have had work for me.** She possesses the most complete combination of **academic intelligence** and the **ability to work well with others** that I have seen in a student intern."

Jay Walker | Environmental Manager
Ohio Department of Environmental Management (ODEM)
Office of Water Quality | December 16, 20XX

78

Community Planning Intern. *Melanie Lenci, Denver, Colorado*

Note the signature. The writer had the applicant go online and use a free signature generator that created a JPG version of her signature to distinguish her letter from other electronic submissions.

Aniyah Alexander
19 Lawnside Drive
Balmain, NSW 2040

Mobile: 0414 981 062
Home: (02) 9999 9999
E-mail: aniyah@optusnet.com.au

[Date]

[Company Personnel]
[Company Department]
[Company Name]
[Address]
[Suburb, State, Postal Code]

Dear _____,

When I joined the International Society of Logistics Trading (ISLT) in 20xx, it was in bankruptcy with only 152 members. Today it is a $2M international organisation with a membership base of 1,600 members. I transformed ISLT into a strong organisation, with a positive cash flow and outstanding member retention. This success was mainly due to leading the establishment of a 501c3 for the organisation and in the planning and execution of events and programs that generated more than $1.5M in annual revenue and increased asset position from zero to $1.3M.

Prior to working for ISLT, I provided business perspective, strategic visioning, and events management to the ASA Underwriter Association that led to the business becoming a successful and viable organisation through increased membership and community visibility. Through my leadership of the Award Committee, the organisation repeatedly won awards in the annual award recognition programs for Achievement, Public Service, Public Relations, Education, and Members, which were granted to local and state groups by the National Association of Life Underwriters. Prior to my appointment, they had won only two awards in 80 years.

These two examples clearly demonstrate the value I can bring to your organisation. My strengths are in the planning and execution of fund-raising and special events, and in managing the administration of an organisation or event to meet business goals and objectives. I am a creative visionary with a strong team spirit that has an innate ability to take charge, interpret complex issues, and identify opportunities, while still focusing on the actual raising of revenues and membership.

As such, I would welcome an interview to discuss your current needs and my potential contributions. Thank you for your time and consideration of my application. I look forward to speaking with you soon.

Yours sincerely,

Aniyah Alexander
Encl.

79

Executive Director. *Jennifer Rushton, Sydney, New South Wales, Australia*

The applicant wanted a position in fund-raising/events management. The letter shows her ability to turn around poorly performing organizations and increase membership, participation, and revenue.

Cindy Springs
2016 Warm Avenue
Seattle, WA 88888
(555) 555-5555
cindysprings@msn.com

April 16, 20xx

Steve Franklin
Canyon Sheriff's Youth Foundation
1632 Barley Drive
Seattle, WA 88888

Dear Mr. Franklin,

As a highly organized professional with experience in coordinating fundraising events and office management, I invite you to consider the enclosed resume in support of my application to secure a position with Canyon Sheriff's Youth Foundation.

I have successfully implemented and monitored strategic objectives and projects to meet the diverse needs of the Seattle Chamber of Commerce as the Manager, consistently completing projects within or under budget. My experience and knowledge will bring immediate improvements to your current and future projects. Please consider the following in addition to my enclosed resume:

- **In-depth project management,** planning, organizing, and evaluating programs for effectiveness and efficiency. Held presentations with officials and community leaders addressing all concerns and showcasing solutions.
- **Decisive, innovative, and dedicated team leader,** inspiring strong team morale as shown by building a team of professionals, coupled with promoting high-quality work supported by a community-oriented attitude.
- **Developed strong relationships with customers,** subordinates, senior management, volunteers, council officials, and community representatives through outstanding communication skills and business etiquette.

It is with great interest that I encourage you to consider my resume, as I am confident that your organization will benefit from my focus on achieving company objectives as a dedicated leader and team member. I am certain that a personal interview would more fully reveal my skills and desire to join your team, and I will call next week to set a mutually convenient time.

Sincerely,

Cindy Springs

Enclosure

80

Fund-Raiser and Office Manager. *Denette D. Jones, Mountain View, Hawaii*

This three-paragraph letter is enhanced with bulleted statements after the second paragraph. Boldfacing enhances the key topic of each bulleted statement, making the topics readily visible.

Benjamin Hall

56 Sunny Dr. ◆ Poughkeepsie, NY 12601 ◆ 555-555-5555 ◆ ben@aol.com

February 20, 20xx

Ms. Taylor Coleman, Director
The American Heart Society
12 Tucker Drive
Wappingers Falls, NY 12590

Dear Ms. Coleman:

I am a beauty industry professional who is writing to express interest in employment opportunities within your organization. My goal is a promotional position where I can use my marketing expertise and industry contacts in the area of events planning. With my commitment to social advocacy and enthusiasm for cause-related marketing, I believe that I could positively contribute to your endeavors.

For more than six years I have been working as an events planner for various social causes and issues. Currently, I am responsible for leading the marketing and fund-raising efforts for b•cause—a foundation that I established. Throughout my career I have served in a volunteer capacity in an effort to generate philanthropic support and galvanize industry professionals to embrace issues affecting our community.

My career accelerated after Revlon recognized my ability to spot trends and deliver results. Revlon signed me as its National Fund-raising Director. In only a few years, I conceptualized and brought to fruition countless fund-raisers and events, raising more than $500,000. I was successful in planning and executing these programs through a substantial knowledge of the beauty industry (its business, leaders and experts) and a broad understanding of fund-raising.

While I have an innate ability to take charge of and interpret complex issues, my skills focus on the actual raising of revenues through donor acquisition, corporate giving and personal solicitation. Equally notable has been my ability to identify opportunities, gain high-profile support and negotiate corporate sponsorship. More specifically, I have consistently demonstrated an ability to establish credibility and confidence with individuals or large groups. Further, I am experienced and comfortable in dealing with top public and private community leaders.

Enclosed is a copy of my resume for your review. I look forward to the opportunity to provide you with further details of my professional value and personal commitment during an interview. I will call to determine a mutually convenient time to meet. Thank you for your time.

Sincerely,

Benjamin Hall

Enclosure

81

Events Planner. *Kristin M. Coleman, Poughkeepsie, New York*

Striking in this letter is the amount of white space in relation to the great amount of information it supplies. The writer accomplished this feat through smaller-than-average type and narrower left and right margins.

35–12 Cottonboll Drive
Selma, AL 00000

Yasheika Ojimobi

Banquet Management Specialist

yasheika@partytime.com

Phone: (000) 000-0000
Cell: (000) 000-1111

January 14, 20xx

Victor Gibson
Director of Human Resources
Sheridan Corporation
1674 Eldridge Avenue
Montgomery, AL 00000

Dear Mr. Gibson:

In speaking recently with Maxine Ray, who works for Jake Levitz, your Convention Services Manager, I learned that there may be several positions open for persons who are skilled in setting up banquets or managing on-site activities for convention services and trade shows. Because I was intrigued by these opportunities, I am acting on Maxine's suggestion to send you my resume and this letter of interest.

Having spent the past 15 years performing every imaginable task associated with putting together successful banquets and events attended by hundreds of people, I know I have the essential qualifications to be an asset to your organization. As you review my resume, you will see the scope of my involvement and the versatility I can offer. I take great pride in my work, and I am totally dedicated to meeting and even exceeding the expectations of a demanding clientele for their social or corporate functions.

Throughout my career, I have been most effective in orchestrating a team effort while recognizing individual talents to accomplish project goals. The key to my success has been my ability to efficiently manage multiple and varied activities, all taking place simultaneously. Given the opportunity, I can demonstrate this in any project situation calling for broad cooperation.

In addition, I am receptive to new learning experiences; welcome challenges; and have no objection to travel, late hours, or weekend work.

I would appreciate meeting with you personally to discuss your organization's plans and how I may be able to contribute to their accomplishment. I will call you within the next week to determine your interest and perhaps arrange a time when we can meet. Thank you for any consideration.

Sincerely,

Yasheika Ojimobi

Enclosure: Resume

82

Banquets and Events Planner. *Melanie Noonan, Woodland Park, New Jersey*

Extra-wide left and right margins provide satisfying white space in this letter. The first paragraph mentions a referral, and the next three paragraphs play up the applicant's merits. See Resume 3 in Part 3.

Ashina Hartnett

555 55th Avenue, Rochester MN 55555
(555) 555-5555

January 24, 20xx

Mr. Samuel Gleason
James T. Conference Coordinators
555 Salome Boulevard
Chicago IL 66666

Banquet and Conference Coordinator

Dear Mr. Gleason:

My work with a highly diverse clientele has been very rewarding, and the experience has reinforced my need to work in an independent capacity that draws together decision-making, problem-solving, and superior people skills.

Staff and the general public respond positively to my managerial, leadership, and communication style. I would like to continue working in a business or people-related position with public visibility, and have enclosed a resume for your review. Some of the other qualities I offer are

- Ability to listen closely and react to what people actually say or mean
- Diplomacy, discretion, and consistent style
- Positive attitude
- Flexible nature attuned to changing markets and needs
- Attention to details and concerns
- Efficient multitasking and performance under pressure
- Professional manner, with strict adherence to confidentiality
- Awareness of the importance of professional networking—willingness to attend Chamber of Commerce and other relevant meetings

I've enjoyed assisting in the sales department of a major hotel the last two years and have been called on to fill in when the Conference Coordinator needed additional help with the multitude of details for an unusually large conference. I have not only done some of the "grunt" work but also conferred with various clients, set up the technical logistics, handled last-minute changes, and coordinated with the banquet department. Testimonials from the Conference Coordinator and General Manager will back up my skills and abilities and will verify their opinion that I would be a good fit for a full-time banquet and conference coordinator.

I am highly responsible and trustworthy, and clients and employees alike feel comfortable that I'll do what I say and that promises won't "fall between the cracks." My genuine concern for quality customer service and improved worker motivation is readily apparent, as is interest in professional development and ongoing learning.

It is difficult to determine from resumes career potential and in which areas a person can make a difference to a company. I am looking forward to meeting with you to discuss your needs, to exchange information, and to address any questions.

Sincerely,

Ashina Hartnett

83

Banquet and Conference Coordinator. *Beverley Drake, Hot Springs Village, Arkansas*

The applicant was moving from sales to conference work. Unique "multisheet" bullets suggest that each bulleted quality is multifaceted. The third paragraph refers to relevant experience.

Beverly Chase Ryan

0000 Big Horn Road
Bldg. 12, Apt. C
Vail, Colorado 89898

(555) 555-8888   beverlyryan4@aol.com   Cell: (555) 555-7777

January 12, 20xx

Leonard R. Victors, Human Resources Manager
AAA Giant Events, Inc.
222 Johansen Boulevard
Vail, Colorado 89898

Dear Mr. Victors:

I was thrilled to find your firm's advertisement in the *Vail Sunday Times*, January 12, 20xx, for a Senior Winter Events Consultant. My broad management experience in events planning, coupled with my enthusiasm for working in the skiing industry, clearly matches your stated requirements for the ideal candidate to fill this position.

Most of my professional adult life has been occupied with sports, sports marketing, public relations, successful promotional endeavors, and executing all operations within a high-end catering business in Newport, Rhode Island. My athletic achievements and participation in numerous activities in college point to my early accomplishments in building a solid foundation for the intensive responsibilities of planning and successfully executing such events as AAA regularly engages in.

In addition, my experiences as advertising account executive for North American Skiing Companies, director of retail marketing for a radio station, and director of public relations for a baseball team have strengthened my abilities to meet any challenges that may lie ahead in my focused ambition to go further in this growing field of sports events planning.

I would appreciate meeting with you to discuss my candidacy for the position as Senior Winter Events Consultant with AAA Giant Events, Inc. I will call your office to request a meeting date convenient to you.

Thank you for considering my application. I eagerly look forward to our meeting and the opportunity to discuss my credentials and career aspirations for this position.

Sincerely,

Beverly Chase Ryan

Enclosure: resume

84

Senior Winter Events Consultant. *Edward Turilli, Bonita Springs, Florida*

This letter displays the applicant's enthusiasm toward the advertised opening and the prospect of pursuing further her field of athletics. She mentions key experiences for sports events planning.

——RICK BARRINGTON——————————

555 Brooks | Missoula, MT 55555
(000) 555-5555 | rbarrington@xxx.com

September 20, 20XX

Boston Celtics
Human Resources
000 Cosway Street
Boston, MA 00000

Dear Mr. Grousbeck,

Professional basketball is more than a game—it is entertainment. It has the power to deliver excitement and passion while creating energy and intensity in the stands, on the court, and on the screen. Owners of established sports franchises know that success is more than a winning scoreboard—it is creating a dynasty and brand that define the fans and organization as a whole. As a candidate for the Boston Celtics internship, I promise to deliver results to organizational goals beyond your expectations as an energetic, dedicated individual with proven success in deadline-driven, sports entertainment environments.

My qualifications in event production, live entertainment, and media relations would make me a valuable asset for the Boston Celtics. From small-scale events to Fortune 100 productions, I have been recognized as an innovative, self-motivated young professional with a strong work ethic and outstanding interpersonal skills. As your intern, I will make it my mission to use my personal record of success to assist the Boston Celtics, one of the greatest organizations in sports, in their quest for an XXth NBA World Championship.

I am prepared to put all my energy and passion into the Boston Celtics organization. Although my résumé and experience speak for themselves, an opportunity to talk with you personally will confirm the talent, experience, and qualifications I bring to the internship. Thank you for your time and strongest consideration.

Sincerely,

Rick Barrington

Rick Barrington

Enclosure: résumé

85

Sports Events Planner Intern, Boston Celtics. *Cheryl Minnick, Missoula, Montana*

This student wanted his letter to stand out in a field of thousands of applicants. The focus is his understanding of basketball as entertainment and the Celtics. He got an interview and the job.

SUSAN NORRIS

55 South Denton Street, #00, Farside, NC 55555
555.555.5555 • susannorris@xxx.com

MARKETING CONSULTANT / EVENT COORDINATOR / SPONSORSHIP MANAGEMENT

October 7, 20XX

Mr. John Jones
Tourism Director
City of Farside
00 Main Street, #X-0
Farside, NC 00000

RE: Special Events Coordinator position

Dear Mr. Jones:

Like many other citizens of Farside, I have a hopeful vision of Farside as a resort and business destination considered "first in its field." Unlike many other citizens, however, I can support that vision with 15+ years of accomplishment and leadership. I know how to bring in new events, oversee existing events profitably, generate effective marketing strategies, and manage sponsor and media relationships that retain their loyalty and attention. I believe these skills can be useful to Farside on its road to responsible growth, just as they were for the Florida Dodgers, the Sun Bowl, Timex and Lusianne International Tennis Championships, and a Super Bowl or two. "Great," you say, "But Farside isn't a high-dollar metropolis."

True (thank goodness), but the accomplishments that are *closest* to my heart are the following:

- When asked by a local bank to create a special event to celebrate their sponsorship of the Super Bowl that year, I came up with an interactive football clinic involving 1,000 inner-city youth. It was so successful that the Football League adopted it as an official Super Bowl event for the following three years and asked me to organize it in those cities, always working with local organizations.

- I organized a Filipino community festival in York City for the Miami host committee.

- I managed a nationwide journalism scholarship program for the US-Canada Open (golf).

- I garnered sponsorship for Jacksonville inner-city youth for the Jacksonville Cooks basketball camps, with involvement by the Police Athletic League.

The enclosed résumé provides more of the details about these accomplishments, and of course I am eager to talk with you in even greater detail in person. The point is that special events have similar issues, regardless of whether the events take place in a metropolitan area or a small town. They are *always* local, and local can be complicated. I have the relationship, strategic, and fiscal skills to navigate those waters.

I left my marketing profession for another full-time profession, and I'm proud to say the results of that job have grown into happy contributors to their community. Now I have the time and the marketing skills to be of service. May we talk?

Thank you for your time, interest, and consideration. I look forward to our conversation.

Best regards,

Susan Norris

Susan Norris

enc. Résumé

86

Special Events Coordinator. *Dayna Feist, Asheville, North Carolina*

After a big-city career and an 18-year sabbatical to raise two children, this applicant was competing with residents of a small town for a coveted position. This letter got her an interview.

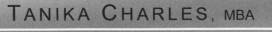

TANIKA CHARLES, MBA
DYNAMIC EVENT PLANNER

"It is our attitude at the beginning of a difficult task which, more than anything else, will affect its successful outcome."

-William James

September 27, 20XX

Laura Bell
Human Resources Manager
XXXCorp
00 Swan Road
Las Vegas, NV 00000

Dear Ms. Bell:

As a visionary event planner with a powerful 10-year history of masterminding innovative events, I am pleased that XXXCorp requires a **Corporate Event Manager** to meet and exceed company-wide strategic goals. Please accept this letter and the attached résumé in consideration for this intriguing role.

XXXCorp has a reputation for achieving business results with a performance and customer-driven focus. The attached résumé illustrates my talents in these key areas. I have significant experience successfully planning events in various sizes and complexities from large-scale musical concerts to overseas executive symposiums.

My event portfolio demonstrates the experience I bring to XXXCorp:

➨ *Musical Events: April Laping, Cindy Deon, Hendrix Sound, Jules Black, Jim Conway*

➨ *Promotional Events: Microsoft Corporation, Estee Lauder Companies, Bell, Virgin Mobile*

You will find that I have a flair for flawless execution of events and a reliability that will provide your organization with peace of mind. My inclusive, hands-on, and team-oriented leadership style enables me to turn vision into reality.

I believe there is an excellent fit between my leadership skills and your need for a dynamic and engaging Corporate Event Manager. I welcome the opportunity to meet in person to discuss this exciting position and will follow up with a phone call to confirm your receipt of my résumé. I look forward to speaking with you in the near future to arrange a meeting at your convenience.

Regards,

Tanika Charles, MBA

Enclosure: Résumé

55 **Forest Link Road, Las Vegas, NV 55555** ▪ **Mobile: 555-555-7777** ▪ **Home: 555-555-5555** ▪ **E-mail: events@xxx.com**

87

Corporate Event Manager. *Tanya Sinclair, Pickering, Ontario, Canada*

An eye-catching header, a relevant quotation, bulleted items showcasing some of the applicant's key clients, and contact information in a text box are distinctive features of this letter.

CONFIDENTIAL

Chelsea Connors

000 Sturbridge Commons Henniker, New Hampshire 00000
✉ cconners41@xxx.net ☎ 555.555.5555 (cell)

Monday, XX August, 20XX

Mr. Charles W. Morgan
General Manager
The Gold Medal Hotel Group, LLC
0000 Breeds Boulevard
Suite 000
Boston, Massachusetts 00000

> …**$250K** in new revenue…**penetrated and held** a new, saturated **market** …**exceeded a** Saudi prince**'s every expectation**…**$70K in new** catering **bookings**…increased revenue **$20K** in only six months

Dear Mr. Morgan:

You've just read the headline version of contributions I've made in the catering and event planning field—in the last three years alone. If that kind of track record would serve The Gold Medal Group, I would like to join your team as your newest Catering and Event Sales Manager.

There is no secret to what I do. I am driven by a passion to serve *all* my customers: the clients who pay the bills, the vendors and business partners who share in the success, and the company for which I work.

That passion isn't just an in-vogue word. I was a very successful sales professional for Proctor & Gamble for more than a decade. They promoted me three times. But my heart has always been in catering and event planning. So I invested two years in learning every aspect of the business, mastering a comprehensive, rigorous certificate program at Northeastern University.

Only then did I feel ready to take on serious responsibilities with one of the nation's top hotel and resort chains. Then, I mastered serving the most demanding, sophisticated customers by holding management positions in upscale country clubs.

Now I want to return to my first love: catering and event planning at the corporate level. Right at the top of my résumé are five pledges of value you'll see me deliver from the start. Backing them up are five examples of problems solved and new revenue earned.

But when it comes to something as important as serving The Gold Medal Group, words on paper cannot substitute for people speaking with people. Therefore, I would like to hear about your requirements in your own words.

May I call in a few days to arrange a time for that purpose?

Sincerely,

Chelsea Connors

Encl.: Résumé

CONFIDENTIAL

88

Catering and Event Sales Manager. *Don Orlando, Montgomery, Alabama*

This applicant wanted to transition from logistics and sales at a major corporation to a corporate position in the hospitality industry. A text box displays notable achievements.

LilyGrace Deihl
Cell: (555) 555-5555 Home: (555) 555-7777
555 Pepper Court
Kerrville, TX 55555
lilyg@xxx.com

---

*"LilyGrace **consistently exceeded goals** in fundraising endeavors for us. Our volunteers **loved working with her**, and she endeared herself to those clients we served."*—Robert N. Reid, Executive Director, Wish on a Star Foundation

*"LilyGrace's strong customer relationships have been **instrumental in building our client base within the community.** LilyGrace is known for working with clients and **delivering stellar results** through her ability to listen to clients, assess needs, and suggest services or products available…"*—Larry Hanes, Owner, Hanes in the Hills Bed & Breakfast

---

March 24, 20XX

Mr. Grant Kayson, Guest Services Director
The Hills Inn Resort and Conference Center
000 Hwy 00 North
Kerrville, TX 55555

Dear Mr. Kayson,

Amanda Ashworth in Human Resources suggested that I contact you directly regarding the Senior Event Coordinator position opening. As my resume indicates, I have a demonstrated commitment to my customers' and my employers' goals. That track record is consistent in my career endeavors as well as in my life as a whole; I dedicate myself to whatever tasks are at hand, marshal my resources, and stay with projects until they are completed.

I am accustomed to fast-paced environments where deadlines are a priority and handling multiple jobs simultaneously is the norm. I am a dedicated listener and an accomplished problem solver. Realizing that everything from consistency in training to time management affects the bottom line, organization and extraordinary attention to detail are my paramount professional philosophies.

The position with your organization caught my attention as I will be relocating to the Asheville area to be near family. I have a loyal customer base of travelers and would love to offer Smoky Mountain Resort & Conference Center as a new destination.

Resumes help you sort out the probables from the possibles, but in no way do they judge the caliber of a candidate. I look forward to discussing our mutual interests further and am available at your convenience for a personal meeting.

Thank you for your time and attention to my materials.

Sincerely,

LilyGrace Deihl

89

Senior Event Coordinator. *Devon Benish, San Antonio, Texas*

This letter is a networking letter triggered by a referral. The writer put as part of the heading great quotations from former employers to excite the reader about the applicant.

Troy McDonaldson, M.P.A.
555 S. Copperland Lane
Gold Basin, New York 55555
555-555-5555
troymcdonaldson@xxx.com

NEW BUSINESS DEVELOPMENT
"Good business is good when it's good for all concerned"

October 4, 20XX

Ms. Lacea Hower
American Center for Genetic Studies
5555 Orpington Boulevard
White Leggern, Illinois 55555

RE: Manager, Consumer Tradeshows

Dear Ms. Hower:

On the recommendation of Hank White, President of the ILPAF, I am forwarding my resume to be considered for the above-referenced position. I was excited to learn that you are seeking someone with a strong entrepreneurial spirit to lead the launch of the organization's first public tradeshow and educational event, as this seems to be an ideal match for my qualifications.

Not only have I successfully provided high-ROI advertising, sponsorships, and exhibit space for tradeshows, I also have a background working for an association management company, a master's degree in public administration, and a previous career as a physical education teacher. In addition, I currently design and implement interactive education programs for healthcare associations, including the New York Chapter of Pediatric Medicine.

Select accomplishments have included:
- **Partnering with technical vendor to pioneer creation of virtual conference and mobile apps to increase engagement of association members.** (Austin Parkus Interactive)
- **Leading sales team in adding 30% in new revenue to client associations by designing customized conference packages.** (Association for Growth)
- **Attaining 20% increase in partnerships by analyzing market segments and delivering custom-built bundled media packages.** (Martin Sexton Convention Center)

The attached resume includes additional examples of ways my successes in leading sales teams and securing valuable partnerships have generated revenue both for my employers and client associations. I would welcome the opportunity to speak with you in more detail and will call next week to follow up. Should you wish to contact me earlier, I can be reached at the telephone number and e-mail address listed above. Thank you for your time and consideration.

Sincerely,

Troy McDonaldson, M.P.A.

Enclosure

90

Manager, Consumer Tradeshows. *Charlotte Weeks, Chicago, Illinois*

The position was for someone to launch the organization's first tradeshow. The writer mentioned results from similar initiatives the applicant had taken, plus relevant valuable experience.

ELIZABETH COOPER

55 Hillcrest Drive   (555) 555-5555
Biloxi, MS 55555   elizabeth@xxx.net

November 15, 20XX
Mr. Alan Schmidt, CEO
Brady Memorial Hospital
0000 Riverview Parkway
Biloxi, MS 00000

Dear Mr. Schmidt:

In recent years, America's healthcare crisis has left multimillion-dollar shortfalls in the cost of providing charity and emergency care on public hospitals around the nation. As a member of the Association of Healthcare Philanthropy, I learned that Brady Memorial Hospital is facing this type of challenge, with its government aid greatly reduced. For this reason, I am submitting this letter and attached resume in response to your online posting for a Director of Development.

For the past 7 years, I have held a leadership position in developing relationships with prospects and donors to support a $40 million campaign for St. Mark's Hospital. My qualifications strongly match your requirements in that I have significant experience in the following areas:

- All development activities involving foundations, corporations, individuals, physicians, campaign committees, employees, and the community
- Major gift solicitation, annual fund reporting, and proposal writing
- Production of fund-raising plans, budget, literature, direct mail packages, campaign materials, and slide show presentations
- Research and cultivation activities
- Planning of public announcements to the media for the entire campaign
- Recruitment, supervision, and training of support staff and volunteers

With my demonstrated success in soliciting major gifts from various constituencies, our capital campaign was able to raise $3.4 million toward our first-year goal of $4 million in only 8 months. I can attribute this accomplishment to the identification, cultivation, solicitation, and stewardship of individual donors, as well as setting goals and developing plans for an assigned portfolio of approximately 75 current and prospective major donors with a primary focus of giving above the $25,000 level.

I applaud the efforts that Brady Memorial Hospital has made to provide for the healthcare needs of the less fortunate in the Gulf area. Your endeavors are much too valuable to fall victim to financial crisis. I am confident that I can help you achieve your funding goals and would like to contribute my energy, enthusiasm, and organizational and persuasive skills to the Director of Development position. May I meet with you soon?

Sincerely,

Elizabeth Cooper

Enclosure

91

Director of Development. *Melanie Noonan, Woodland Park, New Jersey*

A hospital desperately needed money to stay open. The applicant's career focus was hospital funding. This letter to a CEO has a goal of convincing readers that she can reach major donors.

HARRY STRONG

900 Starling Lane
Indianapolis, IN 00000

harrystrong@yahoo.com

Cell: (555) 555-6555
Office: (555) 555-5555

January 25, 20xx

[Name]
[Title]
[Employer]
[Address]
[City, State ZIP]

Dear Mr. or Ms. _____:

Like many other recent graduates, I am searching for an opportunity to apply my skills while contributing to a company's growth. Unlike others, though, I don't believe that a new bachelor's degree is enough to qualify in today's highly competitive market.

As a result, I have worked diligently to supplement my college education with hands-on experience in financial environments, equipping me with a wide range of skills as a Financial or Business Analyst. Through my employment and educational training, I have developed the qualifications that will make me an asset to your company:

- **Financial Skills and Experience:** More than 2 years of experience in a corporate environment as a financial advisor, along with a solid background in financial analysis, reporting, budgeting, negotiating and business/financial planning. Apply financial tools to identify, manage and maximize investment funds.

- **Keen Research, Analytical and Quantitative Skills:** Adept at reviewing, analyzing and synthesizing financial data, as well as viewing challenges from different perspectives to arrive at creative solutions.

- **Computer Software Tools:** Demonstrated proficiency in learning new applications quickly. Skilled in using Microsoft Word, Excel and Access database software. I also use Morningstar extensively to research data on mutual funds.

- **Proven Communications, Organizational and Interpersonal Skills:** My collective experiences have enabled me to hone my interpersonal, written and verbal communications skills, which include developing financial reports, interfacing with internal and external customers and delivering presentations. Cultivating and maintaining positive relationships with a wide range of personalities have resulted in a large referral network from satisfied clients. Another strength is my ability to efficiently organize and manage my day-to-day responsibilities for maximum productivity.

Based on my talents and dedicated efforts, I have been recognized for my contributions to business growth and success. If you need a highly motivated professional who grasps new concepts quickly; loves to learn; and offers the personal drive, skills and confidence to succeed, I would welcome an interview. I'll contact you in a few days to explore the possibility. Thank you.

Sincerely,

Harry Strong

Enclosure

Financial or Business Analyst. *Louise Garver, Broad Brook, Connecticut*

This letter is for a new graduate who found an opportunity as a Financial Analyst. Bullets and boldfacing draw attention to the applicant's qualifications, which he gained from experience and education.

Angela T. Ingram

0000 Merritt Highway
Orlando, Florida 32821

555-555-5555
atingram@network.com

Director of Employment
Company
Address
City, State ZIP

Dear Director of Employment:

After a successful and satisfying career with Iowa's largest independently owned financial institution, I recently moved to Florida and am looking forward to embarking on a new career here. I am taking the liberty of enclosing a resume describing my background. When you review it, you may notice that I am experienced in and capable of stepping into a variety of areas. Let me elaborate.

Project Management. A consistent thread through my career at the bank was that I was often given the responsibility to oversee projects ranging from implementing new software to managing a major consolidation of branches. I have proven that I have the expertise to manage people and processes, resulting in minimal disruption to clients and/or staff.

Administration. I believe I have succeeded in providing administrative and technical support to management and users at all levels within the corporation. I am skilled in assessing others' needs and developing strategies to meet those needs. My communication skills are well developed, which facilitates my efforts.

Training and Supervision. My experience encompasses both. Because I had no formal technical training, I had to constantly self-teach and update my own skills. That gave me a unique perspective and helped me to become an effective trainer. As my resume indicates, I supervised a high-volume second-shift processing department.

In addition to the traits listed above, my performance reflects a dedication to my employer and a high degree of self-motivation. Performing beyond expectations is the norm for me. After you have examined my material, I hope you will contact me to arrange an interview. I am confident I can make significant contributions to your organization. I can be reached at home (555-555-5555) or on my cell phone (000-000-0000). Thank you for your time and consideration.

Sincerely,

Angela T. Ingram

Enclosure

93

Bank Supervisor. *Janet L. Beckstrom, Flint, Michigan*

The applicant was moving across the country and was qualified to work in diverse capacities. The writer capitalized on the applicant's broad experience and drew attention to it with boldfacing.

MARIAN R. SMITH, CFA

555 Grove Street, St. Louis, MO 55555
Home: 555-555-5555
Cell: 500-500-5000
smithm265@verizon.net

**BUILDING BEST-OF-BREED TREASURY FUNCTIONS
BALANCE SHEET AND LIQUIDITY MANAGEMENT
GLOBAL BANKING RELATIONSHIP MANAGEMENT
CORPORATE FINANCE DEAL EXECUTION
BUILDING & LEADING HIGH-PERFORMANCE TEAMS
ADVANCED PENSION AND RISK MANAGEMENT**

September 25, 20xx

Victor Hellman
President
CRB Limited
555 Conant Ave.
St. Louis, MO 55555

Re: Treasurer Position—Reference Code 55555

Dear Mr. Hellman:

My specialty is bringing cost-conscious leadership to the treasury function of a global corporation. Using my broad, 17-year experience in corporate finance and treasury operations, I am able to envision and implement company-wide solutions that reduce costs, add to the bottom line, and minimize risk.

I have demonstrated an ability to optimize the balance sheet and effectively maintain liquidity within multinational corporations. My notable strengths in communication and relationship-building have resulted in fruitful relationships with both internal clients and external members of the financial and regulatory communities. These skills have also enabled me to build strong international corporate treasury teams.

I am a skilled negotiator with an expert grasp of financial instruments, business opportunities, and the competitive financial landscape. I have been able to close major deals that have been critical to the financial health of the organizations for which I have worked. Some examples of my achievements include the following:

- Closed bond deals valued at $400 million in the tight credit environment of 20xx and 20xx.
- Developed an interest rate strategy that yielded $65 million in new revenue from strategic interest-rate swapping activities.
- Instituted a Global Enterprise Risk Management System to protect the corporation from poor governance practices going forward.

My most recent titles have been Assistant Treasurer at two multinational companies with $3 billion and $6 billion in annual revenues, respectively. These roles offered me unusual opportunities to participate at the highest levels of the corporate treasury function. As the #2 treasury professional in such large global corporations, I was frequently in the position of executing the responsibilities of Treasurer. Although my recent titles read "Assistant Treasurer," I am ready to "hit the ground running" in the top treasury position.

I anticipate with pleasure an opportunity to learn about the challenges CRB Limited is facing and to discuss with you the contributions I could make as Treasurer to the prosperity of your organization. I will call next week to set an appointment.

Sincerely,

Marian R. Smith, CFA

Enc.

94

Treasurer. *Jean Cummings, Concord, Massachusetts*

The applicant wanted to work for a multinational company and wanted her new title to be Treasurer, not Assistant Treasurer. The writer explained the person's qualifications for the top job.

RICHARD KIMBLE
rkimble@aol.com

12 Norwood Avenue   (555) 555-5555 (H)
Oakland, NJ 07420   (000) 000-0000 (W)

November 18, 20XX

Hiring Authority
Company
Address
City, State ZIP

Dear Hiring Authority,

After 20 years as a successful small-business owner, I'm changing career directions to
follow my longtime desire to be a financial planner. To that end, I am currently enrolled
in a CFP program.

Although I have no professional experience as a financial planner, I have frequently
advised others on investment strategies. In my own case, I developed an investment
strategy for my portfolio that yielded an annual return of 10.5% for a 10-year period
ending 12/31/XX. I also managed the disbursement of assets for 2 estates.

I can be characterized as an entrepreneur with sound business judgment, maturity, good
sales skills, and high integrity. I enjoy challenges that require learning new skills and
interacting with the public. I am steady and patient, having built my own business from
the ground up to more than $500,000 in annual revenues.

My goal is an exciting and rewarding position with a company facing new prospects. I
am eager to participate in any training process that will build on my skills and provide the
knowledge I need to be successful.

I prefer to stay in the metropolitan New York City area, but will consider attractive
opportunities in the tri-state region. I would prefer to travel no more than 50% of the
time.

I will contact you in the coming weeks to explore the possibility of an in-person meeting.
Thank you for your consideration.

Sincerely,

Richard Kimble

Enclosure

95

Financial Planner. *Igor Shpudejko, Mahwah, New Jersey*

This professional photographer wanted to transition to being a financial planner without related
experience. The writer emphasized the applicant's maturity and sound business judgment, which
are needed by financial planners.

BRITTANY LYONS

000-000-0000

lyons@email.com
0000 S. Front Street, Tulsa, OK 74107

March 12, 20xx

Ms. Lisa Hart
First Bank of Columbus
1383 Main Street
Columbus, OH 43204

Dear Ms. Hart:

Numbers drive good business decisions … collecting and analyzing data is critical to sound decision making.

My career experience within the banking industry has been broad-based, but it has always involved generating the necessary data to foster decisions that positively impact an organization's bottom line. My ability in this area is well documented in my resume. I have

➢ Held full decision-making authority for *deploying, expanding, and optimizing the banking delivery network* within the Florida region for the past three years.

➢ Ensured the *successful transition of employee incentive plans* following Barnett Bank's merger with Bank of America.

➢ Developed *uniform reporting mechanisms* to promote efficient line-management activities.

➢ *Reengineered and standardized* national sales incentive programs.

➢ Taught *staffing needs calculations and employee utilization* to branch offices to ensure delivery of top-notch customer service while controlling costs.

➢ Created a *cost analysis system* to effectively track internal profitability.

I will be relocating to the Columbus, Ohio, area within the next few months and would appreciate the opportunity to discuss how I might deliver similar results for your organization. May we talk? I will be in town the week of March 24 and will call to set up an appointment with you.

Sincerely,

Brittany Lyons

Enclosure

Ability** is what you're capable of doing.* ***Motivation *determines what you do.*
*****Attitude** determines how well you do it.* — Lou Holtz

96

Bank Executive. *Cindy Kraft, Valrico, Florida*

A number of features make this letter distinctive: the partial line in the contact information, the business axiom in boldface, the bulleted items enhanced with italic, and the Lou Holtz quote.

KIMBERLY A. CARTER

888 West Road • Anywhere, Michigan 55555 • 555.222.2222 • kac@email.com

January 8, 20xx

Marcy Johnson
ABC Accounting Company
333 Capital Avenue
Anywhere, Michigan 55555

Dear Ms. Johnson,

As a well-qualified credit account specialist, I demonstrate my ability to effectively communicate with clients, resolve payment issues, and collect past-due payments. I bring more than 18 years of accounts receivable experience in addition to being involved in all processing stages of collections. The scope of my experience includes, but is not limited to, commercial, automotive, and manufacturing environments.

My focus is to deliver results and provide superior service by quickly identifying problem areas in accounts receivable and developing a solution strategy to ensure that issues are resolved. My expertise lies in my strong ability to build rapport with clients, analyze accounts, and manage all aspects related to my appointed position and areas of responsibility. I find these qualities to be my greatest assets to offer employers.

Because of an unforeseen circumstance, I was unable to continue my employment as a cash applications analyst with a well-known automotive industry leader. Since my employment with A-1 Corporation, I have accepted a temporary position as a billing assistant with a local company. My objective is to secure a position in accounts receivable and credit collections with an established company. As you will note, my resume exhibits a brief review of contributions I have made to my employers, and I enjoy challenges.

A complete picture of my expertise and experience is very important. Therefore, I will follow up with you next week. I look forward to speaking with you soon to answer any questions you may have regarding my background.

Regards,

Kimberly Carter

Enclosure

97

Credit Account Specialist. *Maria E. Hebda, Trenton, Michigan*

This letter is strong because of four carefully crafted paragraphs. These indicate in turn the applicant's experience, areas of expertise, career objective, and follow-up plans.

HARRY STRONG

900 Starling Lane
Indianapolis, IN 55555

harrystrong@yahoo.com

Cell: (555) 555-6555
Office: (555) 555-5555

January 25, 20xx

[Name]
[Title]
[Employer]
[Address]
[City, State ZIP]

Dear Mr. or Ms. _____:

Like many recent graduates, I am eager to begin my career in finance. Unlike others, I realize that a new bachelor's degree is not enough to qualify in today's highly competitive market. As a result, I have worked diligently to supplement my college education with hands-on experience in financial environments, equipping me with a wide range of skills as a Financial Analyst. Through my employment and educational training, I have developed the qualifications that will make me an asset to your company.

Financial Skills and Experience

More than 2 years of experience in a corporate environment as a financial advisor, along with a solid background in financial analysis, reporting, budgeting, negotiating, and business/financial planning. Apply financial tools to identify, manage, and maximize investment funds.

Keen Research, Analytical, and Quantitative Skills

Adept in reviewing, analyzing, and synthesizing financial data as well as viewing challenges from different perspectives to arrive at creative solutions.

Computer Software Tools

Demonstrated proficiency in learning new applications quickly, I am skilled in using Microsoft Word, Excel, and Access database software. I also utilize Morningstar extensively to research data on mutual funds.

Proven Communications, Organization, and Interpersonal Skills

My collective experiences have enabled me to hone my interpersonal, written, and oral communications skills, which include developing financial reports, interfacing with internal and external customers, and delivering presentations. Cultivating and maintaining positive relationships with a wide range of personalities has resulted in a large referral network from satisfied clients. Another strength is my ability to efficiently organize and manage my day-to-day responsibilities for maximum productivity.

Based on my talents and dedicated efforts, I have been recognized for my contributions to business growth and success. If you need a highly motivated professional who grasps new concepts quickly, loves to learn, and offers the personal drive, skills, and confidence to succeed, I would welcome an interview. I will call you in a few days to set a convenient time.

Sincerely,

Harry Strong

98

Financial Analyst. *Louise Garver, Broad Brook, Connecticut*

This letter is a reformatting of Cover Letter 92. Boldfaced bulleted items there become bold centered headings here, making important information more conspicuous.

MR. GAHRAM MEESHAN

0000 Central Avenue   555-555-5555
Glendale, California 91208   g_meeshan@earthlink.net

March 10, 20xx

HORIZON MORTGAGE LENDERS, INC.
522 N. Purdham Avenue
Glendale, California 91203

Attention: Robert Vesag, Sales Manager

RE: Loan Officer—Monstertrak no. 1039888

Dear Mr. Vesag:

Once in a while, someone wakes up to find himself living in the wrong life.

As a forensic biomechanics assistant and a personal trainer, I have extensive experience in dealing with people, difficult or otherwise, as well as in research and data collection. These are skills that would be easily transferable to the loan industry because I would also have to deal with people and data, albeit in a different environment.

My current goal is to explore new career options that fit better with my personality. I like numbers but would rather deal with them in a financial environment.

In your ad under qualifications, it states "No experience necessary." As my resume indicates, I am a quick learner and problem solver while dealing with new concepts, systems, and procedures; therefore, a good fit exists between your requirements and my abilities. I do have a bachelor's degree, although not in the discipline you prefer. Again, this should not be an obstacle as I have a strong desire to learn and to succeed.

I will call you on Thursday to set up an appointment and further explore the possibilities of our working together.

Thank you for your time and consideration.

Sincerely,

Gahram Meeshan

Enclosure

99

Loan Officer. *Myriam-Rose Kohn, Valencia, California*

This applicant was a forensic biomechanic's assistant and wanted to become either a broker or a loan officer. The letter, therefore, mentions transferable skills, the reason for a switch, and motivation.

Susan E. Williams

0000 Indianwood Road
Clarkston, Michigan 48348

555-555-3333
susiew@network.net

August 11, 20xx

Dear Director of Employment:

A BBA degree, 20+ years of experience in the banking industry, and a comprehensive understanding of probate law—that's what I have to offer your organization. After a rewarding career at Michigan National Bank, I find myself in the position of seeking new career opportunities. My resume is enclosed for your review.

My recent experience at the bank has been in the Personal Trust/Probate department. In my capacity as Trust Officer, I was responsible for personal trust, estate, and investment accounts. I settled estates, coordinated the administration of legal documents, and directed the disbursement of funds according to the trust and/or applicable laws (among many other things). This comprehensive background would be a distinct asset to your firm.

In addition to my fiduciary responsibilities, I took a personal interest in every client. There were cases that necessitated my intervention to arbitrate differences between feuding beneficiaries. Sometimes I was called on to schedule doctor appointments or arrange for home repair. But serving the client (or the client's estate as the case may be) was always my top priority.

When you review my resume, you will see that I also managed the corporate trust division and provided administrative support in the employee benefit area. This experience adds to my versatility.

Thank you for taking the time to review my credentials. I hope you feel a personal meeting would be beneficial; I am available at your convenience. If you have any questions—or when you are ready to schedule an interview—please give me a call at 555-555-3333.

Sincerely,

Susan E. Williams

Enclosure

100

Trust Officer. *Janet L. Beckstrom, Flint, Michigan*

The applicant had extensive experience in a bank's trust/probate department. She was looking for a position with a law firm that could benefit from her experience and transferable skills.

RAYMOND MARLIN

12 Main Street
New York, New York 00000
(555) 555-5555 • raymon44@cox.net

February 8, 20xx

Mr. Fred Johnson
President/CEO
Reynolds Corporation
666 Mason Road
New York, New York 00000

Dear Mr. Johnson:

Perhaps your company could benefit from a strong chief financial officer with a record of major contributions to business and profit growth.

The scope of my expertise is extensive and includes the full complement of corporate finance, accounting, budgeting, banking, tax, treasury, internal controls, and reporting functions. Equally important are my qualifications in business planning, operations, MIS technology, administration, and general management.

A business partner to management, I have been effective in working with all departments, linking finance with operations to improve productivity, efficiency, and bottom-line results. Recruited at The Southington Company to provide finance and systems technology expertise, I created a solid infrastructure to support corporate growth as the company transitioned from a wholesale-retail distributor to a retail operator. Recent accomplishments include the following:

- **Significant contributor to the increase in operating profits from less than $400,000 to more than $4 million.**

- **Key member of due diligence team in the acquisition of 25 operating units that increased market penetration 27% and gross sales 32%.**

- **Spearheaded leading-edge MIS design and implementation, streamlining systems and procedures that dramatically enhanced productivity while cutting costs.**

A "hands-on" manager effective in building teamwork and cultivating strong internal/external relationships, I am flexible and responsive to the quickly changing demands of the business, industry, and marketplace. If you are seeking a proactive finance executive to complement your management team, I would welcome a personal interview. I will call to explore the possibility of a personal interview. Thank you for your consideration.

Very truly yours,

Raymond Marlin

Enclosure

101

Chief Financial Officer. *Louise Garver, Broad Brook, Connecticut*

This senior-level applicant wanted a finance executive position that encompassed all areas of finance and not just treasury operations (his most recent position). He was successful in reaching his goal.

DAVID JOHNSON
5 Mulberry Street
Simsbury, CT 00000
(555) 555-5555
davidj@compusa.com

February 3, 20xx

Mr. George Meadows
Chief Executive Officer
Danaher Corporation
678 City Center
Hartford, CT 00000

Dear Mr. Meadows:

As a manufacturing executive, I have consistently delivered strong performance results through my contributions in cost reductions, internal controls and technology solutions. The comparison below outlines some of my accomplishments as a Chief Financial Officer in relationship to the position requirements.

Your Requirements	My Qualifications
Full range of finance, accounting and treasury experience; operational focus; strong internal controls.	Built and led strong finance organizations, creating solid infrastructures and strengthening internal controls. Instituted formal budgeting, forecasting, cash management and other management processes. Proven record for designing growth strategies and financial consolidations to achieve business objectives.
	Recruited by Halstead Company to provide expertise in acquisitions, financing and MIS and to orchestrate an IPO. Comprehensive background in all areas of finance, accounting and treasury. Recognized for strengths as a consensus/team builder and effective arbitrator/negotiator.
Mergers and acquisitions experience.	Acquired extensive experience in the analysis of new business opportunities and with mergers and acquisitions throughout career history. Effectively merged and streamlined two divisions, which resulted in substantial savings and positioned company for future growth.
	Spearheaded acquisition of several operating businesses with sales ranging from $1 million to $220 million, which included personally handling all negotiations, performing due diligence, developing tax structure and coordinating legal and accounting activities.
MIS background.	Led installation of state-of-the-art MIS technology in different companies. Improved inventory management, boosted sales and cut annual operating expenses through MIS technology implementation.

I would welcome a personal interview to discuss how my experience would contribute to the achievement of your company's objectives for growth and success. I will contact you next week to set up an interview.

Very truly yours,

David Johnson

Enclosure

102

Chief Financial Officer. *Louise Garver, Broad Brook, Connecticut*

Some resumes and cover letters for executives have smaller type to fit in more information. This letter is an example. This two-column format was successful in generating interviews and offers.

Beverly Armstrong, C.P.A.

0000 Harbour Walk Road
Weston, CT 06883

555-555-5555 • Cell: 000-000-0000
bevarmstrong@yahoo.com

January 17, 20xx

The Azure Group
P.O. Box 21648
Weston, CT 06883

Dear Hiring Professional:

The position of **Director of Finance** advertised online accurately describes my skills and abilities. I may be the ideal candidate for you—I not only have the experience you request but also additional perspective from other fields and positions to draw on.

Your Needs	**My Qualifications**
Minimum of a B.A. in Accounting or Finance	◆ Certified Public Accountant
	◆ Bachelor of Business Administration from Colby with a concentration in Accounting and Finance
5–7+ years of progressively responsible experience providing high-level financial analyses	◆ More than 14 years in a variety of financial positions of escalating responsibility for large and small companies in different fields
	◆ VP of Finance and Controller for $250 million public company, managing monthly financial close, daily cash flow analysis, overall financial and profitability analysis, acquisition and systems integration, coordinating audits, health and property & casualty insurance, and human resources
	◆ Results include negotiating competitive contracts to reduce expenses from $250K–$400K annually, reducing cash outlay by $1.25 million due to creative financing deals, and achieving post-merger synergies of $3–$4 million annually
A strong insurance background	◆ More than 4 years at Commercial Insurance company, promoted to Director of Reinsurance, reported directly to CFO
Ability to create and implement new procedures and systems	◆ At Director and VP levels, implemented new processes to improve cash management, credit card processing, staffing, cost reduction, automated reporting systems, and many others
Experience in reviewing contracts and agreements	◆ As Director of Acquisitions, reviewed and revised documents, including all confidentiality/nondisclosure agreements, letters of intent, and stock/asset purchase agreements
	◆ In VP of Finance and Controller positions, reviewed and improved cash management procedures, health insurance agreements, reinsurance contracts, and fronting agreements

103

Director of Finance. *Gail Frank, Tampa, Florida*

This two-column format extends to a second page. The size of type would be too small if you tried to fit all of this letter's information on one page. The visible "weight" of the second column gives the impression that this candidate's qualifications more than adequately

Beverly Armstrong, C.P.A. page 2

555-555-5555 • Cell: 000-000-0000
bevarmstrong@yahoo.com

<u>Your Needs</u>	<u>My Qualifications</u>
High degree of personal integrity and effective interaction skills with executives, clients, vendors, and other internal/external parties at all levels	♦ Excellent relationship-development, problem-solving, negotiation, and presentation skills; manage sensitive relationships with executive management, directors, employees, clients, bankers, insurance regulators, venture capitalists, investment bankers, joint-venture partners, and acquisition targets

My resume provides further details of my accomplishments. I look forward to discussing yet another career opportunity with you. I will e-mail you to set a time we can sit down for an interview.

Sincerely,

Beverly Armstrong

Enclosure

meet the prospective employer's needs. If you feel that long paragraphs slow down the reading of a letter, you can see that the tempo of reading across columns from left to right is quicker, which makes the format successful.

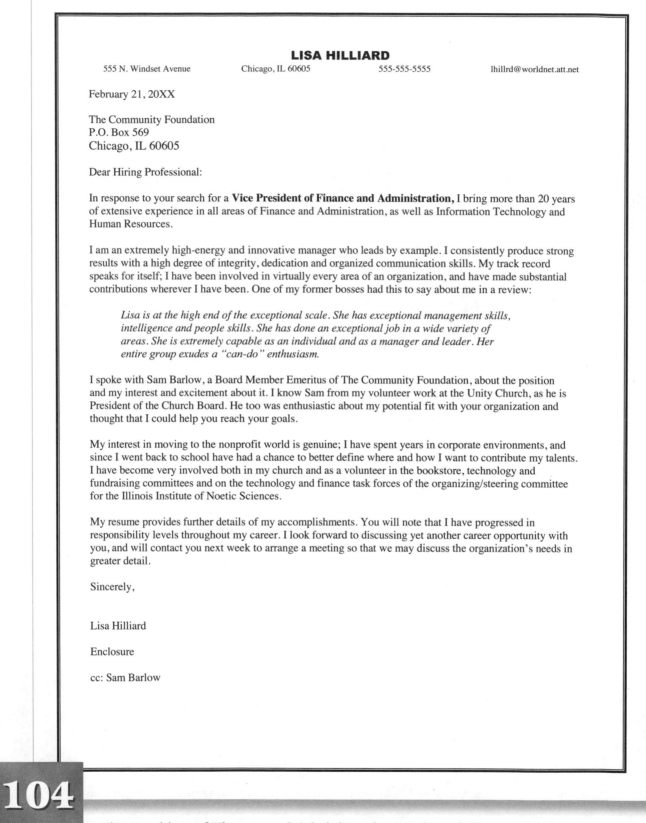

LISA HILLIARD

555 N. Windset Avenue   Chicago, IL 60605   555-555-5555   lhillrd@worldnet.att.net

February 21, 20XX

The Community Foundation
P.O. Box 569
Chicago, IL 60605

Dear Hiring Professional:

In response to your search for a **Vice President of Finance and Administration,** I bring more than 20 years of extensive experience in all areas of Finance and Administration, as well as Information Technology and Human Resources.

I am an extremely high-energy and innovative manager who leads by example. I consistently produce strong results with a high degree of integrity, dedication and organized communication skills. My track record speaks for itself; I have been involved in virtually every area of an organization, and have made substantial contributions wherever I have been. One of my former bosses had this to say about me in a review:

> *Lisa is at the high end of the exceptional scale. She has exceptional management skills, intelligence and people skills. She has done an exceptional job in a wide variety of areas. She is extremely capable as an individual and as a manager and leader. Her entire group exudes a "can-do" enthusiasm.*

I spoke with Sam Barlow, a Board Member Emeritus of The Community Foundation, about the position and my interest and excitement about it. I know Sam from my volunteer work at the Unity Church, as he is President of the Church Board. He too was enthusiastic about my potential fit with your organization and thought that I could help you reach your goals.

My interest in moving to the nonprofit world is genuine; I have spent years in corporate environments, and since I went back to school have had a chance to better define where and how I want to contribute my talents. I have become very involved both in my church and as a volunteer in the bookstore, technology and fundraising committees and on the technology and finance task forces of the organizing/steering committee for the Illinois Institute of Noetic Sciences.

My resume provides further details of my accomplishments. You will note that I have progressed in responsibility levels throughout my career. I look forward to discussing yet another career opportunity with you, and will contact you next week to arrange a meeting so that we may discuss the organization's needs in greater detail.

Sincerely,

Lisa Hilliard

Enclosure

cc: Sam Barlow

104

Vice President of Finance and Administration. *Gail Frank, Tampa, Florida*

To indicate the applicant's breadth of experience and high standards, the writer provided in the center of the letter a quotation in italic from one of her performance reviews. The reader's eye goes right to it.

Anthony Edwards

5555 SW 55 Avenue ▪ Fort Lauderdale, FL 55555 ▪ 555-555-5555 ▪ aedwards@xxx.com

Hiring Manager
Name of Organization
Address
City, State Zip

August 22, 20XX

Re: VP of Finance Position

In today's economy, corporations must establish and operate according to solid financial principles in order to maintain a competitive edge while remaining profitable. I invite you to consider my qualifications and accomplishments as I am certain of my ability to add value to the performance of your organization. My notable accomplishments include the following:

✓ Conceiving, designing and implementing the first computerized casino control and management reporting system in Montreal

✓ Transforming underperforming operations; increasing cash and revenues from zero to more than $5 million within 3 years

✓ Increasing annual profits by $200K within 12 months

✓ Leading and motivating a 22-person sales team to produce annual revenues of $5 million

My vast knowledge of financial operations has propelled my track record of success. Along with my broad range of skills in all aspects of accounting and financial management, I bring the drive, leadership and vision necessary to produce results and positively affect your bottom line. Any of my past employers can attest to my abilities to use my financial and accounting expertise to steer companies to profitability and long-term growth:

"He successfully led a team to timely restructure and refinance our debts, improve our cash flow as well as provide additional capital for expansion."

– Howard Matthews
Chairman, International Corporation, Inc.

I have attached my résumé, which highlights my experiences and accomplishments in more detail for your review. I would love the opportunity to speak with you regarding a potential employment opportunity within your firm. Please feel free to contact me by phone or e-mail.

Thank you for your time and consideration. I look forward to hearing from you soon.

Sincerely,

Anthony Edwards

105

Vice President of Finance. *Melanie Denny, Sunrise, Florida*

The applicant had many years of finance experience. The letter highlights notable accomplishments and makes evident through center-justification a direct quotation from a past supervisor.

TAMMY H. MILSAP

555-555-5555 | tammymilsap@xxx.net | linkedin.com/xx/xxxxx

Re: Senior Consultant, Distribution Channel Marketing Opportunity

Dear Donna,

Thank you for enlightening me about the fantastic opportunity with AllCare Insurance. Your instincts were right: I am certainly interested in the role, and this letter will provide more detail in support of my candidacy.

First and foremost, I am a builder of relationships. From a young age, I have had many great opportunities to initiate and cultivate relationships all over the world! I was raised in a military family and have thrived while living within various cultures on different continents. I continued my fascination for challenges and diverse environments by attending the Blue Ribbon Military School, where my relationship-building savvy was solidified in a base of leadership development.

Shortly after graduating from Blue Ribbon with highest honors, I spent five years with the Army and then launched a micro business while I started my family. In this venture, I grew my consumer sales and key talent recruitment so well that **I attained #1 status in the country out of 50,000 others.** Following this, I applied my successes and talents in networking, leadership, sales, and marketing with my love for strategic relationship acquisition in a career in the financial industry.

At TrueGen Investments, I was rapidly promoted and rotated through several customer-facing, strategic sales, and marketing roles. In my last position as VP, Retail and Small Business Client Strategy, **I developed, implemented, and managed the client strategy for a $35B bank in support of 5,000 employees and 440 branches.** My work yielded these notable results:

- Pioneered recognized industry best practice; saved cost/increased revenue in 40+ branches.
- Strategically retained annual revenue of $70MM in high net-worth clients.
- Managed P&L for multiple channels with annual revenue of more than $85MM.
- Leveraged customer insights to revamp employee training and thus improve client experience.
- Consistently lauded for successful team motivation tactics and leadership by example.

Donna, I am innately passionate about creating and sharing best practices for the benefit of my teams. I am acclaimed for leading organizations to understand and create unique solutions to meet their customers' needs. **I firmly believe that building and maintaining relationships and upholding empowering, evolutionary leadership are two additional keys to my success.** I would welcome the opportunity to speak more with your team about creating customized approaches and solutions to ensure the continued growth and customer delight with AllCare Insurance.

Sincerely,

Tammy Milsap
Enc: Résumé

Leadership | Empowerment | Achievement

106

Senior Consultant. *Kelly Welch, Raleigh, North Carolina*

This applicant wanted an executive role in financial services. The letter, playing up the applicant's relationship-building skills, talents, successes, and results, scored an interview.

5555 Belleview
Cleveland, OH 55555

Martin Kaplan

(555) 555-5555
martin@xxx.net

October 2, 20XX

Ms. Shirley Woodruff
Executive Vice President
Superior Realty and Investment Company
0000 Washington Parkway
Cleveland, OH 00000

Dear Ms. Woodruff:

As a versatile and dedicated finance/operations executive with a 20-year background in commercial real estate management and controllership, I am seeking a new association in need of an organized planner, persuasive negotiator, and skilled financial strategist. Having extensive exposure to leasing, purchasing, and sale of properties through closing, I am especially effective in partnering agreements with various outside professionals to achieve desired goals.

For example, I have

✓ Turned around a situation where weak financial control and ineffective staff were impacting profitability. Within a year, totally revamped the reporting package; hired competent professionals; and brought in qualified consultants in legal, accounting, and insurance matters.

✓ Saved the company millions of dollars by accomplishing a major tax restructuring deal that eliminated double taxation of corporate profits.

✓ Influenced two former tenants to terminate below-market leases several years ahead of schedule at a cost to the company of only $25,000, laying the groundwork for occupancy by a large retailer. Negotiated a 10-year lease agreement with this tenant at $16/sq. ft. to generate total income of $2.4 million.

✓ Found and ultimately purchased a 10,000 sq. ft. office building that was 22% vacant at an opportune time, prior to its upward revaluation. In 10 months, achieved 96% occupancy for an excellent immediate return with significant upside potential in the future.

My enclosed resume will give you further evidence of my proven track record of effectiveness in all financial and operational management aspects of properties that include office buildings, shopping malls, and industrial sites, as well as the smooth functioning of internal processes. In this turbulent economic climate with property values plummeting, real estate investors are looking for solid deals that will result in growth and profitability. I could provide the direction they need now and into the future. I would like to discuss how my qualifications relate to your plans to see if we could develop a mutual interest.

Thank you for your consideration, and I look forward to speaking with you.

Sincerely

Martin Kaplan

Enclosure: Resume

107

Real Estate Finance Executive. *Melanie Noonan, Woodland Park, New Jersey*

After dissolving a 10-year partnership, this applicant wanted to help another firm restore profitability. The letter focuses on his accomplishments and forte in finding undervalued properties.

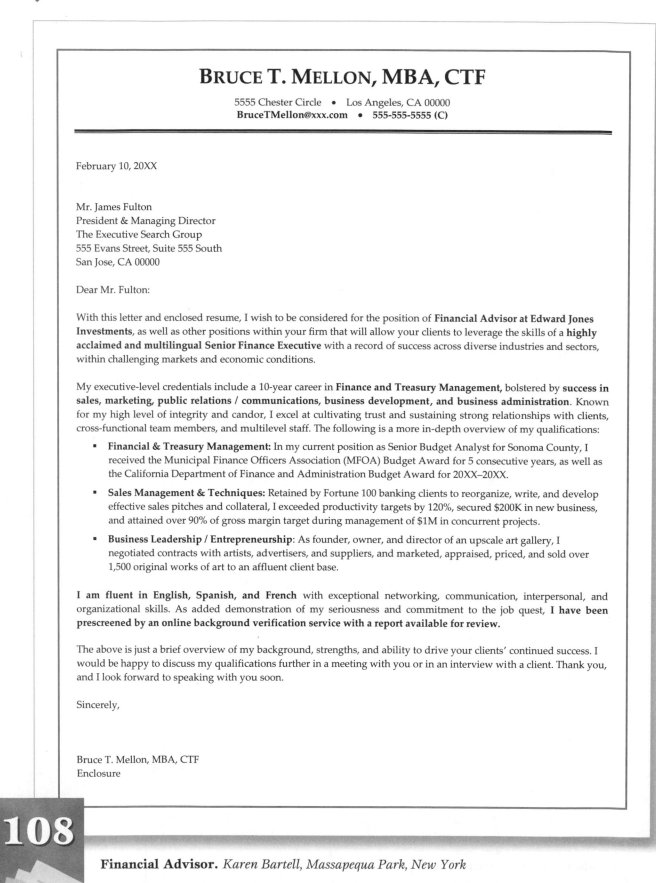

BRUCE T. MELLON, MBA, CTF

5555 Chester Circle • Los Angeles, CA 00000
BruceTMellon@xxx.com • **555-555-5555 (C)**

February 10, 20XX

Mr. James Fulton
President & Managing Director
The Executive Search Group
555 Evans Street, Suite 555 South
San Jose, CA 00000

Dear Mr. Fulton:

With this letter and enclosed resume, I wish to be considered for the position of **Financial Advisor at Edward Jones Investments**, as well as other positions within your firm that will allow your clients to leverage the skills of a **highly acclaimed and multilingual Senior Finance Executive** with a record of success across diverse industries and sectors, within challenging markets and economic conditions.

My executive-level credentials include a 10-year career in **Finance and Treasury Management,** bolstered by **success in sales, marketing, public relations / communications, business development, and business administration**. Known for my high level of integrity and candor, I excel at cultivating trust and sustaining strong relationships with clients, cross-functional team members, and multilevel staff. The following is a more in-depth overview of my qualifications:

- **Financial & Treasury Management:** In my current position as Senior Budget Analyst for Sonoma County, I received the Municipal Finance Officers Association (MFOA) Budget Award for 5 consecutive years, as well as the California Department of Finance and Administration Budget Award for 20XX–20XX.

- **Sales Management & Techniques:** Retained by Fortune 100 banking clients to reorganize, write, and develop effective sales pitches and collateral, I exceeded productivity targets by 120%, secured $200K in new business, and attained over 90% of gross margin target during management of $1M in concurrent projects.

- **Business Leadership / Entrepreneurship**: As founder, owner, and director of an upscale art gallery, I negotiated contracts with artists, advertisers, and suppliers, and marketed, appraised, priced, and sold over 1,500 original works of art to an affluent client base.

I am fluent in English, Spanish, and French with exceptional networking, communication, interpersonal, and organizational skills. As added demonstration of my seriousness and commitment to the job quest, **I have been prescreened by an online background verification service with a report available for review.**

The above is just a brief overview of my background, strengths, and ability to drive your clients' continued success. I would be happy to discuss my qualifications further in a meeting with you or in an interview with a client. Thank you, and I look forward to speaking with you soon.

Sincerely,

Bruce T. Mellon, MBA, CTF
Enclosure

108

Financial Advisor. *Karen Bartell, Massapequa Park, New York*

In this letter to a recruiter, the writer included the fact that the applicant had completed an online background verification report. In a few months the applicant got a new position with a 20 percent salary increase. See Resume 6 in Part 3.

BARB JOHNSON

5555 Martin Circle • Davie, Florida 55555
(555) 555-5555 • bjohnson@xxx.com

Hiring Manager
County Government Office
Address
City, State Zip

August 22, 20XX

Dear Hiring Manager,

Would County Government Office benefit from a resourceful and dedicated administrative professional? If so, I invite you to consider my broad experience and diverse skills, as they may be of interest to you.

As outlined in the enclosed résumé, I possess a strong background in various nonprofit organizations and government entities including city, county, and federal agencies. Notable organizations consist of the Social Administration, County Elections Office, and the School Board of Brender County. In addition, I was recognized for going above and beyond as a devoted member of the community and honored with the 20XX "Heart of the Community Award."

Credited with consistently exceeding client expectations, I have in-depth insight and invaluable knowledge of administrative operations. Please allow me to highlight a few of my talents:

- Meeting/event planning and travel coordination
- Deadline-sensitive time management expertise
- Workflow and office automation proficiency
- Excellent presentation, documentation, and writing skills
- Superior customer relations, conflict resolution, and problem solving

Currently, I am seeking a position where I can continue to bring a sense of commitment, dedication, and professionalism to every aspect of my work. As a member of your team, I am confident that my innovative and results-focused approach would make a significant contribution to the goals of your organization. I welcome the opportunity to discuss any current or future administrative openings with you.

Thank you for your consideration, and I look forward to hearing from you soon.

Sincerely,

Barb Johnson

Enclosure: Résumé

109

Government Agency Administrator. *Melanie Denny, Sunrise, Florida*

The individual wanted to send a "cold call" letter to various government agencies to work in either a nonprofit or government sector. The letter highlights a community award as a selling point.

March 21, 20XX

Mr. William Babinski
Staffing Director
Chambers Medical Clinic
Duluth, Minnesota

RE: MEDICAL TRANSCRIPTIONIST

Dear Mr. Babinski:

Enclosed is a resume for the posted position.

Graduating with honors in 20XX from the medical transcription certification program at Manchester Community and Technical College, I am ready to begin the career for which I have worked so hard.

My medical records experience will be especially helpful in this position. Not only am I highly familiar with patient record management, but also I bring the following:

- ◆ Positive collaboration with physicians and other medical personnel
- ◆ Understanding of team concepts, legalities, confidentiality, hospital code and patient rights
- ◆ Experience working with pneumatic record transport systems
- ◆ Multicultural experience

General business skills complement my experience. This includes data entry, word processing, strong communication skills and accuracy, as well as the ability to monitor my own work. I've established a good track record for a positive attitude, initiative, organizational skills, pride in my work, confidence and team spirit.

I very much look forward to hearing from you regarding this position.

Sincerely,

Nina Altonson

NINA ALTONSON

Chauncey Court #16
Rochester MN 55555

(555) 555-5555

ninaa@minnonline.com

MEDICAL OFFICE PROFESSIONAL

◆ ◆ ◆

BUSINESS SKILLS

Data Entry 12,500 KPH
Telephone Skills
Pneumatic Record Transport System
Facilitation
Problem Solving
Customer Service
Filing (Numeric & Alpha)
Training of Staff

CULTURAL DIVERSITY & LANGUAGE

Four Years of Spanish
Extensive Travel–Western U.S.
Multicultural Experience

110

Medical Transcriptionist. *Beverley Drake, Hot Springs Village, Arkansas*

Making a cover letter look different from others is a challenge. Using a multicolumn format can produce good results. The vertical line can be in a narrow, separate column or as a side border of a text column.

Ariel Adams
111 Washington St.
Hunterville, IL 60030
(111) 222-2222
aadams@email.com

October 27, 20XX

Human Resource Manager
Lucas County Health Department
Human Resources Office
111 Greenich Rd.
Lucasville, IL 00000

Dear Human Resource Manager:

When I read your advertisement for a *Patient Care Representative* on Lucas County's Web site, I thought that you had written the job description with me in mind. As you require, I am fluent in both English and Spanish and have excellent interpersonal skills. Additionally, I have experience in handling cash and performing inventory.

For the past 3 years, I have been caring for an elderly relative who is now deceased. During that time, I gained a considerable amount of experience scheduling appointments and communicating with medical staff and patients. I can be very empathetic and patient with sick individuals who may be confused or upset.

As soon as I complete my GED next month, I will be available to start work. As you will see on my attached resume, I am actively working to improve myself. For 10 hours each week, I have been practicing typing and am confident that I can meet your expectations in this area.

I am eager to make a difference at the Lucas County Health Department. I will contact your office at the end of the week to verify that you have received my letter and resume and to talk to you further about this opportunity. In the meantime, feel free to contact me at (111) 222-2222.

Thank you for your time and consideration,

Ariel Adams

Enclosure: Resume

111

Patient Care Representative. *Eva Locke, Waukegan, Illinois*

The writer cast as strengths the skills this applicant used in caring for a sick relative. Because the applicant lacked GED and typing requirements, these are mentioned as being met in the near future.

SEAN HARRIS

5555 Parksville Avenue, Leesburg, VA 55555 ● (555) 555-5555 ● seanharris@xxx.com

Providing Top-Notch, Patient-Centered Care

June 16, 20XX

Mr. Vernon Byers
Human Resources Manager
Kennestone Hospital
Marietta, GA 55555

Dear Mr. Byers:

Are you looking for a *Patient Advocate* who can ensure that your hospital's healthcare service initiatives are aligned with corporate goals, while committing to your team's overall success?

I offer:

- 5+-year track record of delivering excellent customer service.
- Ability to increase efficiency and productivity, while going the extra mile for your patients.
- Demonstrated record of proactive leadership and sound decision making that shines with superior achievements.
- Energy, enthusiasm, perseverance, and motivation.

My key strength is initiating and implementing changes through process reengineering. This starts with analyzing a unit's current operations, building rapport with employees and patients, and forging strategic alliances that will benefit all departments involved. The accomplishments mentioned on my resume provide evidence of my dedication to succeed.

I am confident that I can make an immediate difference to your team. I will call you June 23 to schedule a meeting at your convenience. Please feel free to contact me at **(555) 555-5555** if you would like to speak with me sooner.

I look forward to meeting with you to discuss how I can help you achieve your most pressing technology goals. Thank you for your time and consideration.

Sincerely,

Sean Harris

Enclosure

112

Patient Advocate. *Leeza Byers, Marietta, Georgia*

With only three years of experience in healthcare, the applicant wanted a new position in healthcare in another state. The letter highlights transferable skills from prior work experience. See Resume 11 In Part 3.

CANDACE R. DOLGREEN, MBA, MS
NURSING HOME ADMINISTRATOR
—Science and business woven together with passion and empathy—

Date, year

Ms. Delia True
QualCare Rehabilitation and Nursing Center
000 Harbranch Street
Edison, NJ 55555

Dear Ms. True:

Why are you passionate about your industry? What is your vision for the future of eldercare? I want to know. I would love to discuss your thoughts on eldercare and related issues that affect your facility and the state of New Jersey. I know that you, as a preceptor, understand the challenges that confront you daily...and you realize the challenges those entering the field will face some day.

Throughout my career, I have sought to merge my interests in business and life sciences with my desire to help others. My heart and passion have always been with the elderly. Driven by this passion, I would like to discuss my interest in entering the NJ-AIT program with you.

In support of this interest, would you be able to share a cup of coffee with me? As a future NJ-AIT intern, I want to know how I could help you to achieve some of your goals because your success would be my success.

Would you be available to meet with me this week or next? I am available on Tuesdays, Wednesdays or Fridays. I will also be following up this letter with a phone call to understand what is most convenient for you, and I look forward to meeting with you. Thank you very much for your time and consideration.

Warm regards,

Candace R. Dolgreen, MBA, MS

Enc: Résumé
Enc: Starbucks card

"As I look into the rearview mirror, it is clear that my scientific and business backgrounds were but a prelude. I have applied these experiences to my passion for working with the elderly, helping them achieve more satisfying lives." CRD

555 Traynor Way ◆ Freehold, NJ ◆ crdolgreen@xx.com ◆ 555.555.5555

113

Elder Care Administration Intern. *Kelly Welch, Raleigh, North Carolina*

To get attention and show genuine interest, this applicant included a $5.00 Starbucks gift card with this letter. Because of her innovative approach, she won an interview and got the internship.

John Davidson, BS, RT (R) (CT)

000 Miller Street ♦ Schenectady, NY 55555 ♦ (000) 000-0000 ♦ 000000000@xx.com

July 15, 20XX

Human Resource Representative
Department of Human Resources
Albany Medical Center
00 New Scotland Avenue
Albany, NY 00000

RE: Medical Imaging Tech V, #XXXX and Medical Imaging Tech II, #XXXX

Dear Human Resource Representative:

I am responding to the Medical Imaging Tech V and Medical Imaging Tech II positions advertised on Albany Medical Center's website. I believe my skills, experience, educational background, and professional credentials make me an ideal candidate. I am a former employee of Albany Medical Center and seek a return to full-time employment in medical imaging.

As a highly skilled and accomplished Radiologic Technologist, I offer more than 20 years of successful experience at various healthcare facilities. I am currently employed part-time at the Merzig Clinic, where I perform a wide range of diagnostic X-rays and DEXA scans. My most recent full-time experience includes serving as a Diagnostic Radiologic Technologist at the Stratton VA Medical Center. In this role I managed the evening shift for several years and performed a full range of diagnostic X-rays and DEXA scans. Other duties included serving as a Key Operator for the PACS system, filling in for CT as needed, and teaching CPR to healthcare providers throughout the medical center. In prior experience as a Special Procedures Technologist at Schoharie County Community Hospital, I performed diagnostic X-rays, CT scans, nuclear medicine, and quality assurance. I am an extremely reliable employee and have had less than three unscheduled sick days during my career.

With excellent communication skills, I am talented at building rapport and establishing positive relationships with patients, co-workers, and other healthcare providers. Additionally, I am the X-ray Visions Columnist for *ADVANCE for Imaging & Radiology Oncology* and can bring Albany Medical Center to a national audience every month. In fact, I have previously published a pair of articles on Albany Medical Center's pediatric radiology department. My educational background and professional credentials include a bachelor's degree, an associate's degree in Radiologic Technology, New York state licensure as a Radiologic Technologist, and CPR certification. My deep commitment to high-quality patient care and making a positive difference in the lives of others will be a valuable asset to your team.

I feel confident I will make an immediate and positive contribution to Albany Medical Center. I believe my qualifications meet your current needs and would like to further discuss my background in a meeting with you. Thank you for your time and consideration. I look forward to your reply.

Sincerely,

John Davidson, BS, RT (R) (CT)

114

Medical Imaging Technician. *John Femia, Schenectady, New York*

This radiologic technologist was currently working part-time and wanted to reenter the medical imaging profession with his first firm. This letter plays up his skills and 20 years of experience.

CAMILLE DEROSA

35 Flower Trail Lane ◆ North Babylon, New York 11703 ◆ (555) 555-5555
cderosa@optonline.net

Name
Company
Address
City, State ZIP

Date

Dear Sir or Madam:

In May, I will graduate from the State University of Stony Brook with a **Bachelor of Science in Cytotechnology, with a minor in Biology.** I am seeking to pursue my long-term personal and professional goal of a challenging career as a **Cytotechnologist** *within a hospital environment for the variety of specimens and the opportunity to participate in fine needle aspiration procedures.* Let me briefly highlight the skills, values and contributions I will bring to your healthcare facility:

- Dedicated commitment to a long and successful career as a **Cytotechnologist.**

- Excellent patient relations/evaluation, time-management, troubleshooting, interpersonal and communication skills, developed through experience at **Good Samaritan Hospital as a Cytology Prep Assistant.**

- Ability to perform independently or as part of a team, building cooperative working relationships among management and support staff in order to meet goals and achieve successful results.

- Aptitude to collaborate with physicians to implement protocol; provide new product evaluations and procurement.

- Proven success in prioritizing time and completing intense workloads under severe pressure to attain goals and meet project deadlines, achieving desired results.

- An energetic, hardworking and self-motivated work ethic, coupled with a flexible approach to assignments.

Because a resume can neither fully detail all my skills and accomplishments nor convey my potential to your **Cytology Department,** I would welcome a personal interview to further explore the merging of my *education, experience, ambition* and *enthusiasm* with your facility's objectives. I will call next week to inquire about a mutually convenient time.

Very truly yours,

CAMILLE DEROSA

Enclosure

115

Cytotechnologist. *Donna M. Farrise, Hauppauge, New York*

The two-line page border, boldfacing and italicizing of key information and keywords, and bulleting of skills and worker traits make this letter attractive, strong, and easy to grasp at a glance.

Elizabeth Santiago

11 Riverside Drive
New York, NY 10023

(555) 555-5555
esantiago@xyz.com

April 23, 20XX

Michael Kahn
Director of Human Resources
St. Luke's–Roosevelt Hospital Center
Roosevelt Division
1000 Tenth Avenue at 58th Street
New York, NY 10019

Dear Mr. Kahn:

After reading about your organization's new health care initiatives, as described on the hospital's Web site, I was excited to learn of an opening for a Clinical Laboratory Scientist. My background in developing and implementing testing and instrumentation procedures can bring an immediate benefit to the hospital as it strives to improve patient care. I am enclosing my resume for your review.

With 15 years of experience in the hematology and pathology departments of two major teaching hospitals, I am able to prioritize workflow and resolve problems to ensure the efficiency and accuracy of department operations. In particular, I have reviewed and revised operating procedures to achieve regulatory compliance. Among my key accomplishments are the following:

- Managed installation and implementation of new coagulation system, including writing procedures and training staff. Coordinated with multiple departments for successful completion within a one-month time line.

- Integrated a standardized coagulation system across two hospital campuses to ensure better patient care and quality assurance.

- Established, wrote, and set up a preventative maintenance schedule for hematology instrumentation to ensure the quality of performance.

I look forward to the opportunity to talk with you in person about the contribution I can make to your hospital. I will contact you in the near future to schedule an interview.

Thank you for your consideration.

Sincerely,

Elizabeth Santiago

Enclosure

116

Clinical Laboratory Scientist. *Wendy Gelberg, Needham, Massachusetts*

The applicant did background research on the prospective employer's website and links her accomplishments directly to the mission of the company. Bullets point to the accomplishments.

KATHERINE TEOJEN
555 Caswell Avenue
Charlotte, NC 28888
(000) 000-0000
katherinet@ncnet.com

March 27, 20XX

Dr. John Irving
Director of Clinical Recruitment
Carolinas Medical Center
Charlotte, NC 28888

Dear Dr. Irving:

On the high seas, navigation is very important. In fact, few persons could play a more significant role than the captain of a large cargo vessel.

When the cargo vessel approaches the mainland or nears port, a towering beacon of golden light flashes and revolves to guide ships and warn of obstacles. Here, the lighthouse and its keeper bring the ship through the maze of rocks, atolls and barnacled debris, to safe harbor.

The speech-language pathologist is comparable to the lighthouse keeper; she is the beacon, the guiding light, with the training to show the way to those less fortunate. I understand, intimately, the importance of such training. At age six, to correct the mispronunciation of the letter "r," I went to a speech therapist. This was a pivotal moment, for I realized that *I* could be helped and that speech-language problems were correctable.

Over the years, this interest has grown and taken on a new meaning. Two years ago, I volunteered for Operation Smile, a project in which local physicians travel to Third-World countries and perform reconstructive surgery (usually pro bono) to correct cleft palates of children.

Since then, I have worked as a volunteer at Lake Forest School for the Deaf, teaching basic life skills using sign language. And at Mercy Speech & Hearing Center, a clinic sponsored by the United Way, I currently volunteer, observing and evaluating children with articulation and audiology problems.

Since August 20XX, while completing requirements for a master's degree, I have been employed at The Center for Speech Excellence in Charlotte, administering tests and tutoring children in the Fast-Forward Program, an intensive six-week interactive program, with emphasis in receptive language skills, auditory processing and central processing disorders. Working under the auspices of Pamela Wright, a speech pathologist, I have shadowed her while working with children with cochlear implants. The Center treats hearing-impaired children and also works with adults (e.g., accent reduction, voice pitch alteration and stuttering).

My goal is to provide diagnostic, therapeutic and associated counseling services within a hospital or other clinical setting. I am particularly interested in working with children with articulation, fluency, language, voice and neurological deficits. If your hospital needs a speech pathologist—to be that "guiding light"—I would appreciate the opportunity to discuss your needs in a personal interview. I look forward to meeting with you. A brief resume of my background is enclosed.

Sincerely,

Katherine Teojen

Enclosure

117

Speech Pathologist. *Doug Morrison, Charlotte, North Carolina*

The ambition of this young speech-language pathologist to help others overcome obstacles (because of her own early problems with speech) is embodied in the opening and closing analogy.

JENNIFER E. EMERSON, LPN

000 PEABODY AVENUE
MELROSE, MA 00000
(444) 888-2222

CELL: (444) 888-0000
E-MAIL: JEMERSON@AOL.COM

February 5, 20XX

Madeline Detweiler, Practical Nurse Administrator
Lowden Family Health Centers
4444 South Main Road
Pohasset, MA 00000

Dear Ms. Detweiler:

I am writing in response to your advertisement in *The Melrose Daily News* for a full-time Licensed Practical Nurse. I believe that I can fill that position well due to my education, health care experience, and professional sincerity.

A recent LPN graduate of the Pohasset Regional Technical School in Taunton, MA, I currently hold a license in Massachusetts and have also applied for a New Hampshire license.

My demonstrated strong organizational and communication skills derive from my successful employment experiences in business offices, as my enclosed resume confirms. These skills, coupled with my LPN education and training, should prove to be of great benefit to your family health center.

I am confident that you will agree that my qualifications match your requirements for this position. Therefore, I would greatly appreciate an opportunity to meet with you to fully reveal my keen interest in the health care field and to determine how I may fit your staff profile. I can be reached by e-mail, home phone, or cell phone days or evenings to arrange for an appointment. If I do not hear from you by Monday, February 15, I will call your office to request a meeting at a time convenient to you or another member of your staff.

Thank you for considering my application for employment at Lowden Family Health Centers.

Sincerely,

Jennifer E. Emerson, LPN

Enclosure: resume

118

Licensed Practical Nurse. *Edward Turilli, Bonita Springs, Florida*

The challenge was to convince a recruiter that the entry-level applicant's proactive manner in obtaining her degree and another state license outweighed her minimal nursing experience.

Frances C. MacSorley

1212 Juniper Circle
North Kingman, CT 66666
francesmac@earthlink.com

(000) 222-1111   Cell: (000) 222-3333

January 27, 20XX

Philippe J. Desjardin
Director of Human Resources
New Haven Memorial Hospital
111 Brently Street
New Haven, CT 00000

Dear Mr. Desjardin:

This letter is in response to your advertisement in *The New Haven Sunday Times*, January 27, 20XX, for a Licensed Practical Nurse to be employed at the Leone Mathieu Life Care Center.

I believe that my qualifications are strong for this position, for my 15 years in practical nursing have given me excellent professional experience in addition to my personal career objective of providing and maintaining the highest level of nursing care and quality of life to patients under my charge. My total nursing experience has been, and continues to be, full-time, direct patient care.

Always deeply committed to the nursing profession, I have striven to keep abreast of the latest data through in-service learning and reading various journals and selected publications. Courses taken in the liberal arts are in direct preparation for my Associate degree as a Registered Nurse. Moreover, they have broadened my capacity to deal with humanitarian issues that are so much a part of healing.

If you agree with me that my credentials are sound for this position at the Leone Mathieu Life Care Center, I would very much appreciate an opportunity to meet with you to discuss my candidacy for this opening at Memorial Hospital. I can be reached by e-mail, at my home after 5 p.m., or at any time by my cell phone to schedule an appointment at a time that is convenient to you.

Thank you for considering me for this position. I look forward to meeting with you soon and will contact you to schedule an interview.

Sincerely,

Frances C. MacSorley

Enclosures: resume / application

119

Licensed Practical Nurse. *Edward Turilli, Bonita Springs, Florida*

After 15 years in practical nursing, the applicant wanted another LPN position while she worked on her registered nursing degree. The letter shows her commitment to nursing and humanitarian issues.

Louella Dodds, RN

555 Harrison Street, Apt. 555		Home (555) 000-5555
Los Angeles, CA 55555	louella@xx.net	Mobile (555) 555-0000

February 21, 20XX

Ms. Margaret Tremont, Director of Nursing
University Hospital Emergency Department
000 Broadway
Los Angeles, CA 00000

Dear Ms. Tremont:

The current issue of *Nursing Spectrum* featured an article on the shortage of qualified nurses in trauma centers. The article specifically mentioned University Hospital as one that is experiencing a great need for nurses with this specialty to meet the needs of more than 60,000 emergency patients yearly. Before raising my family for the past five years, I had been an emergency room nurse, and I am seeking to reenter this career. Please consider me an interested candidate for any open nursing positions in your Level I trauma center. My resume is attached for your review.

I have been keeping up to date on new nursing interventions and pharmacology through attendance at medical education seminars held by the Emergency Nurses Association. I currently work in per-diem assignments through the Comprehensive Healthcare agency, mainly in critical care areas.

My extensive former background includes frequent challenging cases involving inner city residents who were ignorant to medical care until stricken with life-threatening illnesses, in addition to victims of vehicle accidents, violent acts, or drug overdoses. With my triage experience, I can quickly assess urgency of patients' needs, and then prioritize which situations are more critical than others and/or require immediate physician referral. It is easy for me to determine if complaints are false or not urgent, saving the time and energy of other medical personnel. Also, I can run codes whenever necessary.

As an empathic care provider, I offer emotional support and a calming effect to patients and their families while explaining procedures, often in high anxiety or noncooperative situations. Upon their discharge, I educate patients and their caregivers on basic nursing functions to be performed at home and preventive measures or alternative options to cope with future medical challenges.

My superiors have noted in my evaluations that I have keen observation skills and appropriately respond to symptom changes and declines in patients' vital signs. If considered for hire, I am certain my knowledge, skills, and team-player attitude will greatly enhance the work environment at University Hospital's Emergency Department. I am flexible as to shifts and have no problem working nights. May I hear from you soon concerning a personal interview?

Sincerely,

Louella Dodds

Enc: Resume

120

Trauma Center Nurse. *Melanie Noonan, Woodland Park, New Jersey*

After raising a family, this applicant wanted to return to full-time employment. This letter outlines her qualifications, particularly her no-nonsense approach in recognizing real patient needs.

Winthrop "Lee" Kent
0000 Carlton Circle — Memphis, Tennessee 00000
winlee@extra.com — ✆ 000.000.0000 – 555.555.5555 (Cellular)

Friday, January 30, 20XX

Dr. Charles Fleming, MD
Medical Associates of Crofton, P.C.
500 Elm Street
Suite 400
Crofton, Alabama 36100

Dear Dr. Fleming:

If you could "design" the best practice manager for Medical Associates, would the following meet your needs?

- ❑ A **cash-flow expert** who combines the realistic outlook of an auditor with the profit-building drive of an entrepreneur,

- ❑ A **productivity multiplier** with a proven track record of leading diverse employees to greater productivity and loyalty,

- ❑ A manager with a gift for **freeing decision makers** for the tasks only they can do, and

- ❑ A dedicated administrator who can replace the distractions of business with **peace of mind** that comes from lessened liability and greater profits.

You have just read the 76-word version of my resume. You'll find the complete document on the next pages. What you won't find are the usual "summary of qualifications" and lists of responsibilities. In their places are more than a half dozen documented contributions that helped move organizations forward.

I enjoyed working for the state. And I was promoted twice in just eight months because the state valued my contributions. But my real calling is working in the private sector.

Because I have a natural desire to fill people's needs, I would like to hear about Medical Associates' special requirements in your own words. I will call in a few days to find a few minutes to do that.

Sincerely,

Winthrop Kent

Encl.: Resume

121

Medical Practice Manager. *Don Orlando, Montgomery, Alabama*

This letter helped a state employee transition to a medical practice manager. The letter opens with an engaging question, and the answers—as bulleted items—appeal to the needs of the reader.

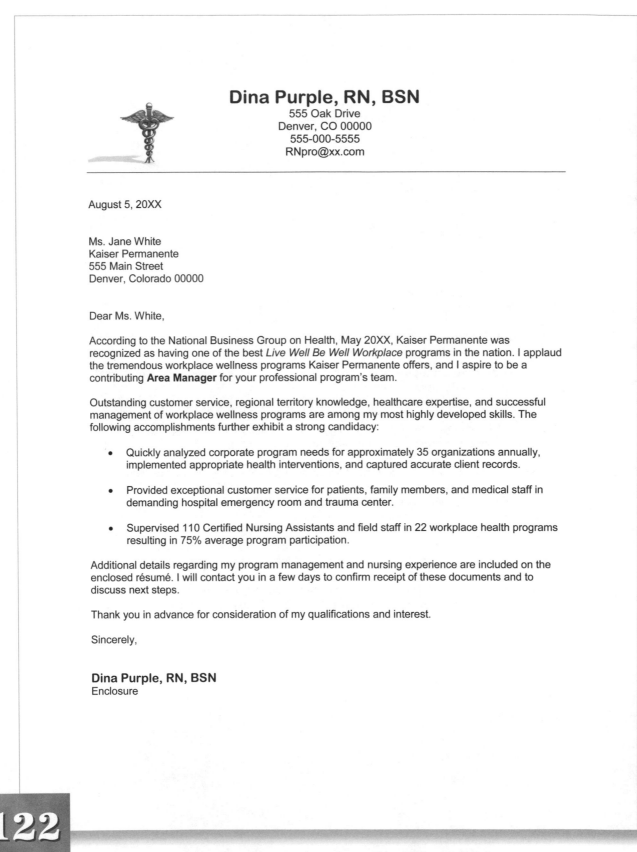

Dina Purple, RN, BSN

555 Oak Drive
Denver, CO 00000
555-000-5555
RNpro@xx.com

August 5, 20XX

Ms. Jane White
Kaiser Permanente
555 Main Street
Denver, Colorado 00000

Dear Ms. White,

According to the National Business Group on Health, May 20XX, Kaiser Permanente was recognized as having one of the best *Live Well Be Well Workplace* programs in the nation. I applaud the tremendous workplace wellness programs Kaiser Permanente offers, and I aspire to be a contributing **Area Manager** for your professional program's team.

Outstanding customer service, regional territory knowledge, healthcare expertise, and successful management of workplace wellness programs are among my most highly developed skills. The following accomplishments further exhibit a strong candidacy:

- Quickly analyzed corporate program needs for approximately 35 organizations annually, implemented appropriate health interventions, and captured accurate client records.

- Provided exceptional customer service for patients, family members, and medical staff in demanding hospital emergency room and trauma center.

- Supervised 110 Certified Nursing Assistants and field staff in 22 workplace health programs resulting in 75% average program participation.

Additional details regarding my program management and nursing experience are included on the enclosed résumé. I will contact you in a few days to confirm receipt of these documents and to discuss next steps.

Thank you in advance for consideration of my qualifications and interest.

Sincerely,

Dina Purple, RN, BSN
Enclosure

122

Healthcare Program Manager. *Ruth Pankratz, Fort Collins, Colorado*

After 15 years of nursing, this applicant wanted to manage healthcare programs. The letter showcased her management skills. She got an interview and became one of the five leading candidates.

```
Julie Windham
1111 Madison Avenue
Boise, ID 00000
(000) 000-0000
jwindham@earthlink.net


January 30, 20XX


Human Resources Department
Access Health Care
2323 Woodhaven Street
Boise, ID 00000

Dear Human Resources Representative:

It is with great interest that I forward my resume for consideration as Program
Director. Currently, as Admissions Coordinator for the ABC Rehabilitation and
Care Center, I spearhead marketing efforts for this health care service
provider, ranked #1 in a heavily competitive market, drawing clients from all
parts of Idaho. My results have been significant and include the following:

* Occupancy rate increase from 90% to 98% (highest rate among facilities in
Idaho);


* Patient increase from 6-7 to 18-19 through strategic marketing communications;


* Cost-effective service rate wins through tactical negotiations with insurance
companies.

My resume is attached to provide you with specific details concerning my
background and qualifications. Thank you for your time.

Sincerely,

Julie Windham
```

Program Director. *Daniel J. Dorotik, Jr., Lubbock, Texas*

This e-mail letter in text (.txt) format shows that online letters (and resumes) are preferably shorter than those in traditional format. Readers like window-size documents that require little scrolling.

FOSTER M. CLAYTON
9 Cranberry Lane ▪ Oxford Hills, PA 19666
Home: (555) 888-9999 ▪ Mobile: (555) 555-6666 ▪ E-mail: Clay212@aol.com

December 16, 20XX

Ms. Liz Carter
MHS Recruiters
999 Old Nathan Road
Suite 333
Eagleville, PA 19777

RE: Orthopedic/Musculoskeletal Product Line Director
        Main Health Systems

Dear Ms. Carter:

It is with great interest that I submit my resume and collateral materials for consideration as Orthopedic/Musculoskeletal Product Line Director at Main Health Systems. It is my understanding that the successful candidate will possess qualifications and experience that closely match those detailed in my resume, and it would be my pleasure to meet with you to discuss this exciting opportunity.

Highlights of my professional career include

- ◆ More than 20 years of top-flight management experience in the healthcare services and products industries.

- ◆ Expertise in the start-up of new healthcare ventures and accelerated growth within existing provider organizations.

- ◆ Delivery of strong revenue and profit growth within extremely competitive healthcare markets.

- ◆ Strong qualifications in new business development, strategic planning, marketing, risk management, program development, and teaching.

- ◆ Broad-based general management skills in human resource affairs, training, financial planning and analysis, and presentations to various boards and professional groups.

- ◆ Extensive network of professional, technical, and medical contacts throughout the healthcare community.

My leadership style is direct and decisive, yet I am flexible in responding to the constantly changing demands of the industry, customers, and the market. I am familiar with most regulations governing healthcare practice and have been actively involved in several professional organizations within the field.

I look forward to speaking with you to discuss this opportunity and will call next week to request a meeting. I would be pleased to provide professional references, additional biographical information, and work samples in preparation for an interview. Thank you for your consideration.

Sincerely,

Foster M. Clayton

Enclosure

124

Orthopedic/Musculoskeletal Product Line Director. *Karen Conway, Bend, Oregon*

This letter's first paragraph directs the reader to the resume, and the bullets draw the reader's attention to the applicant's most relevant experience, expertise, qualifications, and skills.

VALERIE ENDICOTT, ND, MBA

555 NW 5th Avenue, Apt. 55 | Portland, ME 55555 | 555.555.5555 | info@xxx.com

June 28, 20XX

Dr. Eric Weitzman
Health Elements
555 Oaktree Road
Portland, ME 55555

Dear Dr. Weitzman,

As a naturopathic physician, advocacy for health, wellness, and preventive care programs has long been a passion of mine. Appreciating that this passion is in direct alignment with Health Elements' own mission to elevate community well-being, I would like to present myself as a viable contender for your group's new **Director of Corporate Health Programs**. You will find that my experience in primary medical healthcare, an MBA in Healthcare Administration, and leadership capabilities in strategic planning and business management directly illustrate the talents you seek. Furthermore, I offer you the following critical strengths:

Operational Leadership: As Naturopathic Physician / Office Manager at Pearlman Health Clinic (PHC), I formalized new business procedures and restructured teams to boost performance efficiency and **cut $500K in operational costs in less than nine months** through strategic supplier negotiations.

Staff Empowerment: From scratch, successfully built and **groomed 10 personnel at PHC to top performance** via talent acquisition strategies and mentorship programs in medical insurance and administration to positively impact productivity and support business growth.

Financial Results: Resurrected the budget for the Continuing Medical Education (CME) department as the part-time CME & Alumni Affairs Officer at the University of Portland (UP) from a **$70K+ deficit to positive growth of $150K+ within just seven months**.

Presentations / Training: Convey the critical healthcare message as an invited to speaker to numerous national conventions. **At UP, increase the medical community's knowledge base by organizing monthly continuing education programs with renowned presenters across various healthcare disciplines.**

Product / Technical Proficiency: **Recognized industry expert on natural medicine, nutraceutical pharmacology, and dietary supplements**. Repeated success deploying cost- and time-saving EHR solutions that saved tens of thousands and hundreds of man-hours. Skilled in alternative insurance coding and billing.

Professional / Political / Community Affiliations: Remarkably **well-networked in the preventative medicine, medical insurance, wellness, and primary care communities**—having served on policy-making healthcare leadership committees as well as federal and state legislative committees, and attended myriad lobby days to establish networks within the political arena.

I am as devoted to community engagement and business expansion as I will be to your team and would welcome an occasion to apply my skills and expertise with well-respected community healthcare advocate such as yours. My personal offer to you in return, a partner who is prepared to assume complete responsibility for directing your strategic business needs and executing pioneering new wellness initiatives for community business leaders. I would enjoy meeting you to discuss my qualifications in greater detail and will follow up with you on Tuesday to schedule a time to meet.

Sincerely,

Valerie Endicott, ND, MBA

Enclosure: Résumé

125

Director of Corporate Health Programs. *Sandra Ingemansen, Leeds, West Yorkshire, England*

This letter helped a Naturopathic Physician/Office Manager become a Director of Corporate Health Programs with a leading medical consulting group for Fortune 500 companies.

JOHN A. WILLIAMS, RCFE, LNHA

555 Washington Street ▪ San Diego, CA 55555 ▪ (555) 555-5555 ▪ john.williams123@xx.com

September 14, 20XX

Mr. James Barnes
Park View Senior Living
555 West Harbor Drive
San Diego, CA 55555

Dear Mr. Barnes:

I was excited to learn that Park View Senior Living is hiring a new Executive Director. The opportunity sounds like a perfect fit for me, and I have heard good things about your facility from Sam Jacobson, who was my instructor for a recent healthcare course.

Based on your recent job posting on your website, I have all the qualities you are looking for in an ideal candidate, as outlined below:

Your Requirements	My Qualifications
▶ A passion for working with seniors	▶ A passion for providing the best possible quality of life for seniors
▶ Previous management in a healthcare or assisted-living community (70+ units)	▶ More than 7 years of management experience at a 130-bed convalescent hospital
▶ Managed a large team of employees (50+)	▶ Currently lead a team of 215+ employees
▶ Ability to maintain a high occupancy through marketing strategies	▶ Have been able to achieve a census of up to 96% through effective marketing strategies
▶ Current RCFE in California	▶ Possess current California RCFE
▶ Bachelor's degree in business or healthcare	▶ BS in business management; now halfway through MBA

Please see my résumé for more details of my qualifications. I hope to have an opportunity to share with you how my leadership abilities could benefit Park View Senior Living. Thank you for your time and consideration.

Sincerely,

John A. Williams, RCFE, LNHA

Enclosure

126

Executive Director, Assisted-Living Facility. *Kelly Donovan, Ontario, California*

The goal was a position similar to the one the applicant had. The letter refers to a contact with the new facility and compares the applicant's qualifications with the new company's requirements.

PAUL JOHNSON

14 Westlake Drive
Framingham, MA 01702

Email: paul@johnson.com

Cell: 000 000 0000
Residence: 555 555 5555

11 February 20xx

Mr. David Paul
ATCT Hospital
18 Saddleback Road
Framingham, MA 01702

Re: Chief Executive Officer

Dear Mr. Paul:

For almost 20 years, I have been at the forefront of initiatives that have positioned organizations to support significant growth, and have turned around floundering and problematic divisions to regain the respect of the people they serve. I have conceived new ideas to strengthen core services to customers, project-managed new infrastructure initiatives, and maintained the morale of "the troops" despite periods of instability and change.

Considered a senior executive with a combination of vision and corporate realism, I have been acknowledged for my capacity to harness the enthusiasm and talents of others, identify core issues, and exploit the necessary resources available to stretch funds and achieve management objectives in healthcare and medical environments.

Experience of this magnitude hasn't been developed overnight; successes have been hard won, and commitment has been tireless. Yet the rewards of seeing an idea take hold of people's imaginations for better and more responsive service delivery remains to this day one of my greatest motivators, and it is a skill I'm keen to demonstrate for my next employer as I meet the next challenge of my professional life.

Eager to tackle new opportunities, my last major role as Vice President, Business Delivery, consulting primarily to medical, healthcare, and education sectors, has now concluded. I have transformed what was a new business unit into a vital, responsive operation that delivered strong productivity increases and growth in just two years.

And now the time is ripe for a new challenge. Broad-based knowledge across diverse sectors and specialist executive consultancy experience in healthcare and medical sectors position me well for joining your leadership team.

Experienced in hospital operations; case management; and all the economic, procedural, and staff issues inherent in such environments, I believe I can bring a unique skill set to the role of hospital CEO. Having worked closely with senior executives in major healthcare facilities and hospitals, I know and understand the complexities of the healthcare system, the infrastructure, and how to position the organization for genuine growth. I see significant opportunities in aligning myself with ATCT Hospital, opportunities I'm keen to tackle and achieve measurable successes in, for our mutual benefit.

Naturally I would be delighted to explore your needs in detail at an interview and can arrange to meet at a mutually convenient time. In the meantime, my resume is attached for your review, and I can be contacted at the numbers provided. Thank you for your time and consideration, and I look forward to speaking with you soon.

Sincerely,

Paul Johnson

127

Chief Executive Officer. *Gayle Howard, Southbank, Victoria, Australia*

The challenge of this cover letter was to convince the reader that this senior consultant, who had worked in healthcare for many years, was qualified to assume the role of a hospital CEO.

CINDY WANG
55 East Zhongshan Road, Shanghai, Peoples Republic of China 555555
5555 Main Street, San Diego, California 55555 USA
USA: +1-555-555-5555 • China: +86-555-555-5555 • Cindy@xxx.com

August 16, 20XX

Mr. John Smith
China CEO
ABC Health Management
000 East Beijing Road, Jingan District
Shanghai, China 55555

Dear Mr. Smith:

Speed to market, cost challenges, political and economic ambiguity, and cultural misunderstandings are just some of the complexities facing healthcare companies looking to capitalize on the rapid growth and market size in the Far East. I would welcome the opportunity to explore how I can help ABC Health Management manage these intricacies.

I am a strategic senior leader with 20 years of experience delivering solid business results on behalf of high-growth start-ups as well as Fortune 500 multinationals. My most recent post was as CEO of Sinohealth BioTech, an innovative healthcare management firm in China. I also have a track record of significant contribution with Diversified Equipment International in China and CH2M Hill in the USA.

Having led cross-functional teams across product development, supply chain, manufacturing, and quality, my key competencies begin with P&L management, strategic planning, market intelligence, and talent development. Perhaps you would be interested in just a few highlights from my background:

- At Sinohealth BioTech, the owner of the start-up handed me a blank slate and I quickly built the organization into a high performance team of 26 that are driven by creativity and the sprit of entrepreneurship.

- Also with Sinohealth BioTech, as part of the business formulation stage I gained extremely critical recognition and support from Chinese national and municipal governments. In addition, I successfully signed world-renowned chemist Dr. Sarah Jones as a company shareholder and chief science consultant.

- With Diversified Equipment, I helped position the brand in China as a leading construction equipment manufacturer. Market share increased from less than 10% to more than 30%. This drove the company's investment in three greenfield sites. I also held P&L responsibility managing a 450-employee manufacturing facility, developing it from early production phase into a stable manufacturing site.

- As a result of my work with Diversified Equipment, I was selected to participate in the prestigious *Global Leadership Program* of the Stanford University Graduate School of Business. This supported my professional development into a forward-thinking business leader (beyond being a day-to-day operations manager).

Among my strengths are communication and negotiation skills across all levels of internal and external stakeholders and knowledge of local government relationship protocols regarding how to develop and maintain win-win business relationships. My east-west educational background and work experiences drive my understanding of cultural differences. This understanding helps develop a strong local business focus without compromising global standards.

At your convenience, I would be most interested in speaking with you. I will call your office to see if that may be possible.

Sincerely,

Cindy Wang

128

Senior Healthcare Manager. *Peter Hill, Honolulu, Hawaii*

The challenge of this cold-call letter was to keep the applicant, a businesswoman with cross-cultural experiences, from being pigeonholed as a manufacturing and operations person.

CATHERINE SITTON
555 N. Johnson Avenue, Apt. 5
Brookhaven, Pennsylvania 19333
(555) 555-8888
cate_sitton@penn.net

December 16, 20XX

Sodexo Marriott Corporation
ATT: Franklin Hunt, Director of Personnel
5 Landon Way
Princeton, NJ 08888

Dear Mr. Hunt:

I would like to express my interest in joining Sodexo Marriott in a management capacity. I am particularly interested in a senior-level position involving corporate dining, catering, and banquet events. Enclosed is my resume, reviewing my extensive background and accomplishments in staff and operations management, for your consideration.

As an effective manager and chef, I have a proven track record in all facets of the food service industry. My greatest strength would have to be my ability to generate employee loyalty and create a team environment. Equally strong is my ability to control labor and food costs. I am especially proud of the fact that former staff members often request to join me when I accept a new assignment. I provide extensive training, direction, and feedback; they are clearly aware of my expectations and interest in their welfare.

Other key attributes include attention to detail, the ability to work effectively in high-pressure situations, a high level of motivation, and emphasis on sanitation. Here are several career highlights that may be of interest:

- ◆ Significantly reduced Workers' Compensation costs in all locations through close attention to safety.
- ◆ Acquired an excellent reputation as a chef, skilled in the areas of menu planning, timing, presentation, and food quality.
- ◆ Hired as a consultant to assist a new center-city restaurant during its start-up phase.
- ◆ Developed training manuals and completed staff training for all positions.

On a final note, it goes without saying that guest satisfaction is key to a successful operation. I consistently stress to my staff the importance of communicating effectively with guests. Not only does the guest feel unique and special, but also it demonstrates confidence on the part of the employee. That equates to a successful dining experience and repeat business, which has been the norm in each of my operations.

I believe my education and background have provided the tools and experience necessary to manage a large-scale operation, and I would welcome the opportunity to discuss employment prospects at Sodexo Marriott in a personal interview. I believe your organization would be an ideal work setting for someone with my skills and personality.

I'll look forward to meeting with you and will contact you to set a mutually convenient time for an interview.

Sincerely,

Catherine Sitton

Enclosure

129

Hotel Manager. *Karen Conway, Bend, Oregon*

A series of short paragraphs makes this longer-than-average cover letter relatively easy to read. The bulleted items provide relief from the series and draw attention to career highlights.

Michael J. Fisher, C.M.C.

56 Madison Avenue
Summit, New Jersey 07901
(555) 555-5555
mjfcmc@earthlink.net

[Date]

[Name]
[Title]
[Address]
[City, State ZIP]

Dear [Name]:

Enclosed is my resume for your review. I am confident that my extensive experience as an executive chef and hotel/restaurant manager would serve as an asset to a position in your organization. My career began 23 years ago as an apprentice training under several notable, internationally known chefs. Since that time I have been involved extensively in the area of food services management and marketing.

I am currently General Manager and Corporate Executive Chef of Hague Nieuw-York. In 20XX, I was hired to start up this 225-seat restaurant. The casual dining establishment is part of Avanti Brands, Inc., USA. I am responsible for all financial reporting and instituted key control systems to meet the standards of the parent company. Additional achievements include gaining excellent media publicity, creative menu development, and directing on- and off-site catering for many New York City premieres. I was asked to coordinate all aspects of our new construction and assist in the design aspects of the kitchen.

As Director of Operations for Town Square Katering and Times Square Restaurant in Hoboken, New Jersey, my staff and I expanded the business to accommodate parties ranging from 10 to 4,000 people and grossed more than $1.5 million in sales.

Working as Vice President of Operations and Executive Chef for Pine Ridge Country Club, I oversaw all profit-and-loss functions for a 165-seat, a la carte restaurant and a 1,000-seat banquet facility. The club had an 18-hole championship golf course that I managed, with an active membership of 1,000 members.

I gained extensive international experience working as Executive Chef for Ordini's, a five-star-rated restaurant in New Zealand, preparing food for the Prime Minister, various heads of state, and visiting dignitaries. I obtained my New Zealand Master Chef's Certification. In addition, I served as an Executive Pastry Chef and Chef for a Hawaiian hotel owned and operated by the Sheraton Corporation.

Thank you for your consideration. I look forward to speaking with you personally regarding my qualifications and how I can contribute positively as a member of your management staff. I will contact you next week to inquire about the possibility of a personal interview.

Sincerely yours,

Michael J. Fisher, C.M.C.

Enclosure

130

Executive Chef and Hotel/Restaurant Manager. *Beverly and Mitchell I. Baskin, Marlboro, New Jersey*

Inferior cover letters wallow in generalities and abstraction. This letter is unusually interesting because of its many references to restaurants in specific locations around the world.

KRISTEN MOORE

5555 Winter Road • Hermitage, Pennsylvania 55555 • 555-555-5555
kmoore@aol.com

August 31, 20XX

Mary Brenner
Five Star Restaurant
5555 Michigan Avenue
Chicago, IL 55555

Dear Ms. Brenner:

I have been fortunate throughout my career in hospitality to work in positions that challenged me and benefited from my passion for management and inventive solutions. I delivered programs that captured market share, accelerated revenue growth, and won dominant competitive positioning. While secure in my current position, I am confidentially seeking a new career opportunity.

By combining my expertise in strategic planning, team building, leadership, and time management with my expertise in budgeting and cost control in the restaurant business, I have significantly contributed to boosting my employer's performance. The strength of my character, my commitment to quality, and my endless ideas and enthusiasm will be an invaluable asset to your establishment.

As a service-oriented professional who focuses on people, let me highlight some of my specific skills relative to a restaurant environment:

> ➢ Recruit a nucleus of staff to effectively and efficiently support the needs of the restaurant. Established reputation for a motivational, hands-on management style that inspires teamwork and builds confidence in others.

> ➢ Emphasize training of all personnel in food preparation, front/back house operations, and problem solving for peak customer satisfaction.

> ➢ Adept at controlling food and beverage costs while maintaining the highest level of customer service.

> ➢ Skilled at marketing and advertising. Identify demographics of target clientele. Recognize need for changes to menu and facility to capitalize on current as well as upcoming trends.

In reviewing the enclosed resume, I am confident you will determine that my qualifications match those established by your restaurant for your next Manager.

I would be delighted to meet with you to expand on the snapshot of my experiences noted in this resume. I will call you next week to set an appointment. Until we speak, I thank you for your time and consideration. I look forward to our conversation.

Sincerely,

Kristen Moore

Enclosure: resume

131

Restaurant Manager. *Jane Roqueplot, West Middlesex, Pennsylvania*

The goal for this letter was to focus on four main areas of need (see the bulleted statements) at the target organization, as identified through the applicant's market research.

José Margoles
5555 Irish Ave. • Rochester, NY 00000

jose.margoles@xx.com
555-555-0000

March 25, 20XX

Red Robin Gourmet Burgers
000 S. Fiddlers Green Circle, #000N
Greenwood Village, CO 55555

Managing profitable restaurants has been my life. Whether opening a brand new facility or turning around a lackluster one, I approach work every day ready to embrace new challenges. That's why Melanie Alsted, Red Robin general manager here in Rochester, has urged me to submit my credentials for your review. After learning about the company from Melanie, several former colleagues, and your website, I am excited for the chance to use my skills and experience in a management position with Red Robin.

I am amazed at the similarities between your business model and my background. Your criteria for a successful Red Robin management team member and examples of my relevant achievements include:

Provide outstanding leadership for team	☒ Received five corporate Team First awards
Be passionate about the industry	☒ Committed to creating positive, enjoyable dining experiences for my customers
Inspire others through coaching and counseling	☒ Mentored at least five employees to earn promotions to General Manager and District Manager
Create a profitable environment	☒ Named General Manager of the Year
Deliver an exceptional customer experience	☒ Ranked in the top 20% of stores for guest loyalty
Maintain high standards of cleanliness, sanitation, food quality, and facility management	☒ Earned Gold Cleanliness award for sanitation
Possess 2+ years of restaurant management experience	☒ Effectively managed restaurants for more than 20 years

As an 18-year employee with Joe's Crab Shack—16 years as General Manager—I gained a reputation for building dedicated teams and resolving issues that stood in the way of profitability. Although I officially retired from Joe's, I am far from ready to stop contributing. I'm eager to get back into the trenches. Therefore, I hope you will consider my interest in joining your management team. You can be assured I have the drive, experience, and entrepreneurial perspective to uphold Red Robin's ranking as one of the country's top 10 highest-rated chains.

Sincerely,

José Margoles

Attachment

132

Restaurant Manager. *Janet L. Beckstrom, Flint, Michigan*

With this cold-call letter, the applicant wanted to get on the company's radar for a future management position. The table matches his accomplishments to the company's criteria.

ERIC A. PRYOR, CCM

45 Ellenger Street •• Hartford, CT 55555
Home: 555.555.5555 •• Mobile: 555.555.7555 •• ericapryor@aol.com

[Date]

[Name]
[Title]
[Organization]
[Address]
[City, State ZIP]

Dear _____:

A general manager with an impeccable record of performance in all areas of operations, service, and financial management is essential to your club's continued growth and success.

As a club management professional with a career history rich in achievements at prominent clubs, you will find on my resume more than a dozen documented examples of my success in **driving membership and revenue growth** while **reducing costs, ensuring efficiency and productivity,** and **promoting unparalleled member service.**

Here's what your club needs … Here's what I offer …

➢ Designation as a Certified Club Manager with extensive and consistent results in ensuring peak standards of operations, efficiency, productivity, quality, and service.

➢ Delivering bottom-line results throughout my career in club management: $10 million in total revenues, $2.9 million in annual membership dues, and $3.4 million in food and beverage.

➢ Demonstrated strengths in financial management and budgeting as evidenced by my ability to reduce/control costs without sacrificing member satisfaction or quality and ensure fiscally sound operations.

➢ Recognition as a natural leader/team builder with managerial strengths combined with the ability to attract, motivate, develop, and retain quality talent who are dedicated to achieving common business goals.

➢ Leadership that earned Region Club of the Year awards and #1 ranking in member satisfaction.

➢ Selection by the Club Management Association as the training club for the North Region.

My success stories arise from my core business beliefs: fostering a positive, productive working environment through hands-on leadership *and* creating an exceptional membership experience to drive bottom-line results. As a result, my efforts have been recognized with multiple awards during my club management career, including "Club of the Year," "Manager of the Year," and "Creativity in Management."

If your client's club could benefit from my talents, I would welcome the opportunity to discuss my potential contributions. I will call to explore the possibility of a face-to-face meeting.

Sincerely,

Eric A. Pryor, CCM

133

Certified Club Manager. *Louise Garver, Broad Brook, Connecticut*

The person was between assignments. The letter highlights the credentials that set him apart from the competition. He seemed a perfect match and landed an interview out of 150 applicants.

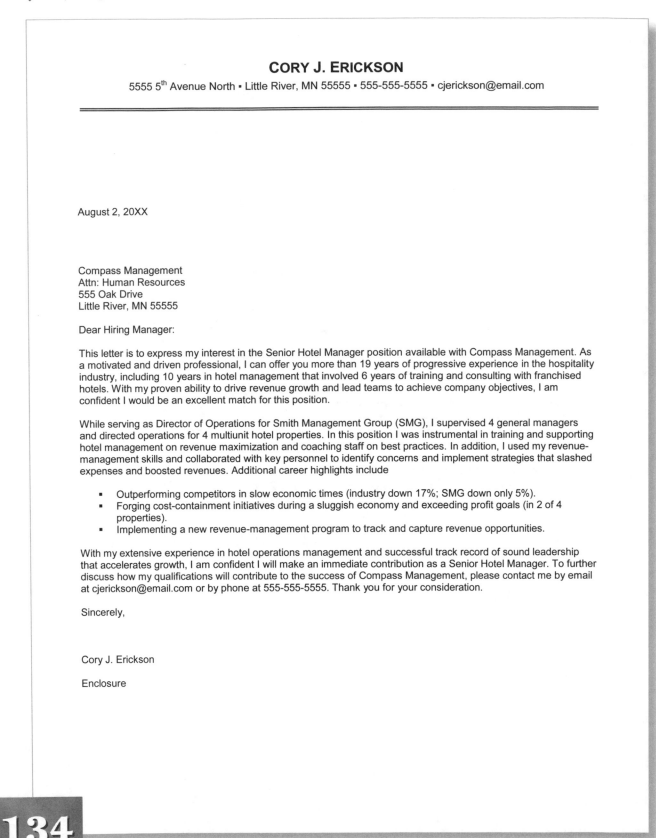

CORY J. ERICKSON

5555 5th Avenue North ▪ Little River, MN 55555 ▪ 555-555-5555 ▪ cjerickson@email.com

August 2, 20XX

Compass Management
Attn: Human Resources
555 Oak Drive
Little River, MN 55555

Dear Hiring Manager:

This letter is to express my interest in the Senior Hotel Manager position available with Compass Management. As a motivated and driven professional, I can offer you more than 19 years of progressive experience in the hospitality industry, including 10 years in hotel management that involved 6 years of training and consulting with franchised hotels. With my proven ability to drive revenue growth and lead teams to achieve company objectives, I am confident I would be an excellent match for this position.

While serving as Director of Operations for Smith Management Group (SMG), I supervised 4 general managers and directed operations for 4 multiunit hotel properties. In this position I was instrumental in training and supporting hotel management on revenue maximization and coaching staff on best practices. In addition, I used my revenue-management skills and collaborated with key personnel to identify concerns and implement strategies that slashed expenses and boosted revenues. Additional career highlights include

- Outperforming competitors in slow economic times (industry down 17%; SMG down only 5%).
- Forging cost-containment initiatives during a sluggish economy and exceeding profit goals (in 2 of 4 properties).
- Implementing a new revenue-management program to track and capture revenue opportunities.

With my extensive experience in hotel operations management and successful track record of sound leadership that accelerates growth, I am confident I will make an immediate contribution as a Senior Hotel Manager. To further discuss how my qualifications will contribute to the success of Compass Management, please contact me by email at cjerickson@email.com or by phone at 555-555-5555. Thank you for your consideration.

Sincerely,

Cory J. Erickson

Enclosure

134

Senior Hotel Manager. *Connie Hauer, Sartell, Minnesota*

Bullets help to make this applicant's accomplishments stand out. The letter was a response to a company ad, and the accomplishments highlight this person's ability to outperform competitors. See Resume 7 in Part 3.

Cliff Stanton

February 1, 20xx

John Smith
Hyatt Hotel
1234 Larimer Street
Denver, CO 80000

Re: Position HY123456

Dear Employment Director:

It's all about heads and beds and customer satisfaction in the hospitality industry. It takes an innovative and tenacious manager to face successfully the tremendous challenges confronting today's leading hotels. I have made a career out of turning around faltering properties, raising service standards, increasing organizational efficiency, and significantly improving bottom line profits.

I am currently the General Manager of the Executive Hotel, Denver. The owners have decided to convert the property into an assisted-living facility, and while they have asked me to stay with the property, my passion for the hotel business necessitates that I move on. I am seeking a management position with an upscale hotel such as yours.

My resume speaks to my history of decisive leadership as well as strong financial and operating results. Most notably I have

- Turned unprofitable properties into consistently performing, multimillion-dollar organizations.
- Streamlined operations and eliminated duplicate functions to reduce costs and increase productivity and revenue.
- Integrated finance and operations, creating proactive business units focused on the bottom line and positioned for long-term growth and profitability.

The value I bring to Hyatt Hotels is broad experience spanning all core business functions with a primary focus on operations and finance. My success is directly attributable to my ability to unify organizations, initiate action, and deliver results.

I welcome the chance to explore any current assignments commensurate with my management skills. I am willing to relocate for the right opportunity.

Thank you for your time and consideration, and I look forward to hearing from you.

Sincerely,

Cliff Stanton

Enclosure

P.O. Box 1234 · Denver, CO 00000 · Home (555) 555-5555 · Mobile/Pager (555) 555-5550 · cliffs@yahoo.net

135

Hotel General Manager. *Roberta Gamza, Louisville, Colorado*

The applicant wanted to move to a luxury, full-service hotel chain. To get the reader's attention, the writer began by getting to the point about what is important in the hospitality industry.

Shanna Collins
000 Sharps Boulevard NE
Norfolk, Virginia 55555

✆ (555) 555-5555

December 20, 20XX

Mrs. Linda Thorndyke
Director of Human Resources
Heritage Companies
PO Box 555
Houston, Texas 55555

RE: Human Resources Assistant

Dear Mrs. Thorndyke:

I am very interested in re-careering to the Human Resources field and have enclosed a resume for your review. Originally an accountant, I am now returning to the paid workforce after a period of extensive community and volunteer work.

Balancing a number of general business skills, I also have a valuable complement of human-service-related strengths, including the following:

facilitation, interviewing and assessment	training and tutoring
patient and customer service	client research and analysis
client data gathering and consultation	listening and communicating

One of the main things I missed in accounting work was direct interaction with people and the opportunity to feel as if my work would make a difference in the lives of others. My nature is one of compassion, patience and responsibility. Solution-oriented, I believe that all problems can be worked out. Research and assessment skills, time management, decision making and multitasking add to the value of my people skills. Adding more flexibility, my working style is one that easily lends itself to either an independent or a group work environment.

Others describe me as highly professional, sensitive to the needs of others, a positive thinker, detail-oriented and dependable. I feel that my maturity and combination of business and people skills are assets and would like to meet with you to discuss your needs, including how I might contribute to those goals.

I will contact your office to see whether additional information is needed and to determine a suitable time to meet with you.

Sincerely,

SHANNA COLLINS

Enclosure

136

Human Resources Assistant. *Beverley Drake, Hot Springs Village, Arkansas*

After a period of volunteer work, this accountant wanted to return to the workforce but in the field of human resources. The letter identifies her transferable strengths, skills, and worker traits.

Available for relocation

Sue Allard

000 Roberts Road, Martinville, Alabama 00000
☎ 334.555.5555 (home) — 334.555.6666 (cell)
suealla@clark.com

November 2, 20XX

Ms. Deborah Montiel
States Bank
44 Charleston Street
Montgomery, Alabama 00000

Dear Ms. Montiel:

I want to make it as easy as possible for States Bank to add me to its team as a Human Resources Assistant. Moving toward that goal starts with my resume.

I wanted to give you something more valuable than the usual job titles, responsibilities, and college course work. That's why I've included examples of HR-related problems solved. At school, my problem-solving skills were reviewed by senior HR professionals who were paid to evaluate my work against tough industry standards. At work, everyone saw my workforce management abilities—from supervisors to coworkers to customers. In fact, it was my work experience that motivated me to get a degree in Human Resources while I continued learning on the job.

My development program is almost finished. I have just obtained my BS in Human Resources. But I want to start putting my energies and skills to work in that field as soon as I can.

So, as a next step, I would like to hear about States Bank's specific HR needs in your own words. I will call in a few days to set up time to do that.

Sincerely,

Sue Allard

Encl.: Resume

137

Human Resources Assistant. *Don Orlando, Montgomery, Alabama*

The applicant had a recent HR degree but never had held an HR position. The third sentence in the second paragraph counters any view that college instruction is out of touch with the real world.

REBECCA B. STILLS

0000 Prosperity Road • Monroe, NC 28888 • (555) 555-5555 • rbstills@gmail.com

April 20, 20XX

Ms. D. Finnegan
TICS Corporation
P.O. Box 7488
Charlotte, NC 28241

Dear Ms. Finnegan:

Why did Abraham Lincoln win log-splitting contests so easily?

You've heard the reason: He knew exactly where to place his wedge to give his blows the most power. When Lincoln won these contests, he was the same age as I am now; and I, too, want to enter a log-splitting contest.

I have a good, strong wedge and a sturdy hammer, but I need a log: a company whose growth I can contribute to and build a career with.

In the first place, I want to get into the field of human resources—as a generalist—starting as a *human resource assistant.* I have strong computer skills (Word, Excel) and the ability to master new things. In addition, I possess strong communication skills, honed through four years as a waitress and as a customer service representative within a fast-paced, quality-minded call center environment.

In May, I will receive my baccalaureate degree in Psychology; I lack only one three-hour course, which is offered at UNCC in the evening this summer. During my college years, I worked to provide 75% of all expenses, so I have grown accustomed to long hours and hard work. And during this time I have been molding my wedge: working as an HR intern (please see enclosed resume) and learning about employee benefits plans and procedures.

This, then, is my wedge into the field of human resources: to be a human resource assistant, acquire experience and advance to more responsible positions. Your company and its opportunities can be my log.

Will you let me enter the contest?

I look forward to meeting with you and will call to set up an appointment.

Sincerely,

Rebecca B. Stills

Enclosure

138

Human Resources Assistant. *Doug Morrison, Charlotte, North Carolina*

This recent graduate was keenly interested in entering the field of human resources. The letter displays her motivation, strong interest, enthusiasm, youthful vitality, and career goals.

555 North Circle, Parrish, FL 55555
gracebennett@xxx.com
Mobile (555) 555-5555

Grace E. Bennett

September 6, 20XX

Lisa Donahue, Human Resources Manager
Job Source Development Agency
555 Job Source Drive
Parrish, FL 55555

Dear Ms. Donahue:

During a recent networking event, I had the pleasure of running into a former colleague by the name of Mr. Robert Winters who is now employed by your agency. Through our conversation, I was able to learn more about the Career Counselor opportunity that was advertised. Mr. Winters has encouraged me to apply and referred me to you because of the congruence of my skills with those necessary for the position.

From my attached résumé, you will find that I have been a credentialed Career Counselor for 15 years. My passion for the field has not ceased, and I am excited every day to do the work that I love. I am continually searching for new resources and methods to work with my clients to help them through the process of career development. Further, I research professional development opportunities to upgrade my skills. Dormancy is something that is difficult for me as I strive to continually develop myself and my skill set.

Many certifications and personal qualities qualify me for this opportunity. You will notice that I am a Certified Job & Career Transition Coach and Myers-Briggs Consultant, in addition to being a Certified Professional Resume Writer. I am completing the Certified Professional Career Coach program to add to my repertoire of knowledge. Furthermore, my personality is conducive to the counseling field. I have an innate ability to make people feel comfortable early in our rapport building so we are able to make progress immediately. I have received many positive comments in this regard through recommendations on my LinkedIn profile. Please feel free to access my profile at www.linkedin.com to get additional information about me and my expertise.

Mr. Winters is aware of my application and has offered to discuss it with you. I sincerely appreciate your time and consideration and look forward to the possibility of scheduling an interview.

Sincerely,

Grace E. Bennett

139

Career Counselor. *Haley Richardson, Riverview, Florida*

A former colleague now worked at the counseling agency where this applicant wanted to work. She used his name as a referral and source of information about her qualifications and work ethic.

MARIGOLD TRUMAN

555 Windy Way East ● Brentwood, NY 11717 ● (555) 555-3333 ● HR@TheBranch.net

June 25, 20xx

Ms. Mary Smith
Recruitment Administrator
Human Resources Department
THE BRANCH BANK
One Branch Plaza
Brentwood, New York 55555

Dear Ms. Smith:

The enclosed resume and supporting documentation are presented for your review and consideration for acceptance into The Branch Bank's Human Resources Associates Program. Ideally, this opportunity will develop and strengthen my skills and knowledge while exposing me to a broad spectrum of areas and challenges conducive to professional growth in the field of Human Resources.

I offer a Bachelor of Arts degree in Psychology and tenure with The Branch Bank since June 20xx in the position of Senior File Clerk, Pre-Arbitration/In-Coming Collections Department. Initially, I joined this department as a temporary employee and proved myself as a team player capable of handling a heavy caseload while significantly improving the quality of office procedures. As a result, my current position was created for me on a permanent basis.

Further, to ensure the continuity of positive changes that I have brought to the department, I provide ongoing training to employees, a role I greatly enjoy. To date, I have been recognized and rewarded for my drive to go above and beyond what is expected of me, with recent contributions that include an interim position as a fully trained Auto Call Directory representative. I am confident that my education, record of excellence (including perfect attendance), and personal attributes (strong organizational, overall communication, and computer skills), combined with a firm aspiration to further my career in Human Resources, qualify me as a suitable candidate.

Although this application, along with my personnel file, illustrates my background well, I feel that a personal interview would better demonstrate my knowledge and abilities. Therefore, I would appreciate an opportunity to interview with you at a convenient time. Thank you for your review and consideration. I will contact you soon regarding the next step in the process.

Sincerely,

Marigold Truman

140

Bank Human Resources Position. *Ann Baehr, East Islip, New York*

The unusual horizontal lines are eye-catching. With its filled circle on the left, the top line balances the contact information. With a filled circle on the right, the bottom line balances the top line.

KIMBERLY BLAKELY
000 Romeo Drive
Commack, New York 11725
(555) 555-5555
kimberlyblakely@yahoo.com

[Date]

[Name]
[Title]
[Address]
[City, State ZIP]

Dear Sir or Madam:

Reflecting on my professional experience within the insurance industry, it is at this point in my career that I am seeking to pursue my long-term personal and professional goal of a challenging career within **Human Resources.** Let me briefly highlight the skills, values, and contributions I will bring to your organization:

- Dedicated commitment to a long and successful career within **Human Resources.**

- Excellent customer service/relations, time-management, troubleshooting, and communications skills, developed through many years in the insurance industry as a **Claims Specialist.**

- Ability to perform independently or as part of a team, building cooperative working relationships among management and support staff in order to meet goals and achieve successful results.

- An energetic, enthusiastic approach with proven success in prioritizing time and resources to attain goals and meet project deadlines.

My personal and professional education, work experiences, interests, and strengths have all contributed to outstanding business achievements. I am accountable for diverse responsibilities, including serving clients and the general public. My acquired knowledge and experience as a contributing individual in the business world will prove to be a quality that will enhance the goals and standards of any Human Resources department.

Please take the time to review the aforementioned credentials. I firmly believe you will find them to meet the needs of your company, and I am confident my contributions to your organization will prove to be lasting, if given the opportunity. Thank you for your time and consideration.

Very truly yours,

KIMBERLY BLAKELY

Enclosure

141

Human Resources Position. *Donna M. Farrise, Hauppauge, New York*

This insurance claim specialist wanted a position in any human resources department. Boldfacing highlights Human Resources as a goal. Bullets point to values, transferable skills, and worker-trait contributions.

Hank R. Johnson

123 Main Street ● Annapolis, Maryland 21403 ● (410) 555-1234 ● E-mail: **hank@protypeld.com**

April 1, 20xx

Any Company USA
Attn: John Doe, Human Resources Director
123 Main Street
Any Town, MD 21032

Dear Mr. Doe,

With my background and experience in Human Resources and Operations Management, I am all too aware of the changes that have influenced the industry over the past few years. Never before have we experienced such a phenomenon or so many challenges at such a rapid pace. Today we are expected to accomplish more, often with less, and generally in a shorter time frame. As an experienced professional in these fields, I have routinely been faced with such challenges. I have a proven track record of success because I face every challenge with passion and energy.

My special talents and skills are supported by some outstanding core strengths:

> **Outstanding corporate team contributor—a solutions specialist**
> **Human Resources generalist and recruiting/training professional**
> **Extensive experience with large and complicated payrolls and compensation**
> **Management operations and consulting expertise in competitive environment**

During my employment history, and with every assignment I have accepted, I have devoted my energies toward being a good steward of available resources. I attribute my ability to improve the operational performance of my employer almost immediately to my resourcefulness and creativity.

You will find that I am a decisive, proactive, and result-driven professional, offering a unique blend of academic achievement, technological expertise, practical experience, organizational and motivational leadership, creativity, resourcefulness, and the flexibility for change.

I would like to meet with you so that we can discuss the special needs of Company USA. We should discuss exactly how my experience and qualifications would best contribute to your success. I will contact you by April 15 to confirm that you received my resume and discuss how I can fit into your organization. Thank you for your time and consideration.

Sincerely,

Hank R. Johnson

Enclosure: Resume

142

Human Resources Generalist. *Beth Colley, Crownsville, Maryland*

The first paragraph indicates that the applicant is aware of the current state of the HR field. A list of outstanding core strengths in boldface focuses on what the individual can bring to the company.

RUBY SLATER
RubySlater@email.com

5555 Arguello Avenue	**Residence (310) 555-5555**
Los Angeles, California 55555	**Mobile (310) 555-0000**

[Date]

[Name]
[Title]
[Company]
[Address]
[City, State ZIP]

Dear [Ms./Mr. Name]:

Strong human resources leadership can have a tremendous impact on operating results. By building and managing an effective HR infrastructure, developing successful productivity, efficiency, quality and performance management, I have consistently made a direct contribution to corporate goals. Highlights of my professional career include

- 15 years of senior-level experience as an HR Generalist, providing HR planning and leadership in union and nonunion environments across diverse industries
- Implementation of HRIS technology and applications to improve information flow and use in strategic planning initiatives
- Strong qualifications in employee relations with ability to build confidence and trust between employees and management
- Introduction of loss control, safety and Workers' Compensation fraud programs
- Authoring employee manuals to provide employee guidelines in compliance with changing regulatory environments

Most significantly, I have positioned myself and the HR function as a partner to senior management in working together toward producing top-performing workforces able to meet operating challenges. Currently I am looking for a new opportunity as a senior-level HR professional with an organization seeking talent, drive, enthusiasm and leadership expertise. I would welcome a personal interview to explore such positions with your organization and will contact you to arrange a time to meet. Thank you.

Sincerely,

Ruby Slater

Enclosure: Resume

143

Human Resources Generalist. *Vivian VanLier, Los Angeles (Valley Glen), California*

The applicant was seeking a position as a senior-level HR professional. Bullets point to highlights of her 15-year career. In the last paragraph, she places her HR role on a par with senior management.

María Santaquín

000 Abbot Road ■ Roma, CA 55555 ■ msantaquin@xx.com ■ (555) 555-5555

HUMAN RESOURCES DIRECTOR

Date: August 23, 20XX

Mr. Mark Wise
Wise Recruiting Resources
55 Longer Drive
San Diego, CA 55555

Dear Mr. Wise:

As an expert recruiter and experienced human resources generalist, I was pleased to read of your company's need for both. I am confident that my history of successfully sourcing and placing candidates at all levels, from administrative roles through C-suite, will serve you well. I also look forward to leading your organization's human resources division, from policy development through benefits management.

Examples of my recent successes include:

- Successfully placed COO with very particular client; sourced several choices for client, across a variety of Web media.
- Changed sourcing methods to include behavioral interviewing as well as tests of skills and battery assessments of personality, increasing fit with client companies and reducing turnover 25%.
- Wrote and revised corporate human resources policies in concert with expert consultant and legal team, ensuring superior compliance with all applicable regulations.
- Improved safety compliance, reducing X-MOD to 120.

Of course, these are only samples of the types of successes I am accustomed to delivering. I look forward to doing the same and more for your company. I am interested in speaking with you to discuss the value that my strengths and experience can bring to Wise Recruiting Resources and can be reached in confidence at the above telephone number or email address. I look forward to hearing from you.

With best regards,

María Santaquín
Enclosure: Résumé

144

Human Resources Director. *Amy L. Adler, Salt Lake City, Utah*

A company wanted a candidate who was experienced with both recruiting and human resources. The letter takes a mixed approach, highlighting accomplishments in both areas. See Resume 8 in Part 3.

LATOYA B. JOHNSON, BA

• 5 Main Street • Las Vegas, NV 55555 •
• H (555) 555-5000 • latoya@xx.com • C (555) 555-5555 •

STRATEGIC HUMAN RESOURCES SPECIALIST
"Providing people solutions with bottom-line results!"

September 27, 20XX

Laura Bell
Corporate Recruiter
ABC Manufacturing
55 Swan Road
Las Vegas, NV 55555

RE: **Human Resources Generalist Posting, Job Reference # HRXXXX**

Dear Ms. Bell,

If ABC Manufacturing is seeking a dynamic, results-oriented human resources generalist with strong communication and leadership skills, then I believe we have good reason to meet! Your organization has a reputation for operational excellence as shown by your recent ranking as one of the "50 Best Employers." I would like to exceed expectations by using my talents to support your exceptional work. I feel this position is an excellent career opportunity and match for my skills and HR experience.

Highlights of my human resources background include:

✓ *Progressive leader with more than five years of experience as a human resources professional.*

✓ *Hands-on expertise in all functional areas of human resources with special emphasis on recruitment, training, and employee relations.*

✓ *Exceptional project management skills and the ability to lead, coach, and influence others while communicating effectively toward the achievement of company goals.*

My experience is complemented by a strong education that includes a Bachelor of Arts from Stanford University where I majored in Psychology. I remain current with emerging trends and legislation through my membership with the Society of Human Resources Professionals. As the attached résumé indicates, I am also a lifelong learner who is committed to excellence and believes in actively giving back to the community through volunteer work, which appears to be an important corporate initiative at ABC Manufacturing.

I am eager to discuss this intriguing career opportunity with you further. I will contact your office next week to confirm receipt of my résumé and to discuss scheduling an appointment at your convenience. Thank you for your time and consideration.

Warm Regards,

Latoya Johnson

Enclosure: Résumé

145

Human Resources Generalist. *Tanya Sinclair, Pickering, Ontario, Canada*

The rounded header with the applicant's name, degree, and contact information is eye-catching. The tagline is relevant to the role and speaks to the applicant's work style and value.

Will consider relocation to Dallas

Jud Jackson

5555 Montego Drive, Austin, Texas 00000

judjackson@xx.com ☎ 555.555.5555 (home) – 555.555.7777 (cell)

Monday, XX May 20XX

Mr. Melvin W. Cox
Director of Human Resources
Benchmark, Inc.
000 Northridge Parkway
Suite 000
Dallas, Texas 00000

Dear Mr. Cox:

I would like to join the Benchmark team as your newest HR Generalist.

You'll find six ROI-building actions I'm prepared to demonstrate from day one, right at the top of my résumé. Backing them up are eight examples of broad and deep personnel-related contributions I've made to my employer and our teams.

I've complied with all your online filing requirements. However, I want you to be able to prove to your leadership team that the next HR Generalist you hire will make Benchmark more money than it takes to bring that person on board. That's why I've replaced the usual lists of responsibilities and key words with documented value.

As you read, I hope these central ideas stand out clearly:

- ❑ While I've never had the term "HR" in any of my official job titles, my companies have consistently rewarded me for performing that function well.

- ❑ While others will tell you they are "people persons," management and teams think of me as *their* go-to "people person" — because I help them align their personal success goals with our corporate vision and profits.

- ❑ While others may bring experience serving professionals, my work requires me to deliver top-notch HR benefits to everyone from busboys to vice presidents.

When it comes to something as important as HR, words on paper are not substitutes for person-to-person conversations about your specific personnel needs. May I call in a few days to get on your schedule to explore how I might meet Benchmark's HR requirements?

Sincerely,

Jud Jackson

Encl.: Résumé

146

Human Resources Generalist. *Don Orlando, Montgomery, Alabama*

This applicant had just earned his MBA with a concentration in human resources but never had a job title that included that term. The letter shows how his past experience is relevant to an HR position.

SUSAN BALDWIN

55 Buccaneer Court, Morristown, NJ 00000
Cell (555) 555-5555 · sbaldwin@xxx.com

Seeking a position as a...
HR/BENEFITS COORDINATOR

March 12, 20XX

Mr. John Gold
Human Resources Manager
Thomas Corporation
555 Main Street
Newark, NJ 00000

Dear Mr. Gold,

With a solid background in healthcare insurance plans, 401(k) administration, and pensions, I have the knowledge and abilities necessary for your open position of Benefits Administrator.

I began my career with several positions in payroll before transitioning into a benefits administration role where I thrived for five years. Unfortunately, I was part of a layoff and transitioned back into payroll and most recently, office administration. I am now at a point where I'm exploring new opportunities and would like to return to what I enjoyed the most: **benefits administration.** My résumé is attached for your review. Highlights of what I bring to the table include the following:

- **Conscientious, approachable professional** with demonstrated ability to improve employee communications by explaining benefit offerings and answering concerns about coverage and costs.
- **Trusted team player** recognized by both management and peers alike for the reliable accuracy found in my work, a consistent level of hard work, and unwavering dedication to the job.
- **Well-rounded background** across benefits, payroll, and general office administration complements my ability to resolve problems and find ways to streamline procedures.
- **Strong computer skills** and knowledge of many of the common software platforms in use today.

For these reasons and more, I am confident in my ability to make an immediate contribution to your company and would welcome an interview at your earliest convenience.

I will call your office next week to follow up.

Sincerely,

Susan Baldwin

Enclosure: Résumé

147

Benefits Administrator. *Laurie Berenson, Franklin Lakes, New Jersey*

The letter addressed a career change from healthcare back to human resources. The challenge was to explain why the applicant wanted to return to an earlier field in her career.

RACHEL SWATHMORE

HUMAN RESOURCES SENIOR EXECUTIVE

[Insert Date]

[Insert Contact Name]
[Insert Contact Title]
[Insert Company Name]
[Insert Contact Address]
[Insert Contact Address]

Dear [Insert Contact Name]:

Are you looking for an innovative and multidimensional senior manager who understands and leverages Human Resources strategy and operations management to meet corporate goals?

With more than 15 years of experience as a Human Resources executive with world-class entertainment and hospitality companies including STC Corporation, Trump World, and Wynn Entertainment, I have been directly involved in the formation of corporate vision and strategy, the management of rapid growth from acquisitions, and the direction of daily operations from a human capital perspective. Abilities that I bring to the table include the following:

Corporate leadership and change management impacting thousands of employees:
As the senior HR executive for STC Corporation / Gaming Division, I strategized and integrated distinctly different business cultures, instilling a "one company mentality" throughout the organization.

Identification of business challenges and development of action plans to address those challenges:
As senior HR executive at Trump World, I developed a winning HR strategy for an underperforming operating unit. I also assumed a new regional role to consolidate HR functions for multiple properties.

Provision of counsel and advice to senior corporate executives:
While at Trump World and Wynn Entertainment, I reported to the Chairman / CEO. My independent counsel and perceptions of people and issues were highly respected and carried weight in final evaluations.

Development and management of HR strategies on a global basis:
As Senior Vice President of Human Resources for STC Corporation, I managed HR systems / processes impacting thousands of employees on four continents. I am experienced in multicultural business practices including executive recruitment, management development, succession planning, compensation / benefits, and cultural integration.

Management of difficult business situations involving complex people issues:
As a senior manager, I have tackled many complex, high-value projects. At STC Corporation and Trump World, Inc., I managed the HR-related aspects of the company's dynamic growth through acquisitions where I produced organization-wide support for management's new vision.

[Insert Contact's Name], may we set up an exploratory meeting?

Sincerely,

Rachel Swathmore

---

25 Grove Avenue, Atlantic City, NJ 55555 | 000-000-0000 | E-mail: rachswath@aol.com

148

Human Resources Senior Executive. *Deb Dib, Medford, New York*

This letter template for an HR Senior Executive was ready to send to different addressees. The applicant just provided different information where indicated for each new contact.

Peter Hamilton

50 Chestnut St.
Needham, MA 05550

555-555-5555
phamilton@xyz.com

September 1, 20XX

Maria Constantine
Vice President of Finance
Massachusetts Medical Manufacturing
189 Lexington Ave.
Waltham, MA 02454

Dear Ms. Constantine:

Your description of the Director of Human Resources position at Massachusetts Medical Manufacturing closely matches my background, and I am enthusiastically submitting my resume for your review.

With extensive experience in human resources management, I have the vision and the solid track record of results that can help Massachusetts Medical Manufacturing as it prepares to acquire California Medical Instruments and develop new lines of medical products. In my current role as Director of Human Resources at Boston Medical Devices, I provide the full spectrum of human resources support for our worldwide patient monitoring division. After an acquisition of a German company in 20XX, my mission—which I accomplished—was to blend the cultures, operations, and procedures smoothly to enable our division to meet production deadlines and achieve sales goals.

Specific areas of accomplishment include the following:

> **Acquisitions:** Provided leadership in two acquisitions to develop procedures that identified and implemented best practices, reduced redundancies, and achieved several million dollars in cost savings.
> **Strategic Planning:** Consulted with senior management to design and implement programs and policies concerning recruitment, employee development, diversity, regulatory compliance, conflict resolution, and performance management.
> **Organizational Development:** Integrated teams from Purchasing, Manufacturing, and Engineering to change corporate culture and define common vision of success, resulting in on-time product delivery.

I am confident my background and experience can benefit Massachusetts Medical Manufacturing, and I would like to talk with you to learn more about the company and to explore how I can contribute to its future success. I will contact you next week to set a time to do so. I look forward to meeting with you.

Thank you for your consideration.

Sincerely,

Peter Hamilton

Enclosure

149

Director of Human Resources. *Wendy Gelberg, Needham, Massachusetts*

In researching a prospective company, the applicant learned that it was acquiring another company. The writer highlighted the applicant's experience that was relevant to an acquisition.

KARL SMITH

4/23 Cuttingway Street
Rocklin, CA 95677
(407) 555-6666 (Cell)
smithkarl@hotmail.com

September 2, 20XX

Ms. Sarah Lancer
HR Director
Leading Technologies, Inc.
155 Crystal Road
Hilltop, NY 11787

Dear Ms. Lancer:

Re: HUMAN RESOURCE PROFESSIONAL

Building and sustaining a professional, committed, and top-performing staff to support the demands of a multinational corporation working within constantly changing and demanding environments requires a unique blend of operational planning/management expertise and decisive human resource leadership. Possessing these skills and more, I have managed diverse teams being solely responsible for staff ranging from 100 to 25,000 personnel, demanding expertise across all facets of leadership, training, communications, performance monitoring, policies, procedures, and change management in order to successfully achieve performance goals.

As a talented HR professional I offer strong qualifications and experience across all core generalist functions, organisational change, and productivity/performance advancements, combined with strong cross-cultural communication and interpersonal skills.

My enclosed resume highlights my professionalism, commitment, and proven competencies, to which I add the following achievements:

♦ **HR system and policies development:** Employed as subject-matter expert revolutionizing an existing lengthy and costly employment review process into a robust and transparent system that fast-tracked staff reviews. This initiative realized a **saving of $5.75M in the first year** of implementation and **increased savings by 47% to $8.5M in the second and subsequent years in salaries alone.**

♦ **Staff training and knowledge expansion:** Campaigned and amplified part-time staff's participation and completion of career development courses, expanding number of competent staff, thus increasing operational capability and staff suitability for national/international assignments.

♦ **Staff recruitment and retention:** Acknowledged for the development of innovative and proactive recruitment programs, currently exceeding all other divisions in their recruitment campaigns to secure high-quality staff despite candidate shortages across the board. Successfully increased staff retention and minimized personnel changeover.

♦ **Leadership and team building:** Headed all staffing functions involving 350 full- and part-time staff achieving all corporate performance objectives despite lack of staffing resources, which were overcome by empowering junior managers and adopting supportive leadership approach to successfully lift team morale and collaboration.

I thank you for your consideration and welcome the opportunity to discuss my application in further detail and how I may be able to contribute to the ongoing success of your company. I will contact you by September 15 to set a time when we can talk further.

Sincerely,

Karl Smith

150

Human Resources Professional. *Annemarie Cross, Hallam, Victoria, Australia*

This applicant was transitioning from the military and had few achievements in his first resume and cover letter. The writer pinpointed many achievements and showed areas of competence.

CARRIE HINKSON

Cell: (555) 555-5555 ■ carriehinkson@xx.com ■ http://www.linkedin.com/xx/xxxxx

Contributing to bottom-line objectives through Strategic Performance Management and Enhanced Efficiency

March 4, 20xx

Ms. Lisa Felton
AT&T
555 Peachtree Street, NW
Atlanta, GA 00000

Dear Ms. Felton:

Looking for a **Senior Global Talent Management Director** who can lead the organization's global talent management and leadership development initiatives, align strategies with corporate goals, and commit to your organization's success?

I offer your leadership team:

- 15-plus years of global HR leadership experience at the executive/director consultancy level.
- Track record of delivering mission-critical HR projects in challenging environments.
- Reputation for consistently increasing revenue and achieving considerable cost savings.
- Demonstrated record of proactive leadership, sound decision making, and effective change agent/leader management that shines with superior achievements.

My key strength is initiating and implementing changes through innovative talent management, leadership development, process improvements, and labor resources optimization. This starts with analyzing a company's current operations and processes, building rapport with directors, VPs, C-level executives, and employees, and forging strategic alliances that will benefit the company.

You can be confident that I will be able to make an immediate difference to your team. I will call you March 9 to schedule a meeting at your convenience. Please feel free to contact me at **(555) 555-5555** if you would like to speak with me sooner.

I am looking forward to meeting with you to discuss how I can help you achieve your most pressing organizational development goals. Thank you for your time and consideration.

Sincerely,

Carrie Hinkson

Enclosure

151

Senior Global Talent Management Director. *Leeza Byers, Marietta, Georgia*

The format of this letter showcases the scope of this applicant's skills across several major disciplines in the HR arena, with an emphasis on her organizational development achievements. See Resume 9 in Part 3.

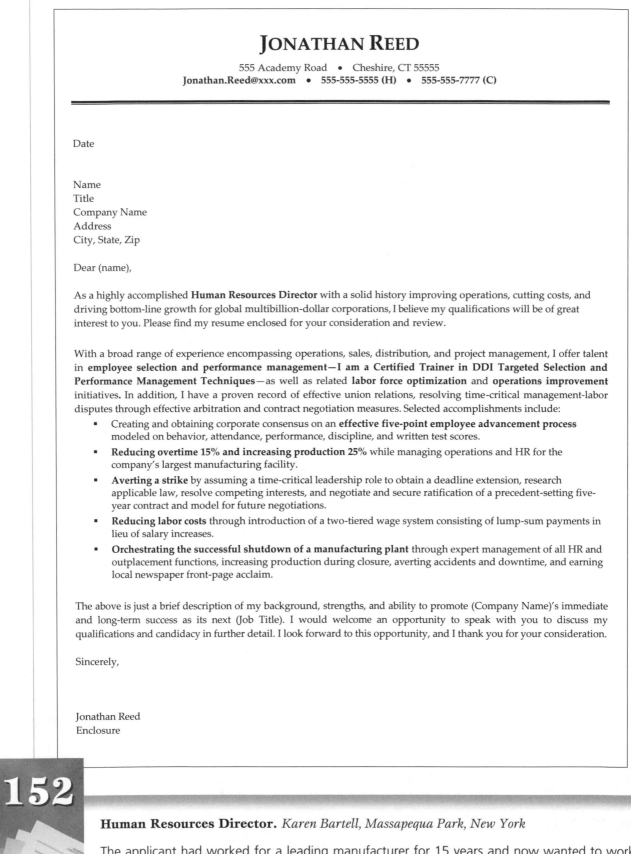

JONATHAN REED

555 Academy Road • Cheshire, CT 55555
Jonathan.Reed@xxx.com • 555-555-5555 (H) • 555-555-7777 (C)

Date

Name
Title
Company Name
Address
City, State, Zip

Dear (name),

As a highly accomplished **Human Resources Director** with a solid history improving operations, cutting costs, and driving bottom-line growth for global multibillion-dollar corporations, I believe my qualifications will be of great interest to you. Please find my resume enclosed for your consideration and review.

With a broad range of experience encompassing operations, sales, distribution, and project management, I offer talent in **employee selection and performance management—I am a Certified Trainer in DDI Targeted Selection and Performance Management Techniques**—as well as related **labor force optimization** and **operations improvement** initiatives. In addition, I have a proven record of effective union relations, resolving time-critical management-labor disputes through effective arbitration and contract negotiation measures. Selected accomplishments include:

- Creating and obtaining corporate consensus on an **effective five-point employee advancement process** modeled on behavior, attendance, performance, discipline, and written test scores.
- **Reducing overtime 15% and increasing production 25%** while managing operations and HR for the company's largest manufacturing facility.
- **Averting a strike** by assuming a time-critical leadership role to obtain a deadline extension, research applicable law, resolve competing interests, and negotiate and secure ratification of a precedent-setting five-year contract and model for future negotiations.
- **Reducing labor costs** through introduction of a two-tiered wage system consisting of lump-sum payments in lieu of salary increases.
- **Orchestrating the successful shutdown of a manufacturing plant** through expert management of all HR and outplacement functions, increasing production during closure, averting accidents and downtime, and earning local newspaper front-page acclaim.

The above is just a brief description of my background, strengths, and ability to promote (Company Name)'s immediate and long-term success as its next (Job Title). I would welcome an opportunity to speak with you to discuss my qualifications and candidacy in further detail. I look forward to this opportunity, and I thank you for your consideration.

Sincerely,

Jonathan Reed
Enclosure

152

Human Resources Director. *Karen Bartell, Massapequa Park, New York*

The applicant had worked for a leading manufacturer for 15 years and now wanted to work in Human Resources. The letter emphasizes his diverse experience as well as multiple HR skills.

DONNA WEICHSEL

000 Heber Avenue
Park City, UT 00000
Cell Phone: 000.000.0000
Email: donna@xx.com

December 30, 20XX

Mr. Joe Smith
Bik Bok Corporation
000 Dalecot Drive
Trumbull, UT 00000

Dear Mr. Smith:

My interest in exploring a new challenge as Global Human Resources Director with Bik Bok Corporation has motivated my writing to you. The enclosed resume briefly describes my expertise in international human resources, expatriate policy design, HRIS administration, and talent management for global business operations. In today's business world, an essential ingredient for success is a combination of a proactive management style with a proven ability to achieve goals and objectives. I am confident that my solid reputation as a fair, innovative, and dynamic leader would make a positive and immediate contribution to your organization.

Selected achievements include:

- Demonstrated longevity and subsequent promotions with 16 years of experience in the oilfield services industry. Expert at analyzing employment infrastructures and processes, identifying areas of weakness, and creating programs that position the company for industry leadership, while maximizing protection against risk/litigation.
- Counseled, trained, and mentored international HR associates with respect to policy administration and mobilization procedures in more than 50 countries.
- Demonstrated success in revitalizing HR infrastructures, as well as creating HR functions from ground level due to mergers, acquisitions, and divestitures. Excel at recruiting and identifying talent and determining the most effective development plans to allow executives to perform at their highest potential.
- Played an integral role in reengineering the benefits structure following XYZ Corporation's acquisition of ABC Industries. Migrated all post-merger employees to the new parent's benefits, and transitioned expatriates and commuters into the Company's global HRIS.

I am adept at handling difficult situations and consider adversity an opportunity—not a challenge. I would very much like to speak with you directly to discuss your organization and how our association could be mutually beneficial. I can be reached at the above phone number, by email, or on LinkedIn with the QR code above.

Thank you in advance for your time and consideration.

Sincerely,

Donna Weichsel

Attachment

153

Global Human Resources Director. *Donna Allen, Heber City, Utah*

This applicant had a lengthy career history. To overcome the perception that older candidates are not technologically up-to-date, the writer used a QR code to connect with the applicant's LinkedIn profile.

Sami Sosa
5941 Glendower Lane
Plano, TX 75093
Res: (555) 555-5555
Cell: (555) 000-0000
s.sosa@iee.org

[Date]

[Name]
[Company]
[Address]

Dear Hiring Executive:

I am exploring leadership opportunities with your company. With a strong background in the launch of software applications and services such as Intelligent Networks, as well as operational support systems in North and South America, Europe, Asia, Africa and the Middle East, I maintain excellent customer relationships and deliver on commitments. As a hands-on team builder with solid management, operation and product development skills, I am certain I could make a valuable contribution to your goals. Areas of expertise and transferable skills include

P&L Responsibility	Strategic Planning	Problem Analysis & Resolution
Budget Planning & Forecasting	Project Management	Team Leadership
Product Management	Product Development	Business Development
Training & Development	Network Applications	Systems Integration
Technology Management		

Throughout my career I have

→ Combined in-depth technical knowledge with operational business knowledge.
→ Managed P&Ls of more than $400 million and staff of 1,500 throughout the world.
→ Developed an exceptional ability to build strong, long-term customer relationships.

My peers can confirm that I thrive in an atmosphere of challenge. An in-depth knowledge of all phases of business activity, along with specialized abilities that set my performance apart, enables me to offer a truly unique talent. I'm confident I can bring to the table a package of skills, experience and abilities that will provide you with an invaluable resource.

I will follow up with you in a few days to answer any questions you may have. In the meantime, you may reach me at (555) 555-5555 home, (555) 000-0000 cell or through email at s.sosa@iee.org. I look forward to our conversation and thank you for your time and consideration.

Sincerely,

Sami Sosa

Enclosure

154

Information Systems/Technology Position. *Steven Provenzano, Streamwood, Illinois*

The opening paragraph is impressive because of its global connections. The three-column list of areas of expertise and transferable skills is useful because it can be modified for each targeted employer.

ROBERT J. LITTLEFIELD

0000 Indiana Avenue ◆ St. Paul, MN 00000 ◆ (000) 000-0000 ◆ name@aol.com

January 30, 20XX

Mr. Ted Morrison, IT Director
ABC Computers
3434 Smith Street
St. Paul, MN 00000

Dear Mr. Morrison:

I read your advertisement for a Software Developer with considerable interest, as my background and skills meet your requirements for this position. Therefore, please accept my resume for your review and allow me to explain briefly the positive qualities I can bring to your company.

Because my resume contains the specifics regarding my BBA degree, educational awards, and technical competencies in areas such as object-oriented programming, I will not need to go into detail here about these particular items. Instead, I'd like to point out a few of my qualities not covered on the resume that I would contribute to help your organization meet its development project objectives:

- **Highly focused work ethic**—I maintain a strong focus on "getting the job done right" in a field where the back-and-forth nature of the project cycle can lead to getting sidetracked and committing errors.
- **Ability to modify communications**—I am skilled in altering my communications to gain understanding from end users with minimal IT knowledge and team members with limited English skills.
- **Enthusiastic attitude**—I truly enjoy software engineering and the challenges inherent in an ever-changing, leading-edge field. To this end, I always enjoy learning about emerging industry trends.

Companies today need more than "technologists" to ensure the success of high-priority goals; they need individuals who can also master the teamwork, the communications, and the relationship-building side of projects. I am the type of person who would bring this balance of technical and nontechnical skills to help your firm achieve success.

I am available immediately for a personal interview and offer you competence, dedication, and a strong work ethic. Thank you for your time and consideration, and I look forward to the opportunity to meet with you. I will call you to set an appointment.

Sincerely,

Robert J. Littlefield

Enclosure

155

Software Developer. *Daniel J. Dorotik, Jr., Lubbock, Texas*

A resume typically presents details not found in a cover letter. This cover letter is different in indicating qualities not covered in the resume. Bullets and boldfacing call attention to these qualities.

L e o n a r d   C u r t i s

123 Circle River Drive · Littleton, CO 00000
555.555.5555 · Lencurt@msno.com

January 21, 20XX

John Jones
Vice President, Software Development
Axis Technologies
Table Mesa Drive
Boulder, CO 00000

Re: Position 1234, Software Development Manager

Dear Mr. Jones:

I am passionate about developing products that provide real-world solutions and have an impact on customers' business. Understanding the challenges our customers face, combined with practical implementations of product concepts and technologies, is key to successfully designing and delivering value-rich, profitable products.

I noted with great interest your advertisement in the *Denver Post* for a Software Development Manager. My technical management expertise, leadership skills, and extensive experience in VC++ are an excellent fit with your position.

My strengths are in creatively applying or modifying industry products to job requirements and incorporating new technologies quickly and proficiently. My track record as outlined in the enclosed resume demonstrates that I can

- Manage programs from initial concept through deployment at customer sites.
- Supervise/mentor cross-functional teams as well as software and hardware engineering teams.
- Serve marketing with my technical expertise, influencing product development, client presentations, and contract negotiations.

I admire the corporate culture and core beliefs that Axis Technologies exemplifies. I am eager to apply my knowledge and expertise, and I welcome the opportunity to explore my potential contributions with you.

Thank you for your consideration; I look forward to speaking with you soon.

Sincerely,

Leonard Curtis

Enclosure

156

Software Development Manager. *Roberta F. Gamza, Louisville, Colorado*

The person was applying to a company known for its friendly and laid-back corporate culture and wanted to refer to the company's culture in the letter. Short paragraphs help to make it easy to read.

Bruce Barnes
000 Ichabod Crane Lane
Montgomery, New Jersey 08502
000-000-0000
E-mail: Bruce_Barnes45@email.com

Date

Name
Company
Address
City, State ZIP

Dear Sir/Madam:

As a senior **Operations and Systems Professional,** I understand that success depends on the ability to merge the strategic with the practical, to understand needs and expectations in the corporate environment, and to communicate those needs to appropriate managers. I believe that my background and accomplishments reflect a commitment and an ability to find solutions to these challenges.

My career includes 15 years with Merrill Lynch, four of those years as First Vice President of Fund Operations, Systems, and Infrastructure. More recently, I served as President of GovXcel, a specialty software firm; and as Chief Information Officer / Senior Vice President of VerticalNet, an Internet company that acquired and maintained 59 virtual scientific and engineering communities. In all positions, I was responsible for streamlining their operations.

One of my greatest strengths is hiring and developing motivated, long-term employees and building strategic teams. I have developed contacts in several industries, enabling me to work with people on all levels. Among the people I have managed are Ph.D. scientists and engineers, systems and technical professionals, and accounting personnel.

Many of my assignments have been with start-up operations. I approach my work with a strong sense of urgency, working well under pressure and change. I am a forward thinker and a team player who has a strong commitment to my people and the organizations I work for.

Thank you for your consideration. I look forward to meeting with you personally so that we may discuss how I can make a positive contribution to your corporation. I will call next week to inquire about a convenient time to meet.

Sincerely yours,

Bruce Barnes

Enclosure

157

Operations and Systems Professional. *Beverly and Mitchell I. Baskin, Marlboro, New Jersey*

In five short paragraphs, the applicant indicates his views on success, the shape of his 15-year career, his people skills, his worker traits, and his anticipation of a positive interview with the reader.

STEVE BRODY

999 Royal Augusta Road, #234   stevebrody@email.com   Home: 555.222.8888
Pinehurst, Ontario A1A 1A1   Cell: 444.777.5555

February 2, 20XX

Ronald Kleinberg
Senior VP, Technology Management
IBC Technology
600 Century Place
Pinehurst, Ontario
B2C 3D4

Dear Mr. Kleinberg,

Stan Morrisey of Suntech and Ellis Cantasi of Levinson Solutions both suggested that I contact you, as they believe that my skills, expertise, and leadership in technology development are a perfect match for IBC. Having reviewed your Web site, I am impressed with your successes and aggressive plans for the future and would like to draw your attention to the value I can offer.

Put simply, my expertise lies in delivering high-performance, enterprise-class technology solutions, and throughout my career, I have leveraged the following skills and experience to exceed expectations in service bureau, government, and national retail environments:

> - More than 15 years of experience in leading and developing enterprise data centres, voice and data communications, and information-storage technologies
> - Shrewd business skills with a solid grasp of the "business" of technology
> - Full-cycle project management, including strategic planning, design, implementation, and maintenance
> - Superior leadership capabilities with outstanding people skills and a customer-centric focus

Results have been consistent and significant, and include the following:

> - **Recently negotiated $12 million annual savings** in strategic print-sourcing initiative
> - Spearheaded consolidation of two corporate print shops, realizing an **annual savings of $600,000**
> - **Under-cost critical UNIX and data warehousing acquisition** project by $2.5 million
> - Introduced and supported new **debit and POS technologies across 8,000 retail registers nationally**

I invite you to review the attached resume, which further outlines the value I can offer your technology team, and would welcome the opportunity to discuss how I could contribute to IBC's future growth and success. If you are interested in a dedicated professional with a reputation for generating real results, then I believe we would have much to discuss.

I thank you for your time and look forward to the opportunity to meet in person. I will contact you in the near future to set a time for an interview.

Sincerely,

Steve Brody

Encl.

158

Technology Development Position. *Ross Macpherson, Whitby, Ontario, Canada*

The letter first refers to some mutual acquaintances and then indicates the applicant's expertise and achievements. The company had no opening, but he got an interview to discuss another position.

BRAD LAWRENCE

776 Ellington Drive
San Diego, CA 55555

555.555.5555

E-mail: lawrence@comcast.net

June 10, 20XX

[Name]
[Title]
[Employer]
[Address]
[City, State ZIP]

Dear Mr. or Ms. _____:

Providing strategic planning, design innovation, and cost-effective technology solutions that improve performance and achieve business objectives are among the qualifications that I would bring to your company as Information Systems Manager.

As a business-focused technology management professional with more than 10 years of progressive experience in rapidly growing environments including the pharmaceutical industry, I have successfully

- Built and directed the IT function from start-up, forging strong relationships with business units and leading large-scale projects such as SAP ERP implementation at 2 sites—on schedule and well under budget.

- Pioneered the design and leveraged existing technology and knowledge base with internal resources to implement Infor10 ERP system that enabled company to retain a $40 million account and provide the foundation for rapid implementation methodology while gaining a competitive market advantage.

- Rescued a failed e-commerce project, resulting in restored customer confidence and retention of a $350-million-a-year account. Solution is now utilized as an enterprise standard to provide cost-effective Web access for all customers.

My success thus far results from an ability to see the "big picture" and deliver the greatest value out of IT solutions quickly. As a result of my unique accomplishments with SAP and Oracle software, I was invited to deliver customer-success-story presentations for both organizations.

Although secure in my present position, I am confidentially exploring new challenges in information systems management. May we meet to discuss the value I would add to your company's IT organization? I will call to set a mutually convenient time.

Sincerely,

Brad Lawrence

Enc.

159

Information Systems Manager. *Louise Garver, Broad Brook, Connecticut*

The individual wanted to transition from a manufacturing environment to a pharmaceutical company. The writer mentioned pharmaceutical industry experience and relevant projects.

MARY LAWSON, 84 Swan Lane, Blaine, MN 55555
(555) 555-5555   Email: mllaw@network.com

February 5, 2013

Mr. Charles Phillip
Gantry Communications
303 Mountain Pass
Denver, CO 55555

INFORMATION TECHNOLOGY IN EDUCATIONAL AND NONPROFIT SECTORS
MARKETING ▶ ANALYSIS ▶ DATA ▶ APPLICATIONS

Dear Mr. Phillip:

Promoted 11 times in 21 years by Nelson International Technologies, I have an extensive background in information systems and project-based work. Since leaving traditional employment in 2008, I've been challenged by entrepreneurial ventures, career exploration, and civic work.

Enclosed is a resume detailing my strengths and abilities, with particular emphasis on marketing and technical skills. Other relevant areas of knowledge and expertise include the following:

- ▶ Leadership, consulting, and relationship building
- ▶ Strategic analysis and creativity
- ▶ Speech writing, presentations, instruction, and training
- ▶ Data synthesis and research
- ▶ Applications for academic learning approaches
- ▶ Marketing programs and client relations

Achievements, awards, and recognition attest to my ability to think "out of the box," apply theory, test concepts, and contribute to breakthrough ideas. Leading edge ... change-oriented technology ... resourceful ... self-motivated—these are qualities describing my style and approach to whatever I do.

An interview would provide the opportunity to exchange information, address issues, answer questions, and determine applicant suitability. I am most interested in discussing your company's goals and needs and will call within the next week to schedule a time to meet. I look forward to speaking with you.

Sincerely,

Mary Lawson

Enclosure

160

Information Technology Position. *Beverley Drake, Hot Springs Village, Arkansas*

A banner between the reader's address and the salutation indicates the applicant's target fields and areas of expertise. After the second paragraph, bullets point to additional areas of knowledge and expertise.

Kate Dobson
0000 Autumnbrook Drive ▪ Atlanta, GA 00000 ▪ (000) 000-0000 ▪ name@aol.com

January 30, 20XX

Human Resources Department
ABC Solutions
3434 Pinetree Avenue
Atlanta, GA 00000

RE: Position as Systems Administrator

Dear Staffing Representative:

It was with great interest that I noted your advertisement for the position of Systems Administrator. I believe I am the ideal candidate for your consideration, with qualifications correlated to your requirements. Thus, please allow me to explain briefly how I might contribute to your firm's operational performance.

Throughout my career, my expertise has been in providing systems integration solutions for multimillion-dollar clients. As a Senior Systems Integrator for IBM, I have instituted technology assimilations and changes for our clients that produced cost savings and positioned them for success in their respective markets. I would now like to use my systems management and integration skills to help your company maintain a strong customer base and improve productivity.

Additionally, my background in help desk administration, project management, and IT applications could benefit your firm in specific need areas. I enjoy being a diverse "team player" within an organization and contributing to my employer's success in various capacities.

To provide you with details concerning my qualifications and accomplishments, my resume is enclosed. I will contact you next week to follow up on this letter of inquiry; perhaps we could arrange a meeting to discuss our mutual interests.

Thank you for your time and consideration. Please do not hesitate to contact me if I can answer any questions.

Sincerely,

Kate Dobson

Enclosure

161

Systems Administrator. *Daniel J. Dorotik, Jr., Lubbock, Texas*

This letter is a response to an ad. Short paragraphs mention in turn the applicant's qualifications; areas of expertise and skills; background and worker traits; and resume, providing details.

Victoria A. Future

0000 Woolery Lane, Dayton, OH 45415
Phone: (555) 555-5555 | E-mail: vfuture@jitaweb.com

Date

Contact
Company
Address
City, State ZIP

Re: Network Administrator position

Dear Mr(s). _____:

In desktop support and as a network administrator, I handled a number of technical, maintenance, and support issues for the corporate and branch computers at S³ Business Techs. I configured and installed hardware, software, and peripherals—and diagnosed and troubleshot complications pertaining to the local area network (LAN). I worked with virus-protection software and utility programs, ensuring that company policies and procedures were followed and that each new feature addressed technological advancements.

Stepping up to the plate, you'll discover that I've applied key performance by installing the LAN system at S³ Business Techs in only 7 months, saving $1.5 million in fines by integrating an EDI system and Ordernet mailboxes. I saved up to $256,000 the first year by implementing a self-help process for end users that eliminated the need for costly technical support on small problems.

Skills recap includes the following:

- Managed LAN network life cycles on a Windows platform, from software and hardware applications to equipment layout and technical support

- Have in-depth knowledge of LAN maintenance and troubleshooting, including desktop support, configuration, and workstation issues, from initial problem analysis to final end resolution

- Integrate amongst technical support, ensuring that multiple tasks and parallel deadlines are met and in line with technological advancements and company growth

Contact me at (555) 555-5555 should you require clarification of my skills or would like to schedule a meeting time for us to discuss this position.

Sincerely,

Victoria A. Future

Attachment

162

Network Administrator. *Teena Rose, Springfield, Ohio*

This direct letter indicates immediately the applicant's experience and quantified accomplishments. Bullets point to network experience, network knowledge, and technical-support expertise.

James Madison, CCNA, MCSE

00000 Autumnwind Drive • Houston, TX 00000 • (000) 000-0000 • name@ev1.net

January 24, 20XX

ABC Systems
2323 Smith Avenue
Houston, TX 00000

RE: Senior WAN Engineer position, ID #6970

Dear Hiring Authority:

It was with great interest that I read about your opening for a Senior WAN Engineer, as my background and abilities meet your requirements for this position. Please allow me to explain briefly what I can offer your organization.

With several years of experience as a Network Engineer, Manager, and Administrator, I have demonstrated the ability to fulfill business goals through network solutions, maintain excellent client relationships, and make bold decisions to achieve corporate and client objectives on critical projects. The following accomplishments illustrate these skills:

- As a Network Engineer and Director of Engineering Services with Cisprint, I completed a complex VPN Installation project involving 20 bank locations within an aggressive one-week deadline.
- As a Network Engineer and Special Projects Manager with IED Communications, I received commendations for my work on implementing Cisco VPN networks using ASA and VPN Routers.
- As a Network Administrator for Top Networks, I built loyal client relationships through constructing, installing, and configuring desktops, workstations, servers, and all network-essential equipment.

I have found that the most effective skills for a network engineering position lie in an understanding of both the technological and business goals within an organization. What I would bring to ABC Systems is a combination of technical expertise and business intelligence to help fulfill your company's ongoing and future objectives.

I have enclosed my resume to provide additional details regarding my background and qualifications, and I welcome the opportunity to interview for this position.

Thank you for your time and consideration.

Sincerely,

James Madison

Enclosure

163

Senior WAN Engineer. *Daniel J. Dorotik, Jr., Lubbock, Texas*

This well-organized letter displays ABC, A+B+C thematic structure. Three roles indicated in the second paragraph (Network Engineer, Manager, and Administrator) appear again as bulleted items.

AMANDA LEE JANSEN   555 Olde Floppy Drive • Suite 000 • Montréal H5H 5H5

January 5, 20XX

Mr. Jean-François Hébert
Director, Web Development
Technova Corporation
555 Compu Techway
Silicon Valley North
Ottawa, Ontario K0K 0K0

Dear Mr. Hébert:

I want to be your next **Software Developer/Programmer,** a position I saw advertised on your "Job Opportunities" Web page. As the attached resume indicates, I am presently working as a *Senior Java Programmer Analyst* with Best Bullion Bank. I am involved in a $6 million project, migrating web applications from Netdynamics to Websphere. My resume details a wide range of programming and related projects in which I have participated during the last 15 years.

Throughout my career, I have

- Undertaken projects critical to the success of my employers and their clients.
- Adopted a team-oriented approach toward problem solving.
- Proactively shared relevant knowledge and findings with fellow developers, who frequently approached me for guidance.
- Developed clean code that has been virtually bug-free.
- Demonstrated passion for learning new technologies and finding better ways to use old ones.

Having written software for users extensively, I now wish to focus on scripting tools for other developers. I have done what these developers do, and I know what they need. I have the knowledge and experience to devise methods whereby they will be able to do their job faster and better. In particular, I like working with Java. I especially like the fact that the source code is open.

Since entering the IT field, I have taken an interest in examining source codes for software at all levels, including operating systems (e.g., Linux) and development tools (e.g., JDK). Writing for an O/S without examining source code is analogous to completing a jigsaw puzzle, start to finish, with one's eyes closed.

Another analogy involves a comparison between recent editions of MS Word and WordPerfect. Although Word now makes it easier to view codes than did prior versions, it lacks the advantage that WordPerfect has in permitting a high degree of user control. In Word, you never know exactly which codes are embedded in your document or where they are. In WordPerfect, not only do you know their syntax, but you can delete and replace them at will, making for a cleaner, tighter document. Just as serious word processors prefer WordPerfect, serious developers check source codes for components of the environments in which they work.

My qualifications and experience are documented in the attached resume. I am confident that, on reviewing it, you will agree I have the potential to become a worthy member of your team. I will call to set a convenient time to meet, so that we could discuss how I might best serve Technova Corporation.

Sincerely yours,

Amanda Lee Jansen

164

Software Developer/Programmer. *Howard Earle Halpern, Toronto, Ontario, Canada*

The applicant knew exactly what she wanted and indicated her technical preferences and biases, screening out incompatible employers. This letter resulted in two successive contracts.

TIMOTHY L. MICHAELS

000 King Street • Fairport, New York 14450 • 555-555-5555 • timm2@localnet.net

January 25, 20XX

Mr. I. M. Important, CIO
Important Industries, Inc.
1234 Industrial Parkway
Rochester, New York 14699

Dear Mr. Important:

Capitalizing on a 12-year career with Eastman Kodak Company that has encompassed Systems Administration, IT Project Management, and Business Analysis experiences, I am seeking to use my broad-based IT knowledge in a challenging position with your firm. In pursuit of that goal, I have enclosed for your review a resume that outlines my professional background.

Some of the key capabilities that I can bring to a position with your firm include the following:

- **Supporting precision manufacturing operations, including clean room environments. During the start-up and launch of Kodak's thin film manufacturing facility, I was accountable for setting up and maintaining process control, inventory management, and resource planning applications that contributed to the efficient and profitable operation of that plant.**

- **Managing database tools that allow sales and marketing teams to capture customer information, track market trends, and plan sales/marketing strategies. In my current assignment, I maintain applications that are utilized by 100 managers in the field, plus close to 100 marketing and headquarters staff, to manage relationships with a customer base exceeding one million total accounts.**

- **Implementing and maintaining HR applications and e-mail utilities to serve up to 500 end users. As a Senior Systems Analyst with the team that launched the Office Imaging Group, I had responsibilities in these areas, including controlling user access and establishing accounts.**

- **Serving in Business Analyst roles that have included using innovative IT solutions to streamline and optimize various materials-forecasting functions.**

I believe that the knowledge and expertise developed over the course of my career can be a valuable asset to a smaller firm on the rise. I would enjoy meeting with you to explore how I can best serve your current and future needs, and I encourage you to contact me to arrange an initial interview.

Thank you for your time and consideration. I will call you soon to explore the possibility of an interview.

Sincerely,

Timothy L. Michaels

Enclosure

165

IT Project Manager/Systems Administrator. *Arnold G. Boldt, Rochester, New York*

To avoid a bland list of technical proficiencies, the writer presented this applicant in the context of his project-management and customer-relation skills. Bullets and boldfacing make these skills stand out.

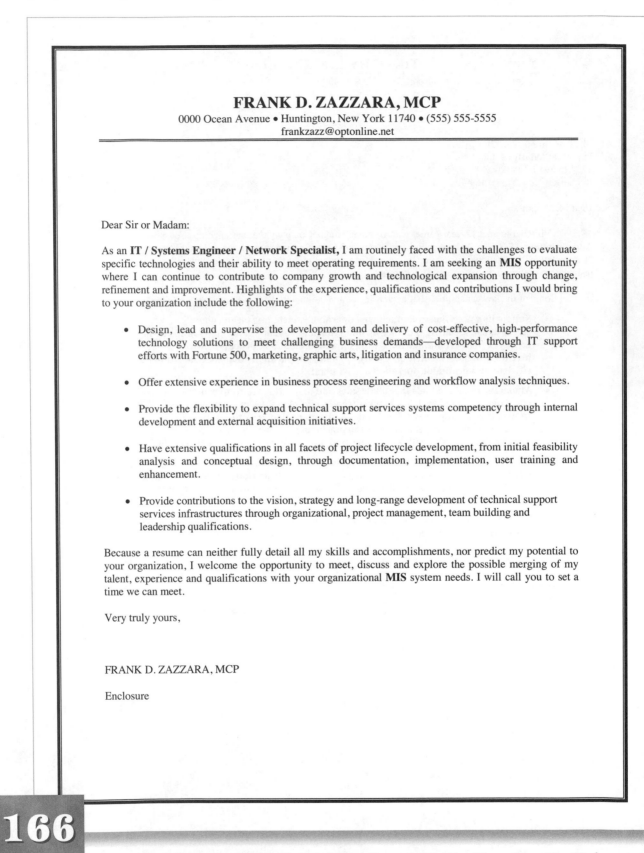

FRANK D. ZAZZARA, MCP

0000 Ocean Avenue • Huntington, New York 11740 • (555) 555-5555
frankzazz@optonline.net

Dear Sir or Madam:

As an **IT / Systems Engineer / Network Specialist,** I am routinely faced with the challenges to evaluate specific technologies and their ability to meet operating requirements. I am seeking an **MIS** opportunity where I can continue to contribute to company growth and technological expansion through change, refinement and improvement. Highlights of the experience, qualifications and contributions I would bring to your organization include the following:

- Design, lead and supervise the development and delivery of cost-effective, high-performance technology solutions to meet challenging business demands—developed through IT support efforts with Fortune 500, marketing, graphic arts, litigation and insurance companies.

- Offer extensive experience in business process reengineering and workflow analysis techniques.

- Provide the flexibility to expand technical support services systems competency through internal development and external acquisition initiatives.

- Have extensive qualifications in all facets of project lifecycle development, from initial feasibility analysis and conceptual design, through documentation, implementation, user training and enhancement.

- Provide contributions to the vision, strategy and long-range development of technical support services infrastructures through organizational, project management, team building and leadership qualifications.

Because a resume can neither fully detail all my skills and accomplishments, nor predict my potential to your organization, I welcome the opportunity to meet, discuss and explore the possible merging of my talent, experience and qualifications with your organizational **MIS** system needs. I will call you to set a time we can meet.

Very truly yours,

FRANK D. ZAZZARA, MCP

Enclosure

166

IT Systems Engineer/Network Specialist. *Donna M. Farrise, Hauppauge, New York*

Boldfacing and bullets help to focus this applicant's multifaceted letter. The letter relies especially on the bulleted items to highlight the applicant's experience, qualifications, and possible contributions.

Lydia Cunningham
4444 Alapaha Drive
Golden, Maryland 00000
[000] 555-5555 — [000] 555-6666 (Mobile) — lcunningham4012@propser.net

Wednesday, 07 March 20XX

Drayton Nabers
Director of Finance
c/o State of Maryland Personnel Department
Post Office Box 00000
Annapolis, Maryland 00000-0000

Dear Mr. Nabers:

As soon as I saw your announcement for Chief Information Officer, I made writing this application my first priority. Because my natural inclination is to anticipate and try to fill needs, I thought you deserved a good deal more than the standard application and resume.

I designed my resume in a new way. Gone are the usual "summary of qualifications" and sterile lists of responsibilities. In their places, starting right at the top, are eight capabilities I want to offer the Governor and the people of Maryland. Backing them up are 14 sample contributions made to organizations of all kinds—from large public-sector agencies to small businesses to nationally known IT leaders. Finally, I wanted you to have a detailed list of my technical skills. Nevertheless, there is important information no resume format or application form can transmit well.

I've already begun a personal, professional development program. I designed it to make me productive right from the start. I am studying the National Association of State Chief Information Officers' Transition Handbook, Governor's Transition Team IT Assessment Template, and the Chief Information Officer Transition Handbook. And I've begun to form professional relationships with CIOs in several states. They've given me invaluable insights into tough problems they are dealing with right now—problems that are similar to ones we face in Maryland today.

Normally, I would take the next logical step and ask for a little time on your schedule so that I could hear about your specific IT needs and goals in your own words. However, I am sensitive to the instructions that accompanied the announcement. If a personal meeting isn't possible now, I encourage you to test me for yourself in an interview soon.

Sincerely,

Lydia Cunningham

Enclosures:
1. Application for Examination
2. Resume
3. IT Capabilities the State of Maryland Can Use at Once
4. College-Level Course Work Applicable to CIO Performance

167

Chief Information Officer. *Don Orlando, Montgomery, Alabama*

The challenge was to find a way to get the hiring decision maker's attention. The letter shows that the applicant was already learning about state government and could be effective at once.

Robert P. Barnes, CBCP

Certified Business Continuity Professional

1434 Madison Boulevard
Orlando, FL 38917
Residence: 555-555-5555
Mobile: 000-000-0000
RobertPBarnes@earthlink.net

April 8, 20XX

Samuel Ryan, CIO
Global Financial Services, Inc.
495 Central Avenue
Orlando, FL 38917

Dear Mr. Ryan:

Development of a comprehensive, state-of-the-industry business-continuity program is critical to a company's ability to achieve its core mission. Employee safety, shareholder value, corporate reputation, revenues and profits, data integrity and IT systems—these are some of the corporate interests that an effective business-continuity program is designed to protect. My expertise is the ability to deliver, within a complex multinational organization, innovative business-continuity plans that are integrated with overall corporate strategy and aligned with corporate goals.

In my work as Business Recovery Manager at Morgan Summers Financial Services, I established just such a program. My groundbreaking thinking and writing promoted business-continuity planning as a strategic, business-driven process in which IT played a supporting role. My contributions helped ensure that the company would mitigate risk, survive potential disruptions and recover in a timely manner. Achievements included the following:

— Developed and executed business-continuity plans for an organization with $176 billion in assets under management, 40 business units, 800 employees and 19 different IT systems running 200 applications.

— Promoted my visionary concept of the role of business-continuity planning throughout the organization and achieved buy-in for plan initiatives from 40 business units (including six IT business units) and two disaster-recovery vendors.

— Implemented a multifaceted employee-awareness program to help ensure that employees knew how to implement plans in the event of a business disruption.

I came up through the ranks as an IT professional and earned both my M.B.A. degree and my Bachelor's degree in Business Computer Information Systems. As an experienced BCP manager who is a Certified Business Continuity Professional, I am well credentialed for assuming a leadership position in business-continuity planning.

Please contact me if you are interested in my demonstrated ability to help a company mitigate risk and protect critical assets. I look forward to an opportunity to speak with you in person about your business requirements and will call in two weeks. Thank you.

Sincerely,

Robert P. Barnes

Enclosure

168

Business Recovery Manager. *Jean Cummings, Concord, Massachusetts*

This cover letter is for a position in an increasingly important field: business continuity planning. Dashes serve as bullets to indicate the applicant's achievements with "heavy numbers."

Eric Gransome

555 Mountain Avenue ✧ River Edge, NJ 00000
Home (555) 555-5555 ✧ Cell (555) 555-5555
EGransome@xx.com

Senior Client Service Project Manager
Experience leading and integrating high-profile projects and initiatives involving new technologies

March 12, 20XX

Ms. Jane Turning
Director of Information Technology Recruiting
IT Partners
555 West Broadway
New York, NY 00000

Dear Ms. Turning,

I'd like to introduce myself as an effective IT Solutions and Project Manager candidate with strengths in new product adoption, clarifying business needs, project development, monitoring, and reporting. With recent high-profile project experience reporting up to C-level management, I have the expertise and knowledge necessary for a senior client service role with one of your clients.

My résumé details my accomplishments as a professional with more than 15 years of experience in data center environments. Highlights of my strengths include:

- **Technical Acumen.** With a hands-on mechanical and electrical aptitude, known as "Mr. Fix-it" no matter what the problem. Also skilled in aligning IT solutions with business strategy.
- **Strong Performer.** Consistently assigned largest projects in terms of number of servers affected and executive visibility out of a team of 12 project managers. Recently managed 6 concurrent projects involving more than 2,400 services and was selected to lead 2 new global initiatives.
- **Stabilizing Personality**. Open, patient, and tolerant of differences, with a natural quality of being nonjudgmental. Sensitive to the feelings of others, calming, and adept at reconciling factions.

Based on this record of success, I am confident in my ability to make an immediate and lasting contribution within one of your client companies and would welcome an interview at your earliest convenience. I look forward to speaking with you soon.

Sincerely,

Eric Gransome

Enclosure: Résumé

169

IT Solutions and Project Manager. *Laurie Berenson, Franklin Lakes, New Jersey*

This is a cold-call letter to an IT recruiting agency. The three bullets point to information that shows that the applicant has not only technical strengths, but also relationship skills.

Mark Resnik

55 North Mercer Ave. | Olmsted Falls, OH 55555 | 555.555.5555 | mresnik@xx.com

John Doe
President
ABC Company
555 Elm St.
Chicago, IL 55555

Dear Mr. Doe:

It is with great enthusiasm and interest that I am responding to your recent post for an Information Technology position within your organization. As a professional with an extensive history across IT leadership, customer service, business analysis, supplier performance assessment, and various other operational areas, I bring talents and expertise that would benefit your company.

My diverse background includes strengths in aligning technology and business objectives, designing and integrating IT systems, managing the quality of products, and directing projects and programs. Furthermore, I am an adaptable and mobile employee who is capable of building rapport and networks in new places with individuals from all backgrounds. Indeed, I am outstanding when it comes to speaking to groups. Matched with excellent skills in problem solving, organization, and leadership, I am confident that I can make an immediate and positive impact as a member of your team.

Highlights of my career include:

♦ Valued for keen business acumen and IT prowess, which has led to the success of multiple initiatives.

♦ Improved operational performance by spearheading technical projects that saved millions of dollars, slashed labor hours, and boosted communication and daily business efficiencies.

♦ Ensured customer satisfaction by evaluating and monitoring products for quality and compliance.

As you can see from my resume, these are but a few achievements from my accomplished career. My goal is to produce more results for your company. I would welcome the opportunity to speak with you in person to discuss how my qualifications could benefit. Thank you for your time and consideration. I look forward to hearing from you soon.

Sincerely,

Mark Resnik

Enclosure: resume

View and/or print my resume: www.resumexxx.com/xxxx

Mark sees opportunities for improvement not only in his area, but in other areas of business. This includes personal development, processes, and marketing.

Mark is quality conscious and expects his people to be customer oriented and more quality conscious.

His team is better engaged, and Mark's newer hires seem to be winners in many people's eyes.

RESULTS FROM 20XX PERFORMANCE EVALUATION

170

Information Technology Position. *Jane Roqueplot, West Middlesex, Pennsylvania*

This applicant had been downsized. The writer included a recent, positive performance evaluation to show that the applicant's current situation of unemployment was not a result of any poor performance.

MICHAEL PETERMAN

555 WILTON COURT ▪ NEW YORK, NY 00000

H: 555.555.5555 ▪ C: 555.555.5500
peterman.mike@xx.net

March 14, 20XX

<Contact Name>
<Title>
<Company Name>
<Address>
<City, ST Zip>

Dear <Contact Name>:

As an innovative and resourceful senior business and technology leader, I offer a successful track record in providing streamlined operations, introducing system efficiencies, and maximizing productivity. I bring to <<Company Name>> extensive strategic and creative thinking with strong problem-solving abilities, in addition to a history of actual contributions. I welcome new challenges in achieving a desired set of goals.

My background encompasses leadership success across multifunctional areas of expertise, including IT network and operations management, budget administration, business continuity, and systems integration. Throughout my career, I have earned a solid reputation for my ability to rapidly adapt to new technology, develop operational strategies, and manage high-profile projects from original concept through implementation. My strong ability to understand client needs and propose solutions that increase efficiency in a cost-effective manner will be an asset to your company.

I am convinced that my extensive industry experience, along with my Master of Science in Management and Information Systems, will allow me to achieve outstanding results. As an accomplished Regional Vice President of Information Technology for National Cable Corp., I was directly responsible for developing and implementing business plans and technology improvement initiatives, resulting in successful systems integrations and risk mitigation. Using a hard work ethic in pursuit of excellence, superior organizational and managerial skills, and leadership talents are the keys to providing your firm with exceptional results and high goal attainment.

Other highlights of my background that may be of interest to you include recommendations, such as the following:

- *"Michael clearly demonstrates a strong foundation of the technology required to build out solutions according to well-defined architectures, as well as leading-edge solutions. Michael has worked to build highly collaborative teams consisting of expert consultants and vendors, as well as leveraging internal subject matter experts and technical resources to work toward a single, consistent solution."* – John Smith, Chief Executive Officer, Regional Cable Company

The accompanying résumé will provide further details of my responsibilities, skills, and accomplishments. I would very much appreciate the chance for a personal interview to discuss your organization's needs. Should you have any questions, please do not hesitate to contact me. Thank you, in advance, for your time and consideration.

Sincerely,

Michael Peterman
Enclosure

171

Senior Business and Technology Executive. *Alexander Kofman, San Bruno, California*

This ad-response letter conveys the applicant's broad areas of expertise and focuses on his leadership abilities. The testimonial from an ex-boss shows clearly the applicant's abilities. See Resume 10 in Part 3.

James McAllister
555 Clark Road – Fitchburg, WI 55555

jimmymac@xxxx.net
555-555-5555

February 11, 20XX

Ms. Monica Templeton, Director
Human Resources
American Family Insurance
555 Madison Parkway
Madison, WI 55555

Dear Ms. Templeton:

During a conversation with Ronald Avery, an agent at Hometown Insurance, Rebecca Iglesia indicated there is an opening for an Assistant Adjuster at American Family Insurance based out of your corporate office. She suggested I submit my resume for consideration. It is attached for your review.

You'll see that I have a strong small-business background. I think it's interesting that I run my company following the same core values that American Family promotes. There is no doubt in my mind that's why my company has been in business 24 years—we respect our customers and are committed to providing excellent service based on integrity and fairness.

My qualifications go beyond a similar business philosophy. As part of my job, I routinely conduct inspections, identify scope of work, and generate estimates. I communicate with not only my customers, but also suppliers, contractors, and employees. Being able to manage competing priorities comes with the territory. I'm able to examine situations with a critical eye from multiple perspectives, a skill that would definitely benefit a claims adjuster.

Understanding that education is key in today's tough economic environment, I recently returned to college and will complete an associate degree in business next summer. That, coupled with my extensive experience, demonstrates I have the right combination of education and experience to excel in this position. I'm confident I can easily learn any industry-specific information that I might not be familiar with.

I hope you will consider my interest and contact me for an interview. I'd appreciate the opportunity to relate why my background is such a good fit with American Family Insurance and share my enthusiasm for joining the team of such a highly regarded organization. Thank you for your time and attention.

Sincerely,

James McAllister

Attachment

172

Assistant Adjuster. *Janet L. Beckstrom, Flint, Michigan*

The applicant had been a carpenter who owned his own business. Because of the downturn in the construction industry, he was seeking a position in the insurance industry. The letter names an acquaintance and refers to the company's core values.

DAVID L. LINDEMAN

55 South Albright Road ◆ Mercer, PA 55555 ◆ dlindeman@xxx.net ◆ 555.555.5555

Mike Kuzio
Abc Insurance Company
00 Cochran Road
Pittsburgh, PA 55555

Dear Mr. Kuzio:

When Jeff Huff, an area Abc Adjuster, notified me about positions becoming available through you, I was eager to send you my resume for review. With more than 18 years of experience in assessing, estimating, and repairing vehicle damage, I am energized and ready for an appropriate position, such as an Insurance Adjuster or Claims Manager. My resume is enclosed.

I have demonstrated that I am not only proficient in repairing vehicles but also in accurately assessing damage and negotiating estimates with insurance companies. I have the ability to identify the "real" extent of damage in relation to the claim, and to ensure all repairs are completed properly, thoroughly, and to the highest standards. For these reasons, managing people and appraising damage have become regular duties of my job.

In this capacity, I have learned to identify which members of my team are best suited to get each job done, and I then delegate work according to their strengths. I have also spent the last eight years managing teams of four to eight people in the concrete design and construction industry.

My superiors have recognized me as someone who can think innovatively and employ deductive reasoning to determine the cause of damage and the most efficient way to conduct repair work.

Key accomplishments to date:

- ✓ Earned 16 certifications from seven organizations in the automotive and security tech industries and am currently enrolled in the AIC certification course with the Insurance Institute of America.

- ✓ Developed a specialized method of installing certain weld-on parts, saving time, reducing material waste by nearly half, and increasing customer and technician satisfaction.

- ✓ Own and operate a successful concrete design and construction business (eight years).

> *"David has always demonstrated a high degree of integrity and honesty. He has also displayed excellent negotiating skills, and his ability to handle and estimate repair claims has always been consistently thorough and accurate.*
>
> *I am giving David my highest recommendation without reservation. He has the experience, knowledge, and ambition it takes to excel in the insurance industry and would be a tremendous asset to any company."*
>
> Ronald B. Morrison, Jr., Cincinnati Insurance

The organizations I've worked for greatly benefited from my ability to assess damage, manage projects and people, and complete high-quality work. Your organization, should it choose to leverage these strengths, will enjoy the same.

If you are searching for an Insurance Adjuster or Claims Manager with a strong hands-on understanding of vehicle repair work and excellent negotiation skills, please contact me to arrange an interview. I look forward to hearing from you.

Sincerely,

David L. Lindeman

View and/or print resume: www.resumexxx.com/xx

173

Adjuster or Claims Manager. *Jane Roqueplot, West Middlesex, Pennsylvania*

The individual had never worked in the insurance industry but, as an auto body expert, was experienced in estimating automobile damage. The letter points out each of his strengths.

Danielle Quinones

danielleq@homenet.com

Current Residence:
515 Abernathy Court
Richland, NJ 00000
(000) 000-0000

After March 1, 20XX:
70 Turtleback Trail
San Jose, CA 00000
(000) 000-0000

January 3, 20XX

Stevenson, Pellegrino & Delacruz, P.C.
Attorneys at Law
194 Morse Avenue
San Jose, CA 00000

Attention: Law Office Administrator

Please accept this letter and resume in application for the position of Legal Administrative Assistant you posted recently on the Internet.

Although I presently reside in New Jersey, I will be relocating to California in the near future. I am extremely interested in the position you describe and precisely meet your qualification requirements. As I plan to complete my undergraduate education at Los Gatos University and then continue on to pursue a law degree, this position seems like an ideal opportunity to expand my knowledge in the various aspects of a legal practice.

In my current position as a legal secretary for an attorney specializing in personal-injury litigation, I have had extensive experience in organizing workflow and meeting multiple deadlines. I can assess what needs to be done and take appropriate action with minimal direction. Having no prior legal experience, I quickly learned on my own initiative how to open and keep track of a large number of case files varying in complexity. Managing a variety of responsibilities in an environment with deadline pressures is a challenge that I truly enjoy.

I hope you will give me the opportunity to prove my ability to make a significant contribution to your organization. If you are interested in speaking with me further, I will gladly fly to California to interview for this position. Please contact me by leaving a message with Joe or Katy Ventura at (000) 000-0000. They will also serve as my personal references.

Sincerely,

Danielle Quinones

Enclosure: Resume

174

Legal Administrative Assistant. *Melanie Noonan, Woodland Park, New Jersey*

The opening paragraph identifies the position, and the second paragraph tells of the applicant's relocation plans. The third mentions crucial experience and skills.

CHRYSTAL SCOTLAND

55 Horrace Drive
Brentwood, New York 55555
(555) 555-5555
CS@LawandOrder.net

Date

Name
Company
Address

As a second-year law student at The Long Island University School of Law, I look forward to realizing my long-held dream of practicing law. As I move toward receiving my Juris Doctor in May 20XX, my career focus has remained steadfast with a strong interest in the emotionally charged world of Family Law. After careful research, I have chosen to seek a summer position with your law firm that will allow me the opportunity to further develop myself professionally. Ideally, this position will build upon recent undergraduate internship experience working within a progressive Domestic Violence Clinic headed by the Long Island Law Service Committee.

In this position, my oral advocacy skills, technique for conducting witness examinations, and ability to effectively negotiate on behalf of clients played a vital role in achieving a favorable outcome for my client when given the opportunity to try a case in Family Court. This achievement, coupled with my experience as a Student Editor on Long Island University's *Family Court Review,* solidified my interest in Family Law.

Prior experience includes three years as an Administrative Assistant with The Law Offices of McLaughlin & Meyers, P.C., a position held while attending school full-time. In this capacity, I exercised strong research, communication, and problem-resolution skills, along with the ability to handle pressing assignments in the office and at the courthouse. It is with your firm that I hope to continue in this vein as I strive to further my education and develop myself professionally.

The accompanying resume illustrates well my experience, academic achievements, and community service. However, I feel a personal meeting would better convey the value I could bring to the appropriate position. I welcome the opportunity to participate in a confidential interview to discuss in person the possibility of my joining your law firm.

Thank you in advance for your consideration. I will contact you soon.

Sincerely,

Chrystal Scotland

175

Legal Administrative Assistant. *Ann Baehr, East Islip, New York*

This law student was looking for a summer position to continue her professional development. The letter shows that she is already an effective worker who could help a law firm significantly.

JULIE R. MICHAELS

555 S. Global Trail ♦ Broomfield, CO 80455 ♦ Home 303.000.5555 ♦ jm999@comcast.net

[Date]

[Manager]
[Company]
[Street Address]
[City, State ZIP]

Re: [name of position] advertised on [date]

Dear [person or title],

Through my studies for certification as a Paralegal, I have gained strong skills in conducting legal research and a broad knowledge of the legal system. My professional goal is to apply this knowledge in order to provide quick and efficient research and administrative assistance for my next employer. Highlights of my background include the following:

> ➢ Completed courses in Business Law; Contracts; Criminal Law; Constitutional Law; Real Property; Legal Research; Civil Litigation; Wills, Trusts & Estates; and Domestic Relations through the Paralegal Technical Institute. I maintained a 4.0 G.P.A. throughout this coursework.

> ➢ Repeatedly recognized as a quick learner with strong analytic and problem-solving skills. Possess excellent skills in technology and a variety of computer applications.

> ➢ Gained excellent feedback regarding timeliness and quality of completed projects throughout work history.

> ➢ Broad exposure to variety of cultures and races gained from military experience and worldwide travels. Strong ability to relate to persons with diverse backgrounds and on different levels.

The accompanying resume will provide you with the additional details of my accomplishments and skills. I would welcome the opportunity to meet with you and learn how I can make a positive contribution to your firm. I will call next week to inquire about the possibility of a meeting.

Thank you for your time and consideration.

Sincerely,

Julie R. Michaels

176

Paralegal. *Michele Angello, Aurora, Colorado*

The applicant had just finished school and wanted a law position, but lacked practical experience. The writer emphasized completed course work, a high GPA, and skills desirable to a law office.

Arthur J. Norton, Esquire
555 Donaldson Lane
Hermitage, PA 55555

555.555.5555

The Family Center, Inc.   August 31, 20XX
Box CAD
55 Reade Street, 5th Floor
New York, NY 55555

Dear Personnel Manager:

After practicing law in the Commonwealth of Pennsylvania for more than three years, I am hoping to return to the State of New York. Please accept the enclosed resume for consideration for your advertised full-time position of Staff Attorney.

I am confident you will find that my qualifications meet those established by The Family Center, Inc., for this position:

• Interest in public-interest law, family law, or HIV/AIDS law	✓ Knowledgeable regarding custody, protection from abuse, landlord-tenant issues, supplemental security income, welfare, unemployment compensation, bankruptcy, and debt collection.
• Strong commitment to public service	✓ Through varied internships in New York and currently at Northwestern Legal Services, I have developed a passion for assisting people to ensure their rights.
• Strong organizational and writing skills	✓ Inherent ability for meticulous organization resulting in concise, analytical communication and presentations /arguments in written and oral format.
• Strong interpersonal skills	✓ Consistently demonstrated my ability to put clients at ease and gain their trust by employing skills to develop rapport for effective representation.
• Juris Doctor degree from accredited law school	✓ Awarded Juris Doctor by City University of New York School of Law.
• License to practice in New York State	✓ Admitted to New York State Bar in August 20XX.

I am eager and enthusiastic to assist individuals and families with serious illnesses, such as AIDS, in protecting their rights within the legal system.

I welcome the opportunity to meet with you to further relate how I can quickly become a contributing member of the legal team at The Family Center, Inc. I will call you September 5 to set a time.

Sincerely,

Arthur J. Norton, Esq.

Enclosure: Resume

177

Staff Attorney. *Jane Roqueplot, West Middlesex, Pennsylvania*

A family center solicitation indicating qualifications for a position enabled the writer to set up a two-column match between the job's requirements and the applicant's abilities and experience.

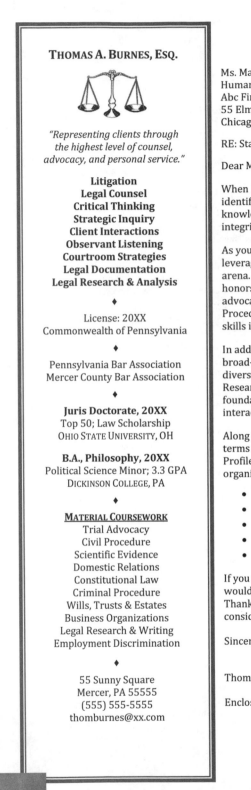

THOMAS A. BURNES, ESQ.

"Representing clients through the highest level of counsel, advocacy, and personal service."

Litigation
Legal Counsel
Critical Thinking
Strategic Inquiry
Client Interactions
Observant Listening
Courtroom Strategies
Legal Documentation
Legal Research & Analysis

◆

License: 20XX
Commonwealth of Pennsylvania

◆

Pennsylvania Bar Association
Mercer County Bar Association

◆

Juris Doctorate, 20XX
Top 50; Law Scholarship
OHIO STATE UNIVERSITY, OH

B.A., Philosophy, 20XX
Political Science Minor; 3.3 GPA
DICKINSON COLLEGE, PA

◆

MATERIAL COURSEWORK
Trial Advocacy
Civil Procedure
Scientific Evidence
Domestic Relations
Constitutional Law
Criminal Procedure
Wills, Trusts & Estates
Business Organizations
Legal Research & Writing
Employment Discrimination

◆

55 Sunny Square
Mercer, PA 55555
(555) 555-5555
thomburnes@xx.com

Ms. Mary Jane Smith
Human Resources
Abc Firm
55 Elm Street
Chicago, IL 55555

RE: Staff Attorney

Dear Ms. Smith:

When I came across your recent post for a Staff Attorney within your firm, I identified my legal background as an ideal match for the position. As a knowledgeable and talented Attorney, I offer quality legal services focused on integrity, professionalism, and respect for clients to your firm.

As you can see from my resume, I am an award-winning Attorney who leverages a solid academic background and hands-on experience in the legal arena. I was recognized as a top performer in law school, receiving such honors as membership to The Order of Barristers for excellence in oral advocacy and CALI awards for attaining the highest grade in both the Civil Procedure and Jurisprudence Seminars. My competitive spirit and notable skills in public speaking would be of great benefit to Abc Firm.

In addition, you would gain the advantage of a multifaceted professional with broad-based competencies across legal arenas and functions. Through diverse scholarship and experiences as an Attorney, Legal Intern, and Research Assistant, I bring a wealth of knowledge and versatility. With a foundation in focused research, courtroom strategies, negotiation, and client interaction, I would be a welcome addition to your staff.

Along with hard skills in law, I also want to express that I am a great match in terms of my behavioral style. A recent *Success Insights*™ DISC Personal Style Profile, which assessed my inherent behavior, revealed the value I bring to an organization as:

- Strong, knowledge-driven ethic.
- Always looking for logical solutions.
- Objectivity. Poised as "the anchor of reality."
- Defines, clarifies, gets information, and tests.
- Gains trust and ability to influence decisions/actions through rapport.

If you are searching for a thorough, conscientious, and resourceful Attorney, I would welcome a personal meeting to further discuss my qualifications. Thank you for taking the time to review my resume and for your consideration. I look forward to hearing from you soon.

Sincerely,

Thomas A. Burnes, Esq.

Enclosure: resume

View and/or print my resume: www.resume.xx/xxx

178

Staff Attorney. *Jane Roqueplot, West Middlesex, Pennsylvania*

As a recent law school graduate without real employment experience, the individual needed to have many keywords and soft skills emphasized. The letter resulted in an immediate job offer.

TIM PARIS, ESQ.

tim_paris@xxxx.com Relocating to Los Angeles 000-000-0000

August 16, 20XX

Hiring Director
Fortunati Tax Advisors
0000 Kent Ave., Suite 000
Los Angeles, CA 00000

Re: **International Tax Manager, Los Angeles, CA**
Reference Number: TDS-J-DSE-00000]

Dear Hiring Director:

I am writing to apply for your International Tax Manager position in Los Angeles.

As you can see from my enclosed resume, I have just graduated from Harvard Law School with an LLM in Tax. In particular, I intensively studied current international tax issues and trends. This new degree strengthens my knowledge and skills related to complex multinational corporations like those served by Fortunati.

My LLM in Tax complements my eight years as a tax attorney, years in the financial sector, and undergraduate degree in finance. I have built a reputation as an adviser who can, among other things, harmonize the often disparate requirements of regulations with a keen eye on minimizing clients' tax burdens and preserving their wealth. I look forward to bringing my expertise and enthusiasm to Fortunati.

During visits to friends and family, I have become impressed by the vitality and the global reach of the city and am excited about the challenges of working in it. Thus, I have begun the process of admittance to the California bar as part of my move to Los Angeles in the fall.

I would like to come in and share my ideas with you while learning more about Fortunati and your needs. I will call next week to see if we can meet.

Sincerely,

Tim Paris, Esq.

Encl.

0000 Merrill Ave, Boston, MA 00000

179

International Tax Manager. *Shauna C. Bryce, Annapolis, Maryland*

This applicant was relocating to Los Angeles and wanted a position with a major firm. Boldfacing makes the sought position stand out. With short paragraphs, the letter is easy to read.

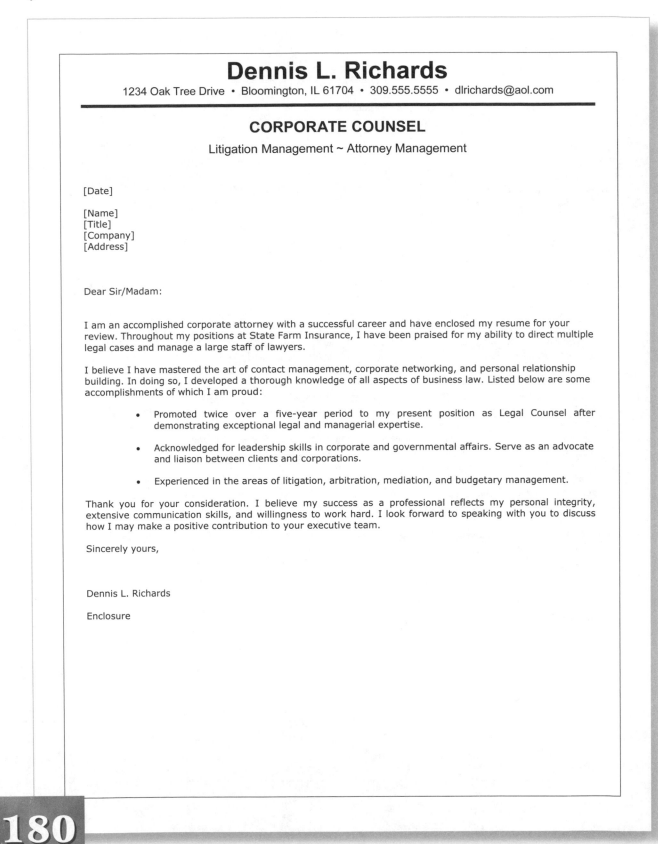

Dennis L. Richards

1234 Oak Tree Drive • Bloomington, IL 61704 • 309.555.5555 • dlrichards@aol.com

CORPORATE COUNSEL

Litigation Management ~ Attorney Management

[Date]

[Name]
[Title]
[Company]
[Address]

Dear Sir/Madam:

I am an accomplished corporate attorney with a successful career and have enclosed my resume for your review. Throughout my positions at State Farm Insurance, I have been praised for my ability to direct multiple legal cases and manage a large staff of lawyers.

I believe I have mastered the art of contact management, corporate networking, and personal relationship building. In doing so, I developed a thorough knowledge of all aspects of business law. Listed below are some accomplishments of which I am proud:

- Promoted twice over a five-year period to my present position as Legal Counsel after demonstrating exceptional legal and managerial expertise.

- Acknowledged for leadership skills in corporate and governmental affairs. Serve as an advocate and liaison between clients and corporations.

- Experienced in the areas of litigation, arbitration, mediation, and budgetary management.

Thank you for your consideration. I believe my success as a professional reflects my personal integrity, extensive communication skills, and willingness to work hard. I look forward to speaking with you to discuss how I may make a positive contribution to your executive team.

Sincerely yours,

Dennis L. Richards

Enclosure

180

Corporate Counsel. *Beverly and Mitchell I. Baskin, Marlboro, New Jersey*

This applicant was a successful lawyer with management skills. Managerial expertise is a theme that appears repeatedly in this letter: in the first two paragraphs and in the first and third bulleted items.

JAMES M. RYAN
55 Roman Drive • Chicago, Illinois 00000
jamesmryan@email.com • (555) 555-5555

September 26, 20XX

Rita Jefferson
Director of Attorney Recruitment
Office of the Attorney General
555 West XX Street
Chicago, Illinois 55555

Dear Ms. Jefferson:

In response to your search for an Assistant Attorney General in the Public Aid Bureau, I offer specialized experience in child support enforcement and a history of meeting and exceeding performance objectives. As such, I am confident in my ability to become a top-contributing member of your team. The enclosed resume provides a summary of my background and qualifications for your review.

Throughout my career, I have proven myself to be a top performer who quickly grasps complex concepts and responsibilities. Whether tasked to manage a demanding caseload of 3,200 active child support cases, eliminate a substantial backlog of cases referred by DHFS, create training materials for a staff of 60 employees, or coordinate law student participation in a veterans' volunteer project, I have consistently exceeded expectations.

My experience with the Adams County State's Attorney's Office demonstrates my value in the workplace. Following a routine externship, I was offered an ongoing paid internship opportunity. Three months before graduation from law school and in a tough job market, I was offered a full-time attorney position. Even before the bar results were posted, my performance earned me the second largest caseload in the division.

Highly dependable and trustworthy, my background includes holding a Top Secret security clearance and earning operational and administrative promotions in the U.S. Air Force.

At this time, I am seeking new career challenges and would welcome the opportunity to discuss your needs and how my talents can meet them. Please contact me using the phone number or email address provided above to arrange an interview. I look forward to speaking with you soon. Thank you for your consideration.

Sincerely,

James M. Ryan
Enclosure

181

Assistant Attorney General. *Michelle P. Swanson, Edwardsville, Illinois*

This newly licensed attorney was applying for a position that required much more experience than he had. After using this letter that focuses on relevant internship experience, he got an interview.

CLIVE EUSTIS, ESQ.

00 Lamplight Ave., Apt. #0 ▪ Annapolis, MD 00000 ▪ 000.000.0000 ▪ clive@xxxx.net

August 16, 20XX

Inara Smith, Esq.
Mist, Nakai, Lyme, and Rox, PC
000 Pine Street, XXth Floor
Baltimore, MD 00000

re: Litigation/Case Manager Position—Baltimore

Dear Ms. Smith:

I am writing to apply for the litigation/case manager position in your law firm's Baltimore office.

As you can see from my enclosed resume, I am an experienced litigation/case manager with a particular love for complex securities litigation and regulation. Although I began my career as a commercial litigator, I quickly found that the project management role was perfectly suited to my skills and interests. I am known for working with attorneys to develop a strategy for getting the job done well and quickly, for pulling together and managing diverse resources, and for both traditional and multimedia trial support.

During my 25 years of law firm experience, I have led numerous large, time-sensitive projects, including the following:

- Managed 97-attorney, multiple-office team in 2-month review of approximately 650,000 email messages utilizing in-house review platform.

- Managed team of 25 attorneys in 6-month online review of approximately 700,000 email messages utilizing vendor-hosted, Web-based review platform.

- Trained and managed 40-person review team for 4 weeks for voluminous SEC production.

- Planned and executed 6-day, on-site (Seattle, WA) collection and subsequent scanning, processing, and database management of more than 200,000 pages of local counsel's case file developed over 30 years in *pro bono* death-penalty case.

I expect my ability to juggle the needs of attorneys and their clients, my experience, and my enthusiasm would be assets to the Firm. I would like to come in and share my ideas with you while learning more about the Firm and your future challenges. I will call next week to see if we can meet.

Sincerely,

Clive Eustis, Esq.

Encl.

182

Litigation/Case Manager. *Shauna C. Bryce, Annapolis, Maryland*

Bullets point to four significant projects that are quantified in specific numbers related to personnel, time (days, weeks, months, and years), and materials processed (e-mail messages and pages).

Corena Gold   000 Waterfront Drive, Philadelphia, PA 00000 ~ 000.000.0000 ~ corena@xxxxxx.net

August 16, 20xx

Human Resources Manager
United States Court of Appeals for the Third Circuit
Room 000
000 West Main Street
Philadelphia, PA 00000

<u>**Re: Chief Circuit Mediator, Vacancy Announcement No. XX-0000**</u>

Dear Human Resources Manager:

I am writing to apply for the Court's Chief Circuit Mediator position.

I am a lawyer with more than 16 years of experience in complex litigation (both trial and appellate levels), mediation, arbitration, and negotiation. Moreover, through my extensive work in all three "seats at the table" (i.e., court arbitrator, counsel, and party), I have developed the ability to create the consensus necessary to resolve matters in mediation, thereby avoiding the costs of continued litigation.

Having served as a court-appointed arbitrator, as a litigator representing individual and corporate clients, and as in-house counsel to major companies, I have built:

➢ An appreciation for the purpose and process of mediation, and the responsibilities of the mediator to both the court and parties;

➢ An understanding of a wide variety of substantive civil law issues;

➢ A broad experience with the Federal Rules of Civil Procedure, the Federal Rules of Appellate Procedure, and the Federal Rules of Evidence;

➢ An ability to weigh the merits of allegations, defenses, and legal theories, as well as the likely admissibility, credibility, and availability of evidence to support them;

➢ An understanding of litigation strategies and costs; and

➢ An ability to determine reasonable settlement values.

Productive mediation requires the mediator to excel in all these areas. But conflict resolution also requires understanding of factors not easily assigned a dollar value: parties' emotional investment, motivations behind the litigation, and individual personalities. Also needed are creative, goal-oriented problem solving and a tremendous amount of patience. Using these skills, I have successfully brought difficult personalities to agreement.

I would very much appreciate the opportunity to discuss with you how my experience can best support the needs of the Court and to learn more about the position and future challenges. I look forward to hearing from you. In the meantime, my resume is enclosed for your review.

Sincerely,

Corena Gold

Encl.

183

Chief Circuit Mediator. *Shauna C. Bryce, Annapolis, Maryland*

The first extended paragraph attests to the applicant's ability to solve problems and contain costs. The rest of the letter speaks of her understanding, broad experience, and skills.

ALLAN LOWE

555 North Avenue • Orlando, Florida 55555 • 555.555.5555 • allanlowe@xxxx.com

September 1, 20XX

Mr. Barry Nash, Director
National Oceanic and Atmospheric Administration
555 Ocean Avenue
St. Petersburg, Florida 55555

Dear Mr. Nash:

I could not have been happier to see the posting for the internship with the National Oceanic and Atmospheric Administration (NOAA) on the agency's website. As I complete my Bachelor of Arts degree in Criminal Justice from the University of Central Florida, I have been seeking an experience that will let me put my classroom knowledge into practice. Attached to this cover letter and résumé you will find a letter of recommendation from a faculty member and mentor, Dr. Phillip Rhodes, as he also referred me to this opportunity.

Since enrolling in the Criminal Justice program, I have excelled. I have been involved in on-campus and off-campus activities, participated in mock trials, and also started a local chapter of the Criminal Justice Club, of which I am the president. Although my schedule is hectic and I have to find ways to multitask to accomplish my goals, I thrive on the variety and challenge. Leadership, innovation, and communication are three of my strongest skills that I have demonstrated throughout my education, and I would love to put them to good use at your agency.

Faculty members have commented on the caliber and quality of the work that I produce, which can be seen in my electronic career portfolio. In addition to these items, I recently was featured in the Criminal Justice Student Journal for my research on dwindling fish populations. The enforcement of maritime law is one of my passions, and I would love to bring my educational experience to the internship opportunity and work toward the goals of the agency, as laid out on the NOAA website.

I am thrilled about this field and can think of no better place than NOAA to hone my skills and contribute to the profession. I look forward to the possibility of discussing my qualifications and skills further during an interview. Thank you for your consideration.

Sincerely,

Allan Lowe

Please feel free to peruse my portfolio by using the QR Code or by visiting www.xxxx.com/xxxxx

184

Intern. *Haley Richardson, Riverview, Florida*

This student approaching graduation wanted an internship. An interested reader could scan the included QR Code with a smartphone to view the student's portfolio online.

FOREST GOODWIN

555 Elm St., Pandora, OH 55555 ❖ 000-000-0000

Dear Hiring Professional,

Although I have been successful in my current position as Police Chief for Pandora, Ohio, the opportunity to contribute to the law enforcement of Ottawa, Ohio, a slightly larger community, excites me. I have respect for the law and do what it takes to see that a community under my watch is safe.

During my 10 years in law enforcement, I have worked in four different communities—Pandora, Crestview, Ottoville and Delphos—which has given me the opportunity to work with a diverse population. It has been my experience that people may not always agree with my decisions, but they will agree that I am fair and that I know the law.

You will find me to be organized, detail-oriented and personable. I am able to work well with a variety of individuals, which helps me maintain relationships throughout the community. My professional experience and dedication to service have enabled me to become a more highly effective law enforcement officer.

I thank you for taking the time to read over my resume and consider me for a position within your Police Department. If you should have any other questions, please feel free to contact me at 000-000-0000. I look forward to speaking with you again soon.

Sincerely,

Forest Goodwin

Enclosure

185

Police Chief. *Nicole Niemeyer, Kalida, Ohio*

The applicant was a seasoned law enforcement officer with great experience. The writer stressed a personal touch to make clear the applicant's appeal to small communities.

JIM JOHNSON

555 Oak Street		Cell: 555.555.5555
Reno, Nevada 55555	jjohnson@xxx.xx.com	Home: 555.555.0000

Committee to Elect George Jones
55 Main St. Suite 55555
Reno, Nevada 55555

Dear Selection Committee:

Throughout my career, I have committed myself to a high standard of results-oriented leadership. By adhering to a work ethic that respects hard work and expects exceptional quality, I have successfully contributed to improving the operations of the City of Reno Police Department. At this point in my career, I seek new challenges and feel that I can make significant contributions as Reno's next Police Chief. During my 18-plus years as a member of the management team with the City of Reno Police Department, I have honed my leadership skills that, together with my dedication to law enforcement, would enhance my effectiveness as the next Police Chief.

As you review the enclosed resume, you will get an overview of my law enforcement career. These highlights and notable accomplishments are indicative of the quality, caliber and strength of my management skills to plan, organize, direct, staff and coordinate police operations, to enforce statutes, laws and regulations designed to protect life and property, and to preserve peace and to prevent crime. In addition, my commitment to interacting with community groups will enhance the relationship between the police department and the community.

I am skilled at analyzing situations and implementing an effective course of action. I look forward to the potential to play a broader role in determining departmental goals and objectives, orchestrating changes, fostering programs that will impact public safety and initiating policies that improve morale throughout the organization.

In anticipation that there will be questions for me, I welcome the opportunity to meet with the selection committee to address those questions. Until then, I thank you for your time and professional consideration.

Sincerely,

Jim Johnson

Enclosure: resume, references

186

Police Chief. *Jane Roqueplot, West Middlesex, Pennsylvania*

The mayor discreetly asked this well-qualified law enforcement professional to submit materials for several posted cabinet positions. With the aid of this letter, he was hired.

Victor Passenti

●●

00-00 West Lake Avenue, Yardley, NJ 55555 ■ (555) 555-5555 ■ victor@xxx.net

January 12, 20XX

Ms. Linda Daniels
Township Administrator
Municipal Building, Room 00
Yardley, NJ 55555

Dear Ms. Daniels:

I am extremely interested in the soon-to-be-vacant position of Police Chicf and hereby present my qualifications in this letter and attached resume.

I have been employed by the Yardley Police Department since 1992, progressing to my current position of Detective Captain in 2001. I am FBI certified, and my experience is a balance of operations and administration. My major skill is in criminal investigations, where I have achieved my most significant successes, in particular, with the Narcotics and Organized Crime Divisions.

Techniques that have been most effective for me include:

- Skill in identifying confidential informants and obtaining evidence for criminal prosecution.
- Constant awareness of surroundings and any disruptive occurrences, helping to thwart illegal activities.
- Adept in handling potentially volatile situations using a nonjudgmental approach in dealing with suspects.
- Superior analytical and organization skills to help reconstruct and sequence events.
- Methodical follow-up and proficiency in correlating facts and processing information effectively.
- Sound interview techniques when conducting fact-finding interrogations with suspects and hostile witnesses that lead to admission of criminal activity.
- Empathy and caring attitude toward victims.
- Thoroughness in collection, examination, and preparation of evidence for criminal prosecution.
- Ability to testify in court in an intelligent and reliable manner that is believable by judge and jury.

As head of my unit, I possess an action-driven leadership style that commands presence, yet I am approachable and nonthreatening to my detectives. I demand professionalism and accountability of my officers; if warranted, I initiate disciplinary action. My superiors recognize me as a team builder and proactive problem solver, as evidenced by my numerous awards and commendations.

If considered for promotion to Police Chief, I have the vision to take the organization to the next level, leading law enforcement efforts that will continue to be a credit to the citizens of Yardley. In light of my stellar record of achievements, I look forward to a positive decision from the Township Board.

Sincerely,

Victor Passenti

Enclosure: Resume

187

Police Chief. *Melanie Noonan, Woodland Park, New Jersey*

With 20 years of experience, this applicant was highly qualified to take the next step of his career. This letter is about his skills, techniques, and character traits that contributed to his success.

PATRICK M. WILLIAMS

SECURITY MANAGEMENT EXPERT

55 Raymond Road ■ Chicago, IL 55555
555.555.5555 ■ patrickwilliams@xxx.com

June 29, 20XX

Mrs. Claire Donahue, HR Adviser
The Nelson Trust
555 Euston Street
Chicago, IL 55555

Dear Mrs. Donahue,

Given my 12 years of dedicated service and loyalty as Senior Security Adviser to The Nelson Trust and a proven record of accomplishment in all areas involving the provision of safety and security services, I am writing to convey my qualifications and experience that directly mirror all the requirements you seek for the role of **Security Manager.**

Through my experience and continuous charity industry training over the years, I have remained abreast of and solved many issues that the Trust has faced. I have been instrumental in bringing forward viable ideas to ensure the utmost safety for both personnel and visitors by initiating collaborations with the Office Services Manager to deploy new policies and protocol across multiple Trust sites. I would be surprised if you were able to find a more dedicated Security Manager than I will be, or one more ready to contribute to security service excellence by implementing best practice safety standards that ultimately ensure business continuity. Some of my strengths and achievements include:

- Teaming up with all departments to jointly **originate and institute security policies that focus on compliance** with industry, legal, and Trust needs.
- Ensuring that the Trust's **Health & Safety Policy is adhered to** with full commitment to uphold organization-wide objectives during risk assessment and safety guidance functions.
- Cultivating **partnerships with local law enforcement** to remain tapped into newest security developments and threats.
- Fostering the utmost credibility and trust from senior management, colleagues, Trust staff, and visitors alike due to **engaging, transparent communications** and **unyielding follow-through** on every project I undertake.

Along with my **Illinois Armed Security Guard License** issued by the Illinois Department of Financial and Professional Regulation, I have obtained an **Associate of Science in Security Management.** I strongly advocate further professional training through regular attendance at seminars and courses—for personal and staff development—and have introduced new training initiatives for all security employees encompassing responsibilities and policies associated with roles and site requirements to drive forward performance levels. Additionally, I am First Aid trained and serve as Fire Marshal for all Trust sites.

I am a professional, personable team motivator and supervisor with proven departmental management and policy development skills, a commitment to a high level of proactive service, and a supporter for clear and concise communications. I can produce solutions to problems where others have failed, and I will educate and motivate my teams to do the same.

The accompanying résumé will give you an outline of my potential for making worthwhile contributions in the role of the Trust's **Security Manager.** I believe it would be mutually beneficial for us to meet to further discuss my ideas on ensuring a safe and secure environment for staff and visitors as well as protecting the Trust's premises and property. I look forward to our conversation and thank you for your time and consideration.

Kind regards,

Patrick M. Williams
Enclosure: résumé

188

Security Manager. *Sandra Ingemansen, Leeds, West Yorkshire, England*

The writer used boldfacing for the applicant's education, license, and leadership abilities to cover the requirements set forth in the job posting. Two months after the letter was sent, the applicant was offered the position.

BILL STEADMAN, CPP

CORPORATE EXECUTIVE ● CHIEF SECURITY OFFICER

"Security is always too much...until it's not enough."
—Daniel Webster

«Date»

«First_Name» «Last_Name»
«Title»
«Company»
«Postal_Address»

Dear «Courtesy_Title» «Last_Name»:

In these perilous times, today's socially and financially conscientious enterprise is obligated to take a serious, urgent, and comprehensive approach to protecting infrastructure, property, and people from internal and external threats. Globally, companies are reprioritizing corporate security in their plans and actions, despite the soft economy.

Today's conundrum? Do more with less—again! This is where I come in! Through 20+ years of experience in the planning, deployment, and management of full-scale corporate security programs, I can provide <Name of Company> with the capacity to efficiently and cost-effectively avoid / mitigate risk and loss. In addition, I bring the added value of senior-level executive achievement, advanced academics, and an understanding of technology.

The following are highlights of my successes:

- Served as Head of Security for all of Your Cable's corporate entities and assets and managed related strategies, projects, inventories for corporate headquarters, and two operating divisions. Controlled $7 million capital and expense budget.

- Assisted SVP of Security (solid line to CEO) with enterprise-wide budget and team oversight ($24+ million / 800+ employees).

- Contributed to $1+ million in annual cost savings related to corporate security.

- Formed and managed an internal organization—Intelligence Services Group—as a solution to employee and vendor security issues.

- Planned and managed technology-based security—personnel, proprietary, and intellectual property protection—systems projects representing investments, some in excess of $1 million.

- Contributed to strategic plans and actions for high-profile venues and events (e.g., West Side Arena, Lyman Recital House, and Senior GMA Tournament). Consulted on Metropolis Plaza security issues after the 20XX bombing.

<Name of Contact>, if you see value in the breadth of my experience, scope of my knowledge, and caliber of my management qualifications, please get in touch so we can set up a meeting. I look forward to discussing your needs and my solutions, and you can expect to hear from me soon. I can guarantee you a substantial ROI.

Sincerely,

Bill Steadman

Enclosure

vulnerability assessment ● access security ● event security ● workplace / employee security
executive protection ● electronic surveillance / countermeasures ● competitive intelligence / countermeasures
emergency preparedness ● crisis response ● intellectual / proprietary property protection

25 Bristol Road, Smallville, New Jersey 33333 ● Home: 444-444-4444 ● Cell: 777-777-7777 ● E-mail: bstead@verizon.net

189

Corporate Security Officer. *Deb Dib, Medford, New York*

Contact information is put at the foot of the page so that the Webster quotation can go at the top. This quote sells the need for security right upfront. The bulleted successes and the keywords near the foot are strong.

CST. DANIEL TURCOTT #544

000 King Street, Apt. #212   Phone: (555) 444-8888
Augusta, Ontario A1A 1A1   Pager: (905) 444-5555

January 12, 20XX

RE: PROMOTIONAL REVIEW BOARD

Dear Sir/Madam,

It is with great interest that I submit my qualifications for the Promotional Review Board. I am a highly skilled and highly regarded police officer with recent experience working as an Acting Sergeant and considerable international leadership experience. In all capacities, I have consistently distinguished myself as a dedicated, well-organized, and highly capable leader.

In addition to the experience and expertise outlined in the attached resume, I offer strengths in the following specific areas:

> **Leadership**—Through my current role as Acting Sergeant with the Augusta and Pinehurst Community Police Services, and additionally from my experience in Kosovo as the Chief of Border Police Unit, I have demonstrated strengths in leading officers through example, coaching, and the clear communication of expected performance standards. In delegating responsibilities and specific tasks to subordinate officers, I am mindful of developing officers and ensure that they are part of the team. I provide leadership by example, showing compassion and respect for fellow officers while maintaining good guidance and direction.

> **Communications Skills**—My communication is clear and concise, and I have excellent listening skills. In Kosovo, I was responsible for representing our United Nations Border Policing efforts in politically tense meetings with Yugoslav, Macedonian, NATO, and UN representatives. These meetings were extremely volatile at times and required the highest levels of diplomacy, clarity, and interpersonal expertise.

"Mr. Turcott enjoys a natural ability to interact and converse well with people of all walks of life. His interpersonal skill is the trait that is far superior and the envy of many."
> Everson W. Summerset, Inspector
> Chief of Training for United Nations Mission in Kosovo

> **Organizational Skills**—I have consistently been commended for my organizational and logistical skills. While in Kosovo, I effectively managed all resources and coordinated the activities of 130 officers and 60 police vehicles across five international border crossings. Most recently, I reviewed and updated 433 ARPS files on outlaw motorcycle gang members and their associates.

"There were always logistical problems and bureaucratic issues to be handled. These circumstances never deterred Turcott from accomplishing his mission, even under difficult circumstances."
> Willis B. Redfield, Senior Case Agent, Narcotics Division
> New York Police Department

> **Above-Standard Proven Work Record**—As a Uniform Officer, I maintain one of the highest levels of statistics with regards to drug and criminal investigations within my division. Additionally, I am consistently identified for special projects and investigative work within my division, the Intelligence Unit, and other police services.

Page 1 of 2

190

Police Sergeant. *Ross Macpherson, Whitby, Ontario, Canada*

This Police Constable had to "apply" for a promotion to Sergeant. Because hundreds of officers applied for the promotion and the letter and resume carried so much weight, the standard one-page length was replaced with a powerful two-page letter that included achievements and

Cst. Daniel Turcott #544

000 King Street, Apt. #212
Augusta, Ontario A1A 1A1

Phone: (555) 444-8888
Pager: (905) 444-5555

continued...

➢ **Dedication**—Extremely self-motivated and driven to succeed, I have a consistent desire to improve skills and exceed expectations. Proven flexibility and adaptability.

➢ **Self-Discipline**—I was personally selected by Division Inspector to develop, coordinate, and implement a 6-week Street Level Drug Investigation within the Pinehurst community. As Officer in Charge, I successfully managed budget allocation, vehicle rentals, and undercover buys, and directed junior and senior officers in the execution of all search warrants.

➢ **Conflict Resolution**—I successfully created a 130-officer Border Police Unit in Kosovo, requiring advanced conflict-resolution skills in a post-war restoration scenario. Given that no such police unit existed in the region when I arrived, our presence in such a volatile region created considerable conflict among residents and the international police officers I was responsible for training and supervising. In spite of these obstacles, I was able to create an effective Border Police Unit covering five international border locations between two sovereign countries.

[Officer Turcott's] sensitive, honest, and positive team approach garners the mutual respect between himself and others that permit effective conflict resolution."

Everson W. Summerset, Inspector
Chief of Training for United Nations Mission in Kosovo

I am confident that my work experience, reputation, and dedicated work ethic will exemplify the type of officer you require. Thank you for your consideration.

Sincerely,

Constable Daniel Turcott #544

Page 2 of 2

testimonials in seven top functional areas. Boldfacing and underlining make these areas stand out. Italic is used for the important testimonials. This candidate got the promotion over more than 200 other officers.

JONATHAN A. EAGEN
4444 Martin Road • Allentown, PA 19222 • (666) 888-0000

March 17, 20XX

George Washington, Secretary of Homeland Security
White House
ATT: Office of Homeland Security
1600 Pennsylvania Avenue
Washington, DC 20502

Dear Secretary Washington:

As you build your Homeland Security team, it is my hope that you are looking for individuals like me—people who have been in the trenches and who are willing to "do what it takes" to accomplish a task. If you spoke to Jack Long in Lt. Governor Justine's office, he would tell you that I *am* that person and that I would be a strong contributor to this uncharted and unprecedented challenge you face.

Until August, I was a Research Analyst and Campaign Coordinator for Senator Don Thornton. Following Senator Thornton's retirement, I served as a Campaign Coordinator for Representative Lisa Carpenter, working closely with the Republican State Committee. At this point, I am ready for a new challenge, and I can envision no other personal or professional opportunity more fulfilling and rewarding than being a member of the Homeland Security team.

From the time I was a young man, I have had an interest in public service. You will note in my resume that I have served as a Councilman and Committeeman in my home borough. Although I didn't realize it at the time, I was taking the first steps toward a career serving the public and my country. When I envision the perfect job and work environment, there are three things that rank high on my list of priorities:

- I work best on a team...particularly one that is targeting a meaningful goal such as homeland security;

- I *must* be aligned with a leader who is known for his/her integrity, character and strength of purpose...an individual who leads by personal example; and

- I want to be given the opportunity to tackle any challenging, responsible assignments that I'm deemed capable of handling. I make it my business to learn all I can about my organization's mission, strategies and functions so that I can work from a standpoint of knowledge.

On a personal level, you should be aware that I am single, available for travel and open to working extra hours to accomplish the team's objective. To say I am organized and work well under pressure would be an understatement. I've had to be in order to balance full-time employment with my educational requirements. And whether large projects or small—you can count on me to get the job done. I have a "can-do" attitude and plenty of persistence, and I enjoy doing the footwork.

I would be proud to join this top-flight team concerned with protecting our nation and its citizens. I have enclosed my resume, outlining my experience and credentials, for your consideration. I realize that a resume is only a brief overview, so I can be available to meet with you for a personal interview at your convenience. Please note that I have submitted my resume online as well. I look forward to talking with you in the near future.

Respectfully,

Jonathan A. Eagen

Enclosure

191

Homeland Security Position. *Karen Conway, Bend, Oregon*

Referrals in the first two paragraphs help to catch the reader's attention. The letter then turns to building a case for regarding this applicant as a worthy candidate for a Homeland Security position.

BRUCE T. THOMASON

98 Ben Franklin Drive • Austin, TX 78734
Home: (555) 222-2222 • ThomasonB@aol.com • Work: (555) 333-3333

<Date>

[Company Name]
[Department]
[Address]
[City, State, ZIP]

Dear [Name],

It is with great interest that I am forwarding my resume for consideration as Major within your agency. As a highly motivated Director of Informational Systems within your law enforcement agency, and having served in many capacities within this agency, I am confident that I possess the skills, the knowledge, and—most important—the dedication and commitment to ensure that citizens are provided with safe, efficient, quality protection.

My desire to make a difference in the community and in the lives of the people in that community led me to a career in law enforcement. The teamwork, dedication, and commitment involved in serving the community make this work extremely rewarding, as does the continual effort to be the "Best of the Best." Law enforcement is a physically demanding and dangerous occupation, requiring physical fitness, discipline, and teamwork. My team-building, leadership, and motivational skills will be an asset to the position, as will my stamina and capacity to act decisively in emergency situations.

With more than 25 years of law enforcement experience, I will bring to this position extensive expertise and departmental knowledge. With a vision of a progressive Sheriff's Office with a continuing tradition of exemplary service, I believe my values of honesty, embraced diversity, respect, commitment, and full accountability, combined with knowledge gained from extensive experience, will guarantee my ability to do this important work.

Throughout my career, I have demonstrated my ability to handle full responsibility and leadership. My responsibilities have been diverse and have included departmental management, strategic planning, project management, and financial analysis. Having successfully executed tactics to cut costs and improve efficiency, I possess the ability to conceive and implement business solutions to problems while working closely with personnel and projects, building a reputation for quality and overall results. My mission is for a Sheriff's Office by and for the people, committed to justice by serving and protecting our community.

Thank you for your time and consideration of my application. I look forward to discussing in detail with you the ways in which I can make a significant contribution to your agency, and I invite you to contact me, at your convenience, at either of the above numbers.

Sincerely,

Bruce Thomason

Enclosure

192

Police Officer, Major. *Jennifer Rushton, Sydney, New South Wales, Australia*

The individual was applying for an internal position as Major within his agency. He wanted to show both his commitment to law enforcement and his ability to lead and implement changes.

DAVID MARTINEZ

45 Hillside Lane
Wilmington, MA 55555
(w) 555-555-5555 (h) 555-500-5000
e-mail: dm45@verizon.net

EXECUTIVE/VIP PROTECTION
TEAM & TASK FORCE LEADERSHIP
SECURITY OPERATIONS MANAGEMENT
NATIONAL & INTERNATIONAL INVESTIGATIONS
TRAINING PROGRAM DEVELOPMENT/DELIVERY
SECURITY POLICY/PRACTICE DEVELOPMENT

September 25, 20XX

Thomas Jones, Secretary of Public Safety
State of Connecticut
Executive Office of Public Safety
3 State Street, Suite 5555
Hartford, CT 55555

Dear Secretary Jones:

I understand that your office will shortly be seeking a Director of the Office of Commonwealth Security. I would bring to the position key competencies in the areas of terrorism-prevention strategy development, security operations management, and interagency cooperation.

My expertise is protecting large and small groups against terrorist attack. For more than 25 years, I have worked for the United States Secret Service in a range of capacities. Currently I am Assistant to the Special Agent in Charge of Hartford's Protection and Intelligence Squad. During my career, I served on multiple task forces where communication and cooperation were critical to achieving results. Earlier, I conducted high-profile fraud and forgery investigations. Highlights of my achievements include the following:

- Contributed as a member of the U.S. Secret Service Airport Security Review to the analysis of security breaches and the development of remediation plans.

- Resurrected and reenergized a financial organized crime task force that had lost the support of key stakeholders. With my skills in leadership, communication, negotiation, and collaboration, I was able to bring back to the table three federal agencies and the Hartford Police Department, among others.

- Developed a strategy for protecting the 2004 Presidential Debate in Hartford from disruption. Executed security operations in a large, coordinated effort. Deployed agents from several public agencies to secure an environment in which media, celebrities, and political staff numbered in the thousands.

- Protected a former U.S. president as leader of a protective detail. Managed operations, scheduling, and training for agents. Developed a plan for relocating the former president in the event of a national crisis.

I understand that developing a coordinated strategy to protect the state from terrorism will be a key mission for the new Director. With my intimate understanding of issues surrounding protective security operations and my expertise in strategizing and executing large protective operations, I am well equipped to take on the task.

I would also be able to make important contributions in another critical area: promoting communication and collaboration between agencies to obtain proper intelligence and then acting expeditiously and collaboratively to develop seamless security solutions. I have a strong track record of coordinating efforts with multiple stakeholders to get work done.

I look forward with interest to speaking with you in person and will call to set an appointment. Thank you for considering my strong interest in the position.

Sincerely,

David Martinez

193

Director of the Office of Commonwealth Security. *Jean Cummings, Concord, Massachusetts*

The individual wanted to move up to the top security job in the state. The writer brought together all the pieces of his experience that qualify him for this position. Note the bulleted highlights.

TED PELLETIERE

Home:
000 Mullen Road
Peekskill, NY 00000

E-mail: pellted@cox.net
(555) 555-5555

Mailing Address:
P.O. Box 445
Peekskill, NY 00000

March 23, 20XX

New York Times
Box 990
New York, NY 00000

RE: INVESTIGATIONS MANAGER

As a professional with extensive hands-on and supervisory experience in law enforcement, private industry, and the military, I believe that my expertise is a match for this position. Accordingly, I have enclosed for your review a resume that summarizes my skills and accomplishments in investigations management.

I have achieved a successful record as an investigator and supervisor in delivering results to corporate clients as well as in community and executive protection. My skills encompass undercover criminal investigations • background checks • fraud investigations • arrests and extradition • fugitive location and apprehension • electronic surveillance and detection • employee dishonesty.

Currently as Chief Inspector at the State's Attorney's Office, I direct a team in security, safety, and investigation operations. As a supervisor, I am accountable for the development, training, and supervision of a diverse workforce. I also am well versed in security program planning and critical incident/crisis management based on my experience as a member of the Federal Anti-Terrorism Task Force.

Previously employed with the New York Police Department, I progressed through increasingly responsible law enforcement positions that included development of the training division, establishing and overseeing the department's narcotics unit, and training new staff. In addition, my diverse experience includes providing successful investigative services for corporate clients in the insurance industry, as well as conducting criminal/counterintelligence investigations during my military reserves tenure.

I am confident that my expertise and professionalism would allow me to meet the challenges of this managerial role and protect your clients' interests. Thank you for your consideration. I will contact you later this month to explore the possibility of a personal interview.

Sincerely,

Ted Pelletiere

Enclosure

194

Investigations Manager. *Louise Garver, Broad Brook, Connecticut*

This applicant wanted an investigations management position in a corporate setting. The letter refers to the individual's experience, skills, current position, and previous NYPD employment.

ALLEN JURGENS

0000 Red Barn Road   555-555-5555
Agua Dulce, California 91350   ajurgens@netzero.net

January 5, 20XX

Benson Security
35000 Sierra Highway
Agua Dulce, California 91350

Proficient Loss-Prevention Expert
Committed to Helping You
Achieve a Healthier Bottom Line!

Each year, retailers lose an estimated $26 billion in merchandise to shrinkage, primarily through theft and employee error. This means 1 to 2 percent of total sales are lost, and for larger companies, this loss totals in the millions. Some companies find themselves in this predicament because of an ineffective loss-prevention program or lack of one.

Here's how I can help…

- Draw on practical experience to identify and solve loss-related problems.
- Develop and implement sound strategies to arrive at effective solutions.
- Use effective management techniques to train loss-prevention staff.
- Collaborate with team members to address current problems and anticipate future challenges.

I believe in the Golden Rule and have always applied it; it was one of the first things I instilled in my staff. Throughout my law enforcement career, I have focused on empowering my subordinates to succeed by encouraging them to develop their strengths and grow professionally. In many cases where individuals were dissatisfied, I resolved the underlying problems and turned their attitude around. This approach consistently produced highly effective, supportive teams under my command.

Qualifications I bring to your company [use name of company if you have it] include

- Proven performance in fast-paced and high-stress working environments.
- Strong analytical skills with exceptional attention to detail.
- High motivation and ability to aggressively take on great responsibility.
- Hands-on experience with classified documentation.
- Experience in intelligence report writing, including in-depth reports on high-interest areas of operation.

Based on my experience, strong work ethic, and commitment (no one will "outwork" me), I am confident that I can add significant value to your security function. If appropriate, I would like to schedule a meeting to discuss your needs and the contribution I can make to the success of your organization. Should any questions arise regarding the information on my résumé, please contact me; otherwise, I will call you next week [if you have or can look up contact number] to set up an appointment. I look forward to speaking with you soon.

Sincerely,

Allen Jurgens

Enclosure

195

Loss Prevention Expert. *Myriam-Rose Kohn, Valencia, California*

This letter's pattern includes these items in turn for the reader: your problem, how I can help, my work with subordinates, my qualifications, and my confidence in being useful to your organization.

Thomas J. Sonner

333 West Boulevard
Hansing, WA 98888-8888
(777) 777-7777
email: TJS777@email.com

March 18, 20XX

General Manager
Senior Gardens
77 Mystery Drive
Hansing, WA 98888

RE: Community Relations Director

I enclose my resume in response to your March 8 ad in *The Hansing Bee* for a Community Relations Director. It seems a surprisingly good match for my background, and I would welcome an opportunity to discuss it with you personally.

My considerable experience as a highly successful, respected, and beloved pastor / counselor / teacher, briefly summarized on the enclosed resume, testifies to my relationship-building expertise—I am confident in my ability to represent Senior Gardens to prospective residents and their families. My work with diverse populations has honed my innate ability to recognize needs and present workable solutions—I can easily relate to your customers. Of course, successful networking with civic and religious leaders in local and state communities, office personnel, administrators, executives, children, and adults is one of my fortes.

With my experience in recruiting volunteers, public speaking, presentations, and training, I have well-developed powers of persuasion—easily translated to sales and marketing skills— and certainly ministry and teaching can be considered long-term-care industries.

I hope you can see the potential here for my making a significant contribution to your business. I will give you a call in two weeks to schedule a time we can meet to discuss the opportunity further. Thank you for your consideration.

Sincerely,

Thomas J. Sonner

enc: resume

196

Community Relations Director. *Janice M. Shepherd, Bellingham, Washington*

The applicant was a Roman Catholic priest who had decided to transition to secular work. This letter was successful in getting an interview for him, and he was successful in landing the job.

Paul Patton

15711 Clinton Avenue
Houston, TX 00000

Home: (000) 000-0000
Email: name@aol.com

January 14, 20xx

Dr. Ken Woolforth
Vice President for Enrollment Management
University of Houston
P.O. Box 00000
Houston, TX 00000-0000

Dear Dr. Woolforth:

It was with great interest that I learned about the opening for a Director of Professional Services, as my qualifications match your requirements for this position. Please allow me to explain briefly how my skills and abilities can contribute to the success of the University of Houston.

In reviewing the requisition for this position, I noted that you are seeking a candidate with the ability to "apply universal business principles to a variety of environments"; as the Director for my advertising firm and a General Manager in several other capacities, I have held full responsibility for a broad range of business disciplines and functions, including marketing, accounting, budgeting, sales, production, customer service, staffing, and general administration. In addition, I meet the following specific requirements:

Your Requirements:

- 7 years of management experience
- Bachelor's degree from accredited university
- Knowledge of printing, copying, and mailing processes
- High level of financial and administrative management skills

My Qualifications:

- 15+ years of experience in various management positions
- BS from the University of Houston
- Experience in printing, mailing, and copying functions as Director of XYZ Advertising
- Track record of meeting tight budgets, streamlining processes, and ensuring workplace efficiency

My resume is enclosed to provide you with additional details regarding my background and achievements, but I am certain that a personal interview would more fully reveal the diversity of my management experience and the unique contribution I can make to your university. Thank you, Dr. Woolforth, for your time and consideration.

Sincerely,

Paul Patton

Enclosure

197

Director of Professional Services, University. *Daniel J. Dorotik, Jr., Lubbock, Texas*

This letter was a response to an ad. The writer used a Your Requirements… My Qualifications format to draw attention to the excellent match between the applicant and specific ad requirements.

Elizabeth A. Gulickson

| 5555 Massachusetts Ave. | lizgulickson@xxxx.com | (H) 555.555.5555 |
| Fort Collins, CO 55555 | | (C) 555.555.0000 |

January 24, 20XX

Mr. Matthew Townsend, Principal
Rocky Mountain Academy
5555 Mountain Trail
Fort Collins, CO 55555

Dear Matt:

As you know from our conversation the other day, I am interested in being considered for the Director of Admissions position you recently posted on the Rocky Mountain Academy website. I'd like to take this opportunity to summarize my qualifications. My resume is enclosed, and it fills in the details.

The goal for the Director of Admissions as stated on the position description is to increase student enrollment at the school. What a great time to begin this initiative, with a new location on the horizon. As media attention builds, we can capitalize on that increased visibility by beginning to talk with current families and community members about all that Rocky Mountain Academy has to offer.

Who better to promote Rocky Mountain than someone who has such a long track record with the school? Because I have been affiliated with it in so many different capacities, I embrace the mission and tradition of RMA. As a result of my involvement in the community, I am a familiar face in many circles. Through my business, I have many ties with business and community leaders. I easily build rapport and gain the trust of people.

Although that personal connection is important, the position description indicates the new Director of Admissions should also have a background in marketing and sales. Most of my career has been in commercial real estate. In my company, making the sale comes second to filling the client's needs. I think that kind of long-term relationship building and consultative selling would be extremely effective to open doors and secure commitments from families.

I have a personal stake in the school's success and will continue to work hard in any capacity to help support its future. I welcome the chance to talk with you about my suitability and enthusiasm to fill this vital role. Thank you for your consideration.

Sincerely,

Elizabeth A. Gulickson

Enclosure

198

Director of Admissions. *Janet L. Beckstrom, Flint, Michigan*

In a declining real estate market, the applicant wanted permanent employment in a new field. The letter emphasized her track record with the school and relevant facets of her experience.

Shemaka Drew
414 Chapel Hill Road Morraine, Georgia 30000 ▪ [678] 555-5555 ▪ sd200@charge.com

Friday, April 9, 20XX

Mr. Charles W. Moran
Chairman, Board of Directors
The Wentworth Foundation
2230 Corona Boulevard
Suite 100
Atlanta, Georgia 30000

Dear Mr. Moran:

I want to be the one who translates your vision for The Wentworth Foundation into results as your Executive Director. Over the years, I've done just that for not-for-profit entities that range from a large university to a humane society to a minority arts festival to a science museum to a family and career services provider.

How well did I do? On the next pages, you'll read about some two dozen documented contributions. But I thought you deserved more than a typical resume, with its sterile lists of job titles and responsibilities.

In their place are examples of donors found and retained, funds raised, staff and volunteers inspired, services expanded—in short, everything The Wentworth Foundation should have to be the center of excellence in the field. However, even a specially tailored resume format can't show *how* I've built my track record.

Behind the results is this professional code that guides all I do:

- ❑ Building financial support is good; keeping financial support growing is better.
- ❑ Making your organization more visible is good; having it synonymous with its function is better.
- ❑ Recruiting volunteers is good; keeping them is not only better, it's more fun.

Now I am ready to put all my energy to work for The Wentworth Foundation. However, when it comes to your special needs, words on paper are no substitute for personal conversations. I will call around the middle of next week to hear about your organization's special needs.

Sincerely,

Shemaka Drew

Encl.: Resume

199

Executive Director, Foundation. *Don Orlando, Montgomery, Alabama*

The applicant had many positions during the last few years. The letter refocuses attention away from the applicant's job history and to the benefits the person can bring to the foundation.

SENTA WEIL

555 Hammel Drive   www.sentaweil.com   (310) 555-5555
Beverly Hills, CA 90210   senta@weil.com

John Jacob Jingleheimer
555 Michael Drive
Beverly Hills, CA 55555

September 7, 20XX

Dear Mr. Jingleheimer,

I am a skilled supervisor, trainer, and motivator combining Ph.D., MBA, and JD degrees with extensive service in public, private, and nonprofit venues. I offer an outstanding history of successfully managing projects from conception, through development, to implementation. I am especially skilled at negotiations and strategic planning and am an inveterate problem solver and decision maker with an unexcelled record of reducing operating costs, increasing productivity, and bringing mission-critical projects in on schedule and within budget.

Although most people are either dreamers or doers, I am both. I am a compassionate and visionary leader who tirelessly works on many projects to benefit our community by combining a lifelong and heartfelt commitment and dedication to helping others with exceptional communication talents, outstanding interpersonal skills, and a proven ability to convey complex concepts in understandable terms.

Generally recognized as an "idea/strategy" person, I also possess the know-how and wherewithal to implement my ideas. In fact, my entire history is one of creating something where it did not exist before. Although I can follow the lead of others, my main value is in creating new and pioneering methods to achieve goals by working the "big picture" and effectively managing staff to assist me. I combine exposure to many experiences, an excellent education, and a self-starting personality to get done what needs to be done.

If you are searching for an innovative leader who will generate growth and profit, please contact me to arrange an interview. I am eager to learn more about the challenges facing your organization and to discuss how I can make a difference.

Sincerely,

Senta Weil

Enclosure

200

Corporate Director. *Janice Worthington, Columbus, Ohio (with Jason and Jeremy Worthington)*

The writing challenge was to provide an all-purpose letter for a position in either a public sector or a corporate environment. The applicant wanted the letter to be generic but also remain powerful.

CRYSTAL M. DAVIS

2721 Terra Firma Drive, Lawrenceville, NJ 08640
Tel: 609.771.5555 ▪ Email: crystaldavis@bellnet.com

September 2, 20XX

Mr. Tom O'Kane
Human Resources Manager
Firmenich Incorporated
P.O. Box 5880
Princeton, NJ 08543

Dear Mr. O'Kane,

Kirsten Alexander of Human Resources suggested that I contact you regarding the open position of **Administrative Manager.** If you have need of a well-qualified professional with **German and French language skills** and experience in office administration, customer service, sales, training, and marketing, then we should meet. My resume is enclosed for your review. Highlights include the following:

- ☑ More than **eight years of experience** in organization, coordination, communication, and customer service with Devoneaux, an international exporter of consumer goods. Consistent focus on creating and maintaining profitable client relationships. Supervised and trained 15 administrative assistants and customer service reps in stellar client communications.

- ☑ A resourceful **problem-solver** with a track record of getting positive results, including a record-setting 75% collection rate on accounts 90 days past due.

- ☑ Ability to **build confidence and trust** at all levels with domestic and international customers, and demonstrated experience in promoting results-oriented environments. Achieved lowest turnover rate for administrative assistants and customer service reps in company's history.

- ☑ **Proven communication skills,** including fluency in French and German. Up-to-date technology skills in MS Office Suite (Word, Excel, Access, PowerPoint, and Outlook), Internet, e-mail, and multiple peripherals (scanners, digital cameras, and printers).

My career success has been due in large part to building supportive relationships and tackling persistent problem areas with creative approaches. I am seeking the opportunity to transition my experience, skills, and enthusiasm into a new organization where I can have an impact on company growth.

I will call your office next week to answer any initial questions you may have and to set up a mutually convenient appointment. Thank you for your consideration.

Sincerely,

Crystal M. Davis

201

Administrative Manager. *Susan Guarneri, Three Lakes, Wisconsin*

The job had been posted for some time before the applicant learned of it. The writer used a third-party reference, bullets, and a testimonial to capture attention. The applicant got the job.

RON BATTISTA

999 Augusta Crescent
Pinestone, Ontario L1N 8G7

Home: (555) 666-4444
Cell: (555) 777-9999

March 3, 20XX

Salvatore Bosso
Bosso Associates Inc.
333 Bayfield Avenue
Suite 1550, P.O. Box 16
Pinestone, ON A1A 2B2

<u>**Re: Manager, Technical Services**</u>

Dear Mr. Bosso,

To be a truly effective manager, you have to get your hands dirty.

Throughout my management career, this has a been a major key to my success—getting in the trenches, spotting opportunities for improvement and cost savings, leading the team by example, and knowing firsthand that things are running at optimum levels. If this is the type of manager you're looking for, then I'd welcome the opportunity to speak with you about the contribution I can make.

In recent management positions, I have been responsible for overseeing and optimizing the logistics and operations of expansive, high-volume environments. In every position, I have considered my mandate not only to manage activities, but to find opportunities to improve processes, eliminate redundancies, cut costs, increase revenues, and improve service. The results have been dramatic:

- **Slashed distribution costs by $500,000 for National Review**
- **Inherited district with lowest customer satisfaction rating and turned it around to first place in less than one year**
- **Increased dealers from 600 to 1,150 in less than 7 months**
- **Reduced inventory costs by $16,000 within one year**

I believe I can offer you the very same level of expertise, and I am confident that the results would speak for themselves. I would welcome the opportunity to meet in person to discuss the value I can bring, and I am available for a personal interview at your convenience.

Thank you for your consideration. I will contact you soon to set an appointment for a personal interview.

Sincerely,

Ron Battista

Enclosure

202

Technical Services Manager. *Ross Macpherson, Whitby, Ontario, Canada*

The candidate wanted to convey in the opening paragraphs his hands-on management style. The bullets then communicate strong quantified achievements he has provided for previous employers.

Michael Fisher

555 Melody Lane
Hubbard, Ohio 55555
(555) 555-5555

August 30, 20XX

Mr. Mark Johnson
Duferco Manufacturing
5555 Youngstown Road SE
Warren, OH 55555

Dear Mr. Johnson:

Throughout my career in manufacturing, I have demonstrated exceptional knowledge of a variety of processes and kept current on changes in technology. Combining technical with management expertise, I am confident I can deliver positive contributions to your company as its next Vice President.

As a manager, I capably direct, motivate, coach, facilitate, train, and coordinate the efforts of multifunctional teams performing multiple assignments and ensuring optimum performance, while keeping an eye on the bottom line. I have strong expertise in managing capital and operating budgets, inventory, cost results, service results, safety issues, customer satisfaction, and labor relations.

I work to identify and implement methods to enhance optimization of production yields and finished product while minimizing downtime and improving scrap management. As a direct result of these efforts, notable results were achieved for several major accounts, leading to increased productivity for numerous parts production per month. Let me share some of these:

1. General Electric   *Locomotive Mainframe Casting and Electric Motor Housings*
   - Reduced costs   • Improved timely deliveries
   - Modified production process   • Dramatically reduced scrap
   - Visited customer and identified areas where they could use help

2. Siemens   *Electric Motor Housing*
   - Slashed costs and scrap   • Developed new business
   - Designated as contact person for any questions or concerns from the customer

3. Ingersoll-Rand   *Air Compressor Castings*
   - Worked on their team to manufacture product to tighter tolerance, allowing them to reduce their machine times while reducing scrap

4. Energy Industries   *Gas Booster Compressor Castings*
   - Collaborated with their engineers to reduce leakage problems

At this point in my career, I seek new challenges and look forward to meeting with you to discuss how I can contribute to your company and make a positive impact on your bottom line. In response to your request for salary history, my compensation has been within industry norms for each position, ranging from mid 70s to low 80s, and I assume you will offer a competitive compensation package. Thank you for your time and consideration in reviewing my qualifications in the enclosed resume. I will call you next week to explore the possibility of an interview.

Sincerely,

Michael Fisher

203

Vice President. *Jane Roqueplot, West Middlesex, Pennsylvania*

The writer showcases the applicant's accomplishments to demonstrate his ability to meet the company's standards and goals. Results are grouped by company and category of parts.

Jon W. Nederstein
0000 Winchester Court, #2B
Alexandria, Virginia 22314-5780
(555) 555-5555

March 22, 20XX

Todd Norling
Human Resource Director
Artesia Drilling Equipment Company
14502 Highway 14 East
Stafford, Texas 77700

Dear Mr. Norling:

Over the years, I have seen many examples of great leadership. What separates the truly successful from the rest is a higher level of contribution toward the organization's most important goals. Are you looking for a vice president of operations who can motivate a team to implement plans that not only meet but also exceed growth and financial goals? If so, I am the person who can deliver these contributions.

As you will note on the enclosed resume, the breadth of my expertise covers a wide area of responsibilities. I am a hardworking, ambitious leader and motivator. I am consistently recognized for team building, creative problem solving and a high degree of expertise in the manufacturing field. Would you like to see some of these events take place in your facility?

- Turnover rate of 12% per month brought to 3% per month
- Scrap rate cut 50%
- Increased output threefold
- Profits raised 200% in 2 years

These accomplishments demonstrate what I have done in the past for other manufacturing facilities and can do in the future for you. At your convenience, I would like to meet with you and explore the possibility of using my experience and knowledge to benefit Artesia Drilling Equipment Company. I will call later this week to see if we can arrange an appointment. Thank you for your time and consideration.

Sincerely,

Jon W. Nederstein

Enclosure: Resume

204

Vice President of Operations. *Michele Angello, Aurora, Colorado*

Bullets in the body of the letter emphasize accomplishments that are commented upon in the resume. The text refers to the applicant making the same type of improvements for the next employer.

BETH SMITHEY

000 Reynolds Court   **Valrico, Florida 33594**   **(555) 555-5555**   **bethsmithey@aol.com**

April 9, 20XX

Cargill Animal Nutrition
ATTN: Florida Position
P.O. BOX 8250
Montgomery, AL 36108

Dear Hiring Professional:

The Cargill Animal Nutrition management position you advertised recently accurately describes my skills and abilities. I am a professional with a strong track record of success who would love to join your company!

Your Needs	Examples of My Qualifications
Team player	◆ Currently a case manager for a juvenile offender release program after completion of boot camp. Have to create a team environment with the juvenile, drill instructor, psychologists, teachers and parents to ensure post-release success. Our program has the highest success rate in Florida.
Adaptability	◆ Ran a retail store and performed any and all functions that had to be completed, from sales to administration to customer service. ◆ Set up and ran a new branch of a company that provided auto financing. Had to adapt rules and procedures to accommodate car dealers and customer needs.
Communication skills	◆ Have developed and given numerous presentations and classes to groups and organizations. ◆ In Human Resources position, gave new-employee orientations, completed and filed paperwork and answered employee questions.
Decision-making skills	◆ All my jobs have required exceptional decision-making ability: from developing case-management and release plans to running a store or managing human resource benefits for employees.
Manage multiple tasks simultaneously	◆ Currently supervise and oversee the cases of up to 30 juveniles who are in different phases of release, simultaneously managing their needs, program plans and paperwork. ◆ Background in Human Resources, where conflict management and multitasking were essential to successful performance.
Conflict-resolution skills	◆ As case manager for a youth offender program, am constantly resolving and mediating conflicts among the juveniles, their parents, the system, teachers and other authority figures.

My resume provides further details of my accomplishments. I look forward to discussing a new career opportunity with you. I will contact you next week to arrange a meeting to discuss your company's needs in greater detail.

Sincerely,

Beth Smithey

205

Project Manager. *Gail Frank, Tampa, Florida*

A poorly worded, "loose" want ad asked for a lot of generic skills. The applicant had little experience in the field. The writer played up the applicant's communication skills and team-player achievements.

MARY JO ALLEN

555 Jamestown Road • Glenwood, IL 00000 • 555-555-5555 (H) • maryjallen@email.com

Date

Name
Title
Company Name
Address
City, State, Zip

Dear (name):

> *"A dedicated employee who steps up to the tasks assigned…Mary Jo has continually held herself to the highest standards…is assertive and proactive in handling issues …demonstrates good judgment…I would work on any project with her."*
> *Jim Milroy, Systems Training Manager*
> *Brookhaven Laboratories*

As a highly acclaimed and award-winning professional with solid progressive excellence delivering cost reductions and process improvements to promote organizational gain, I believe my qualifications will be of great interest to you. Outlined on the enclosed resume you will find a record of achievement in the following key areas:

…. Project Planning and Management … Operations and Staff Administration … Ergonomics & Space Planning … Facilities and Security Administration … Vendor and Supplier Negotiations … Office Management … Organizational Restructuring & Development … Budget & Profitability Oversight … and more.

Throughout my career, I have managed complex restructuring projects, consistently finishing under budget and ahead of schedule. I am known for my skillful coordination of cross-functional teams, synchronizing engineers, architects, designers, vendors, and subcontractors to execute projects smoothly, efficiently, and with little or no business disruption. Committed to personal and organizational progress, I am currently pursuing a Master's Degree in Project Management, maintaining a GPA of 3.90.

As a result of my efforts and company dedication, I

- **Received the Presidential Award in 2000** for the complex headquarter relocation of 1500 employees, as well as Pride of CORP Awards in 2005 and 2006 for a strategic corporate renovation program and other initiatives.
- **Reduced Workers Compensation Claims by 90%** through the development and initiation of a productive Ergonomics program.
- **Cut overhead costs by nearly $900K** through innovative programs and procedures including furniture renovation, insourcing alternatives, and strategic vendor negotiations.
- **Instituted valuable operational improvements** including the Facility Safety Evaluation Program, the Ergonomics Assessment Program, and a maintenance staff directory.

The above is just a brief description of my experience, strengths, and ability to lead your organization successfully into the future as its next (Job Title). I would welcome the opportunity to meet with you to discuss my qualifications and candidacy in further detail. I look forward to this opportunity, and I thank you for your consideration.

Sincerely,

Mary Jo Allen
Enclosure

206

Project Manager. *Karen Bartell, Massapequa, New York*

This letter was nominated for a TORI (Toast of the Résumé Industry™) Best Cover Letter Award. The glowing testimonial from a supervisor sets the tone for this document.

FRANCIS CAMPBELL
http://linkedin.com/xxxx/xxxx/x/555/55x

+44 (0)5555 555 555 ■ franciscampbell@xxx.com
55 Gables Close ■ London, XXX XXXX, UK

*~ Providing dedicated, forward-thinking **Housing & Urban Development** consulting services ~*

August 23, 20XX

Ms. Angela Stevens, VP of Development
Tacker Development Corporation
555 Central Avenue, Suite 555
Newark, NJ 55555

Dear Ms. Stevens,

If you are looking for an outspoken **Community Development Advocate** and **Senior-Level Project Manager** who is qualified to make instant and valuable contributions to your firm's real estate development projects across Newark, your search is over. I offer strong commercial and analytical skills combined with a clear-cut view of business priorities and the ability to drive complex initiatives across multicultural and multisite development projects that stimulate community growth.

I am accomplished in drafting winning bids to secure funding, enterprising when searching for new development opportunities, and extremely resourceful when directing project teams and administering budgets in the multimillions. With **Prince2 Practitioner** qualifications, I bring with me winning skills in streamlining construction site operations and driving end-to-end development efforts—from the predevelopment phase of financial and project feasibility analysis, stakeholder and community engagement, and construction site management to compliance monitoring and property management.

With international experience, I have performed in numerous high-profile **housing refurbishment consulting** roles across various London boroughs, including **the London Borough of Newham—the location of the 2012 Olympics.** I have proven experience responding strategically and tactically to changing priorities and client requirements on both small- and large-scale imperatives within diverse populations and socioeconomic climates. Realizing the need for international adoption of best practice development policies, I functioned as a key member of a team that successfully delivered a **HOPE VI/HUD-inspired program due to its success in the United States.**

Some strategic personal initiatives in Newark include

- **Assisting Newark's Planning & Economic Development Department in drafting a new ordinance that was consequently passed by City Hall;** developing a broad network of industry connections and gaining a deep understanding of local community cultures and requirements as well as compliant policy making during a self-initiated internship.
- Building credibility with Brick City Development Inc. in Newark, subsequently chosen to **sponsor project inception and team meetings on behalf of the Director of Greater Newark Convention & Visitors Bureau** during high-stress Newark Restaurant Week event-planning efforts.
- **Reaching out to Mayor Cory Booker as a catalyst for international policy sharing and execution** between the City of Newark and local London boroughs; connecting with the Brookings Institute in Washington, DC, to jump-start transatlantic exchanges in policy making and research.

In addition, I hold a **M.S. in Social Policy and Planning and a B.A. in Politics & Development** and have gained on-the-job insight to predevelopment and construction processes with a strong focus on eco-construction/sustainable building techniques and materials to deliver affordable, environmentally friendly housing and mixed-use development projects.

My career has been marked by quick promotions and selection for the most challenging assignments because of my reputation for getting things done and having the leadership skills to inspire dynamic team performance. In every case, I have succeeded in meeting tough standards, tight deadlines, and ambitious service-level agreements. I also recognize that it is people who ultimately deliver results, and I am strongly focused on building relationships with clients, colleagues, contractors, community service business partners, resident/tenant groups, and government regulatory agencies.

I will follow up with you in a few days to answer any questions you may have. In the meantime, you may reach me at the above phone number or by email. I thank you for your time and consideration and look forward to what I expect will be the start of many positive exchanges.

Sincerely,

Francis Campbell
Enclosure: résumé

207

Senior-Level Project/Program Manager. *Sandra Ingemansen, Leeds, West Yorkshire, England*

This applicant was networking to get her next consulting role, so the writer put a LinkedIn profile address in the contact information and started the letter with a personal branding statement.

David Lee Thompson
6798 Broad Street West, Milwaukee, WI 53202
414-291-5555 Home ▪ 414-220-3333 Cell ▪ dleethompson2@comcast.net

October 11, 20xx

Hiring Manager
Carrington Ice Cream Products Company
Dubuque, IA 52001

Re: Regional Licensed Manager
Licensed Stores—Dubuque, IA
Ref ID: 00007311RLM

Dear Hiring Manager,

Your job posting for a **Regional Licensed Manager—Licensed Stores, Dubuque (IA)** on Monster.com demonstrates that your company's values match mine and piqued my interest in contacting you.

As an experienced multiunit retail store operations manager, I am most interested in joining an organization where increasing sales does not take a back seat to quality and customer service. Carrington's reputation for brand standards and integrity, as evidenced in the Carrington "Quality Customer Experience," is renowned. I'd like to be associated with your winning team!

My resume is enclosed for your review. With 10 years of experience in the retail sales industry, my background includes direct sales, sales management, operations management, strategic planning, P&L management, merchandising, buying, team building, marketing and promotions, human resources, and customer-relationship management. I have outlined below how my qualifications match your requirements:

Your Requirements	My Qualifications
1. Progressive sales management experience within a retail environment, merchandising, and influencing others to achieve sales and profitability results—10 years.	1. Ten years of progressive sales management experience in consumer retail industry. Currently on target to achieve **double-digit million-dollar gross margin profits** for 20xx. Motivated teams to win district, division, and regional awards and rank in top 5 (out of 190 stores) in earnings.
2. Progressive experience managing multiunit retail operations—minimum of 3 years.	2. Three years of multiunit retail operations experience, combined with 1 year of category management experience for **2,000 stores and 5 distribution centers**. Track record of gaining trust and buy-in from store directors that contributed to award-winning performances for store sales.
3. Supervision—8 years.	3. Ten years of supervisory experience, including positive team-building and effective change management. Participatory management style has led to **increases in morale, productivity and sales,** while **reducing shrinkage to record lows.**
4. Analysis of financial performance—minimum of 2 years.	4. Full P&L management experience for 9 years, overseeing multimillion-dollar operating budgets. Closely monitored cost controls and **captured millions of dollars in cost savings** through careful vendor and product negotiations.

My sales management and retail operations experience has equipped me to drive consumer sales—I would like to do the same for you. May we talk soon? I will call to set an appointment. Thank you for your time.

Sincerely,

David Lee Thompson

208

Regional Licensed Manager. *Susan Guarneri, Three Lakes, Wisconsin*

The numbered, side-by-side comparison chart makes it easy to check off each requirement as met. Phrases in boldface allow for quick scanning of key points and results.

PETER SAMUELS

67 Downey Street ■ West Milton, CT 55555 ■ 555.555.5555 ■ petersam@aol.com

[Date]

[Name]
[Title]
[Organization]
[Address]
[City, State ZIP Code]

Dear Mr. or Ms. _____:

During my 10-year career as a public official, I have acquired broad experience and honed diverse skills that I believe will be of interest to the Town of West Milton. My background, highlighted in the enclosed resume, demonstrates that I possess the necessary strategic planning, financial, project, and people management capabilities that would qualify me to serve as your community's Town Administrator.

What do I offer?

- More than 10 years of municipal government experience as a Selectman and Chair governing the Town of Southington, which is complemented by concurrent private-sector management experience.
- Proactive leadership with proven ability to inspire cooperation, communication, and consensus among personnel and other groups.
- Development and administration of $10 million budget as well as planning and overseeing multiple projects to meet community needs.
- Contributing to economic development by building strong public/private partnerships and negotiating agreements.

Examples of my accomplishments:

- Leadership of several town revitalization projects providing key services.
- Negotiating Tax Incentive Financing Agreements for retaining and attracting employers.
- Sound fiscal management that includes improved benefit programs without cost increases.
- Fostering a work environment that builds team spirit and energizes employees to perform at their best. As a result, our staff is recognized for exceptional responsiveness and positive community relations.

This position as Town Administrator is particularly exciting to me for several reasons. As a native of the community, I am familiar with the area's demographics and general issues facing West Milton. In addition, I still consider the community my "home" as I have an extended family living in the area, am a property owner, and would love to be a resident of the community once again.

I have always had a passion for municipal government service and would enjoy making it my full-time career. Therefore, I welcome the opportunity to discuss my qualifications and the contributions I would make as your community's Town Administrator. Thank you for your consideration.

Sincerely,

Peter Samuels

209

Town Administrator. *Louise Garver, Broad Brook, Connecticut*

The applicant was changing careers from daytime sales management to after-hours town management. The letter focused successfully on accomplishments in municipal government.

FRANK CREESHER
000 South Stewart Way · Sacramento, CA 99999 · (555) 555-5555 · fcreesher@aol.com

March 28, 20XX

Thomas Lindsay
Projects Manager
Evinco Metus
1632 Artic Avenue
Sacramento, CA 99999

Dear Mr. Lindsay,

Leading construction management projects for high-growth companies within the microelectronics industry is my area of expertise. I am currently exploring opportunities where I can contribute significant experience in project management—hence, my interest in Evinco Metus.

As you will note on the enclosed resume, the breadth of my expertise covers a wide area of responsibilities, thereby providing me with insights into the total operation. My experience includes microelectronics cleanroom facilities, hazardous occupancies, laboratories and workspaces to support integrated micro systems research and development, as well as production. Allow me to highlight several key projects of particular relevance to Evinco Metus:

- Project Manager for **Command Semiconductor project** (Manassas, VA) through Marrow Contractors, Inc.;
- Senior Project Manager for **Hysteria E-4 Wafer Fab project** (Eugene, OR) through M+W/Marrow joint venture;
- Pre-Construction Manager for **Miasma Technologies Fab 6 project** (Boise, ID) through Morose.

You will find me to be a dedicated project manager who leads by example and is accustomed to a fast-paced environment where deadlines are priority and handling multiple jobs simultaneously is the norm. I have more than 15 years of experience and throughout my career have built a reputation as an individual who takes charge and responsibility for planning and executing challenging projects and for being a talented and determined manager who accomplishes results.

I am confident that the mixture of my work experiences, along with my strong communication skills, would benefit your company. I welcome the opportunity to meet with you to explore how my expertise and talents could best meet the facilities and construction project needs of Evinco Metus.

I appreciate your time and consideration and look forward to speaking with you soon. I will follow up in a few days to explore the possibility of a personal interview.

Sincerely,

Frank Creesher

Enclosure

210

Construction Project Manager. *Denette D. Jones, Mountain View, Hawaii*

The applicant wanted to move from construction management to project management. Bullets and boldfacing highlight key projects relevant to the targeted company, which is mentioned three times.

Lynn Struck 0000 Eagle Drive 555-555-5555
Sterling Heights, MI 48310 lynnst@network.net

April 12, 20XX

BigCar
Employment Division
1000 BigCar Drive
Auburn Hills, MI 48326

I am contacting you to apply for a production position with BigCar. I have eight years of valuable production experience. My husband, Adam Struck, is a current BigCar employee at Warren Assembly. He suggested I send my resume for consideration.

My first production position was with Plastics Research in its Brighton, Michigan, plant. I learned a lot about assembling parts and operating machinery. Since 20XX I have held a seasonal position with Conrad Foods on a packaging line. To say that I'm a hard worker is an understatement. For example, my first summer on the job I packed an average of 3,000–4,000 jars a day (the standard is about 1,200 jars/day). Because of my performance, the next year I was promoted to Crew Leader, the only seasonal employee to hold that position. I get along well with my coworkers and am constantly on the lookout for ways to improve my performance.

I really enjoy the fast-paced production environment, and it would be great to work for BigCar. Once you've read my material, I hope you will forward my resume to the specific units that need production workers. I am available for an interview and will call you to find a mutually convenient time. Thank you for your time and consideration.

Sincerely,

Lynn Struck

Enclosure

211

Automotive Production Position. *Janet L. Beckstrom, Flint, Michigan*

The applicant wanted a production position in an automotive plant. She mentioned her husband's name because the company offers hiring preference to those recommended by current employees.

Will consider relocating to San Diego

William "Bill" Stockton
0000 Saguaro Loop Mesa, Arizona 00000
✉ billstockton0000@xxx.com ☎ 000.555.5555

Monday, XX February, 20XX

Mr. William "Bill" Stockton
Plant Manager
BrightStar Industries, Inc.
000 Northridge Parkway
Suite 000
San Diego, California 00000

> *Payoffs:* Put an **end to unscheduled shutdowns** and **saved thousands** in expensive repairs…Cut a **30 percent reject rate to 1½ percent in 5 days,** 2 days early—without disturbing production…**Fixed an environmental problem** in just 5 weeks that once cost my employer thousands in EPA fines.

Dear Mr. Stockton:

You have just read the 47-word version of my résumé. I've sent this package to you because I want help you make the production numbers you want for BrightStar.

I love what I do. This is the first real résumé I've ever had; companies always sought me out. So when my recent employer downsized me a few days ago, I took responsibility for matching what I do with what companies need.

That's why the next pages don't look like a typical résumé. I thought you deserved to see 6 profit-building capabilities I want to put at BrightStar's disposal at once as your newest Plant Maintenance Supervisor. Backing them up are 9 examples with payoffs like the ones you just read above.

I'm a lot better at listening to people than I am writing to them. So I'd like to call in a few days to see how I can help you.

Sincerely,

William "Bill" Stockton

Encl.: Résumé

212

Plant Maintenance Supervisor. *Don Orlando, Montgomery, Alabama*

The writer of this cover letter is a master of the unexpected in creating cover letters (and resumes) that avoid stale approaches. Note here the use of "Payoffs" to label achievements.

Jim Salinger
00 Woodlawn Drive • Hope Hull, AL 55555
(000) 000-0000 • jimsalinger555@xxx.com

November 15, 20XX

Myra Cassidy, Vice President
ABS Group
PO Box 000
Montgomery, AL 55555

RE: Operations Manager Position

Dear Ms. Cassidy:

To continue ABS Group's commitment to quality and customer satisfaction, you need managers who are always thinking about the customer's needs. I believe my past accomplishments, combined with a focus on the end user, make me the ideal candidate for your Operations Manager job.

Following my service in the U.S. Navy, I moved up the chain of command at a single company, all the way from Production Worker to Operations Manager.

My career achievements include the following:

- Played a major role in the 2011 startup of a multimillion-dollar manufacturing plant, directing equipment design and layout of the 63,000-square-foot facility

- In 2009, spearheaded the successful turnaround of one of my employer's Canadian facilities, reducing downtime by 85%, raising production by 44%, and increasing sales simultaneously

- Contributed to the plant's earning the coveted Halzmann Prize for excellence in manufacturing in 2012

You can see a more detailed account of my background and skills in the enclosed résumé. Once you've had an opportunity to review it, I hope you'll give me a call. I look forward to discussing how I can help improve ABS Group's bottom line.

Sincerely,

Jim Salinger

Enclosure

213

Operations Manager. *Alexia Scott, Montgomery, Alabama*

Achievements appear stronger when they are quantified, containing numbers, dates, percentages, and dollar amounts. Bullets help to ensure that these quantified achievements are seen.

RICHARD D. PFEIFFER

555 West Randolph Drive | Edwardsville, Illinois 55555
C 000.000.0000 | H 555.555.5555 | rpfeiffer@xxx.com

September 26, 20XX

Jaclyn White
Human Resources
Prudential Building Products, Inc.
555 Palatine Way
Chicago, Illinois 55555

RE: Operations Manager, ID# XXXXX

Dear Ms. White:

I fix broken plants. Throughout my career, whether tasked to turn around a manufacturing facility with significant production issues or take a high-performing facility to the next level, I have consistently delivered strong results. At this time, I am seeking new career challenges, and I believe I am an excellent fit for your advertised Operations Manager job opening.

My expertise lies in reducing costs and headcount while increasing efficiency and production. My contributions to the bottom line are outlined in the enclosed resume, but I want to call your attention to the following achievements:

- **$8M in cost savings** (Wilmot Products, Inc.)
- **200% increase in productivity across 4 plants** (Wilmot Products, Inc.)
- **600% increase in productivity** (Star Manufacturing Co.)
- **50% reduction in headcount** (Star Manufacturing Co.)
- **70% decrease in worker's compensation claims** (SwanCorp.)

I welcome the opportunity to discuss your needs and how my talents can bring immediate and sustainable benefits to Prudential Building Products. Please contact me at your earliest convenience to arrange a personal interview. Thank you for your time and consideration, and I look forward to speaking with you soon.

Sincerely,

Richard D. Pfeiffer

Enclosure

214

Operations Manager. *Michelle P. Swanson, Edwardsville, Illinois*

The first sentence grabs the reader's attention immediately. In just four words, the sentence speaks of the company's biggest need and states how this candidate can address that need.

KELCEE JENKINS, PE

555 Charleston Drive ▪ Lakewood, CO 55555 ▪ 555.555.5555 ▪ kjenkins@xx.net

July 20, 20XX

Lindsey Toole
Director of Human Resources
Select Plastics, Inc.
000 Riverside Drive
Englewood, CO 99999

Dear Ms. Toole:

Luis Kover has alerted me to upcoming opportunities with your organization in a quality-control leadership role. Over the past few years, I have enjoyed watching Select Plastics grow and am excited about the prospect of joining such an innovative, energetic organization. As Select looks to the future, I would like to introduce myself as a resource, bringing a background in process management, quality control, and manufacturing leadership to bolster quality and product outcomes for the organization.

As a leader in manufacturing and global technology companies, I have advanced through facilities management, process engineering, and manufacturing leadership roles. My ability to build effective teams and collaborate across organizations to solve problems has been essential in consistently attaining quality and product development objectives. Highlights of my accomplishments include

- **Cutting waste and downtime** without capital expense, identifying areas for improvement in manufacturing operations, determining the root cause of poor performance, working across departments to gain buy-in and improve solutions, and implementing changes without halting production.

- **Bolstering product development efforts** by adapting operations to meet production needs, managing product-line manufacturing processes, and leading cross-functional projects.

- **Improving quality and controlled product variability** by driving continual improvement of production processes, applying Six Sigma and kaizen principles to evaluate operations, devising solutions that challenged the status quo, and influencing management and shop floor teams.

- **Enhancing performance by establishing meaningful measures,** eliminating unnecessary testing steps, reviewing processes and deviations daily, and educating operators to implement changes and improve production outcomes.

Enclosed is a résumé that details my experience and education. I am excited about what my expertise can bring to your organization and would welcome the opportunity to interview with you to discuss my background in more detail. Thank you in advance for your time and consideration.

Sincerely,

Kelcee Jenkins
Enclosure

215

Quality Control Manager. *Marie Zimenoff, Fort Collins, Colorado*

This professional had been out of the field for a while, running a business, but a networking contact alerted her to opportunities within a targeted organization. Bulleted achievements speak to her leadership abilities.

SHIRLEY A. EDWARDS

H. (555) 555-5555 | shirley@hotmail.com | C. (555) 555-5000
123 Willow Avenue | Las Vegas, NV 55555

INNOVATIVE QUALITY CONTROL MANAGER

September 27, 20XX

Laura Bell
Human Resources Manager
ABC Manufacturing
000 Swan Road
Las Vegas, NV 55555

RE: **Quality Control Manager Posting, Reference # XXXX**

Dear Ms. Bell,

In response to your posting for a Quality Control Manager, I am enclosing my résumé for your review. Given my proven record of leadership and experience in quality control and manufacturing, I am confident that I would be an excellent candidate for this position and an ideal fit for ABC Manufacturing.

I pride myself on being an innovative, results-oriented, and hands-on individual with progressive managerial experience. My management style strongly emphasizes teamwork and relationship building founded upon clear communication and expectations. A review of my résumé will further acquaint you with my background and qualifications for this role.

Your Requirements:

1. Five years of progressive management experience.
2. Quality control training and/or certification.
3. Solid hands-on understanding of the requirements of ISO certifications, along with excellent communication, computer, and leadership skills.

My Qualifications:

1. 10+ years of progressive manufacturing experience and growth.
2. Certified ISO 9001 Auditor through Stanford University.
3. Demonstrated leadership capability in driving business excellence and exceeding corporate goals. Strong training facilitator with solid computer proficiency.

My résumé shows my career growth and experience. What it cannot illustrate, however, is the degree of professionalism, resourcefulness, and dedication that I offer as an employee. A personal conversation will enable us to discuss how I can contribute to the success of your company. As requested, my salary requirements for this role range from $65k to $75k and are negotiable. I look forward to exploring this opportunity with you in the near future.

Regards,

Shirley Edwards

Enclosure: Résumé

216

Quality Control Manager. *Tanya Sinclair, Pickering, Ontario, Canada*

Three of the applicant's qualifications match the employer's three key job requirements. The employer also required salary expectations, which the applicant expressed as a range to prevent elimination.

SHANNON HEWLETT

0000 Fourth Street   New York, NY 10012   555.555.5555   SHewlett@hotmail.com

April 3, 20XX

Mr. John Wyle
Director of Human Resources
Broadcasting Company USA
30 Madison Avenue
New York, NY 10017

Dear Mr. Wyle:

As an experienced Associate Producer with a steadfast career that reflects several years in responsible positions for major clients across new media production, including HBO and Hewlett-Packard, I am enthusiastic about my decision to move my career in the direction of broadcasting.

I bring an accomplished background that encapsulates my ability to conceive, create, and manage the production of independent and high-profile projects with a sense of purpose and a record of achievement. As a renaissance professional who continues to push the envelope of creativity while meeting the demands of workflow and people-management requirements, I continue to prove my ability to cut through red tape and confusion by providing clarity and direction with a demonstrated combination of intellect, artistic talent, and business savvy.

Whether working on proposals, negotiating with vendors, consulting clients, or traveling cross-country to conduct large group training seminars, I deliver results and secure the respect of senior management based on my high performance level. Through hands-on leadership of cross-functional teams, I maintain a cohesive synergy between clients and production teams from point of planning to market launch of multimillion-dollar projects. My ability to work in the present and anticipate what's ahead continuously ensures that deadlines are met on time and within budget with superior results. It is with your organization that I hope to continue in this vein while taking on new challenges in the field of broadcasting.

If, on reviewing my accompanying resume, you feel there is a mutual interest, I would welcome the chance to meet with you to discuss the possibility of my joining your production team as Associate Producer. Thank you for your time. I look forward to speaking with you soon and will call to set an appointment.

Sincerely,

Shannon Hewlett

217

Associate Producer, Broadcasting. *Ann Baehr, East Islip, New York*

The applicant sought to move as Associate Producer from one career (in media production) to another (broadcasting). The letter refers to the many areas in which her experience is relevant to the new field.

Jacqueline S. LeFevre

50 Daytona Street
South Palm Beach, FL 50555
(505) 505-5555
jacquil@yahoo.com

December 6, 20XX

Mr. Dean S. Arnold
Executive Producer
PBC Studios
5000 Ocean Boulevard
Los Angeles, CA 50005

Dear Mr. Arnold:

- Presenting the images and text that optimally tell the story
- Creatively managing to successful fruition multiple projects with overlapping deadlines
- Achieving a vision that is authentic, innovative, and compelling

These are all key strengths that I can bring to PBC Studios in the role of a media strategist. Meld with this my talent for working with high-level decision makers, including celebrities—and an unwavering commitment to producing work of exceptional quality—and I think you'll find me to be a very well-qualified candidate. In addition to highlights presented on my resume, you'll find me to be

- Skilled in developing a powerful media image (or enhancing one to ensure it is totally on-point). I combine strong visual skills with a creative variety of media formats and applications to develop a compelling media image.
- Talented in capturing the right tone and look of a piece that best conveys the desired message.
- An effective communicator and collaborator. I am able to work at all organizational levels while maintaining confidentiality and sensitivity. I have earned a reputation for successfully garnering project approval by all stakeholders.
- A capable researcher and storyteller. I am skilled in defining the project, succinctly telling the story through impactful visuals, and selecting footage and all creative elements that most effectively present the complete picture.

From 20XX through spring of this year, I worked with Streamline Productions, exclusively handling projects for NBC and serving as the editor and, frequently, series editor for a number of high-profile projects. Since then, I have provided freelance production talent to a number of exciting independent projects. Consistent throughout my career has been an ability to keep a project on time and under budget—while delivering outstanding quality. I'd like to bring this same level of talent to PBC. I believe I can provide a degree of innovation and skill that will augment your existing production capabilities in a very complementary manner. Let's speak later in the week.

Sincerely,

Jacqueline S. LeFevre

Enclosure

218

Media Strategist. *Jan Melnik, Durham, Connecticut*

With years of experience with a prominent production company that supported a big-three network, this person wanted a key media position with another big studio. Bullets highlight skills.

NANCY TOLLMAN
555 Circle Avenue, Bradenton, Florida 55555
555.555.5555 ● nancytollman@anyemail.com

September 1, 20XX

Melodie Lang
Marketing Director
XYZ Company
555 Great Company Way
Bradenton, Florida 55555

Dear Ms. Lang:

If you are looking for a Social Media Specialist who has been consistently recognized as an expert in the field, then I would love to work to become a part of your team! Within the last few years, social media has changed the world of business. Something that was seen as a way to keep in touch with family and friends has now changed marketing and promotions. My passion for this field, in addition to my strong qualifications, would make me a great addition to XYZ Company.

As you will see on my attached résumé, I have published many articles and conducted keynote presentations on this topic, all of which have been well received. Of particular note to you and your team are the results that I have generated. My innovative social media marketing plans have made me a recognized presence in this medium. By using Facebook and Twitter alone, I have helped companies achieve a 300% return on investment. Online coupons, contests, and promotional campaigns are my specialty as my focus is the engagement of new and existing customers. I would love to talk further about some specific initiatives I already have in mind for XYZ Company.

My strong work ethic and impeccable attention to detail also make me a strong candidate. I have a keen ability to multitask through different projects. I have developed strong organizational skills to monitor the progress of the marketing campaigns to keep myself and the initiatives on track. For me, teamwork is the best approach as I enjoy working both alongside others and individually to exceed the objectives of my employer. Communication is the way to achieve this, and I strive every day to learn something new.

I would love to talk further about my qualifications and the ways in which I could assist XYZ Company. If there are no current openings, I would be thrilled to talk about the ways in which I could enrich my application for future opportunities. Thank you so much for your time and consideration. I look forward to hearing from you.

Sincerely,

Nancy Tollman

219

Social Media Specialist. *Haley Richardson, Riverview, Florida*

This cold-call letter was sent to a company with no advertised openings. The individual was asking for time with the Marketing Director to present herself for future opportunities.

Jillian K. Young

000 Hawkeye Court   Iowa City, IA 52242   *jkyoung@network.net*
                                                                     555-555-7777

Date

Name
Company
Address

Dear Hiring Manager:

How many times do resumes cross your desk from individuals who have extensive warehouse experience *plus* mail handling experience? I imagine not a lot. So I hope you will review my material and consider my interest in an appropriate position with your organization.

I gained the bulk of my experience during seven years of service in the military, much of which was as a Supply/Warehouse Manager. Not only did I keep track of 10,000 parts in a 10,000-square-foot depot, but I also coordinated repair requests for equipment and vehicles, processing about 300 work orders per day. Additionally, I have been trained in hazardous materials handling, manual and computerized inventory control, and overall warehouse management. Since I left the military in 20XX, I have been a Mail Carrier. One of my periodic assignments is to reduce the accumulation of mail that has been designated *nondeliverable.* It takes research and perseverance, but eventually I whittle down the pile.

My experience in the military cultivated a strong work ethic and helped me develop many personal skills, not the least of which are organization and communication. In fact, my superior officer commended me for my efficient and accurate methods. I have no problems delegating and supervising others.

I will soon be joining my husband in our new home in Cedar Rapids, and I am eager to begin working in the area. I will give you a telephone call to discuss employment opportunities. Of course I can make arrangements to be available for an in-person interview as well. Thank you for your time and consideration.

Sincerely,

Jillian K. Young

Enclosure

220

Warehouse Manager. *Janet Beckstrom, Flint, Michigan*

The applicant had warehousing experience in the Army and worked for the U.S. Postal Service. She could not transfer to a Post Office in her area, so she sought a warehouse management position.

JOHN HENDERSON
555 S. Jackson
Grandview Plaza, KS 55555
Cell: 555-555-5555
Email: hendersonjohn@xx.com

March 28, 20XX

Susan Carter
Human Resources Director
000 St. John Arena
00 Woody Hayes Drive
Columbus, OH 00000

Mrs. Carter:

Thank you very much for all your help these last few weeks. After reading over the job descriptions and requirements you sent me, I am very interested in pursuing the customer service coordinator, seat license coordinator, and production coordinator vacancies with the athletic department. Enclosed with this letter is my resume, which details my education, work experience, and involvement with athletics. I am extremely interested in the challenges of sports administration and feel that I possess the level of enthusiasm, professionalism, initiative, and teamwork to make a significant contribution to the Ohio State Athletic Department.

I am currently an officer in the United States Army and will be leaving the service on June 1. I am a 20XX graduate of the United States Military Academy where I played varsity football and rugby, earning All-American recognition in the latter. I majored in General Law and minored in Systems Engineering. I am confident that I am a prime candidate for any one of the three vacancies with your department. My diverse background and my management and leadership skills will provide your office with a highly motivated and productive professional.

I will be leaving on a 30-day deployment on April 15 but will be in the Columbus area soon following the deployment. I would like to meet with you then. I will contact your office to inquire as to a potential meeting date and time. I thank you for your consideration and look forward to speaking with you.

Sincerely,

John Henderson

221

Athletic Department Coordinator. *James Walker, Fort Riley, Kansas*

This individual had been an outstanding athlete at West Point and wanted a position in sports administration at a university. The letter highlights his athletic and academic achievements, plus his leadership skills. The position he got in ticket sales was a foot in the door.

BRIAN J. RAWLINS
Executive - Leader - Mentor

0000 HighTowers Way, Apt 00, Tacoma, WA 55555
Cell: (000) 555-5555 * Home: (000) 000-5555
BrianRawlins@xxx.xxx

Date:

Roger's Food Corporation
000 One Place Court
Pleasanton, CA 00000

Dear Mr. Smithfield,

I read with great interest an article about Roger's award-winning Supervisory Leadership Development Training Program for Officers in The EDGE insert of the *Army Times*. I feel that I would be an excellent candidate for the training program. As I make my transition into the civilian sector, I would welcome the opportunity to be part of a Fortune 300 corporation that has social responsibility, diversity, and inclusion at the forefront of its core values.

Throughout my extensive and diversified military career, I have consistently demonstrated strong leadership and management skills. My time as a Battalion Commander afforded me the opportunity to develop and successfully execute my management skills, especially in the area of human resources and daily operations. As a Commander, I was ultimately responsible and hands-on with training, motivating, counseling, and developing personnel. Excelling in operations management, I have maintained, forecasted, and distributed budgets and equipment in excess of $120 million dollars.

I am organized, flexible, and mission-focused and work well under pressure. My commitment to excellence is centered with strong ethical standards and impeccable integrity. My attached resume further highlights my former military experience, leadership responsibilities, and achievements.

I would welcome the opportunity to meet with you and discuss my qualifications for the Supervisory Leadership Development Training Program that begins in January.

Respectfully,

LTC Brian J. Rawlins, MBA
Cell: (000) 555-5555
Home: (000) 000-5555

Enclosure

222

Store Manager. *Kara Varner, Hampton, Virginia*

This active duty officer wanted to use leadership-development training to become a store manager in civilian life. The letter stresses his leadership abilities and budget experience.

555 North Career Way Boulevard, Tampa, FL 55555
Home (555) 555-5555, Mobile (555) 555-0000
marycornelius@anyemail.com

Mary K. Cornelius

September 20, 20XX

Ms. Lonny Smith
Director, Corporate Staffing
000 East Drive
Fargo, ND 55555

Dear Ms. Smith:

If you are looking for a professional, detail-oriented administrative assistant who is constantly striving to improve office functions, then you have found your match! The job advertisement on your website was intriguing, and I would like to learn more about the opportunity and determine if my skill set could benefit your organization.

Having spent the last five years as an administrative assistant in the Navy, I think you will find that I am uniquely qualified for this opening. My skills are varied as I was transferred to many different offices because of my ability to easily adapt and learn quickly. Each of these positions allowed me to perfect the office coordination skills that you seek. All of my work was executed exceptionally while following the military protocol of each area, which required extreme attention to detail.

In addition to my technical skills using the Microsoft Office Suite, including programs like Excel and Access, I have a keen ability to establish rapport with my customers and clients. I am able to ask the right questions, whether in person or through electronic communication, to get them the information that they desire. This ability would be especially useful in your office as I could alleviate some of the redundant questions that you might receive, freeing your time for your other responsibilities. I see my role as an assistant to do just that—assist my supervisor and colleagues in whatever way I can.

As I transition to civilian life, I would love to find an employer who could benefit from my skills in calendar coordination, meeting planning, correspondence and document creation, confidential records retrieval, and research. I am a dedicated and loyal employee who will strive every day to exceed the expectations of my supervisor.

Thank you so much for your time and consideration. I look forward to the possibility of discussing my fit within your organization in an interview.

Sincerely,

Mary K. Cornelius

Mary K. Cornelius

223

Administrative Assistant. *Haley Richardson, Riverview, Florida*

The applicant was transitioning from military to civilian life and wanted to continue her career as an administrative assistant. She used words from the job advertisement to convey her value to an employer.

Deputy Director Resource Development

Timothy Cavanaugh
0000 Muroc Drive, Burleson Air Force Base, Texas 00000
000.000.0000 (Office) — 000.555.5555 (Home) — 999.0000 (DSN)
tim.cavanaugh@burleson.af.mil

Monday, 12 July 20XX

Colonel Jordan Cliff
Director of Staff
Headquarters Resource Command
1100 Operations Drive
Burleson Air Force Base, Texas 00000-0000

Dear Colonel Cliff:

Just as you suggested, I have nominated myself for the upcoming GS-14 position that will convert the Deputy DS to a civilian slot. But as I focused on filling out the required resume builder, I became convinced that you deserved a great deal more than just data constrained by character limits of that online form. This package is the result.

Because the next deputy will likely have long-lasting impact on Resource Command, it seemed that two vital pieces of information had to be documented. As a baseline, I had to show my understanding of the kinds of problems I'll be asked to solve. And supporting that baseline had to be vivid examples of my ability to solve similar problems very well.

For the baseline to be valuable, I went beyond the usual consideration of traits or staff skills. I focused on capabilities I must provide to make enduring contributions to the RC mission. You'll find nine of them right at the top of my resume. For proof of capabilities, I had to go beyond just summarizing past problems solved. And so I selected 16 contributions to my organizations that illustrated those capabilities in action.

However, there is some vital information no format, no matter how tailored, can provide. As you read, I hope this central idea stands out clearly: All my efforts are aimed at maximizing long-term returns on every resource investment RC and the Air Force make. I want every tasking, every initiative, to be an opportunity to motivate, lead, and educate others to that same point of view. For me, that vision stands behind every duty, every standard, every KSA, and every classification criterion that might appear in the job announcement.

It's difficult for me to be distracted from the daily business of Resource Command, particularly when that distraction requires me to focus on myself. Therefore, if I have overlooked any information you need, I know you will not hesitate to call on me.

V/R,

Timothy Cavanaugh, Colonel, USAF

Attachment: Resume

224

Deputy Director, Resource Development. *Don Orlando, Montgomery, Alabama*

This retiring senior Air Force officer wanted to stay on in his position as his own civilian replacement. Some Air Force jargon is evident in the letter. For example, "V/R" means "Very respectfully."

DENNIS KRAFT
555 Westside Blvd.
Washington, GA 55555
Cell: 555-555-5555
Email: kraft.dennis@xxx.xx.xxxx

February 10, 20XX

Mr. Arnold Black
Gold's Gym
1234 Muscle Beach Blvd.
Los Angeles, CA 00000

Dear Mr. Black:

I am enclosing my resume in response to your ad for a physical fitness trainer that was listed in last Sunday's *Los Angeles Times*.

In addition to the skills as reflected on my resume, I won first place in the Lightweight classification for bodybuilding while assigned to military service in Korea. Additionally, I placed in the top 10 in the Osan, Korea, all-services competition. While assigned to Fort Carson, Colorado, I held the Lightweight wrestling title while going undefeated for 3 years. I met annual Army requirements for physical fitness by scoring at least 290 out of 300 on each test.

In addition to the resume, I have included several recent professional photographs of myself that will attest to my personal physical condition. I am confident that I can help your clients who desire to improve their physical condition and appearance.

I will call you within the next 2 weeks to follow up on my resume and, hopefully, establish a date and time for an interview.

Sincerely,

Dennis Kraft

225

Gym Director. *James Walker, Fort Riley, Kansas*

Because this man was in excellent physical condition, he looked into physical fitness training and became a gym director.

Marissa Hagan

509 Simmons Avenue
Parkersburg, WV 26101

(304) 555-2222
marissahagan@wahoo.com

August 4, 20XX

Roberta Vickers, Director
Ritchie County Center for the Developmentally Disabled
475 Brookview Terrace
Parkersburg, WV 26101

Dear Ms. Vickers:

My dream of becoming an occupational therapist began while I was still in high school as a volunteer at the Ritchie County Center for the Developmentally Disabled. My older sister, Claire, who was born with Down syndrome, is a resident at one of your group homes. I am amazed at what she has been able to accomplish because of the patience and guidance of your wonderful staff. From seeing her progress, I was convinced that occupational therapy was the right career for me.

Having recently received my associate degree and COTA certification, I am now qualified as an occupational therapy assistant. As you will note from my resume, my training included internships at a nursing home, a rehabilitation facility for brain injuries, and a school for special-needs children. However, my most rewarding experience was at the County Center, where I observed how the therapists assist patients in learning how to lead independent, productive lives. The aspect that is most appealing to me is working with high-functioning adults, such as my sister, who today is able to take public transportation, hold a job, and balance a checkbook. While these are ordinary things we all take for granted, for someone so challenged, they were major achievements.

During my training, I helped various patients increase their strength, manual dexterity, and coordination. Also, through the use of games, puzzles, and computer activities, my patients learned to improve mentally in the areas of memory, perception, decision making, abstract reasoning, and sequencing. Noticing even their slightest gains was extremely gratifying to me.

Besides a genuine desire to help people, I possess additional attributes for success, which include patience, compassion, enthusiasm, creativity, and abundant physical stamina. Nothing could give me greater career satisfaction than to further develop my occupational therapy skills at the County Center. I am available for an interview at your convenience and will call to set up an appointment.

Sincerely,

Marissa Hagan

Enclosure

226

Occupational Therapist. *Melanie Noonan, Woodland Park, New Jersey*

After getting an associate degree and certification, the applicant wanted a position at the center where she had been an intern and her sister is a resident. The letter displays concern.

Keith Robinson

73 Meadows Lane
Milwaukee, WI 53203
Residence (414) 555-1111
Mobile (414) 555-1010

April 16, 20XX

Mr. Albert Gordon
President
Gordon Chemical Company
2060 Route 93
Milwaukee, WI 53203

Dear Mr. Gordon:

Because I understand your concern for the safety of your employees as well as the preservation of the environment, I am writing to you at the suggestion of your plant manager, Mr. John Baynes. You may recall I was the OSHA inspector who visited your workplace on March 27 and was escorted around the building and grounds by Mr. Baynes. As you have probably seen from my report, there are several violations that need to be abated.

When I asked about your safety policies, Mr. Baynes told me that it has been almost two years since they were updated and enforced. He mentioned at one time you had an environmental health and safety manager on your staff, who attended to these matters. However, his position had not been replaced since he left your company, which is my real reason for this letter and enclosed resume. Since your plant manager cannot be everywhere at once, it is obvious that you need someone to fill this vacancy, and I'd like you to know I am a very interested candidate.

My assignments with OSHA have concentrated on the operations of chemical and biomedical facilities, which produce a significant amount of hazardous waste. In addition to business acumen, I have the required knowledge of EPA laws, chemistry, natural sciences, human anatomy, physiology, and math to be effective on the job. Coming from a government agency that most employers regard with trepidation, I have a keen awareness of what needs to be done to bring your workplace up to regulatory standards.

From my tour of your facility, courtesy of Mr. Baynes, I noticed quite a few ways I could make some immediate improvements as well as initiate programs to avoid fines, control accidents, and ultimately reduce your insurance premiums in the future. With your best interests in mind, I will contact you as to when we could get together to discuss my ideas.

Sincerely,

Keith Robinson

Enclosure

227

Environmental Health and Safety Manager. *Melanie Noonan, Woodland Park, New Jersey*

Reference to a third party and a previous visit by the applicant helps to gain the reader's attention. The applicant presents his possible services as a solution to unresolved problems.

Patrick D. Wilder

11 Monroe Street, Salt Lake City, UT 55555

(555) 555-5000 home   patrickw@prodigy.net   (555) 555-5555 cell

March 25, 20XX

Todd Hazeltine
Safety and Health Management
St. Jude's Hospital
16 Rock Lane
Salt Lake City, UT 55555

Dear Mr. Hazeltine:

The purpose of this letter is to introduce myself and then to meet with you about the opportunity for me to provide my expertise in managing safety and health programs to your organization. My confidential resume is enclosed for your review, and I am certain that you will find me very well qualified. Highlights of my resume include

- More than 20 years of experience in Occupational Health and Nursing
- Significant expertise working with OSHA regulations and regulatory compliance
- Ability to develop, conduct and oversee safety and health programs
- Effective communication, preparing technically sound reports, including recommendations for correction of hazards

My professional background, along with my sincere interest in helping others, has enhanced my desire to excel. As a highly motivated professional, I enjoy the challenge of complex, demanding projects.

I am available to meet with you to discuss my qualifications at your convenience and will call to schedule a meeting. I would like to thank you in advance for your time and any consideration you may give me. I look forward to hearing from you.

Sincerely,

Patrick D. Wilder

Enclosure

228

Occupational Health and Safety Professional. *Denelle D. Jones, Mountain View, Hawaii*

Bullets point to resume highlights concerning the applicant's experience, areas of expertise, field-related skills, and communication skills. The rest of the letter shows his motivation and interest.

Cathy Carter
321 Maple Way
Big Lake, IL 00000
555-555-5555 cellular
ccarter@hotmail.com

Date

Mr. George Pappas
Manager
Extreme Workout World
555 Central Avenue
Chicago, IL 00000

Dear Mr. Pappas:

In response to the opening you posted for Fitness Instructor, I have enclosed my resume for your review. I understand that this position requires customer service skills and experience in leading fitness programs, and I believe I have the qualifications you seek.

Having spent the past year learning how to develop sales in the business technology industry, I am now ready to return to the field of fitness—an area I have been passionate about for a long time. In my search, I am targeting positions that will use my knowledge of fitness products and training techniques and my skills in business writing, customer service, and group leadership. I would appreciate the opportunity to discuss how my skills can help you meet the challenges you face in 20XX and beyond.

I will contact you soon to explore the possibility of an interview. Thank you for your time and consideration.

Sincerely,

Cathy Carter

Enc.

229

Fitness Instructor. *Christine L. Dennison, Lincolnshire, Illinois*

The applicant wanted to move to the fitness industry–her real passion–after unsatisfying work in business technology sales after college. The letter stresses skills.

ANGELA S. FAGAN
333 South Street ▪ Philadelphia, PA 19111
Home: (555) 999-3333 ▪ Mobile: (555) 444-1111 ▪ e-mail: afagan@aol.com

January 29, 20XX

Ms. Rose Mayer, Director
Celebrity Associates, Inc.
44 Lake Road
Malvern, PA 19484

Dear Ms. Mayer:

I was excited to discover fabjob.com. I've known for some time that a 9-to-5 job wasn't the right fit for someone with my background and personality, and I would like to explore the possibility of becoming a Celebrity Personal Assistant.

The fabjob.com site certainly clarified the unique skills and expectations of a Celebrity Personal Assistant. Many of the qualifications mirrored my responsibilities as Entertainment/Promotions Coordinator for Harrah's Entertainment. On any given day, I had multiple balls in the air—from coordinating arrangements for celebrities (lodging, transportation, meals) to selecting costumes and overseeing myriad administrative duties associated with a popular entertainment site. I had an excellent reputation for putting out fires and going the extra steps to achieve success. Flexibility and the ability to remain calm were the key elements that allowed me to function effectively in such a high-pressure environment.

On an administrative level, I am organized and meticulous. Careful follow-up is important when coordinating special events and projects, particularly when you are involved with senior-level executives and celebrities. Of course, I am familiar with various technology and equipment, including smartphones, since my background has always involved administrative duties.

Wearing multiple "hats" keeps my daily calendar at maximum capacity, an environment in which I tend to flourish. Overall, I feel my organizational skills and my ability to handle different personalities with varying degrees of understanding and maintenance, regardless of the time element involved, would serve me well as a Celebrity Personal Assistant.

Would you allow me to formally introduce myself? I am very interested in expanding my professional horizons and eager to discuss a future association.

I can be available at your convenience with somewhat minimal notice. My employer is not aware I am contacting you, however, so I would appreciate your confidentiality. A complete resume is enclosed for your review.

Thank you in advance for your consideration.

Sincerely,

Angela S. Fagan

Enclosure

230

Celebrity Personal Assistant. *Karen Conway, Bend, Oregon*

Each paragraph conveys the applicant's enthusiasm toward becoming a Celebrity Personal Assistant. Her organizational skills, technological expertise, and evident maturity temper well her excitement.

Kathryn Tamburro

0000 66th Avenue North ✦ Frankfort, NY 00000 ✦ 555.555.5555

April 2, 20XX

The Ritz-Carlton
3000 Central Florida Parkway
Orlando, FL 32837

Dear Employment Specialist:

I am writing to express my interest in the esthetician position that is posted on your Web site. I was very interested to see this opportunity as my background and qualifications match the requirements outlined in the posting. My goal is to relocate to the Orlando area and secure a position where I can utilize my esthetic training and sales experience.

As you will see from the enclosed resume, I am a newly licensed esthetician (New York State). Since earning my certificate, I have been working in an upscale salon in Millbrook, NY—an affluent town outside New York City. Working in this salon has helped develop my business competency and enhanced my knowledge of service delivery for high-end clientele. In addition to my certification and licensure, I hold a bachelor's degree from Vassar College in Poughkeepsie, NY.

The value I bring to the Ritz-Carlton is not only a broad-based background, but a strong business sense and creative flair. More importantly, I know how to comport myself with high-profile clientele and understand the level of service required from clients seeking world-class spa treatment.

While my esthetic training emphasized specialized techniques and provided exposure to the most up-to-date methods (influenced by Manhattan's progressive market), I also gained valuable product sales experience through the school's operational storefront. Working in the store sharpened my sales, marketing and general business skills. It also contributed to my understanding of the financial impact of daily decisions as well as an awareness of the importance of maintaining positive customer relations.

I am confident that these qualifications will enable me to make immediate contributions toward your overall service goals. I would be happy to make myself available for a personal interview at any time and will call to inquire about a mutually convenient time. Thank you in advance for your time and attention. I look forward to meeting with you.

Sincerely,

Kathryn Tamburro

Enclosure

231

Esthetician. *Kristin M. Coleman, Poughkeepsie, New York*

A task of this letter is to show an upscale employer that the applicant is suitable for the employer's clientele. Every paragraph indicates that she is more than a match for high-profile clients.

Richard Chisholm

15 Clubhouse Drive
Stony Point, NE 00000

(000) 000-0000
richpix@verizon.com

March 10, 20XX

Mr. John Ambrose
News/Picture Assignment Editor
Seward Daily Journal
229 West Rugby Street
Seward, NE 00000

Dear Mr. Ambrose:

As a follow-up to our phone conversation, I am very interested in joining your photo department in a part-time photography position, eventually leading to full-time employment. As you review my resume, please note that I have thorough technical knowledge of shooting and editing as well as a creative personal style to envision and tell a story through the lens.

In the photo-intensive environment of a newsroom, I know the importance of teamwork and the ability to adapt to different formats. I am also accustomed to the pressures of constant deadlines and dealing with temperamental personalities. When problems arise, I remain calm, think clearly, and resolve the issues as quickly as possible. In addition, my flexible schedule will allow me to be available on holidays or at other times you may be shorthanded.

If you are seeking candidates who have a strong passion for photojournalism and subscribe to high NPPA standards, I would appreciate your consideration of my qualifications. I am confident that I can make a significant contribution to your photo department and look forward to discussing potential employment.

Sincerely,

Richard Chisholm

Encl. Resume

232

Photographer. *Melanie Noonan, Woodland Park, New Jersey*

This applicant wanted to give the impression of being someone with creative talent. The writer chose a nonconventional font to convey the idea that his photographer had aesthetic taste and was flexible.

HAROLD VEETER
000 Tidewater Road
Springfield, MA 00000

(555) 555-5555

HARVT@home.com

February 4, 20XX

Mr. Fred Jones
Director of Procurement
Technologies Corporation
3229 Polumba Drive
Springfield, MA 01087

Dear Mr. Jones:

During a recent conversation with Paul Browning, he suggested that I contact you about my interest in a procurement position in your department. Although you may not have an opening at this time, I would welcome the opportunity to learn more about your procurement function and industry.

As you may know from Paul, I recently sold my business and am enthusiastic about the prospect of new challenges. In anticipation of the business closure, I have taken the time to evaluate my career interests, skills and strengths to determine my options.

Procurement was one of my primary responsibilities and a function I enjoyed tremendously. As a result, I have decided to pursue a search in this field. Briefly, my qualifications include a bachelor's degree plus 10 years of experience in supplier/broker relations, cost-effective contract negotiations and managing a multimillion-dollar purchasing volume.

Well-organized with excellent communication and interpersonal skills, I am confident in my ability to add value to an organization. My conversation with Paul reaffirmed my interest in your company, and I look forward to meeting with you to explore the possibilities in relationship to your department's needs. I will call next week to further discuss opportunities with your company.

Sincerely,

Harold Veeter

Enclosure

233

Procurement Position. *Louise Garver, Broad Brook, Connecticut*

This individual wanted to make a career change and used this letter to obtain a networking meeting that ultimately led to a job offer. The purpose of networking is made clear in the first paragraph.

ELIZABETH GREEN

5555 Oak Tree Lane • Northridge, CA 55555
(555) 555-5555 • egreen@email.com

[Date]

[Name]
[Address]
[City, State ZIP]

Dear _____:

If you are seeking a motivated and detail-oriented Purchasing Professional with a proven ability to streamline operations, motivate teams and achieve significant cost savings in a multimillion-dollar environment, then my enclosed resume should be of interest to you.

Common themes that have run throughout my professional career have been outstanding team-building and leadership strengths as well as my ability to see the "big picture"—integrating the purchasing function into corporate goals. Representative of my past accomplishments are the following:

- Directed $200 million purchasing unit for West Coast Entertainment Company...
- Hired, trained and motivated top-performing team members...
- Consistently identified and developed talent in others...
- Employed technology to streamline procedures, including automating the download of purchasing orders to the Letter of Credit system, improving on-time issuance from 20% to 75% within two years...
- Consolidated supplier base from 1,200 to 650 within one year...
- Sourced and developed excellent working relationships with outside and internal vendors...
- Participated in key negotiations...

I am currently seeking a new professional challenge where I can make a positive contribution to future goals and success. I possess a high level of energy and motivation, learn quickly, adapt well to new environments and enjoy challenges. I look forward to a personal meeting, at which time we can discuss your needs and my qualifications in detail. I will call you to set up a meeting. Thank you in advance for your time and consideration.

Sincerely,

Elizabeth Green

Enclosure

234

Purchasing Professional. *Vivian VanLier, Los Angeles (Valley Glen), California*

The middle paragraph with bulleted accomplishments is the key paragraph in this letter. Quantified representative achievements sell the reader on the superior worth of this candidate.

GARRY FUNG

1234 Augusta Crescent
Pinehurst, Ontario A1A 1A1

Phone: (555) 333-7777
Email: gfung@email.com

January 24, 20XX

Joseph Neiman
Chief Technology Officer
Sandoz Investments
123 Young Boulevard, Suite 2305
Pinehurst, Ontario

Dear Mr. Neiman,

- **Is your organization fully prepared to safeguard its technology services, information, and facilities in the event of a disaster?**
- **Are you taking full advantage of high-value and cost-effective vendor agreements?**
- **Do you benefit from high team performance and low turnover?**

If you answered "No" to any of the above questions, then allow me to introduce myself and the expertise I can offer your organization. With a proven and award-winning track record of achievement, I offer a unique combination of expertise in disaster recovery/business continuity planning, vendor management/negotiations, and team leadership. I am currently offering my services to organizations within the Durham region and would like to draw your attention to the value I offer.

Put simply, my expertise is delivering results. In previous positions, I have designed, implemented, and optimized comprehensive enterprise-class disaster recovery and information security procedures, saved millions in vendor negotiations and third-party service agreements, and led a variety of cross-functional teams to consistently achieve and exceed organizational mandates.

If the following interests you, I invite you to review the attached resume, which further illustrates my experience, achievements, and expertise:

- **Expert in disaster recovery, information security, and business continuity**—expertise includes planning, protection, and off-site recovery of technology services, databases, and facilities
- **Superior contract procurement, negotiation, and vendor-management capabilities**—proven record for negotiating agreements that improve service quality and save millions in vendor costs
- **Strong, decisive, and motivating leader**—reputation for building and leading high-performance teams to breakthrough achievement
- Available for **full-time, part-time, contract, and consulting opportunities**

If you believe that you could benefit from a highly motivated and talented professional with a reputation for generating results, I would welcome the opportunity to meet and discuss the specific value I can offer your organization.

I thank you for your consideration, and I look forward to speaking with you soon. I will call you to set an appointment.

Sincerely,

Garry Fung
Enclosure: Resume

235

Vendor Contract Negotiator. *Ross Macpherson, Whitby, Ontario, Canada*

This candidate offered a variety of expertise, so this broadcast letter opens with a few questions to get the reader thinking. The candidate landed five interviews and a lucrative contract in six weeks.

LORI L. DAWSON

555 Loretta Drive | Hermitage, PA 55555

555.555.5555 | lori.dawson@xx.com

Jane Von Jones
President
ABC Company
555 Elm Street
Chicago, IL 55555

Dear Ms. Von Jones:

My 26 years of experience as a purchasing, logistics, and supply chain professional for a leading chemical distributor have been rewarding. I have been recognized as a significant contributor to efficient day-to-day operations. My hope is that you will identify my background and talent as an ideal match as your next Director of Procurement.

With strengths in procurement and distribution, vendor relations, contract negotiation, and safety control, I can obtain the best possible combination of price, quality, and service for your company. In addition, I bring proven skills in leadership, communication, organization, and decisive action that are essential to directing efficiency and productivity for your Purchasing/Procurement department.

My professional experience includes my current position as Director of Chemical Procurement and previous positions as Manager of Purchases and Purchasing Agent. In all of my roles, I have guided the professional development of staff and gained a reliable network of vendors, ensuring the smooth and cost-efficient movement of my employer's supplies. The following is a brief sample of the expertise I offer:

- Subject matter expert on all things relating to chemicals and chemicals procurement
- Leadership to maximize your company's supply strategies, lower cost, and increase supplier reliability
- Proficiency in analyzing material and shipping cost and obtaining the lowest possible purchase cost
- Ability to find the best suppliers, negotiate contracts, and manage shipments
- Personal style strengths to excel in leadership and effective communications

As you will see from my resume, these qualifications only scratch the surface of my extensive suite of skills and knowledge. I am confident that I can make an immediate and positive impact on your organization. I am eager for an opportunity to have a personal meeting to further discuss my qualifications.

Thank you for your time and consideration. I look forward to hearing from you.

Sincerely,

Lori L. Dawson

PROFESSIONAL BEHAVIORAL SUCCESS INSIGHTS ® PROFILE

"Lori wins through hard work and persistence and is not bored staying with one task until it is completed. Because she is receptive and listens well, she excels in gathering information. Lori is good at analyzing situations... Her motto is 'facts are facts.' She prefers to plan her work and work her plan."

Natural Behavioral Style (•) – Supporting Coordinator
Adapted Behavioral Style (★) – Analyzer

The profile commentary and Success Insights® Wheel show that Lori has a genuine strength of effectively drawing upon staff and resources to promote streamlined operations. Her adapted style, matched with her natural style, enables her to achieve significant results in strategic planning and execution in a leadership role.

Complete report available upon request

236

Director of Procurement. *Jane Roqueplot, West Middlesex, Pennsylvania*

This individual learned of a position soon to be available and wanted an interview. The writer used a visual aid to show that the applicant's interpersonal skills made her a good fit for the position.

WALTER E. ELLIS

75 Clover Street
Rochester, New York 14610-4261
555-555-5555 (Home) / 000-000-0000 (Cellular)
walteree@rochester.rr.com

February 27, 20XX

Mr. B. Thomas Golisano
President & CEO
Paychex, Inc.
911 Panorama Trail, South
Rochester, New York 14625

Dear Mr. Golisano:

Capitalizing on a career that encompasses broad-based experience in brand marketing, public relations, and customer relations, I am seeking an opportunity to apply these skills in a marketing communications position that will offer the potential for advancement based on performance. I believe that I possess knowledge and expertise that can be an asset to your firm and have, therefore, enclosed for your review a résumé that outlines my professional background.

Some key points that you may find relevant to a marketing communications role with your organization include the following:

- *Identifying target audiences and developing marketing messages that reach those audiences. In both business-to-business and consumer products settings, I have been successful in researching potential market segments and creating strategies that effectively communicate product features and promote brand awareness.*

- *Implementing innovative, technology-based approaches to marketing, including championing e-commerce initiatives that both augment product sales and afford opportunities to gather information about customers.*

- *Spearheading public relations efforts that coordinate with marketing strategies and advance overall business goals. These have included placement of features in both electronic and print media, participation in high-profile public events, and implementation of "strategic philanthropy" initiatives.*

- *Directing an array of brand management activities, which have encompassed graphic design; copy writing; and production of collaterals, point-of-sale materials, and product packaging.*

I am confident that my experience, education, and enthusiasm will allow me to make a meaningful contribution to your ongoing business success. I would enjoy meeting with you to discuss in detail how my capabilities can best serve your marketing communications needs. Please contact me to arrange a mutually convenient date and time when we might initiate a dialogue.

Thank you for your time and consideration. I will contact you soon to set up an interview.

Sincerely,

Walter E. Ellis

Enclosure

237

Marketing Communications Position. *Arnold G. Boldt, Rochester, New York*

The applicant was transitioning from a marketing position with a small firm to a corporate setting. The challenge was to show that his marketing skills were transportable to a corporate environment.

Tina Nestavez

0000 W. Inman Ave.	Tampa, FL 33609	(555) 555-5555	t.nestavez@juno.com

March 20, 20XX

Mr. Gary Frank
Director of Marketing
Nike, Inc.
One Nike Drive
Seattle, Washington 98744

Dear Mr. Frank:

"Just Do It." That is what I said to myself after hanging up the phone with my friend Jim Heald. He had just described his conversation with you—about needing a new public relations person in Brazil. I had to write after hearing your requirements! Jim said they are the following:

Your Needs	**My Experience**
Communicate in Portuguese and Spanish	✓ Fluent in reading, speaking and writing Portuguese, Spanish and English ✓ Translated an entire book from Portuguese to English ✓ Lived, worked and studied in Brazil
International Experience	✓ B.A. in International Relations ✓ Currently have 100% travel job with extensive foreign travel ✓ U.S. citizen who has lived in Brazil, Japan, Australia and Africa
Public Relations/Liaison/ Communications/Sports Experience	✓ Completed Sporting Goods Analysis on Brazil's economy for U.S. Department of Commerce ✓ Effective multiorganizational liaison as a relief worker in Africa ✓ Resolve ongoing public relations and communications challenges as the "flight attendant in charge," American Airlines

My enclosed resume provides further details of my accomplishments and experience. I look forward to reviewing them with you. I will call you in a few days to see if we can meet next week to discuss how I can help you meet the goals for "Brasil futebol." I'm ready to go!

Sincerely,

Tina Nestavez

Enclosure

238

International Publicist. *Gail Frank, Tampa, Florida*

The applicant needed a letter that made her stand out. The check marks under My Experience serve as a "YES!" for each qualification.

Emily Everly

1 N. Jackson St.
Racine, WI 22222
(333) 333-3333
(444) 444-4444
eeverly@someemail.com

Re: Marketing & Communications Associate

November 23, 20XX

Dear Hiring Manager:

I am interested in the <u>Marketing and Communications Associate</u> position available within Hephert International, Inc. As you can see in my attached resume, I have almost 8 years of experience in a social service position where I am intensively involved with training, volunteerism, and marketing/ public relations. I have been seeking to transition into a corporate environment but wanted to locate an organization with a "heart." After reading the *Comfort stories* and *Being magazine* on your website, I'm intrigued. I would love to talk with you further about how I may fit in at your organization.

I understand that you are looking for someone who can promote, coordinate, and document the volunteer activities of your staff members. I believe my position as a Resource Specialist at Lake County Workforce Development has perfectly equipped me to do that! I serve as an interagency and community liaison for our organization and promote the organization via the website and a biannual newsletter. I also regularly attend and assist with the coordination of community events. The position requires meticulous documentation of confidential information and an ability to clearly communicate with diverse individuals.

Thank you for reviewing my resume. I would love to speak with you personally and will contact you next week.

Sincerely,

Emily Everly

239

Marketing and Communications Associate. *Eva Locke, Waukegan, Illinois*

The applicant had no specific experience in the position for which she was applying. The letter addresses her reason for transitioning and describes her transferable skills.

Katherine Lacey Elliot   999 Kettlepond Circle   (000) 999-6666
Salesbury, CO 22222   Cell: (000) 999-9898
kathy5@earthlink.net

___

February 12, 20XX

Susan Mary Anthony, Human Resources Manager
ABC Advertising Corporation
000 Weybosset Street, Suite 1000
Whitehead, CO 55555

Dear Ms. Anthony:

Your advertisement in the *Whitehead Sunday Globe,* February 11, 20XX, for a copywriter to work in ABC's media relations department excited me, for this position would fulfill my ideal goal. Although a recent college graduate, I believe that my experience and academic training may be just what you are seeking in a candidate to fill this post. Please note that my enclosed resume illuminates my practical field experiences in written communication.

As an English major at Newberg State College, with a concentration in writing, I have worked beyond traditional courses of study by planning and completing independent study projects that took place here and abroad. My cross-cultural studies in Ireland have given me not only a better understanding of education and business in Europe, but also a more global vision of the world marketplace and the tremendous influence that America exercises there. In addition, I would like to share my research article on psychology and the media.

Another independent-study project that has strengthened my base of preparedness for employment in communications was in journalism at *The Salesbury Citizen News.* You may be interested in looking over my portfolio of samples as evidence of substance and style in written communication. I believe that I have excelled in working independently to plan and execute programs on my campus radio show, although I learned that cooperating in teams often brought about stimulating ideas and results.

If you agree that my qualifications meet your standards for this position in the media department, please contact me to make an appointment for an interview at a time convenient to you. I can be reached at my telephone or cell phone, both equipped with voice mail. Thank you for considering my application; I look forward to meeting with you soon.

Sincerely,

Katherine Lacey Elliot

Enclosure: resume

240

Copywriter, Advertising. *Edward Turilli, Bonita Springs, Florida*

This entry-level job seeker indicates her wide experience in communications and zeal to enter this field. Her time in Ireland points to her global awareness as an edge over traditional competitors.

Tim K. Petersen
0000 Groveland Avenue   ◆   Kalamazoo, MI 49004   ◆   555-555-2222   ◆   tkpetes@network.net

March 5, 20XX

Mr. Roger Sanderson
National City Bank
3291 Westnedge Avenue S.
Kalamazoo, MI 49008

Dear Mr. Sanderson:

Marjorie McCarthy suggested I contact you regarding the Public Relations Manager and Communications Specialist positions that were recently posted on your Web site. When you have a chance to review the enclosed resume, you will see that I meet or exceed the qualifications for both positions.

You will notice that over the last 15+ years I have worn many hats. Because the organizations with which I was associated were small, I was responsible for everything from writing press releases to community outreach, grant writing to marketing, and fundraising to budget management. The common thread among these responsibilities: **communication.** Putting the organization's best foot forward was always the priority. I believe my accomplishments (described on my resume) reflect my ability.

My personal assets lend themselves to your positions. For example, you will find that I am

- Highly organized (I had to be to wear all those hats!)
- An accomplished writer (newsletters, marketing material, scripts)
- A strategic thinker (erased red ink and turned a significant profit in 3 years)
- Versatile (all those hats, remember?)

That's why I am confident I can become a successful team member of National City's Communications/Marketing Department. I hope you'll give me an opportunity to speak with you personally so I can elaborate on my qualifications and motivation. I will call you next week to set up a meeting at your convenience. Thank you for your consideration and I'll look forward to hearing from you.

Sincerely,

Tim K. Petersen

Enclosure

241

Public Relations Manager/Communications Specialist. *Janet L. Beckstrom, Flint, Michigan*

The applicant was transitioning from work primarily in a nonprofit arena to work for a for-profit organization. The second paragraph displays a variety of experience from which he could draw.

JESSICA M.SMITH

000 WATER STREET
YARDLEY, PA 00000

JMSMITH44@XX.COM
000.000.0000

BRAND STRATEGIST
Inspired by Possibility ■ *Dedicated to Ideas* ■ *Driven by Expertise*

Date: March 23, 20XX

Consumer Personal Care International
00 Burlington Road
Trenton, NJ 00000

Dear Hiring Manager:

The challenge in creating compelling brand engagement strategies is in seeing customers with "new eyes," with an open-minded perspective and without presumptions caused by our own beliefs. When we are successful in seeing with new eyes, we can formulate persuasive initiatives that address challenges effectively, credibly, and profitably. This is exactly what I have done in the past as a communications strategist, leading teams from smaller businesses and Fortune 500 companies alike—and what I will do for Consumer Personal Care International as its brand strategist.

Recent examples of my successes include the following:

- Developed brand position and site launch strategy for $55MM film distribution company that had remained staunchly offline since its inception.
- Built new strategy team for existing interactive agency, helping it sign high-profile clients such as Gymnastics Star Kids and the Western Movie Maker's leading product franchise.
- Personally signed major technology company for Advertisers National Group, single-handedly adding $4.2MM top-line dollars.

I am very interested in speaking with you to discuss the value that my strengths and experience can bring to Consumer Personal Care International. I can be reached in confidence at the above telephone number or email address. I look forward to hearing from you.

With best regards,

Jessica M. Smith
Enclosure: Résumé

> *"The real voyage of discovery is not in seeking new places, but in seeing with new eyes."—Marcel Proust*

242

Brand Strategist. *Amy L. Adler, Salt Lake City, Utah*

This cold-call letter was to a company to inquire about a need for a brand strategy leader. The applicant could help executives see marketing from new angles rather than old perspectives.

Diane C. Cartwright

0000 Main Street
West Nyack, NY 00000

000.000.0000
dcc41@mydomain.com

April 20, 20XX

Ms. Allison Campbell
The ACME Agency
151 West Third Street
Somerset, NJ 00000

Dear Ms. Campbell:

Creativity. Power. Results.

With more than 10 years of experience in writing business-to-business and direct-mail copy, I have a diversified agency background that has exposed me to several different industries, including health care, financial services, insurance, medical, retail, real estate, and pharmaceuticals. As a seasoned professional, I have consistently created captivating and powerful copy that captures target-market attention and gets the desired results.

Looking for someone who can multitask?

Multitasking has become second nature for me. On average, I balance anywhere from 15 to 20 assignments at any given time. What's more, many of my assignments consist of multiple parts (letters, reply cards, brochures, etc.) and require not only creativity but refined editing skills to ensure that the copy is polished and sharp.

As you required, I have enclosed three representative samples from my portfolio along with my resume. I am confident that, if chosen for this position, I will be able to take The ACME Agency's copy assignments and produce attention-grabbing results.

I welcome the opportunity to discuss with you The ACME Agency's objectives and share how I believe I can contribute to the desired end results. I will contact you to arrange an appointment. I look forward to speaking with you.

Sincerely,

Diane C. Cartwright

Enclosures

243

Business Communications, Writer. *Patricia Duckers, Edison, New Jersey*

The line between this occupational group and the preceding one is thin. Besides writing ad copy, however, this applicant wrote different documents for different industries.

Brittany K. Torres

5-A Riverside Towers
Hackensack, NJ 07602
(201) 555-5555
bkt999@net.net

January 6, 20XX

Sarah Weinstein
Editor-in-Chief
Fashionista Magazine
1500 Seventh Avenue
New York, NY 10000

Dear Ms. Weinstein:

My friends tell me I have a passion for fashion, and I entirely agree. In my spare time, I'm usually found checking out the latest in hairdos to footwear and everything in between. If I'm not at the malls, I'm tuned in to the fashion shows on TV, and of course, I can hardly wait for the latest issue of *Fashionista* magazine to arrive in my mailbox!

As a journalism major, I had exposure to news story reporting, script editing, and press release writing before I landed my first real job as lifestyle editor for my small-town weekly. The pay was minimal, but I had the chance to travel and write freelance articles on topics that interested me, such as wardrobe accessorizing. Most of them were published in various national magazines, including *Fashionista*. Eventually, I relocated to the metropolitan area and am currently employed as a copywriter at an advertising agency with clients in the apparel industry. However, it was always in the back of my mind that someday I'd love to join the editorial staff of a major fashion publication. You can imagine my excitement at seeing your ad in *Women's Wear Daily* for just such a position!

Realizing that I'm up against some serious competition, I am, nevertheless, throwing my hat in the ring and submitting my resume along with a few samples of my freelance articles. If I am considered for the features editor position, an acquaintance of mine, who is a big name in the fashion world, will serve as one of my references. She and I have collaborated closely on advertising campaigns, and I am certain she will vouch favorably for my character, abilities, and work habits.

Thank you for taking the time to review my materials, and I look forward to your further consideration of me. May we meet soon? I will call to determine a mutually convenient time.

Sincerely,

Brittany K. Torres

Enclosure

244

Fashion Magazine Features Editor. *Melanie Noonan, Woodland Park, New Jersey*

The first paragraph indicates specifically the applicant's "passion for fashion." The second paragraph states that the target magazine has already published some of her articles.

Audra Sessoms

audras@xxxx.com • 555.555.5555

August 28, 20xx

Human Resources
American Museum of Natural History
Central Park West at 55th Street
New York, NY 55555

Re: Technical Writer (Information Systems) position

A visit to the American Museum of Natural History when I was a child sparked my interest in science. Having recently completed my undergraduate studies, combining my passion for Marine Biology and English, I was excited to see in your advertised position for a **Technical Writer (Information Systems)** an opportunity to apply my interests and aptitudes in science and communications to make this great museum even more inspiring. After you review my resume, I am confident that you will agree that this position is a good match for my qualifications.

I am extremely versatile, and an employer can expect more of me than just what I am hired for. These qualities are evident in my involvement with State University's newspaper, the *Troubadour,* where I spent 4 years on staff and 1 year as editor-in-chief. During this time, I honed my writing skills and became proficient in both Microsoft Office and Adobe Creative Suite. I also managed all aspects of the *Troubadour*'s biweekly production from scheduling, distribution, circulation, interviewing, copy writing, editing per Associated Press standards, layout and advertising. This was a daunting challenge that I mastered repeatedly.

I would be delighted to discuss how I can contribute to the continued success of the American Museum of Natural History. Thank you for your time and consideration. I will call next week to set up an interview.

Sincerely,

Audra Sessoms

Enclosure: resume

245

IS Technical Writer. *Jane Roqueplot, West Middlesex, Pennsylvania*

The applicant had no actual work history. The writer's goal was to demonstrate specific notable accomplishments while the individual was in school. All three paragraphs display self-confidence.

JOHN C. LAWTON

555 Fortson Street, #6J
Helmsford, CT 55555

jcslawton55@xx.com
555.555.5555

[Date]

[Hiring Manager]
[Title]
[Company Name]
[Address]
[City State ZIP]

Dear [Hiring Manager]:

As a highly effective and innovative general management executive with diverse experience in E-commerce, digital, and traditional marketing, I am writing to express my interest in [Name of Position] with [Company Name]. I have broad qualifications in the areas of business development, strategic planning, marketing, due diligence, and operations; and I have successfully led the creation and launch of online programs, resulting in bottom line growth for Book Publisher, Inc.

You will find that I am a collaborative leader, able to work with a cross-functional, multicultural population to conceptualize, visualize, and produce outstanding results. I offer the following examples of the competencies that will enable me to quickly contribute as part of your senior leadership team:

- Lead current and future online and offline marketing initiatives, including establishing and meeting goals and developing new opportunities in a dynamic and changing marketplace.
- Define the appropriate marketing efforts, including various initiatives such as paid search, natural search, E-commerce, and online efforts.
- Direct marketing and merchandising efforts; directly contributed to 50% in revenue growth at Book Publisher, Inc.
- Review acquisitions and divestitures, including conducting due diligence and contract reviews. Added value as part of the road show team to drive the sale of ABC, the #1 publisher of health books in the US.
- Serve as both a corporate team player and an entrepreneur, bringing knowledge of corporate strategy and operations, creative thinking, and a multifaceted and distinctive perspective to business, negotiating, and corporate venture transactions.

With a well-rounded set of operational, analytical, and interpersonal skills, I am confident that I would make a substantial and meaningful impact on [Company Name]. I would be pleased to have the opportunity to review my credentials with you in a personal interview. Please feel free to contact me at the number above to arrange a time to speak.

Sincerely,

John C. Lawton

Enclosure: Résumé

246

General Manager. *Debra Wheatman, Parlin, New Jersey*

Bullets point to competencies that would enable this individual to contribute to a senior executive team in a publishing firm. Portions of the letter can be adapted as specific positions arise.

00 Elmwood Circle
Sheboygan, WI 55555

(555) 555-5555
ava@xxx.net

June 12, 20XX

Mr. George Bertrand, Editor
The Sheboygan Sentinel
000 West Parkway
Sheboygan, WI 00000

Dear Mr. Bertrand:

Having recently graduated *magna cum laude* from the University of New Hampshire with a B.A. in Journalism, I am back in my hometown and eager to launch my career as a reporter, hopefully with *The Sheboygan Sentinel.*

Because of my exemplary academic record, I earned Phi Beta Kappa distinction and landed the most coveted internship offered to journalism majors—a one-year, paid position as a community reporter for the *Nashua Telegraph*, one of the state's larger daily newspapers with circulation of 90,000 print and online subscribers. During my internship, I was involved in various aspects of the newsroom and given a full range of responsibilities. Working closely with staff reporters, photographers, and editors, I gained practical experience in newswriting, interviewing, and copyediting. Often I was called upon to cover general assignments, features, and human interest stories, many of which were published as front-page centerpieces with my byline. Most importantly, *I never missed a deadline.*

To give you an example of my effectiveness, I collaborated with the city reporter in an awareness-raising campaign. My assignment was to gather information for a major investigational piece on the reassessment of property values in the city of Nashua. This article generated numerous editorials and an overwhelming citizen response to file tax appeals. The editor regarded it as one of the best stories of the year.

During my academic years, I contributed short stories, poetry, and photography to the campus literary magazine and reviewed events for the monthly school newspaper and website. My professors would say I am creative and open-minded with a strong foundation of experience, combined with superior oral and written communication skills. In addition, I have demonstrated the ability to interact effectively and build trust with various personality types.

Because I am energized by fast-paced, time-sensitive environments requiring flexibility, commitment, and teamwork, I feel I would be an ideal candidate for a position in your newsroom. After you have reviewed this letter and my enclosed resume, please allow me to meet with you to further convince you of my qualifications. Thank you for your time and consideration.

Sincerely,

Ava Lindstrom

Enclosure: Resume

247

Newspaper Reporter. *Melanie Noonan, Woodland Park, New Jersey*

The applicant was a recent graduate who was looking for her first real job as a newspaper reporter after returning home from an out-of-state college. She wanted to appear knowledgeable and competent.

JAMES MCMAHAN

jamesmc@roadrunner.com

55 South California Street, Sharon, PA 55555

555.555.5555

Dear Hiring Authority:

**Have you identified a need within your organization for an employee
who has a strong technical and writing background?**

**Perhaps you hoped for your developers to fill that role in
addition to their specialized skills in programming and design.**

I bring the ability to ensure the full appreciation and use of products by providing **solid documentation, developing step-by-step procedures, and highlighting valuable features.** I am confident that your company and end users will benefit from my capacity to **translate complex technical language into clear, concise, and accurate documentation.** In fact, I have been recognized for producing just such focused and **user-friendly software manuals as well as print and online help.**

My success can be attributed to proficiency in quickly gaining a deep understanding of products through research and analysis, training, and working with subject matter experts. By actively seeking and acquiring detailed technical information, I am highly capable of disseminating that information and maintaining thorough and consistent client communication and support.

In additional, my behavioral style has a direct impact on my achievements. A recent behavioral (DISC) profile confirms that my natural style (•) in the workplace is a **Coordinating Analyzer,** and my adapted style (▲) is an **Analyzing Coordinator** *(see The Success Insights® Wheel below)*. This means that I am **genuinely skilled in gathering, organizing, sharing, and standardizing information to build consensus and facilitate change.**

The following career highlights are demonstrative of my behavioral and professional competencies:

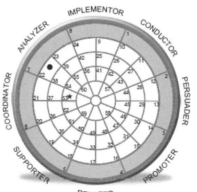

- Attained the historically **best end user satisfaction rating as a Technical Writer** for Lender Processing Services.
- Received promotions at two different companies for **success in interacting with end users in regard to software use and proper procedures** for completing detailed questionnaires.
- Acquired a **solid academic base in technical and writing fields,** including **bachelor's degrees in computer science, English, and English education,** and teacher certification in English literature.

I would welcome the opportunity for a personal meeting to further discuss my qualifications. Thank you in advance for your time and consideration. I look forward to hearing from you soon.

Sincerely,

James E. McMahan

Scan or link to view and/or print my resume: www.xxxx/xxxx

248

Technical Writer. *Jane Roqueplot, West Middlesex, Pennsylvania*

The Success Insights Wheel and its definition within the body of the letter indicate the applicant's inherent analytical and coordinating personal traits. The QR Code provides a link to his resume.

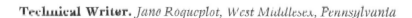

JANET EBERHART

192 CAVENDER TRAIL
MEDFORD, OR 97501

(541) 555-9999
JEBERHART@BEACONREALTY.COM

September 29, 20XX

William Fennimore
Managing Partner
Solid Gold Properties, LLC
6336 Hawthorne Parkway
Portland, OR 97208

Dear Mr. Fennimore:

I recently learned of your expansion plans to open new offices in southern Oregon, and thought you might be interested in my proven track record of substantial business increases in start-up and rapid-growth situations in the residential real estate marketplace.

By way of background, I founded and have been broker of record for a multi-operational real estate company that has grown since 20XX from a 4-person office into a $28 million operation. With my dedicated team of 17 associates and 3 support staff, we handle property management, sales and leasing, and appraisal services. Through intensive marketing, high-gross commission sales, and financial stability, I established the company's presence to qualify for prestigious affiliation with one of the nation's largest franchise networks.

I personally list an average of 30 properties per year. In addition, I oversee 30 to 40 ongoing transactions under contract, intervening to resolve problems that may impact closings. Over 75% of our listings result in sales. In the capacity of officer, I

- Manage all aspects of daily operations, create operating budgets, design expansion plans, and designate funds for company investments;
- Develop and implement programs for lead generation through community involvement;
- Coordinate advertising efforts, including development of collateral materials, direct-mail campaigns, and newspaper ads; and
- Facilitate numerous sales closings by establishing beneficial relationships with executives at financing organizations known to provide alternative lending strategies.

Owing my success to teamwork, I developed a sales training program, capitalizing on each individual's strengths and utilizing appropriate incentives, which has promoted high levels of motivation and productivity and 90% workforce retention. My top producer has shown the potential to follow in my footsteps, so I plan to turn over the reins to her upon finding another challenging opportunity where I could repeat my past accomplishments. Hopefully, it will be with your dynamic organization.

As I am sure you are aware, running a profitable real estate sales office depends heavily on client satisfaction, achieved through building relationships of trust and negotiating win/win outcomes, as well as astute planning and forecasting. I know I have what it takes, and would welcome the opportunity to discuss how my professional skills can contribute to penetrating your new market and positioning Solid Gold Properties for future growth. I will call your office next week to arrange a mutually convenient time to meet.

Sincerely,

Janet Eberhart

Enclosure: Resume

249

Real Estate Broker/Office Manager. *Melanie Noonan, Woodland Park, New Jersey*

The applicant wanted to head a new real estate office in her state. The letter indicates in turn her interest, background and experience, success, managerial ability, and self-confidence.

Chad A. Warner

555 W Cornell Ave., #5 | Bath, NY 55555 | (555) 555-5555 | chadwarner@msn.com

July 19, 20XX

Investment Real Estate Management
5555 States St.
Ithaca, NY 55555

Re: **Asset Manager Position**

Dear Hiring Manager:

Please accept this letter and accompanying résumé as my sincere interest in the Asset Manager position posted on craigslist.org. I have six years of experience in problem solving and overcoming obstacles while managing all aspects of a 26,000 square foot commercial property. Because of the economic climate, my employer has decided to return the oversight of the property to a family-run business model, allowing me to pursue an opportunity to contribute to a property management firm that values excellent customer service and a commitment to developing a positive rapport with its tenants.

As a proactive property management professional, I have frequently been praised by both my employer and the property's tenants for demonstrating my honesty, integrity and dependability and for maintaining a safe and clean environment. My background in sales, financial analysis, and computer programming and networking has allowed me to increase efficiency and generate profitable results for my employers time and again. As a business-minded property manager, I regularly presented research findings, comparative data and market analysis to the property owner to help in making smart investments based on current and forecasted conditions.

My enclosed résumé contains additional information on my experience and skills, and I have recommendation letters not only from the property owner I have served for the past six years, but also from multiple tenants who have appreciated my genuine concern for their needs. I would appreciate the opportunity to meet with you in person and will follow up with you next week to answer any questions you may have.

Your time and consideration are most appreciated.

Sincerely,

Chad A. Warner

Chad A. Warner

Annual Salary Requirements: $50,000–$65,000

250

Asset Manager. *Melanie Lenci, Denver, Colorado*

The applicant was about to lose a job that he had held for six years. This cover letter, along with his resume, helped to ease his anxiety and increase his confidence in his job search.

DAN FARRON

1111 Autumnbrook Drive
Houston, TX 00000

713.000.0000
name@aol.com

January 19, 20XX

Mr. Jonathan Trammel, President
XYZ Corporation
3434 Main Street, Suite 100
Houston, TX 00000

Dear Mr. Trammel:

I noted your advertisement for a Vice President of Operations in *The Houston Chronicle* with a great deal of interest. Your candidate description and position requirements appear to be an excellent match with my background and qualifications.

As Senior Vice President of a diversified Texas real estate firm, I have more than 18 years of expertise in all property types and all facets of commercial real estate investments, including acquisitions, dispositions, development, management, renovation, reuse, finance, and asset management. Some of my skills and experiences that indicate the value I can bring to your company are the following:

- Handled more than 150 commercial transactions nationally, examining every angle and determining appropriate resolutions. I have been successful in acquiring and marketing underdeveloped or mismanaged properties and repositioning them into profitable real estate.
- Built extensive relationships, networks, and alliances with brokers, lenders, and third-party consultants, allowing me to obtain one of the most important value-driven components in real estate: information.
- Developed experience in commercial real estate and demonstrated ability to structure financial loans, venture equity, and troubled debt restructuring, as well as market commercial property.

With commercial foreclosures up, bankruptcies increasing, and long-term interest rates at a 40-year low, opportunity is "knocking at the door" again to recognize and take advantage of these significant market changes and acquire distressed or underperforming properties.

I believe that my experience and qualifications, along with my drive and enthusiasm, make me an excellent candidate for your opening. Perhaps we could arrange a meeting to discuss your current needs and the strategies I could contribute toward their fulfillment. Thank you, Mr. Trammel, for your time and consideration.

Sincerely,

Dan Farron

Enclosure

251

Vice President of Operations. *Daniel J. Dorotik, Jr., Lubbock, Texas*

The opening paragraph claims a match between the applicant and the advertised position. The next two paragraphs, together with the bulleted items, give evidence of expertise and achievements.

Melinda H. Jacobson

0000 Westwood Drive NE Grand Rapids, MI 49505 555-555-4444
melindajacobson@yahoo.com

Date

Name
Company
Address
City, State ZIP

Dear Employment Director:

What does it take to be an excellent appraiser? Accuracy. Thoroughness. Attention to detail. Understanding of the process. I believe you will find that I have these assets and more. That's why I am contacting you—to learn about opportunities in commercial appraising, appraisal review, appraiser management or other related positions with your organization. My resume is enclosed for your review.

You will see that I have been appraising commercial properties for several years. I have found that my skills are particularly geared toward commercial lines in that I am very analytical and I understand how the process actually works. The challenges that commercial appraising present are also exciting.

The breadth of my experience is described on my resume. I have generated many complex files and appraised diverse properties, from vacant land to manufacturing plants and strip malls. In addition to my commercial and residential experience, I have been training appraisers and reviewing/releasing their work. This has presented its own challenges, which have solidified my knowledge of the field.

I sincerely hope you will agree that I have the potential to join your team as a great commercial appraiser. A personal interview would give me a chance to expand on my qualifications and give you an opportunity to see firsthand how motivated I am. I will call you to make arrangements. Thank you for your consideration.

Sincerely,

Melinda H. Jacobson

Enclosure

252

Commercial Appraiser. *Janet L. Beckstrom, Flint, Michigan*

The applicant's experience was mostly in residential appraising, but she wanted to transition to the more profitable realm of commercial appraising. The focus is on previous commercial experience.

Will consider relocation

Richard Montgomery
National Sales Representative

0000 Magnolia Lane, Centerville, Alabama 00000
☎ 555.555.5555 (home) – 555.555.7777 (cell) ✉ Richard_Montgomery@xx.com

Friday, XX February 20XX

Ms. Christine A. Hopkins
Vice President of Sales
TopLine, Inc.
00 Northridge Parkway
Suite 000
Birmingham, Alabama 00000

Dear Ms. Hopkins:

> **Increased revenue** 13.2 percent **after 16 years of decline...raised profits 20 percent in 9 months...strengthened the brand...**gave sales team an **even better edge...Improved speed to market**

You have just read the *Readers' Digest* version of capabilities I want TopLine to enjoy if I can be your National Sales Representative. You'll find in my résumé how I brought in those results and more.

In my résumé I wanted you to see much more than a self-centered objective statement, a vague "summary of qualifications," and tiring lists of job titles and responsibilities. Right at the top of the first page is my pledge of value: five selected abilities you will see me demonstrate every day. Just below them are eight proofs of performance.

Behind those words is this personal, professional code that guides all I do:

❑ Closing each sale is good; leveraging each sale as the first of many is better.

❑ Filling accounts' needs is good; anticipating their needs is better.

❑ Finding real decision makers is good; convincing them TopLine should be their primary vendor is very much better.

I love what I do. My company promoted me six times. I would still be with that company if it hadn't been forced to downsize. However, I see that as an opportunity to serve another organization.

If my philosophy and track record appeal to you, I'd like to hear about TopLine's national sales needs in your own words. May I call in a few days to arrange time to do that?

Sincerely,

Richard Montgomery

Encl.: Résumé

253

National Sales Representative. *Don Orlando, Montgomery, Alabama*

The target company was an Italian maker of high-end kitchen appliances and wanted initial entry into the U.S. market. Every bit of this letter argues that this candidate is the one who can best do the job.

Samuel T. McDowell

555 Diamond River Acres • San Diego, CA 55555
555-555-5555 • stmcdowell36@xx.com

Date

Name
Title
[Company]
Address
City, State ZIP

Dear [Name]:

> *Are top salespeople born or made? After studying the top 1% of salespeople across 23 different industries, Werth learned that most of the top salespeople were doing* the same things—*and what they were doing was* radically different from the other 99% of salespeople. *Conclusion: "Top salespeople are clearly made."*
> — *J. Werth*

I firmly ascribe to this belief and present my track record of exceptional sales results—even during recessionary times, even within one of the most difficult mortgage/home-buying cycles, and even working for one of the most problem-fraught companies in the industry at that time. **Bottom line: As a consistent top producer, I can build long-term relationships, I can sell, and I can deliver unparalleled results.**

At this juncture in my career, I'm ready to make a quantum shift—applying my proven expertise to [Company]'s sales challenges. I can immediately make a difference and deliver valuable solutions in the following ways:

- **Business expansion.** From cold-calling, converting prospects, and building new channels to further penetrating existing accounts, I utilize highly effective and genuine relationship-management expertise to quickly establish rapport, cement value, and close business deals that are mutually beneficial and profitable.

- **Exemplary service.** I treat every transaction with kid gloves, valuing each relationship and each piece of business...and the long-term gain that results from deals with solid foundations backed by exceptional customer service.

- **Unwavering integrity.** From the moment I become part of your team, you'll have my 110% commitment to delivering outstanding results honestly—representing everything that [Company] stands for and promises to its valued clientele. My demonstrated work ethic "knows no quit" (a throwback to many years as a highly focused competitive athlete), and I'll consistently exceed client—and your—performance expectations.

I'm confident of my ability to contribute in an exceptional fashion to [Company] and would value the opportunity to discuss your specific objectives and how my background might represent the right match. I believe in the importance of establishing relationships and connections—and will follow through to learn the best time when we can talk further. Thank you for your consideration.

Sincerely,

Samuel T. McDowell

Sales Professional. *Jan Melnik, Durham, Connecticut*

This letter for no specific opening or network connection introduces an exceptional salesperson whose distinctive sales career has exhibited business-building skills, service, and integrity.

254

JUSTIN POLANIK

555 Chestnut St. ◆ Stoneboro, PA 55555 ◆ 555-555-5555 ◆ juspol@xx.com

Melissa Martin, HR Manager
Butler County Homes
555 Layton Ave
Butler, OH 55555

Dear Ms. Martin:

I am writing to express my interest in the **Sales Representative** position currently available with Butler County Homes. In reviewing the position's job requirements, I am certain my **sales experience** in combination with my **construction background** qualifies me for this opportunity. A summary of my achievements is provided in the accompanying resume, highlighting my abilities in territory development, account acquisition, and client relations. Additionally, I have demonstrated a great ability to

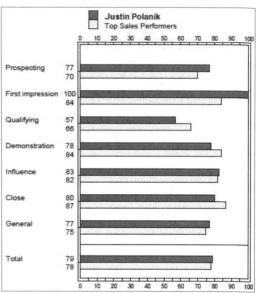

Sales Strategy Index™

- Apply more than 16 years of experience in sales trend analysis, forecasting, and market research.
- Negotiate swift resolution in response to customer concerns.
- Build strategic business partnerships.
- Quickly handle complex business issues to promote customer loyalty.

Leveraging my sales expertise to directly contribute to your organization's existing achievements and to introduce new business development initiatives that meaningfully support your corporate objectives would be most rewarding.

Throughout my career, I have consistently expressed determination, resourcefulness, ingenuity, and a strong commitment to excellence. Given my capabilities, I am confident I will immediately enhance your team's growth and productivity. I look forward to speaking with you regarding my application and qualifications.

I can be reached via email at juspol@xx.com or by calling 555-555-5555. Thank you for your time and consideration.

Sincerely,

Justin Polanik

Enclosure: resume

255

Sales Representative. *Jane Roqueplot, West Middlesex, Pennsylvania*

The Sales Strategy Index is a sales competency test used by sales trainers and employers. The graph of the applicant's test results displays his strengths and knowledge of selling techniques.

SHEILA BEST　　　　　　　　　　　　　　　　555-555-5555

sheilabest@email.com
0000 Rabbit Road, Birmingham, AL 35210

January 21, 20XX

Chairman, Search Committee
Birmingham Chamber of Commerce
106 N. Starline
Birmingham, AL 35210

Dear Chairman:

With strong family roots in Birmingham County and 10 years of broad-based Chamber experience, I feel my qualifications make me an ideal candidate for the president position with the Birmingham Chamber.

Born and raised in Mountain Brook and a graduate of Central High School, I know the Birmingham community very well. As Senior Vice President of the Mountain Brook Chamber of Commerce, I have full P&L responsibility for a $1.6 million budget encompassing production and sales, membership, and operations. While Vice President of Publications and Directory, I directed a staff of 11 in successfully meeting or exceeding annual financial objectives for five consecutive years.

My Chamber experience includes

- implementation of innovative programs and benefits to expand and retain membership;
- sales and production of the only Chamber-produced directory in the United States;
- documented success in establishing long-term, mutually beneficial, and profitable corporate liaisons and alliances; and
- the establishment of a network of contacts to maintain the strong community tie.

I would appreciate the opportunity to discuss in more detail how my experience might benefit the Birmingham Chamber and will give you a call early next week to make sure you have received my resume and to answer any questions you may have. I look forward to speaking with you.

Sincerely,

Sheila Best

Enclosure

256

President, Chamber of Commerce. *Cindy Kraft, Valrico, Florida*

Knowledge of an area and promotional abilities are two key requirements for a chamber of commerce leader. The second paragraph and the bulleted items show the applicant's suitability.

CHRIS PRENTICE

000 Cranberry Street
Salt Lake City, UT 84117

Email: cprentice@hotmail.com

Mobile: (555) 555-5555
Residence: (000) 000-5511

5 February 20xx

Mr. Fred Hall
Director of Sales & Marketing
TechIT, Inc.
4024 South 2100 Street
Salt Lake City, UT 84117

Re: Senior Business Development Manager

Dear Mr. Hall:

As I read your advertisement, it becomes evident that the candidate you seek needs proficiency in many areas. A clear resolve for quality, revenue growth, and profits, coupled with continuous improvement and firm leadership, will be essential to ride the turbulence of the market as we enter these troubled times.

At the same time, consultation, communication, and teamwork will underpin trust, cooperation, and the development of a shared vision, so that your company's long-term growth can be achieved.

In short, the market today is not for the faint-hearted, yet the current crop of challenges to the IT industry are not insurmountable if an individual with my experience, capability, and tenacity takes on the role.

Commercially, I am the seasoned manager you seek. I have extensive national experience in introducing products to market and winning prominence against established competitors. I have built distribution networks, fought hard-won battles to win market share and brand acceptance, and demonstrated the type of maturity that can win consensus in the most highly charged of atmospheres.

Team-focused, I am a strong proponent of the power of people, believing in the "all hands on deck" philosophy to achieve common goals.

Fresh from my last assignment as the Director of New Business for a provider of information systems to the SME market, I have a renewed sense of confidence toward tackling new challenges.

Naturally, I would be delighted to meet with you to review your needs in detail, and I have enclosed a copy of my resume to provide a basis for future discussions. I will call you in the next couple of days to see if our schedules can permit a brief meeting.

I look forward to speaking with you soon.

Sincerely,

Chris Prentice

257

Senior Business Development Manager. *Gayle Howard, Southbank, Victoria, Australia*

Eight short paragraphs quicken the reading tempo of this letter and make it seem shorter than it is. Five of the paragraphs are only one sentence. The impression is that this person does not waste time.

Jane A. Simmons

9007 Rainor Road ▪ Chapel Hill, NC 00000 ▪ Home: 555.555.5555 ▪ Mobile: 555.555.5555 ▪ janeasimmons@aol.com

---

"Having worked with Jane in a very dynamic and fast-paced environment, I was always impressed with her ability to look straight at the goal and help guide the team to the objectives that were set out to achieve. This ability was invaluable to the group when working with various organizations, people, and processes, to build cohesive business and marketing plans spanning the entire worldwide organization. Jane has the leadership to build a common understanding of the customers and the marketing organization we were working with, as well as to assist the organization in defining strategies and programs to address this market."

Fred Jones, VP-Marketing,
Center Technology, Inc.

"Jane could be counted on to take an assignment, project, complex problem and pull the right resources together (people and funding) to drive to success. She works to understand the customer needs, requirements, and pain points and then addresses those in creative new ways. She drives her team and her projects with great independence and with an eye for quality, ultimately delivering exceptional results on behalf of the end user customer and our company. She is an extraordinary team player and one of the most talented individuals I have had the pleasure to work with in my 18 years."

Ellen Lawrence, Worldwide
VP-Marketing,
Center Technology, Inc.

Date

Name
Title
Company Name
Address
City, State, ZIP

Dear Mr. or Ms. _____:

As a business and marketing leader in program management and process improvements that result in increased revenues and reduced costs, I can offer a wealth of knowledge and skill sets to your company. My expertise in leading companies through periods of growth and change have prepared me for any number of challenges that your company may be facing.

Highlights of my achievements during my rapid growth at Center Technology, Inc., include the following:

As Marketing Manager for the global business unit:

- Led a global team of marketing and product managers to redefine the program scope, which increased storage revenue by more than $50 million incrementally in 6 months.

As Marketing Manager for the hardware program:

- Directed the reduction of more than 120 marketing programs with a $13 million quarterly budget down to 8 marketing programs with an $8 million budget.
- Implemented promotions and extensive training programs to increase cross-sell of PCs and support services by more than 25%.

As Business Planning Manager:

- Leveraged the company's global account organization and sales force to increase global accounts revenue by more than 12%.
- Improved relationships between the Americas' regional business and marketing teams through the implementation of best practices.

If you need a strategic marketing executive with strong business acumen and out-of-the-box problem-solving talent blended with extraordinary team leadership and the ability to execute tactically, then I am your candidate. I would welcome the opportunity to discuss how my vision, creativity, and skill sets could benefit your organization. May we meet?

Sincerely,

Jane A. Simmons

Enclosure

258

Strategic Marketing Executive. *Louise Garver, Broad Brook, Connecticut*

This individual wanted to move up to the next level in her career path in technology. The letter emphasizes her leadership skills and results, supported by two testimonials from company VPs.

STEVE A. JOHNSTON

5555 Franklin Avenue • Largo, MD 55555 • sajohnston@xx.com • 555-555-5555

August 14, 20XX

Ms. Cheryl Moore
Human Resources Manager
US Largo Bank
555 S. Market Street
Largo, MD 55555

Dear Ms. Moore:

Business development with a client-centered approach is my area of expertise. Whether the challenge has been to build a new client base for a start-up company, manage a high-performing sales team, or accurately forecast the economic environment, I have consistently exceeded expectations and produced strong monetary results. I present to you my resume for consideration for an Account Executive or Sales Management position at US Largo Bank.

Over the last 10 years, I have performed strongly in these areas:

> **Sales:** Exceeded sales goals and increased the number of clients for Credit Employers Credit Union, a multibillion-dollar bank, and Pay Your Way Solutions, a start-up company, both in Largo, MD.

> **Profit Enhancement:** Contributed to 30% sales increase for Final, a new detergent brand.

> **Quality Control:** Successfully streamlined administrative functions and identified process changes, avoiding $1.5 million in customer deductions at Pay Your Way Solutions.

> **Customer Service and Teamwork:** Built collaborative relationships with clients, vendors, sales teams, and collaborating departments.

At this time, I am looking to begin a new challenge in sales management where I can continue my track record of success, direct a team of representatives, and add to the financial growth of a company. I am willing to relocate anywhere in the southeastern portion of the United States and would welcome the opportunity for an interview. Please contact me at 555-555-5555 to schedule a meeting at your convenience.

Respectfully,

Steve A. Johnston

Enclosure

259

Account Executive/Sales Manager. *Lakeisha Mathews, Baltimore, Maryland*

This letter was a response to an ad. The boldfacing of categories in the quantified bulleted items helps to make visible at a glance the areas in which the applicant has excelled.

MARY J. JACKSON

555 Country Lane, Port Jefferson, NY 55555
555-555-5555 ✧ mojo@xx.com

SALES MANAGEMENT PROFESSIONAL
Maximize Revenues ✧ Rescue Faltering Territories ✧ Increase Productivity

July 19, 20XX

Ms. Robin Kuglerman
Managing Director at Zeppo Industries
000 Meow Boulevard
New York, NY 00000

Dear Ms. Kuglerman:

Your recent advertisement for a Director of Sales indicates your desire for an accomplished sales professional with leadership experience in the B2B services arena. I am a strong candidate with proven success increasing revenue and driving corporate growth. I am your next Director of Sales.

Client satisfaction and new business development—both are accomplished with a customer-centric attitude, consultative sales strategies, and team leadership. I have earned a reputation for mentoring and coaching teams to achieve corporate objectives and developing talent for career advancement. By example, I delivered strong results as Regional Sales Manager in the following areas:

- Raised office rank within region from last place to first place.
- Increased revenue in my company's key product line from $1.8 million to $14.2 million.
- Developed direct reports who were recognized with promotions and recruited into positions of increased scope and responsibility.

My background demonstrates my ability to propel organizations toward success. Senior-level management recognizes my talent for building rapport and motivating successful teams. My peers will say that I am hands-on, results-oriented, and driven to succeed. I am passionate in my efforts to increase revenue share, build strategic partnerships, and create positive results for my team and employer.

The enclosed resume describes my qualifications in more detail. I am available and eager to discuss this exciting opportunity with you. Thank you for your consideration.

Sincerely,

Mary J. Jackson

Enclosure

260

Director of Sales. *Michelle Riklan, Morganville, New Jersey*

In this ad-response letter, bullets call attention to the applicant's strong results as a Regional Sales Manager. Quantifying increased revenue provides an impressive statistic to support the bold opening paragraph.

Kristen Dennison

5 Center Street
Keatsville, New Jersey 55555
kdennison@xx.com, 555-555-5555
www.linkedin.com/xxx/xx

Account Management | Sales | Marketing
Expanding Awareness. Building Relationships. Driving Revenue.

October 4, 20XX

Mr. Stephen Windsom
Glorious Custom Widgets
555 Widget Avenue
Yooper, New York 55555

Dear Mr. Windsom:

With a history of developing new business worth millions of dollars, I am looking to do the same with a leading organization such as Glorious Custom Widgets. Your open position for an Account Manager, which I learned about from Monster.com, seems to be an ideal fit for my qualifications. These include hands-on sales and marketing experience in the widget industry as well as a bachelor's degree in marketing. In addition, I have been involved in package development from conception through completion.

My passion for meeting client needs is what drives me to create innovative solutions. I build relationships with decision makers, determine exactly what their "pain points" are, and set about solving their problems. My distinctive ability in this area has led to the following successes:

> **Securing largest contract in company's history, despite heavy industry competition.**
> **Expanding profit margins 20% by evaluating and revamping pricing model.**
> **Playing key role in successful nationwide launch of new equipment line; products enabled packaging companies to add decorative effects onto package inline on sheet-fed press.**

The attached résumé includes additional examples of ways my abilities have generated revenue for my past employer. I would welcome the opportunity to speak with you in more detail and will call next Thursday to follow up. Though I currently reside in New Jersey, I am open to relocating and am able to move with one week's notice. Please note, I have conducted numerous business trips throughout the U.S. as well as in Europe and Asia, and I am open to any amount of travel. Thank you for your time and consideration.

Sincerely,

Kristen Dennison

Enclosure

261

Account Manager. *Charlotte Weeks, Chicago, Illinois*

The applicant had a marketing background and loved sales and new business development. The letter focused on her drive, greatest achievements, and interest in a job with travel.

PAUL D. LEWIS

555 Clare Street • Melville, New York 44444 • (333) 222-4444 • salespro@soldout.net

Date

Name
Company
Address

Dear Name:

Success is broadly founded in hands-on leadership with a firm belief in performance ownership and accountability. With a career track in senior sales management positions with System-Tel, Virtual-Communication, and Global Wireless, my well-honed consultative sales style and drive to succeed have proven effective in building and sustaining C-level relationships and revenue gains across highly competitive vertical markets.

Perhaps your organization is seeking to recruit a sales executive with these talents to develop and lead its sales organization to success in the face of emerging competition and uncertain economical climates. If this is the case, you will want to consider me as a viable candidate. But first, let me briefly highlight my 13-year sales career with the aforementioned leading organizations to give you a better idea of who I am and the value I would bring to the appropriate executive sales position.

- Over-quota Annual Sales Track Record with System-Tel

2011	**173%**	2009	**142%**	2007	**129%**	2005	**120%**
2010	**166%**	2008	**135%**	2006	**131%**	2004	**133%**

- Develop and execute sales solution strategies for mid-tier and large-scale corporations.
- Train, coach, mentor, and lead more than 30 top-gun sales professionals.
- Cultivate alliance relationships with industry partners.
- Conceptual, technical knowledge of enterprise-wide, technology-based software solutions.

I realize you must be inundated with resumes—some good, some not—and find it increasingly difficult to decide on top talent. As such, I strongly encourage a meeting—either in person or preliminarily by telephone following your review of my accompanying resume, to discuss how I can contribute to the growth of your organization's bottom line.

I will call you next week to explore the possibility of an interview. Thank you in advance for your time and consideration. I look forward to meeting with you soon.

Sincerely,

Paul D. Lewis

262

Sales Executive. *Ann Baehr, East Islip, New York*

The applicant was a senior sales manager looking for a sales executive position. His success at sales is a recurrent theme in the first two paragraphs. Boldfacing of percentages highlights growth.

JILLIAN DANZER
555 Elyssa Way • Staten Island, NY 55555
jilliandanzer@example.com • 555.555.5555

~ SALES GENERATION ■ VISUAL STRATEGIZING ■ BRAND AMBASSADORSHIP ■ TEAM EMPOWERMENT ~

September 01, 20XX

Mr. Alan Miller, Human Resources Director
Steve Madden Ltd.
000 Barnett Avenue
Long Island City, NY 00000

Dear Mr. Miller:

As I consider options that offer new and exciting opportunities to expand my career, I am excited by your job posting for **Senior Key Account Executive.** My retail and wholesale background, leadership, and relationship-based rapport-building talents directly mirror the requirements you seek. The enclosed résumé reflects my ability to make a significant contribution to your brand's positioning and sustained growth. Noteworthy qualifications include

- **Taking a collaborative and adaptable approach to seller/buyer dynamics**—talents refined through a 16-year history across visual merchandising and marketing as well as store sales, territory, and account management roles for *Sketchers* and *Nine East.*

- **Earning recognition for "getting things done,"** characterized by others as a potent problem solver; always striving to develop new ideas, capture new opportunities, and negotiate new partnerships to build territory volume to record levels.

- **Inspiring others to push themselves** through training and leading by example with endless dedication, attention to detail, unparalleled customer service, tremendous work ethic, and pursuit of perfection.

- **A lifelong career developing customer relationships** across diverse geographies with consultative, straightforward communications that promote development of strong and lasting rapport and trust.

- **Repeated success transforming opaque ideas into concrete results** daily with enterprising foresight, innovation, and continual collaboration.

As you may have noticed, my career success has been due in large part to building strategic relationships and tackling persistently difficult areas with resourceful approaches. The requirement to be able to turn one's hand to a number of concurrent priorities, customer accounts, and demanding goals has been paramount—and I have delivered in these areas time and again.

While secure in my current position, I am confidently investigating new challenges. You will find that I am as committed to my career as I will be to Saint Madden Ltd. and would welcome the opportunity to apply my skills and expertise for a world-renowned luxury brand such as yours. I offer you in return a colleague armed with senior management capabilities, focus, and ability to drive performance in all areas of account management, visual merchandising, and field marketing within both retail and wholesale environments.

I will be in contact with you on Tuesday to further clarify my ability to contribute to your organization. In the meantime, I thank you for your time and consideration and look forward to what I predict will be the first of many positive conversations.

Sincerely,

Jillian Danzer
Enclosure: résumé

263

Senior Key Account Executive. *Sandra Ingemansen, Leeds, West Yorkshire, England*

This individual was performing at a senior-management level without having such a job title. The writer strategically places below the contact information keywords indicating her primary strengths.

ERIC J. MANSON

Cascade Towers, 0000 76 Avenue, Bloomington, MN 55555
Cell / Voice Mail 555 555 5000 • Home 555 555 5555 • E-mail: ejmn@concord.net

February 2, 20XX

Mr. Roberto Oltone
Telecommunications Department
Superior Networks
82 Jason Street
Kansas City, Missouri 55555

MARKETING AND SALES MANAGEMENT

Dear Mr. Oltone:

I am most interested in the position advertised recently in the *Sun-Times* and have accordingly attached a professional resume for your review.

With more than 20 years of executive-level experience in marketing electronics and communication equipment and service, I've negotiated numerous contracts; achieved solid revenue growth; and bought, sold, and merged companies. My major strengths fall into the following arenas:

- Marketing and Sales
- Business Development
- Finance
- Training and Development
- Management and Leadership

Personal skills enhance my expertise in marketing management. I am known for having tenacity, a tremendous work ethic, an aggressive solution-oriented focus, and a team-oriented manner. My aversion to micromanaging has generated loyalty from others, as has the ability to listen to suggestions and concerns of customers, managers, and staff. With an intuitive nature and vision for the future, problem solving and decision making come easily to me.

I will be calling your office to determine your interview schedule for this position and look forward to discussing the company's needs and in what ways I might contribute to those plans. Please let me know if you need further information before then.

Sincerely,

Eric J. Manson

264

Marketing and Sales Manager. *Beverley Drake, Hot Springs Village, Arkansas*

In this response to a newspaper ad, bullets point to major strengths. The third paragraph tells about the applicant's managerial abilities, people skills, and additional strengths.

ANDREA DONNA

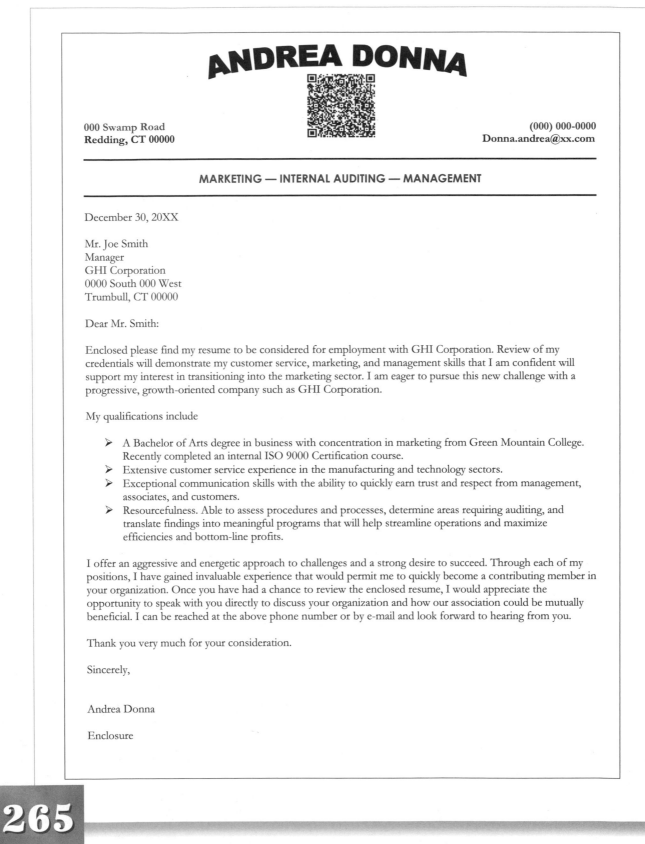

000 Swamp Road
Redding, CT 00000

(000) 000-0000
Donna.andrea@xx.com

MARKETING — INTERNAL AUDITING — MANAGEMENT

December 30, 20XX

Mr. Joe Smith
Manager
GHI Corporation
0000 South 000 West
Trumbull, CT 00000

Dear Mr. Smith:

Enclosed please find my resume to be considered for employment with GHI Corporation. Review of my credentials will demonstrate my customer service, marketing, and management skills that I am confident will support my interest in transitioning into the marketing sector. I am eager to pursue this new challenge with a progressive, growth-oriented company such as GHI Corporation.

My qualifications include

➢ A Bachelor of Arts degree in business with concentration in marketing from Green Mountain College. Recently completed an internal ISO 9000 Certification course.
➢ Extensive customer service experience in the manufacturing and technology sectors.
➢ Exceptional communication skills with the ability to quickly earn trust and respect from management, associates, and customers.
➢ Resourcefulness. Able to assess procedures and processes, determine areas requiring auditing, and translate findings into meaningful programs that will help streamline operations and maximize efficiencies and bottom-line profits.

I offer an aggressive and energetic approach to challenges and a strong desire to succeed. Through each of my positions, I have gained invaluable experience that would permit me to quickly become a contributing member in your organization. Once you have had a chance to review the enclosed resume, I would appreciate the opportunity to speak with you directly to discuss your organization and how our association could be mutually beneficial. I can be reached at the above phone number or by e-mail and look forward to hearing from you.

Thank you very much for your consideration.

Sincerely,

Andrea Donna

Enclosure

265

Marketing/Internal Auditing Position. *Donna Allen, Heber City, Utah*

The applicant was transitioning from customer service to marketing/internal auditing. The QR Code in the contact information indicates that the individual was staying ahead of industry trends.

Lisa A. Santos

555 Victoria Avenue
Augusta, Ontario A1A 1A1
lisasantos@email.com
Home: 555.666.9999
Cell: 555.999.7777

March 3, 20XX

Terrance Flaherty, CEO
Consultronix
345 Pine Valley Road, Suite 4460
Augusta, Ontario
B2C 3D4

<u>**Re: Director of Marketing**</u>

Dear Mr. Flaherty,

I love a challenge!

Whether leading the marketing and promotional initiatives for the Canadian arm of one of the world's largest management consulting firms, spearheading the corporate development efforts of a $25 million fundraising campaign to fight polio, or coordinating high-profile executive luncheons and promotional events with the "who's who" of Canadian business, I approach each challenge with the same "get it done" attitude.

It is exactly this determination—combined with exceptional skills in marketing, promotions, business development, and executive relationship management—that has enabled my successes to date, and that in turn I can offer to your firm. From what I have read in the industry journals of your plans to enter new technology and telecom markets, you need someone who can step in now and create a singular market presence—and with the IT-Com Conference coming to Augusta this September, it needs to be done quickly.

In short, as my attached resume attests, here's what I can offer you:

- **Expertise in creating high corporate visibility and brand recognition**—proven ability to create the appropriate marketing vehicle or event, secure widespread media attention, and stimulate excitement around a product or service

- **A creative mind for promotional opportunities and marketing campaigns**—solid track record for conceiving and organizing high-profile executive luncheons, industry roundtables, and special events

- **Exceptional market research and analysis skills**—critical for appropriate market segmentation and targeted marketing/promotional campaigns

- **Strong project management and leadership capabilities**—organized, focused, and able to pull teams together around a common goal

Please feel free to contact me at your earliest convenience to arrange a personal meeting, and I would be glad to discuss why I'm the person for the job. I already have a number of ideas that should interest you.

I thank you for your consideration and look forward to speaking with you soon.

Sincerely,

Lisa A. Santos

Encl. Resume

266

Director of Marketing. *Ross Macpherson, Whitby, Ontario, Canada*

The unique first paragraph grabs the reader's attention. Bullets and boldfacing highlight what the applicant can do for the company. This letter stood above the rest; in the end she got the job.

Available for relocation to the Dallas area   C O N F I D E N T I A L

Lily Duart   1200 Westie Circle, Montgomery, Alabama 00000
[000] 000-0000 (home) — [000] 000-5555 (cell) — [000] 555-5555 (fax) — 001@scratch.com

Monday, 15 March 20XX

Mr. Norman French, CEO
Carley Products, Inc.
625 Express Highway
Building 333
Dallas, Texas 00000

Dear Mr. French,

In a few seconds, you are going to see a half dozen capabilities I would like to put under Carley's control, followed by three indicators that reflect my success as a Director of Sales and Marketing in nationwide competition. Finally, I thought you deserved to see a half dozen documented contributions to the bottom line. But the story behind the results is as important as the numbers themselves.

I believe that most people—even your sales and marketing staff—can probably do much more than they think they can. And I believe the personal rewards they earn at those new levels will keep them producing at very high rates. I found my philosophy works wonders, regardless of the product being sold or the market being worked or the competitors' actions. Now that I've reached near the top in one industry, I'm ready for the fun of applying what I've learned in new fields.

It all starts with building mutual, beneficial relationships. Therefore, let me suggest this: May we talk soon so that I can learn more about Carley's special needs? I'll call in a few days to find a time when our schedules align.

Sincerely,

Lily Duart

Encl.: Resume

267

Director of Sales and Marketing. *Don Orlando, Montgomery, Alabama*

The applicant had very strong ideas about her philosophy of sales and marketing. By setting these out boldly, the writer appealed to companies that shared the applicant's outlook.

CONFIDENTIAL   *A VAILABLE FOR RELOCATION*

Alex McLean

0000 Duart Drive   Montgomery, Alabama 00000   topdog0000@west.com   000.000.0000

Thursday, April 8, 20XX

Ms. Laura Worth
Sales Manager
Blue Sky, Inc.
1227 Amelia Island Parkway
Suite 200
Jacksonville, Florida 00000

Dear Ms. Worth:

For years, I've been making sales happen in the immediate future. But there's another reason why I have met or exceeded significantly rising sales goals every year for the last decade: I now generate add-on sales for products I championed from an idea to reduce an inventory. Results? I built my district from scratch and led my company from $0 sales to $75M in sales annually.

My company obviously likes what I do. And maybe it's because I love sales so much that now, frankly, I am bored. That's why I am "testing the waters" with this application.

Because I thrive on anticipating requirements, I was thinking about Blue Sky's needs as I considered the form of my resume. Gone are the tiring recitations of job titles and responsibilities. In their places are a half-dozen examples of contributions measured in millions of dollars.

As you read, I hope some central ideas stand out clearly. First, I make it my business to get competitive intelligence faster than my competitors. Second, I make it my business to know my customers' operations almost as well as they do. Third, I make it my business to lead customers to choose my company through clear and compelling evidence that they think is their own good idea.

If Blue Sky can use someone with my track record, I'd like to explore how I can meet your specific sales needs. May I call in a few days to arrange a time to do that?

Sincerely,

Alex McLean

Encl.: Resume

CONFIDENTIAL

268

District Salesperson. *Don Orlando, Montgomery, Alabama*

The goal of this letter was to show that the applicant sold at many levels and used what he learned in the market to help his company beat the competition. Note the strong next-to-last paragraph.

TERRY NARBOW
0000 Jasmine Drive
Agoura Hills, California 91301
(555) 555-5555 (000) 000-0000
tnarbow@aol.com

January 23, 2012

M&R Associates
23457 Abelia Road
Calabasas, California 91304

Attention: Ms. Carolyn Hatten

Dear Ms. Hatten:

Achieving sales and marketing success in today's competitive marketplace requires a creative and strategic thinker who has the ability to establish profitable relationships, accelerate revenue growth, and maintain value-added service.

The company I left in 2011 was quite healthy, but despite record sales and profitability, there were few challenges on the horizon. I could have drawn a fine salary while serving secure accounts, but I was motivated to seek greater challenges. So I resigned in order to complete my B.A. in Business with an emphasis in Marketing as quickly as possible because this was my new chosen path.

Let me assure you, however, that I can make a compelling presentation of my candidacy whether I am selected for a position or not. My background encompasses research, development of categories of questions, creation of forms, merchandising, and displays. My innate ability to know what to ask allows for finding the most efficient way to improve procedures. Whatever the task—research, brand management/recognition, sales—it is my constant focus until completed.

Highlights that may be of particular interest include the following:

- Integration of diverse business practices, systems, and infrastructures to create top-performing organizations.
- Success in leveraging advanced technologies with core business operations.
- Cross-functional expertise in sales, new business development, and general management.
- Introduction of innovative marketing, business development, and promotional strategies that accelerated growth within existing business units and delivered revenues beyond projections.
- Realignment and expansion of third-party distribution network, capturing 20% revenue growth and strengthening competitive market position.

I understand that I may not be able to enter the marketing or brand field at a managerial level. All I am asking for is an introduction to one of your clients. Communication skills are one of my strengths (I continually take public speaking courses at various colleges), and I possess the will to succeed.

At this point in my career, I am interested in exploring new opportunities where my creative drive and energy can be further utilized and where I can continue to grow professionally.

Thank you for your consideration.

Sincerely,

Terry Narbow

Enclosure

269

Sales and Marketing Position. *Myriam-Rose Kohn, Valencia, California*

The opening paragraph is a miniprofile, and the second paragraph indicates the value this applicant placed on a bachelor's degree and career growth. Bullets point to areas of experience and success.

Lesley Mitchell

555 Mass. Ave.
Stamford, CT 55555
(555) 500-0000
Lesley52Mitchell@aol.com

September 25, 20XX

Samuel Jones
Pharmaceutical Sales Recruiter
Jones Solutions
555 Williams Road
Stamford, CT 55555

Re: Position as Pharmaceutical Sales Representative

Dear Mr. Jones:

If you are working with a company seeking an entry-level pharmaceutical sales representative, you may find my achievements interesting. The most important qualification I have for the role is my record as a top sales performer. I combine skills in executing the sales cycle with a passion for building strong customer relationships. Also, I recently earned my Bachelor of Arts in Communication. I believe that these qualifications together are a good predictor of my future success in pharmaceutical sales.

To date, I have 5 part- and full-time years of experience at high-quality retailers. During that time, I produced top sales numbers while concurrently serving as sales manager. Here are some highlights of my career to date:

- Earned the #1 ranking out of 30 sales reps while also achieving the highest numbers for units and dollars per transaction. These results attest to my sincere interest in conveying the unique selling points of my products and in helping the customer through the whole sales cycle from initial inquiry to post-sales customer service.
- Ranked #3 out of 20 in a part-time sales role *while* managing the entire sales staff, earning praise for high-level customer service, and planning 2 sales events targeting professional and academic markets.
- Achieved 200% of the full-time staff target for opening new accounts while working only part-time.

Customers respond to me and are interested in what I have to say. They quickly realize that I am well-informed about my products and know how to counter any concerns or objections they may have. I have also found that I am able to gain access to decision-makers because of my relationship-building strengths, professionalism, assertiveness, and persistence.

I am known for my leadership; proactive, self-directed style; and collaborative team skills. At this time, I am poised to begin a pharmaceutical sales career with an already honed professional image and professional-level sales skills. I am confident that I would prove to be an excellent hire for a pharmaceutical company. I will contact you to find out whether you are aware of any opportunities for which I would be an excellent, low-risk choice. Thank you for your kind consideration.

Sincerely,

Lesley Mitchell

270

Pharmaceutical Sales Representative. *Jean Cummings, Concord, Massachusetts*

The letter was to a recruiter from someone seeking to break into pharmaceutical sales. The writer's strategy was to explain the value of the applicant and to counter any doubts.

Jayne Smyth
101 Main Street
Friendship, CT 06000
555-555-5555
JSmyth@123.zzz

February 10, 20XX

Hallmark Cards, Inc.
ATTN: Human Resources Director
P.O. Box 100000001
Kansas City, MO 64141

Re: Positions for **Sales Professionals**

Dear Human Resources Director:

When you care enough to send the very best...send me!

The opportunity to represent Hallmark Cards, the perennial industry leader, would be a dream come true. Because I share your philosophy that only my best is good enough to offer, I have consistently been a top-producing sales representative for my current employer, constantly exceeding sales quotas and earning recognition from clients, peers and supervisors. Accomplishments have included the following:

- Among 50 sales representatives, rank in the top three for the past two years, supporting the achievement of departmental sales goals averaging $500,000 per month.
- Regularly produce 30% or more over daily sales goals.
- Selected to manage key national accounts.
- Commended by peers for providing sales assistance/support with accounts in a competitive environment.
- Chosen to mentor new hires.

I offer you solid sales experience, a strong customer focus and effective leadership skills, in combination with an "only the best will do" work ethic. I eagerly anticipate the opportunity to discuss your goals for your new territory and the ways in which I might help Hallmark achieve and exceed them. I will call next week to explore the possibility of an interview. Thank you for considering my qualifications.

Sincerely,

Jayne Smyth

Enclosure

271

Sales Representative. *Debra O'Reilly, Brandon, Florida*

The targeted company required outside sales experience, which the applicant lacked. The letter emphasized her sales success and good match for the company. Within a week, she got the job.

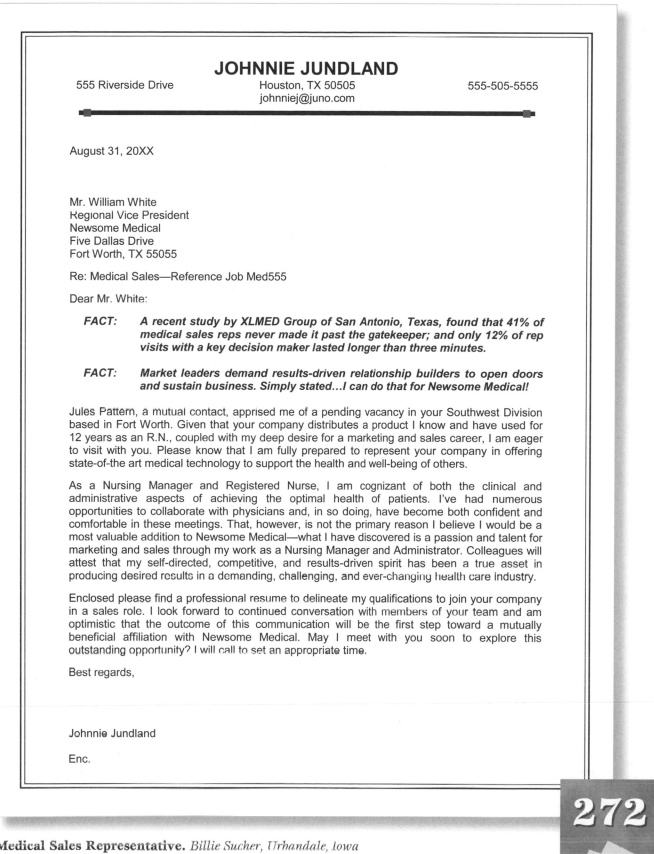

JOHNNIE JUNDLAND

555 Riverside Drive   Houston, TX 50505   555-505-5555
johnniej@juno.com

August 31, 20XX

Mr. William White
Regional Vice President
Newsome Medical
Five Dallas Drive
Fort Worth, TX 55055

Re: Medical Sales—Reference Job Med555

Dear Mr. White:

> **FACT:** *A recent study by **XLMED Group** of San Antonio, Texas, found that 41% of medical sales reps never made it past the gatekeeper; and only 12% of rep visits with a key decision maker lasted longer than three minutes.*

> **FACT:** *Market leaders demand results-driven relationship builders to open doors and sustain business. Simply stated...I can do that for Newsome Medical!*

Jules Pattern, a mutual contact, apprised me of a pending vacancy in your Southwest Division based in Fort Worth. Given that your company distributes a product I know and have used for 12 years as an R.N., coupled with my deep desire for a marketing and sales career, I am eager to visit with you. Please know that I am fully prepared to represent your company in offering state-of-the art medical technology to support the health and well-being of others.

As a Nursing Manager and Registered Nurse, I am cognizant of both the clinical and administrative aspects of achieving the optimal health of patients. I've had numerous opportunities to collaborate with physicians and, in so doing, have become both confident and comfortable in these meetings. That, however, is not the primary reason I believe I would be a most valuable addition to Newsome Medical—what I have discovered is a passion and talent for marketing and sales through my work as a Nursing Manager and Administrator. Colleagues will attest that my self-directed, competitive, and results-driven spirit has been a true asset in producing desired results in a demanding, challenging, and ever-changing health care industry.

Enclosed please find a professional resume to delineate my qualifications to join your company in a sales role. I look forward to continued conversation with members of your team and am optimistic that the outcome of this communication will be the first step toward a mutually beneficial affiliation with Newsome Medical. May I meet with you soon to explore this outstanding opportunity? I will call to set an appropriate time.

Best regards,

Johnnie Jundland

Enc.

272

Medical Sales Representative. *Billie Sucher, Urbandale, Iowa*

The individual had no prior experience in medical sales but wanted to secure a position in this highly competitive field. This sale-driven letter helped to secure an interview.

GABE CONNOR

1219 Wall Street Heights, New York, NY 10005
Home: (917) 333-9999 • gconnor@gmail.com • Cell: (917) 222-1111

Date

Company Personnel
Company Department
Company Name
Address
City, State, Postal Code

Dear _____,

When I was promoted to the Senior Sales Manager position at IBM, the company was fraught with major client communication and business challenges. I was personally selected to rebuild account loyalty with key clients Corbro and AMMO and drive hardware sales. I strengthened relationships to the point where I achieved more than $25 million in sales and gained the trust and confidence of AMMO into new initiatives and opportunities that will account for an additional 35% in revenue.

In my previous role at IBM, I turned around a major product suffering a 5-year decline in sales to regain product value recognition that increased sales by 35% and brand awareness by 40%. The product catapulted from one of the lowest-profile brands within IBM with customers looking to move off the platform to one where client representatives were asking to implement non-iSeries workload on iSeries, a notion that previously would not have been considered with representatives.

Prior to this I was recognized for improving operational areas by developing new approaches to finding and attracting new business within target markets, implementing appropriate marketing and sales strategies to achieve growth in sales revenue and improve market share, and proactively developing and building customer relationships by delivering customer solutions.

These examples clearly demonstrate the value I can bring to your organization. My strengths are in devising creative solutions to overcome obstacles, adapting to circumstances, and achieving business growth. I have earned a reputation as an intuitive business strategist who has consistently left each division in an infinitely improved position. I bring to your organization more than 20 years of IT managerial experience, outstanding analytical and strategic thinking, and a ruthless focus on achievement of revenue and profit goals.

My resume is enclosed to provide you with details of my skills and accomplishments, but I am certain that a personal interview would more fully reveal my desire and ability to contribute to your organization. I will call in the coming week to set up an appointment. Thank you for your time and consideration of my application, and do not hesitate to contact me if you have any questions. I look forward to speaking with you soon.

Sincerely,

Gabe Connor

Encl.

273

Director of IT Sales. *Jennifer Rushton, Sydney, New South Wales, Australia*

The person was a senior manager who could turn around declining IT product areas, deliver results, and strengthen client relationships that generated revenue. The letter makes this clear.

CONFIDENTIAL   Job #100-12   *Ready to relocate*

Robert Savage

000 Martin Terrace, Starkley, Alabama 00000   robert_savage@zipx.com   334.555.5555

Monday February 16, 20XX

Ms. Laura Worth
District Sales Manager
TopLine Pharmaceuticals, Inc.
500 Northridge Parkway
Suite 400
Montgomery, Alabama 36100

Dear Ms. Worth:

I would like to join the TopLine Pharmaceuticals team as your newest pharmaceutical sales representative. To give you confidence that I am the right person to interview, this letter anticipates your needs in the following areas:

Your likely requirements:	My capabilities:
• **Strong sales experience.**	• Proven record in closing the most difficult kind of "sales": persuading all my customers to give up their property at a reasonable price and avoid costly legal battles.
• Ability to **master steep learning curves** in new fields.	• Three years of handling rapidly increasing responsibility with absolutely no formalized training.
• Dedication to **reach tough goals independently.**	• Embarked upon a personal, professional development program to learn about your industry from pharmaceutical reps, professional organizations, and trade magazines.

My resume has the details. It may not look like others you have seen. I thought you deserved a good deal more than the usual unsupported summary of "professional qualifications," standard job titles, and unfamiliar responsibilities. In their places are a half-dozen profit-building capabilities I am ready to offer now, backed up by selected examples of performance.

If my approach and track record will benefit TopLine, I'd like to hear about your specific sales requirements. May I call in a few days to arrange a time to do just that?

Sincerely,

Robert Savage

Encl.: Resume

CONFIDENTIAL

274

Pharmaceutical Sales Representative. *Don Orlando, Montgomery, Alabama*

This applicant never had the word "sales" in any of his job titles. To compensate, the writer introduced a table that matched the individual's abilities with likely corporate needs.

DORIS C. KITTERING

7721 Templeton Street
Milwaukee, WI 53202

Mobile: (414) 291-2222
E-mail: dorisckitt@mynet.com

October 22, 20XX

Mary Theresa Wright
Social Technology, Inc.
5050 Wacker Dr.
Chicago, IL 60601
E-mail: mary@socialtech.com

Dear Ms. Wright,

Your online job posting at CareerBuilder.com for a **Regional Sales Director** is such a good fit with my background, you might be skeptical that I could really exist! Let me assure you, I am most interested in this challenging position (I thrive on challenges) and have just what you require…and more.

My resume is enclosed for your review. You will notice that my experience, training, and personal attributes meet all of your stated requirements and preferences, and even surpass them.

Your Requirements & Needs	My Qualifications
▪ Paid nonprofit experience in direct service environment	▪ Five years of experience in **paid nonprofit social services agency** and 10 years of experience with government-funded human services agency in direct service delivery. Increasing the effectiveness of nonprofits resonates with my values and life mission.
▪ Bachelor's Degree in Social Sciences	▪ **Bachelor's Degree** in Psychology.
▪ Sales experience—minimum 5 years	▪ 12 years (part-time and full-time) in inside sales, retail sales, membership sales, and sales management. **Top-performing producer** in all sales environments.
▪ Working knowledge of software programs	▪ Experienced using **The Clinical Manager** (database software for Case Managers), as well as **MS Office** (Word, PowerPoint, and **Outlook**). Quick study in new software programs and applications.
▪ Industry knowledge	▪ 15-year background in social services industry, both nonprofit and government-funded positions.

As a former human services Program Director and current Case Manager, I am thoroughly familiar with the software needs, expectations, and unspoken "pain" of your prospective customers. Because of my background in social services, my credibility and trust-building capacity would be enhanced with your target audience. Couple that with a well-established track record in needs assessment and consultative sales, and I believe you have a winning combination.

May I have the opportunity to make my case? Since I plan to relocate to the Chicago area soon, I would be available for an appointment at your convenience. I will be in town next week and will call to schedule an appointment. Thank you for your consideration.

Sincerely,

Doris C. Kittering

275

Regional Sales Director. *Susan Guarneri, Three Lakes, Wisconsin*

This applicant had a former history in sales and a recent history in social services. The target position integrated technology sales and social services. The letter shows her combination of both.

DANA ROEMER

555 Maple Lane • Sharpsville, CA 55555 • 555.555.5555 • droemer3@xx.com

Jane Doe
President
Abc Sales
55 Main St.
Los Angeles, CA 55555

Dear Ms. Doe:

As an accomplished **Sales Professional** with significant experience leading sales-supported turnarounds, new product launches, business/product development, and account management for global multibillion-dollar companies, my goal is to announce my interest in a position with your company. My research shows that I offer ideal skills to match a position as an **Account Executive** with Abc Sales. With nearly 15 years of combined experience in **sales in the medical fields,** I bring a wealth of talent and expertise of great value to companies in the **medical device, diagnostics, and pharmaceutical arenas.** Furthermore, with additional strengths in competitive analysis, territory development, and team leadership, I can reproduce results for Abc Sales similar to some of my select accomplishments below:

✓ **Increased rankings** – I boosted rank for portfolio performance from 395 in territory to 10th nationwide.

✓ **Successful product launches** – I have introduced new products and gained noteworthy achievements as a result, including Top 10% in national sales performance and Divisional and District Trip Winner.

✓ **Revenue generation** – I have driven volume growth for key products, attaining Top 10% nationally for Ambien CR volume growth and #1 ranking regionally for Ambien CR for 3 consecutive quarters.

> *"Dana prepares for her sales calls and will follow sales procedures. She is very comfortable in a sales environment that allows her mobility and feels comfortable with several proposals [being considered] at the same time. She can move from one prospect to another with ease and feels comfortable shuffling schedules and filling every available time slot with activities."*
> Excerpts from a recent
> Communication (DISC) Style Analysis

These are but a few of my proven, quantifiable achievements. As you will see from my resume, my career has been a series of successes in sales. I'm eager to discuss how my qualifications and skills can benefit Abc Sales. Thank you for taking the time to review my materials. I plan to call within the next few days to learn if we can coordinate our schedules to have a conversation.

Sincerely,

Dana Roemer

View additional accomplishments and/or print my resume at www.xxx.com/xxx

276

Account Executive. *Jane Roqueplot, West Middlesex, Pennsylvania*

This confident applicant made the call planned in the last paragraph. The call became a telephone interview. That led to a flight and an actual interview. One week later, she was offered the job.

AMANDA JONES

000 Cedar Lane • Old Towne, NJ 00000 • mandy000@aol.com • mobile: 000-000-0000 • home: 000-000-0000

Date

Name
Title
Company Name
Company Street Address
Town, State, ZIP

RE: Position title _____ OR Job #_____

Dear Mr. / Ms. _____:

As a Sales Professional with 10+ years of experience in the real estate, retail and service industries, I have consistently met or exceeded aggressive sales targets through my expertise in initiating and developing productive business relationships. Thus, I am an ideal candidate for the position of Pharmaceutical Sales Representative.

Coming from a family of physicians, I am very familiar with the medical environment and am confident that I could add value. My ability to communicate well with highly educated professionals is outstanding. In addition, my organizational skills are superb, and I have been well-liked by all of my employers throughout my career.

The following are some of my career highlights:

- Consistently attained top 10% in rankings of 500+ sales associates.
- Recognized by industry professional association as a top revenue generator.
- Achieved membership in prestigious Million Dollar Sales Club every year in full-time sales.

My interpersonal and communication skills are outstanding and have significantly contributed to my success.

Attached is my resume for your review. I am confident that my demonstrated expertise would add value to your firm and contribute to your continuing success.

I will contact you in the near future and can, of course, be available for an interview at your convenience.

Very truly yours,

Amanda Jones

Attachment: resume

277

Pharmaceutical Sales Representative. *Fran Kelley, Waldwick, New Jersey*

The applicant had successes in sales and wanted to move to pharmaceutical sales. The letter emphasizes her sales skills and physicians in her background.

WILLIAM H. HARRINGTON
1888 Shangri-La Drive · Pleasantville, NC 28888
(555) 555-5555 willyh@argus.net

March 27, 20XX

James L. Starnes
President
Leathercraft Furniture
3030 Haywood Road
Hickory Grove, NC 28601

Dear Mr. Starnes:

I grew up in the furniture business. My grandfather was an executive with Drexel Heritage; my father, a board member of several firms. In spite of my early background, I swore I'd *never* get into the furniture business. But I did. And in the 15 years since I entered the industry (initially **as a salesman for Simmons** U.S.A. and for the past 14 years as a sales representative for Hickory House), I've discovered that selling quality products excites me. Furniture is simply in my blood!

I think you will know from your own experience that it takes years to develop and cultivate extensive contacts, understand the complexities of fabric applications, and become creative in developing marketing strategies.

This is how I fit in: I have just established a sales company, representing leather and fabrics, in North and South Carolina. I am knowledgeable about the residential side of the business, but to expand my outreach I plan to pursue contract opportunities and alternative distribution routes, including auto manufacturers and the garment industry.

I really want to be of help to you—by representing your line in the Carolinas or other areas in the Southeast. I'll call on present and prospective users to tell them about new and existing products. I can provide expert advice without prejudice. It's my job to do just that.

To illustrate my point, let me tell you the story about the firm that installed a large piece of machinery, but after it was set up, no one could start it. Experts were called in from near and far, each fiddling and adjusting, but to no avail. Finally, as a last resort, the company president called a two-for-cent mechanic (or so they thought). In he strolled with his small sledgehammer and walked over to the machine. He studied the unit for several moments and then set his eyes on one spot. He struck three blows with the hammer and, much to the surprise of the onlookers, off she went!

> "Just how much do we owe you?" asked the president.
> "One thousand three dollars," replied the mechanic.
> "What's the thousand three dollars for?" asked the president.
> "Three dollars for three blows, and a thousand for knowing where to hit," the mechanic retorted.

So, in the long run, if a fellow knows his business, it's easy; if not, it's too bad for him <u>and</u> his customer. With 15 years of experience, I know "where to hit" when it comes to marketing and selling furniture and fabric. You are taking no chances when you let me help you.

I am enclosing a resume and list of references. If you think you may be interested in talking about a mutually beneficial relationship, I would be glad to meet with you. I will call in a few days to set a time we can talk.

Sincerely,

William H. Harrington

278

Sales Representative. *Doug Morrison, Charlotte, North Carolina*

A sales rep for 15 years, this applicant wanted to strike out on his own. He formed his own company to represent a manufacturer. The letter conveys his knowledge. (Be sure to read the story in the fifth paragraph.)

Sandra Day

> **17 BROUGHAM TERRACE, #3 ● COSTA DEL ROMA, CA 00000**
> **888-555-1212 ● 888-866-0000 ● SANDRA@HOTMAIL.COM**

Marketing Communications Professional

(Date)

(Contact Person)
(Company)
(Address 1)
(Address 2)

Dear Hiring Professional (or contact name):

I am writing to explore employment opportunities within your organization. As a proven and recognized marketing communications professional, with more than 15 years of combined experience and a solid background as a top performer, I believe I possess the qualifications and experience necessary to become an active and beneficial member of your executive management team.

As a qualified and experienced professional, I have a proven record of accomplishment in new business development, product launch, market penetration, new hire training, and team building and leadership. A highly motivated self-starter with multitasking and follow-through abilities, I consistently achieve both personal and organizational goals, meet timelines, and ensure highest quality/quantity cost per item on deliverables.

A few of my most notable accomplishments include the following:
➢ Planning and executing a successful introduction of **Intro Sports™ High Profile™ FOOTBALL** that debuted on *The Sports Show.*
➢ Developed and maintained high-level media communications, created story proposals, organized conference calls, and wrote article text for U.S. and global publications, gaining international exposure that increased Web traffic by more than 150%.
➢ Spearheaded and executed e-campaign projects for magazines, software, books, and recordings, generating new subscribers, promoting new releases, and achieving a 23% increase in subscriptions.

The enclosed resume briefly outlines my experience and accomplishments. If you have any questions, or would like to contact me to schedule an interview, please feel free to do so, at your convenience.

Thank you for your time and consideration. I look forward to meeting with you soon and will contact you to schedule a time.

Sincerely,

Sandra Day

279

Marketing Communications Professional. *Lea J. Clark, Macon, Georgia*

This singer/songwriter had an artistic background that kept potential employers from seeing her as a marketer. She soon got a job in the marketing department of a fine arts training center.

Lisa A. Guerrero

1111 Martin Lane ▪ Philadelphia, PA 00000 ▪ (000) 000-0000 ▪ name@yahoo.com

Barnes & Noble College Bookstores
3434 Smith Street
Philadelphia, PA 00000

RE: Position as General Merchandise Manager, Job ID 000-000

Dear Human Resources Representative:

It was with great interest that I learned about your opening for a General Merchandise Manager, as my qualifications match your requirements for this position. I am confident I can contribute to the success of Barnes & Noble College Bookstores; therefore, please accept my resume in application for this position and allow me to explain briefly how I meet your requirements and how I can add value to your organization.

As I read your company's advertisement, I noted several connections between what you seek and my background:

Your Requirements:	My Qualifications:
▪ College degree preferred	▪ Bachelor of Arts degree from Temple University
▪ Strong commitment to customer service	▪ Exceeded service delivery goals as Customer Care Manager for Verizon Wireless
▪ 3 years of retail management experience	▪ 4 years as Senior Assistant Manager for retail outlet Shoppers Galore
▪ Team-leadership skills	▪ As manager with Verizon, led team to improved QA scores and 3× sales increase within 3 months of hire
▪ Excellent communication skills	▪ Superb communicator with customers, team members, and upper management
▪ Flexibility is required	▪ Worked varying hours and weekend shifts frequently as manager with Shoppers

Beyond my qualifications, what I can contribute most significantly to your company's future success is my ability to develop great relationships. Whether resolving a customer concern, addressing an issue with upper management, or mentoring a fellow team member, I consistently use a "positive communication" approach that leads to resolved problems and happy customers. In addition, my dedication and work ethic are strong, as my former supervisors will readily verify.

Thank you for your time and review of my qualifications. Please do not hesitate to contact me if you have any questions, and I wish you the best in your candidate search for this position.

Sincerely,

Lisa A. Guerrero

Enclosure

280

General Merchandise Manager. *Daniel J. Dorotik, Jr., Lubbock, Texas*

In this ad response, the writer links the job seeker's qualifications to company requirements line by line. Bullets in both columns help the reader read matching items from column to column.

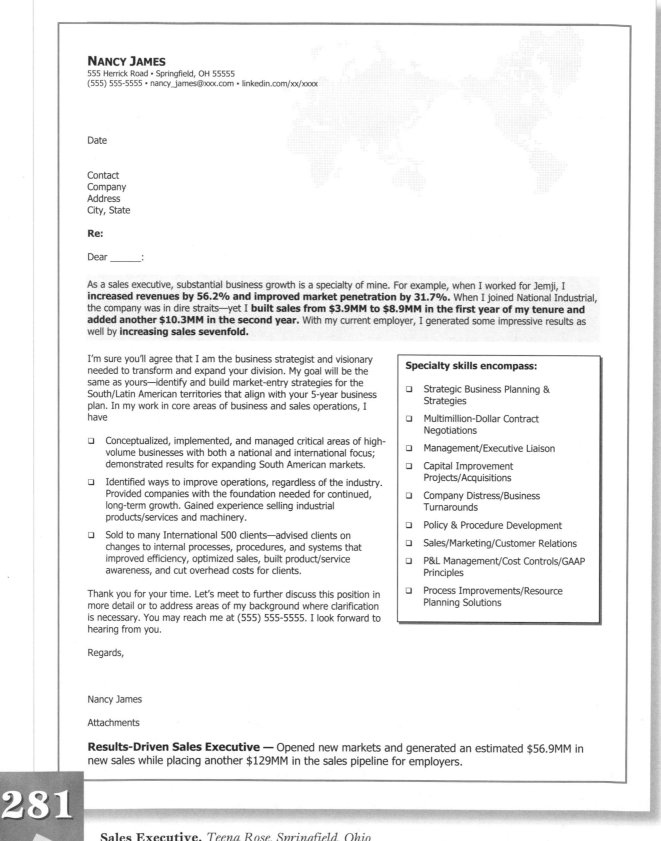

NANCY JAMES
555 Herrick Road • Springfield, OH 55555
(555) 555-5555 • nancy_james@xxx.com • linkedin.com/xx/xxxx

Date

Contact
Company
Address
City, State

Re:

Dear _____:

As a sales executive, substantial business growth is a specialty of mine. For example, when I worked for Jemji, I **increased revenues by 56.2% and improved market penetration by 31.7%.** When I joined National Industrial, the company was in dire straits—yet I **built sales from $3.9MM to $8.9MM in the first year of my tenure and added another $10.3MM in the second year.** With my current employer, I generated some impressive results as well by **increasing sales sevenfold.**

I'm sure you'll agree that I am the business strategist and visionary needed to transform and expand your division. My goal will be the same as yours—identify and build market-entry strategies for the South/Latin American territories that align with your 5-year business plan. In my work in core areas of business and sales operations, I have

- Conceptualized, implemented, and managed critical areas of high-volume businesses with both a national and international focus; demonstrated results for expanding South American markets.

- Identified ways to improve operations, regardless of the industry. Provided companies with the foundation needed for continued, long-term growth. Gained experience selling industrial products/services and machinery.

- Sold to many International 500 clients—advised clients on changes to internal processes, procedures, and systems that improved efficiency, optimized sales, built product/service awareness, and cut overhead costs for clients.

Thank you for your time. Let's meet to further discuss this position in more detail or to address areas of my background where clarification is necessary. You may reach me at (555) 555-5555. I look forward to hearing from you.

Regards,

Nancy James

Attachments

Specialty skills encompass:

- Strategic Business Planning & Strategies
- Multimillion-Dollar Contract Negotiations
- Management/Executive Liaison
- Capital Improvement Projects/Acquisitions
- Company Distress/Business Turnarounds
- Policy & Procedure Development
- Sales/Marketing/Customer Relations
- P&L Management/Cost Controls/GAAP Principles
- Process Improvements/Resource Planning Solutions

Results-Driven Sales Executive — Opened new markets and generated an estimated $56.9MM in new sales while placing another $129MM in the sales pipeline for employers.

281

Sales Executive. *Teena Rose, Springfield, Ohio*

The distinctive feature in this cover letter is the text box listing specialty skills. The box attracts attention immediately. Boldfacing then captures interest in the quantified achievements in the first paragraph.

CLIFF KLEIN, MBA

5555 East 55th Street, New York, NY 55555 • 555-555-5555 (cell) • cliffklein@xx.com

November 12, 20XX

Sandra Wilson, SPHR
Human Resources Director
Applied Materials, Inc.
555 N. Michigan Avenue
Chicago, IL 55555

Dear Ms. Wilson:

I am writing to express my considerable interest in Applied Materials, Inc.'s ***Senior Account Executive, Enterprise Sales*** position announced on LinkedIn. With more than 15 years of experience brokering multimillion-dollar, high-tech application solutions domestically and abroad, I believe I am an ideal fit for the role.

My high-tech sales career began at LAM Research in 1993 when I made the leap from applications engineer to regional sales manager overseeing a 22-state territory. The early link between my technical and interpersonal skills paved the way for the high-stakes strategic partnerships I create today with multibillion-dollar client companies.

I offer Applied Materials expertise spanning the following areas:

- **Enterprise solutions development for Fortune 500 companies.** I am an integral, profit-focused advisor and technical resource to my clients, which have included Company A, Company B, Company C, Company D, and Company E.

- **Capital equipment agreement development across Europe, Asia, and North America.** I have orchestrated hundreds of $10M–$60M deals, and 5 single transactions valued more than $100M.

- **Portfolio management, resource development, and interpersonal relations.** I have managed expectations from front-line engineer to the C-suite, managed quotas up to $82M, and directed teams of up to 13.

- **Product positioning, internally and on behalf of clients.** I have strategically paired existing products and influenced the codevelopment of new technologies to client needs—realizing profits in the hundreds of millions.

As a senior sales professional at the height of my career, I am happy at Varian, but I am ready to explore a new adventure. I am regularly at the helm of strategy, profit, and risk and would envision similar accountability in a senior account management role at Applied Materials.

My résumé is enclosed for your review, and I hope you will agree that my blend of creative thinking, team leadership, global experience, and technical background presents a compelling match. Please reach me any time at 555-555-5555 or cliffklein@xx.com. I look forward to meeting you soon.

Sincerely,

Cliff Klein

Enclosures: Résumé, Addendum

linkedin.xx/xxx/xxx

282

Senior Account Executive, Enterprise Sales. *Jared Redick, San Francisco, California*

The applicant was a senior business development/sales professional in the semiconductor industry. The word *semiconductor* is not used, however, to allow for a possible move outside that high-tech industry.

Jeremiah Josephs

555 Any Street, Millersville, MD 21108 ● 410-555-5555 ● jj55555@media.net

---

May 15, 20XX

Company USA
Mr. John Doe, Lab Manager
123 Main Street
Baltimore, MD 12345

Dear Mr. Doe,

As an experienced senior-level lab technician in a gas chromatograph lab, I will bring the needed skills and expertise to your lab that your company is seeking. After more than 20 years with Lab Testing, Inc., I've decided that it's time to seek new challenges and responsibilities.

Throughout my career, I have supervised and conducted thousands of tests, drafted and presented hundreds of reports, and trained numerous personnel on the proper use and maintenance of gas chromatographs, X-ray diffraction units, carbon sulfur analyzers, a microactivities unit, and a mercury porsimeter, along with other lab equipment. With careful planning and attention to detail, we have maintained a very high level of safety, expedited testing procedures to meet deadlines, and improved the accuracy of tests performed. I also have a thorough knowledge of chemistry and assisted with the compilation and editing of a procedures manual for two commonly performed lab tests.

In addition to my lab management responsibilities, I have held leadership and management-level positions in a volunteer capacity with many local nonprofit organizations and institutions. I am ready to take my skills and experience to the next level and believe that Company USA is just the place to take that step.

I will follow up with you by June 1 to confirm that you received my information and also to answer any questions you may have at that time. Should you wish to contact me sooner, it's best to reach me on my cell phone at 410-555-5555 or through e-mail at jj55555@media.net. Thank you for your time and consideration for this position.

Sincerely,

Jeremiah Josephs

Enclosure

283

Senior Lab Technician. *Beth Colley, Crownsville, Maryland*

The letter calls attention to this applicant's experience, supervisory roles, familiarity with different procedures, volunteer work, and interest in seeking new challenges and responsibilities.

VICTOR A. WILLIAMS

447 North Diamond Back Road • Bethpage, New York 11714 • (555) 555-5555
vaw555@hotmail.com

Dear Sir or Madam:

As a **Supervising Chemist,** I am seeking the opportunity to apply my skills within a challenging **biotechnology environment.**

My background closely parallels the mechanics involved in biotechnology. I supervise the research, proficiency testing, chemical analysis instrumentation, and related software application to analyze the components and physical properties of community drinking water. Highlights of the qualifications and contributions I would bring to your organization include the following:

- Excellent administration, public relations, and communications skills, developed through experience as a **Supervisory Chemist for the largest, most advanced drinking water laboratory in the U.S.**

- Aptitude to conceptualize and coordinate procedures to meet the changing dynamics of assignments, organizational needs, or specific projects. Proficient analytical, planning, and advisory techniques.

- Ability to prioritize time and resources to meet company objectives while reducing operating budget expenses.

Within the course of my work, I have been extensively involved with technical problem-solving and the handling of multiple projects, effectively communicating my findings to management and interdisciplinary professionals. I am eager to continue to use my knowledge and skills where I can provide the direction to support your organization's plans, strategies, and objectives.

I appreciate your time in reviewing my qualifications and look forward to a personal interview. I will call next week to set a time for an interview. Thank you.

Very truly yours,

VICTOR A. WILLIAMS

Enclosure

284

Supervising Chemist. *Donna M. Farrise, Hauppauge, New York*

This letter uses boldface to call attention to the most important information about the applicant: his name at the top, his occupation, his targeted field of activity, and his current position.

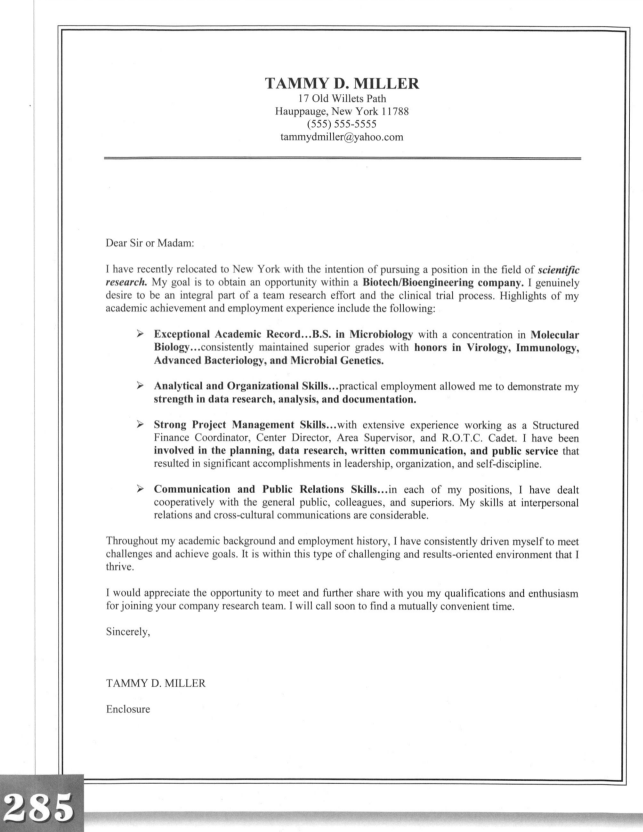

TAMMY D. MILLER
17 Old Willets Path
Hauppauge, New York 11788
(555) 555-5555
tammydmiller@yahoo.com

Dear Sir or Madam:

I have recently relocated to New York with the intention of pursuing a position in the field of ***scientific research.*** My goal is to obtain an opportunity within a **Biotech/Bioengineering company.** I genuinely desire to be an integral part of a team research effort and the clinical trial process. Highlights of my academic achievement and employment experience include the following:

➤ **Exceptional Academic Record...B.S. in Microbiology** with a concentration in **Molecular Biology...**consistently maintained superior grades with **honors in Virology, Immunology, Advanced Bacteriology, and Microbial Genetics.**

➤ **Analytical and Organizational Skills...**practical employment allowed me to demonstrate my **strength in data research, analysis, and documentation.**

➤ **Strong Project Management Skills...**with extensive experience working as a Structured Finance Coordinator, Center Director, Area Supervisor, and R.O.T.C. Cadet. I have been **involved in the planning, data research, written communication, and public service** that resulted in significant accomplishments in leadership, organization, and self-discipline.

➤ **Communication and Public Relations Skills...**in each of my positions, I have dealt cooperatively with the general public, colleagues, and superiors. My skills at interpersonal relations and cross-cultural communications are considerable.

Throughout my academic background and employment history, I have consistently driven myself to meet challenges and achieve goals. It is within this type of challenging and results-oriented environment that I thrive.

I would appreciate the opportunity to meet and further share with you my qualifications and enthusiasm for joining your company research team. I will call soon to find a mutually convenient time.

Sincerely,

TAMMY D. MILLER

Enclosure

285

Researcher. *Donna M. Farrise, Hauppauge, New York*

This letter by the same writer as Cover Letter 284 shows the same technique of using boldface to direct attention to key information. Bold italic is an additional attention-getting enhancement to show the field.

JOHN H. CLARKE, LCPC

0000 N. Buffalo Grove Road
Arlington Heights, Illinois 60004
Telephone: (555) 555-5555 E-mail: JClarke@yyyy.com

April 8, 20XX

James Morgenstern, Ph.D.
Director of Adult Services
Alexian Brothers Northwest Mental Health Center
1606 Colonial Parkway
Palatine, Illinois 60067

Dear Dr. Morgenstern:

I am a Licensed Clinical Professional Counselor and a Master of Arts–Psychology graduate from UIC and am presently conducting a search for a position in an accredited mental health agency or psychotherapy practice. Please review the attached curriculum vitae as it may relate to potential opportunities that might exist within your organization.

My CV indicates that I have 10+ years of experience working in the business world prior to my enrollment at UIC, as well as my current position as a Psychotherapist and previous counseling internship. In my business career, I interacted with many different personality types and developed a keen interest in general psychological issues of adults. I frequently dealt with difficult customers and felt limited in my ability to assist them beyond the boundaries of my employers' products or services. I finally concluded that I could best serve people if I had more knowledge of human behavior, which is why I chose to enter the field of professional psychology. Because your agency provides services for adult populations, I feel that my current experience, academic coursework and business background represent a good fit.

I would welcome the opportunity to further discuss my educational and professional background in relation to the needs of your agency's clientele. I will contact you to determine a time that is convenient to meet. Thank you for your time and consideration.

Sincerely,

John H. Clarke, LCPC

Curriculum Vitae enclosed.

286

Licensed Clinical Professional Counselor. *Joellyn Schwerdlin, Worcester, Massachusetts*

This candidate mentions to potential employers how he transitioned from the business world to the status of Licensed Clinical Professional Counselor (LCPC) while working his way through school.

JASMINE HIGHLANDER

555 Harrison Avenue   Brentwood, NY 55555   (333) 444-5555   advocate@4campuslife.net

Date

Name
Company
Address

Dear Name:

The accompanying resume is presented for your review and consideration for the position of Assistant Director of College Housing. To further illustrate my qualifications, the following outlines the scope of my experience as it pertains to this position's specific requirements.

Your requirements	My qualifications
• Bachelor's degree, or	• Master's degree in Clinical Counseling.
• Four years of experience in lieu of degree.	• Eight years of combined experience in residence hall administration and counseling capacities.
• Promote and develop educational programming and maintain extensive budget.	• Plan, develop, and implement educational programs, and manage an operational budget.
• Administration of three to five residence halls housing approximately 1,000 students.	• Administration of residence halls housing up to 500 students.
• Supervise, develop, and evaluate three to five full-time residence hall directors.	• Supervise, develop, and evaluate 26 Resident Advisors with direct responsibility for four RAs and a Head Resident Advisor (HRA).
• Develop departmental policies and procedures, manage area office including billing, occupancy, and facilities records.	• Direct all aspects of front desk management and facilities maintenance operations.
• Assist in the development and leadership of departmental committees, and serve as manager for student conduct cases.	• Held a one-year position as Vice President of Committees for the Student Government with the State University of New York.

Thank you for your review and consideration. I will call you next week to set a time we can meet. I look forward to speaking with you then.

Sincerely,

Jasmine Highlander

Assistant Director of College Housing. *Ann Baehr, East Islip, New York*

A two-column format is useful for showing how an applicant's qualifications match a company's requirements. This letter shows further that some of the qualifications can exceed requirements.

ANNA M. SANCHEZ

123 Fort Avenue • Anywhere, Michigan 55555 • (555) 555-0000 • asanchez@zzzz.net

February 8, 20XX

John Gomez, Director
Family Community Center
555 Main Street
Anywhere, Michigan 55555

Dear Mr. Gomez,

After serving the Family Community Center for more than 17 years, I have had the opportunity to grow in my profession as an office assistant while helping others in time of need. It gives me pleasure to know I am able to provide much-needed assistance to individuals who turn to our center for support.

My experience has allowed me to work with a large number of adults and children from different ethnic backgrounds, providing assistance to individuals assigned to community service, as well as the elderly. I speak and read Spanish fluently, which is a must because our center serves a great number of Hispanics in the local area.

At this time, I feel my experience and commitment to the Family Community Center have positioned me to take on increased responsibilities. My objective is to secure the Direct Assistance Coordinator position upon its availability, and I welcome the opportunity to discuss my qualifications further. I have enclosed my resume to give you a brief review of my background and experience.

I will follow up with you next week to answer any questions you may have regarding my application. If you would like to speak sooner, please contact me anytime. Thank you in advance for your consideration.

Regards,

Anna M. Sanchez

Enclosure

288

Direct Assistance Coordinator. *Maria E. Hebda, Trenton, Michigan*

This future position was the person's goal after 17 years of service to the organization. She believed that she could take on additional responsibilities and built a case for being considered seriously.

Heather C. Bjorn

999-B Stetson Boulevard
Cranston, SC 55555
(111) 222-3333
heatherb@earthlink.com

March 16, 20xx

Ms. Rebecca Phipps, Director of Human Resources
South Carolina State Department of Social Services
1111 Baltimore Street, 2nd Floor
Cranston, SC 55555

Dear Ms. Phipps:

Please accept this letter of application for employment in the South Carolina Social Services Division for Children and Their Families. My education, training, and experience have built a solid, relevant foundation for employment in this division, as I believe my current enclosed resume proves.

Working with children in multicultural and diverse socioeconomic strata is a challenge in which I am eager to engage as a professional social worker. Although I am content and qualified to continue in my current position with the Easter Seals–SC, Cranston ARC, I feel that my greater strength and enthusiasm lie in assisting youth, as evidenced in my volunteer work with the Children's Crusade. Developing and promoting proper independent living skills is a goal and dream of mine that I shall pursue until I am in such a position to assist youngsters during their crucial, formative time of cultural and behavioral development.

If you feel that my credentials, along with my genuine enthusiasm to work with children, are sufficient to meet your criteria for employment in this field, please contact me when an opening occurs. I can be reached at heatherb@earthlink.com or (111) 222-3333 during the day or evening. I look forward eagerly to meeting with you to discuss my professional qualifications.

Thank you for your time in consideration of my application.

Sincerely,

Heather C. Bjorn

Enclosure: resume

289

Social Services Counselor. *Edward Turilli, Bonita Springs, Florida*

The challenge of this letter was to prove to the recruiter that the applicant, having performed well for Easter Seals in social services, would thrive in a career directly assisting needy, disadvantaged youth.

EVELYN MORRIS

0000 Summit Drive • Englewood, NJ 00000 • (555) 555-5555 • Morris30@aol.com

January 6, 20xx

Ms. Suzanne Reynolds
Director, Social Services
Borrin Correctional Institution
2299 Central Avenue
Englewood, NJ 00000

Dear Ms. Reynolds:

Becoming a social worker has been a lifelong dream of mine, and I have taken the first step toward fulfilling this dream. In May, I will graduate with a bachelor's degree. As part of my educational training, I am seeking an internship at the Borrin Correctional Institution to further develop my clinical social work skills while applying my training to benefit others.

Currently, I am completing a clinical internship at the Borrin Families in Crisis Center. This experience has not only taught me valuable lessons about human life, but has also reinforced my interest in employment in a correctional environment following graduation. My future plans include pursuing a master's degree in clinical social work.

Complementing my education in social work are both employment and volunteer experiences that relate to my career interests while adding to my skill development in this profession. Such experiences over the past several years have included employment as a medical assistant at a physician practice, providing support services to families of children with cancer at a community hospital and volunteering at a crisis-counseling center. In addition, my professors and supervisor at the Borrin Families in Crisis Center have frequently commented on my natural aptitude for a career in social work.

Highly self-motivated with an energetic style, I am eager to learn new skills and enhance my education while contributing to your organization. My strengths also include communications, maturity and the ability to relate effectively with individuals at all levels and cultural backgrounds as demonstrated throughout my prior career in business.

I look forward to discussing an internship opportunity at your institution and appreciate your consideration.

Sincerely,

Evelyn Morris

Enclosure

290

Social Worker. *Louise Garver, Broad Brook, Connecticut*

This prospective graduate was seeking an internship at a correctional facility to develop her clinical social work skills. The letter indicates her experience and strengths. She secured the internship.

Carmen M. Kennedy

carmkenn@hotmail.com

642 Riverview Drive ▼ Parkersburg, WV 26000 ▼ 304.224.0000

April 2, 20xx

Kristi Vanderpool
PO Box 1278
Vienna, WV 26111

Dear Ms. Vanderpool:

To inspire and enable all young people, especially those from disadvantaged circumstances, to realize their full potential as productive, responsible and caring citizens.

The mission of the Boys & Girls Clubs of America is something that I strongly believe in. That is why I read with great interest your recent ad in the *St. Mary's Oracle* for a Teen Outreach Coordinator with the Boys and Girls Clubs of Wirt County. As a native of Wirt County with a lifelong desire to work with children and excellent leadership skills, I believe I have much to offer in this capacity.

A music education major at Marietta College, I prepared for a future career of educating children. I've spent more than 100 hours in the classroom working with, teaching and observing students and have realized that this is where I want to focus my career: working to prepare the youth of today for tomorrow's world. In addition, I have been actively involved in various youth activities throughout my life. It would be an honor for me to be able to contribute to the Boys & Girls Clubs' mission of providing

- *A safe place to learn and grow*
- *Ongoing relationships with caring adult professionals*
- *Life-enhancing programs and character-development experiences*
- *Hope and opportunity*

An interview would allow me to share my qualifications in greater detail and learn more about this exciting opportunity. I will call you next week to follow up. Thank you for your time and consideration. I look forward to speaking with you soon.

Sincerely,

Carmen M. Kennedy

Enclosure

291

Teen Outreach Coordinator. *Melissa L. Kasler, Athens, Ohio*

The writer used information from the mission statements of the Boys & Girls Clubs of America to convey this applicant's dedication. He was called for an interview immediately and given the job.

GEORGE BROWN

5555 Sun Circle, Apt. 55 ◆ Orlando, FL 55555 ◆ 555-555-5555 ◆ GBrown@xx.com

Hiring Manger
XYZ Company
555 Street Name
City, State, ZIP Code

August 22, 20XX

Dear Hiring Manager:

I am writing in regard to the Social Worker position within your organization. Consequently, I ask you to consider my qualifications, skills and accomplishments as you screen candidates for this role.

My bachelor's degree in social work, combined with years of hands-on experience and a genuine passion for helping others, would make me an asset to your organization. Throughout my career, I have accumulated vast knowledge in various aspects of human services as well as key competencies that are imperative to our industry.

Youth Development: During my time at County Group Florida, I was able to concurrently manage up to 30 cases for foster children by proactively building mutually beneficial relationships with child influencers.

Case Management: As an intern at County Charities, I created strengths-based service plans for homeless victims of domestic violence to achieve 100% success rate with client self-sufficiency.

Empathy: At National Hospice Care, I served as a liaison between patients' families and various medical facilities, always offering patient and family support while maintaining a high level of compassion and empathy. As a result, I earned the customer satisfaction certification for outstanding service.

While keeping client needs at the forefront at all times, I *always* uphold the highest level of work ethic, taking pride in the quality and accuracy of my work.

I would appreciate the opportunity to meet with you to further discuss how my knowledge and experiences can add value to your organization. My résumé is attached for your review. Thank you for your time and consideration, and I look forward to hearing from you soon.

Sincerely,

George Brown

292

Social Worker. *Melanie Denny, Sunrise, Florida*

The applicant had extensive experience in the field, and the writer wanted to highlight specific soft skills or competencies, such as empathy, that are important in social work.

Melissa Jackson, MSW

555 Oak Drive ▪ Little River, MN 55555 ▪ 555-555-5555 ▪ mjackson@email.com

June 10, 20XX

Ms. Ann Smith
Quality Care Services
555 North 13th Street
Little River, MN 55555

Dear Ms. Smith:

It is with considerable interest that I respond to the posting for the Social Work position at Quality Care Services. As a compassionate social worker, I believe that my 10+ years of assisting individuals with disabilities makes me an excellent candidate for this position.

As my enclosed resume indicates, my broad-based background of advocating for individuals includes working with children, youth, and vulnerable adults. In my positions, I have had the opportunity to collaborate with numerous outside agencies as I represented the needs of my clients. The following excerpts from letters of recommendation summarize my passion for helping clients:

"I found Melissa to be both understanding and willing to address the matter and work on a resolution that would benefit the clients in the best possible way." ~James Smith, Director, AAA Services

"Melissa's responsiveness was always prompt and appropriate as she efficiently addressed ongoing and changing needs. It was impressive to witness her ability to keep in focus both the immediate and long-term plans, while keeping them in balance with one another." ~Ann Lock, MSW, AAA Services

After spending the past two years at home with my children, I am now eager to return to outside employment and would welcome the opportunity to further discuss how my skills and experience can benefit your clients. Please contact me at 555-555-5555 to arrange an interview at your earliest convenience. Thank you for your consideration.

Sincerely,

Melissa Jackson

Enclosure

293

Social Worker. *Connie Hauer, Sartell, Minnesota*

This ad-response letter includes quotations from letters of recommendation. The applicant's important Master of Social Work (MSW) degree is clearly evident at the top of the letter.

ALLEN T. RANDOLPH
8001 Satchel Drive
Greenfield, MA 55555
Home: (555) 555-5555 • Cell: (555) 555-5000
E-mail: allentr@aol.com

July 24, 20XX

Mr. John Deering
Director of Facility Maintenance
Marietta Manufacturing
Marietta Plaza
Greenfield, MA 98554

Dear Mr. Deering:

Although I opted for retirement at a young age, I have come to realize that I have too much energy and many skills that I still enjoy using. Retirement is definitely not for me. Therefore, your ad for a maintenance specialist caught my attention as I offer the key qualifications your company needs.

Specifically, I have an excellent performance record in the operation and maintenance of building systems and equipment, including electrical, HVAC, telecommunications, pneumatic, electromechanical, and hydraulics. I am also knowledgeable about state building codes, safety, and other regulatory guidelines.

My expertise encompasses multisite facilities oversight, staff supervision, project management, and vendor relations. Examples of relevant accomplishments include reduction in annual maintenance costs and improved functional capabilities while consistently delivering quality service.

Equally important are my planning, organization, and communication strengths. Despite the challenges that can often be encountered, I have completed projects on time and under budget on a consistent basis. I would welcome a personal interview to discuss the value I would add to your company. I will contact you next week to set up a time we can meet.

Sincerely,

Allen T. Randolph

Enclosure

294

Maintenance Specialist. *Louise Garver, Broad Brook, Connecticut*

The individual was a retired person who realized that he wanted to get back to work. The writer created this letter, which communicates the person's talent, energy, and skills. He was hired.

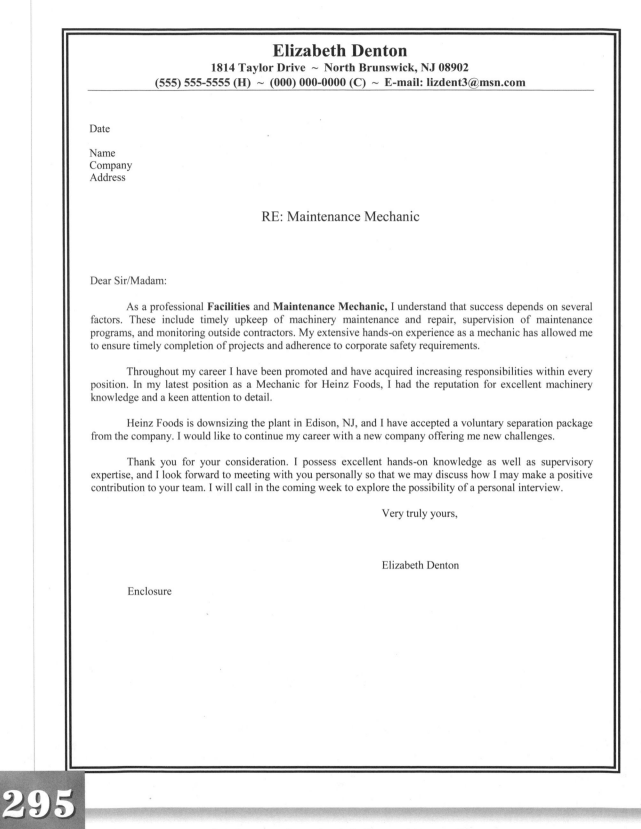

Elizabeth Denton
1814 Taylor Drive ~ North Brunswick, NJ 08902
(555) 555-5555 (H) ~ (000) 000-0000 (C) ~ E-mail: lizdent3@msn.com

Date

Name
Company
Address

RE: Maintenance Mechanic

Dear Sir/Madam:

As a professional **Facilities** and **Maintenance Mechanic,** I understand that success depends on several factors. These include timely upkeep of machinery maintenance and repair, supervision of maintenance programs, and monitoring outside contractors. My extensive hands-on experience as a mechanic has allowed me to ensure timely completion of projects and adherence to corporate safety requirements.

Throughout my career I have been promoted and have acquired increasing responsibilities within every position. In my latest position as a Mechanic for Heinz Foods, I had the reputation for excellent machinery knowledge and a keen attention to detail.

Heinz Foods is downsizing the plant in Edison, NJ, and I have accepted a voluntary separation package from the company. I would like to continue my career with a new company offering me new challenges.

Thank you for your consideration. I possess excellent hands-on knowledge as well as supervisory expertise, and I look forward to meeting with you personally so that we may discuss how I may make a positive contribution to your team. I will call in the coming week to explore the possibility of a personal interview.

Very truly yours,

Elizabeth Denton

Enclosure

295

Maintenance Mechanic. *Beverly and Mitchell I. Baskin, Marlboro, New Jersey*

This applicant had been downsized and was looking for a new, challenging position in which she could use her skills as a mechanic. These are mentioned in the first paragraph.

Ralph Forte
43–74 Belt Parkway
Brooklyn, NY 00000

Home: (000) 000-0000   Cell: (000) 000-5555

January 11, 20XX

New York Post
P.O. Box 4498
New York, NY 00000

Dear Hiring Manager:

In your ad in last Sunday's *Post,* you stated that you needed an experienced elevator mechanic. As you will see when you read my resume, I believe I have the necessary skills and qualifications to excel at this job.

For most of my career, I have been involved in all aspects of elevator installation and maintenance. I have a thorough understanding of all of the requirements necessary for a successful job, and my organizational ability allows me to complete my assignments well within the acceptable time frame.

My present position entails the coordination of equipment and its component parts according to client specifications as outlined on blueprints. I take pride that my work always has passed rigid inspections.

As I am accustomed to preparing logs and reports, paperwork would be no problem. I am considered a good communicator, using this ability to train other personnel and make recommendations to owners/managers to increase efficiency at the installation sites where I have worked. The frequent travel you describe in your ad would not interfere with my personal obligations.

If this position is still available, I would like the opportunity to talk with you in person and discuss how my skills would benefit your company. You may contact me on my cell phone during the workday or at home after 4:30 p.m.

Sincerely,

Ralph Forte

296

Elevator Mechanic. *Melanie Noonan, Woodland Park, New Jersey*

This response to an ad indicates that the experienced applicant is able to perform all aspects of elevator installation and maintenance, including all of the necessary paperwork.

ADAM A. FRANZ

000 Haven Avenue
Stanhope, NJ 00000

automaster@speed.net
000-000-0000

[Date]

[Name]
[Title]
[Company Name]
[Company Street Address]
[Town, State, ZIP]

RE: Position title _____ or Job # _____

Dear Mr. / Ms. _____:

As a state-of-the-art Automotive Technician with 20+ years of experience in maintaining and repairing BMW and Mercedes-Benz automobiles, along with demonstrated ability in mentoring and training junior technicians, I am an ideal candidate for the position of Technical Training Instructor.

My communication and interpersonal skills are outstanding, and I am able to simplify concepts so that students can readily arrive at the solution. My experience teaching *Euro-Auto* in the Edison, New Jersey, school system required that I communicate well to a diverse audience with varying levels of expertise. From the shop floor to the classroom, my students were engaged and motivated by the learning experience.

Throughout my career, I have been recognized by senior management as a technical resource in the industry. Often, I have been called upon to resolve extremely complex technical problems. My success has been measured by attaining consistently outstanding scores on the monthly Customer Service Index. In addition, my frame-off restorations of BMW automobiles and motorcycles are flawless, and I truly delight in teaching others all aspects of automotive work.

Attached is my resume for your review. I am confident that my demonstrated expertise would add value to your firm and contribute to your continuing success.

I can be available for an interview at your convenience. I will e-mail you to set an appointment.

Very truly yours,

Adam A. Franz

Attachment: resume

297

Technical Training Instructor. *Fran Kelley, Waldwick, New Jersey*

This individual was a master mechanic with an impressive list of accomplishments and training. The writer highlighted his years of specialized experience along with his teaching experience.

TOM NEWTON

0000 Whitewood Court • North Brunswick, New Jersey 08902 • 555.555.5555 • newton@gmail.com

QUALITY ASSURANCE PROFESSIONAL
QUALITY CONTROL ~ LABORATORY TECHNICIAN

Date

Name
Company
Address

Re: Quality Assurance Position

Dear Sir or Madam:

Enclosed is my resume for your review. I am confident that my long-term chemical/food experience with various types of manufacturing processes would serve as an asset to your company.

I have 5 years of experience working as a **Quality Assurance Technician** at Northeast Foods, where I performed analytical checks and quality assurance procedures for food and beverage products.

I am considered a quick learner with high concentration skills. In addition, I feel that my interpersonal skills, honesty, and rapport with fellow employees will benefit the company.

Other skills that I have gained though my employment are weighing and blending of batch ingredients according to formula, as well as inventory control. I have always been known for my accuracy and hardworking attitude.

Thank you for your consideration. I look forward to speaking with you personally so that we may discuss my qualifications in greater detail. I will call in two weeks to set up a time that we can talk further.

Sincerely yours,

Tom Newton

Enclosure

298

Quality Assurance Technician. *Beverly and Mitchell I. Baskin, Marlboro, New Jersey*

The applicant was looking for another quality assurance position. Five brief paragraphs tell of his experience, activities, people skills, on-the-job skills, and interest in an interview.

Larry Duvall

41 Grayson Way, Indianapolis IN 55555
larry@yahoo.com ▪ (555) 555-5555

January 23, 20XX

Mrs. Penelope Jackson
Human Resource Manager
Duncan Electric & Gas Company
Corner of Stapleton and Merryman Avenues
Knoxville, Tennessee 55555

Position Desired: ELECTRICAL LINEMAN

Dear Mrs. Jackson:

Since graduating from Mercy County Technical College two years ago, I have worked in the electrical field on a number of emergency and routine projects, including assignments abroad. This experience involves installation, repair and maintenance of transmission and distribution lines and transformers.

Prior experience involves supervising, coordinating and working with considerable responsibility. I believe that many of the personal and work qualities I offer are ones that employers value and have difficulty finding:

Dependability	Flexibility	High Attendance
Work Ethic and Integrity	Dedication	Commitment to Quality and Accuracy

In a global environment that often requires working alongside people with varying temperaments and from various cultures, I'm especially proud to be able to work effectively and efficiently with all kinds of people. My abilities to communicate well with others and to promote team efforts are excellent, and I'm always willing to lend a hand when needed. Leadership experience has taught me patience, diplomacy and tolerance.

I will be calling your office to check on interview scheduling for this position, and I look forward to the opportunity to meet with you to discuss details. If you need additional information, please contact me at the above phone number.

Sincerely,

Larry Duvall

Enclosure: Resume

299

Electrical Lineman. *Beverley Drake, Hot Springs Village, Arkansas*

The applicant indicates in turn his experience, worker traits as transferable skills, people skills, and interest in an interview. His transferable worker traits stand out clearly in three columns.

SANDRA BACHUS, CPP

55 Pinehurst Road
Augusta, Ontario A1A 1A1
(555) 666-9999 • bachus@email.com

February 5, 20XX

Pauline Ho
Senior Human Resources Manager
SciTech Pharmaceuticals
2345 Industry Circle
Pinehurst, Ontario
B2C 3D4

<u>**Re: Senior Component Technician**</u>

Dear Mrs. Ho,

"Sandra is considered an expert in her field...and continues to be the 'go-to' person."

With more than 10 years of experience overseeing packaging specifications, artwork, and production for some of the world's largest pharmaceutical firms, I have developed exhaustive expertise in all aspects of the industry—from technical specifications to quality control, production engineering, artwork, labelling, and distribution.

As the current Senior Component Development Specialist with ABC Packaging Inc., I coordinate 20–30 concurrent packaging projects at any given time for the full range of OTC and prescription products. I am very excited at the prospect of joining your team as your new Senior Component Technician as I am now anxious to apply my expertise to new and more challenging scenarios. The qualifications that distinguish me include the following:

✓ **Certified Packaging Professional** (recertified 20XX) and **PAC Alumni certification** (20XX)
✓ Exhaustive technical knowledge of **packaging components, processes, equipment, and tooling capabilities**
✓ Reputation for identifying opportunities to **improve processes, maximize efficiencies, and reduce costs** based on engineering and production requirements
✓ Skilled in **managing all artwork and creative processes**—familiar with a wide variety of printing processes and alternatives (flexography, gravure, etc.), further encouraging ability to produce top quality every time
✓ Excellent **communication and client/vendor relations** skills, internally and externally

If you are interested in speaking to a highly motivated and skilled professional with a reputation for excellence and continuous improvement, then I would welcome the opportunity to meet to discuss this opportunity in person.

I look forward to meeting with you and will call next week to set an appointment. Thank you for your consideration.

Sincerely,

Sandra Bachus

Encl.

300

Senior Component Technician. *Ross Macpherson, Whitby, Ontario, Canada*

The page border, thick horizontal line, opening testimonial, and bulleted qualifications in boldface helped this candidate stand head and shoulders above other applicants with more traditional letters.

JEFFREY R. SHAW
555 Prescott Road
Greenwich, CT 55555
(Residence) 555-555-5555
(Mobile) 500-500-5000
jrs1966@aol.com

September 30, 20XX

T.R. Patel
CEO
TRP Enterprises
555 West Street
New York, NY 55555

Dear Mr. Patel:

The particular value I offer a technology company is my ability to execute a strategic plan across the enterprise and improve financial performance and customer, partner, and employee satisfaction. I have 10 years of direct P&L and operating management responsibility. My experience spans the software reseller, software licensing/management, and computer hardware industries. I possess an in-depth understanding of the enterprise software market and channel sales and marketing. My experience includes turnaround and transition management.

I have delivered revenue and profit results for a billion-dollar company during periods of intense competition and margin erosion. Most notably, I turned around a failing $750 million North American business unit. Holding P&L, operational, and sales and marketing responsibilities, I was able to achieve these outcomes:

- Accelerated growth of revenue and profits by 33% and continued to produce double-digit revenue growth for five consecutive years.
- Led a reengineering program that reduced operating costs by $18 million within 24 months.
- Delivered technology ROI by reengineering a failing SAP implementation.
- Elevated loyalty scores from major Fortune 500 customers from 60% to 95%.
- Earned coveted top scores from the company's top vendors, including Microsoft and IBM.

Being able to both "zoom out" *and* "zoom in" has enabled me to be successful in creating positive transformations in each of my positions. I view the organization and its market environment holistically, identify areas of waste and underperformance, and translate my assessments into powerful, integrated strategic and tactical plans. Because I am *also* able to "zoom in" and actually execute those change plans operationally, I have been able to create a lean, focused, fast-growth organization.

No change, however, can occur at optimal levels without the active participation of the people who put new initiatives into practice. I know how to improve both employee satisfaction and financial performance by establishing a corporate culture of measurement, accountability, and rewards and then motivating personnel to contribute to the full extent of their abilities.

When the company I led as General Manager was sold to Serus Communications, I played a key role in the transition. Now I am pursuing new challenges. I look forward to speaking with you in the near future about the COO position at JR Patel Enterprises. Thank you.

Sincerely,

Jeffrey R. Shaw

Enclosure

301

Chief Operating Officer. *Jean Cummings, Concord, Massachusetts*

This executive had a broad background in technology and was looking for his next position. The writer presented him as a strong achiever, shown by the bulleted statements.

EVEREST KEENE
55 Square Route • Halifax, Nova Scotia B5B 5B5

September 1, 20XX

Mr. Rory O'May
Director, Machining Division
Celtic Mining and Manufacturing
555 East Boring Beltway
Halifax, Nova Scotia B0B 0B0

Dear Mr. O'May:

I would like to be your next **machine operator,** a position I saw advertised in the *Halifax Chronicle* on August 30.

The attached resume documents seven years of progressively responsible experience in this field. I presently serve as *Cell Leader* and Set-up Person for Atlantic Engine Parts. There, I established a reputation as a responsible, competent employee who could be relied on to produce work accurately and on time. In fact, I received the Eureka! award for averting a crisis that emerged when my colleagues and I were machining new parts for a major corporate client.

We were working to a tight deadline, and I had the privilege of serving as team leader. In the process of machining a particular part, the machining equipment was being damaged. This occurred because the part had been recently manufactured, and our company had not yet been able to acquire appropriate tools to machine it. I had no choice but to adapt existing technology to meet the demand. I accomplished this by modifying the cutting wheel and making adjustments to the computer program that guided the process.

The project was completed on time with minimal scrap, and our client was satisfied with the result.

In solving this problem, I demonstrated not only technical skill, but leadership, because all members of my team had to understand the modifications in order to mass-produce the part in question. It was a group effort, with the part passing from one machine operator to another in order to successfully complete the process. The team had to work harmoniously under pressure to get the job done. My ability to relate well with my colleagues, understand the high level of stress under which they were operating, and be flexible with them during this project played an important role in ensuring everything went smoothly and the job was completed on time.

I enjoy both the technical and interpersonal aspects of machine work and hope ultimately to acquire a supervisory position. I like this field because I am interested in the development of new and better technologies, and I enjoy the challenges that come with advancement. In fact, this was a major reason for my decision to enter the field. To this end, I have acquired a Certificate in CNC Programming from Sinclair College and completed a number of related technical courses.

My qualifications and experience are documented in the attached resume. I am confident that, on reviewing it, you will agree I have the potential to become a worthy member of your team. I will call to set a convenient time to meet, so that we could discuss how I might best serve Celtic Mining and Manufacturing.

Sincerely yours,

Everest Keene

P.S. I can be reached at (555) 000-0000.

Attachment: resume

302

Machine Operator. *Howard Earle Halpern, Toronto, Ontario, Canada*

The applicant "saved the day" by figuring out how to avoid damage to his employer's equipment. This story highlights the individual's leadership and ability to motivate others under pressure.

ALEXIS M. SMITH
0000 Archway Drive ▪ Charlotte, North Carolina 28888 ▪ (555) 555-5555

April 5, 20XX

www.alltel.com/careers

ATTN: Placement Professional

Someone once said, "There are no great companies, just the people who work for them." Sounds as if the person who said this was referring to an organization—like Alltel—that espouses the philosophy of cooperative teamwork.

Your advertisement in *The Charlotte Observer* (April 4) for a Coordinator–Number Administrator certainly seems to describe such an environment, with an opportunity that rewards team performance.

If so, I'd like to become a member!

Throughout my experience with AT&T, I was given opportunities to contribute to resolving customer problems, provide administrative and technical support, and coordinate processes—through both in-house and field staff, as well as customers. Based on my training in the telecommunications industry, I know how to troubleshoot, monitor, and coordinate line problems. I worked in the Technical Department in the Business Center.

Following retirement from AT&T two years ago, I have continued to upgrade my skills, including advanced training in Word, Access, Excel, PowerPoint, and Windows, among others.

I'm confident that I could contribute effectively to the Alltel team. May we schedule a time to discuss our mutual goals?

Thank you for your consideration.

Sincerely,

Alexis M. Smith

303

Coordinator–Number Administrator. *Doug Morrison, Charlotte, North Carolina*

After 30 years of work, this applicant had "retired." Having energy and youthful vigor, however, she wanted to work for a new team—something that she had always been good at and liked doing.

JACK A. WELCH
555 Harbor Drive
Amarillo, Texas 55555
555-555-5555
Jawelch@xx.com

September 18, 20XX

Mr. Frank Jones
Human Resource Director
000 Main Street
Amarillo, Texas 55555

Dear Mr. Jones:

In response to the recent ad in the *Amarillo Times,* enclosed is my resume for the position of Drilling Superintendent.

In addition to my extensive oil and gas drilling experience, I have handled all human resource matters, including hiring, training, and developing rig crews, particularly with regard to on-the-job training. Seventy-five percent of my drillers were college educated. My team was able to keep the turnover rate at less than 9% when the general rig crew turnover was in excess of 25%.

I have led safety meetings and developed a safety program. I've also instituted stringent drug and alcohol policies and achieved one of the lowest worker's compensation rates in the industry by promoting a health, safety, and environment culture through training, identification and resolution of risks, quality management, effective loss prevention, and role modeling.

I have implemented the operators' drilling programs and managed the company's resources for the drilling activities at the well site, achieving safe, efficient, and effective drilling operations at all times. Company owners' expectations were exceeded on the number of wells drilled, time it took to drill wells, profits, along with my ability to secure outside contracts.

I will call you in the next week to 10 days to follow up on my resume, answer any questions you may have, and establish a date and time for an interview.

Respectfully yours,

Jack Welch

304

Drilling Superintendent. *James Walker, Fort Riley, Kansas*

This applicant had been in the oil and gas industry and wanted to reenter the field after not having worked for several years. The letter stressed accomplishments, and the individual was selected for an advertised position.

From: Dan Carter <dcarter@email.net>
To: mhall@abcauto.com
Subject: Certified Automotive Technician Seeking Opportunity to Grow Business Bottom Line
Attachment: DanCarterAutoTech.docx

Dear Mr. Hall:

I was very excited to see the job opening for an Automotive Technician posted on the Indeed.com website. As instructed, I have attached my résumé to this email message for consideration.

Of particular note are my certifications, which are listed on the first page. I have ASE Certifications in eight different areas of automotive service. The online posting stated that some of these were requirements. I hope that you will find I have more than exceeded this qualification.

Other areas in which I excel are customer service and teamwork. I make it a priority to effectively communicate with my clients to ensure they understand the needs and recommendations related to their vehicles. Furthermore, communication with my team members is also important as we work toward efficient time management to improve the business's bottom line.

Thank you so much for your time and consideration. If you require any further information about my experience or certification, please do not hesitate to ask. I look forward to hearing from you to schedule an interview.

Sincerely,

Dan Carter
555-555-5555
dcarter@email.net

305

Automotive Technician. *Haley Richardson, Riverview, Florida*

This letter in response to an online posting was placed in the body of an e-mail message. The letter was short and to the point and did not require a heading. The candidate's qualifications were listed quickly.

Dear Hiring Manager:

For as long as I can remember, I have had a talent for keeping
things well organized and operating efficiently. Post-it Notes,
schedules, databases, and Excel spreadsheets are a part of my
everyday life. I bring order to clutter and structure to chaos.
If you feel that these skills and talents would prove to be
advantageous to the Macy's West Visitors Center, then I would like
to schedule a time for us to meet.

In addition to strong organizational skills, I offer you

   + More than five years of experience in the travel, hospitality,
and tourism industry.

   + Strong computer skills with a knack for Internet research
and database creation and management.

   + A solid work ethic and a commitment to giving whatever
it takes to get a job done, right and on time.

My professional office skills and strengths are complemented by
a positive, can-do attitude; excellent listening skills; and a
sense of humor. I have built an extensive network in Las Vegas
and have assembled a diverse blend of personal and professional
references to attest to my abilities.

I hope you will see what a valuable addition I would make to your
team of professionals and phone me. I can be reached at
555.555.5555 or 555.555.0000. Thank you for your consideration.

Sincerely,

Kathryn R. Hill

306

Travel Industry Professional. *Norine Dagliano, Hagerstown, Maryland*

This letter was e-mailed in response to a job posted on the employer's website. The letter, a brief
overview of the candidate's skills, got an immediate reply. An interview occurred the next day.

Karrie MacNeal

0000 West Union Street ▼ Athens, Ohio 45701 ▼ 555.555.5555 ▼ kmacneal@msn.com

February 12, 20xx

Ms. Susan Andrews
Human Resources Manager
Flyaway Travel Agency
229 South First Street
Athens, Ohio 45701

Dear Ms. Andrews:

It was with great interest that I read your recent ad in the *Athens Messenger* for a Travel Consultant, and I would like to be considered a serious candidate for this position. My resume is enclosed for your review and consideration.

Simply stated, travel has been my passion for more than 15 years! Even though my educational and career paths have taken me in a different direction up to this point, I have recently decided to follow my heart and pursue a career in the travel industry. Because of my desire to work in travel, I enrolled in the Travel Associate Training Program through Career Quest and will complete it next month.

Throughout my career I have utilized an ability to communicate effectively, both orally and in writing, with people from all walks of life. My counseling skills enable me to identify and respond appropriately to client needs. In addition, the time I spent as a Customer Service Manager allowed me to develop and enhance skills in sales, public speaking, event planning and database management that I believe would also be invaluable in your Travel Consultant position.

With a passion for travel, successful career experience in sales and current industry training, I am confident I would be an asset to your travel agency. Feel free to contact me to set up an interview or to answer any questions you may have regarding my background and experience. If you don't get a chance to call me in two weeks' time, I will follow up with you. I look forward to speaking with you soon.

Sincerely,

Karrie MacNeal

Enclosure

307

Travel Consultant. *Melissa L. Kasler, Athens, Ohio*

The applicant had a strong travel background and wanted to transition from customer-service counseling to travel consulting. The writer focused on travel-related activities and transferable skills.

DESMOND MASSEY

000 Augusta Court • Pinehurst, Ontario A1A 1A1
(555) 888-7777 • dmassey@email.com

March 12, 20xx

Pinehurst Transit Commission
Human Resources Department
Placement Services
1111 Batterley Street
Pinehurst, Ontario
A1A 1A1

Re: Operator / Driver Positions

Dear Human Resources Manager,

Put simply, I love to drive—and with more than 600,000 safe miles of large-vehicle driving experience, a conscientious and safety-minded driving style, and years of experience providing the highest levels of customer service, I believe I can offer you both the skills and experience you are looking for in a PTC Operator/Driver.

I have been fortunate. My unique career has afforded me the opportunity to drive and transport loads throughout Canada and the U.S. in a variety of vehicles, including 18- and 30-wheel trailers. While most of my positions were in operations and customer service, these frequent driving opportunities represented an aspect of the job that I thoroughly enjoyed, and as I now find myself seeking a career change, I am finally in the position to pursue a long-standing desire to drive for a living.

I encourage you to review the attached resume detailing my qualifications, highlights of which include

- ✓ **Extensive large-vehicle driving experience—CDL License, Class A with Trailer and Air Brake endorsements**
- ✓ **Outstanding customer service skills from 11+ years in sales and account management— personable, friendly, and professional**
- ✓ **Able to work flexible work schedules and nonstandard shifts**

I would welcome the opportunity to meet and discuss in person the value I could add as a PTC Operator/ Driver. I am very enthusiastic about this opportunity and am confident that I have the right combination of skills and experience to exceed your expectations.

Thank you for your consideration, and I look forward to hearing from you soon. I will follow up in two weeks to answer any questions you might have.

Sincerely,

Desmond Massey

Encl.

308

Operator/Driver. *Ross Macpherson, Whitby, Ontario, Canada*

After 15 years in a family business, this candidate wanted to turn his passion for driving into a full-time career. The letter conveyed his love for driving and his qualifications, making him stand out.

Candy P. Palate

888.555.5555 ● E-mail: cpp555555@media.net ● 5555 Any Street ● Easton, MD 21601

Talbot County Office of Tourism
Attn: Ms. Brenda Carnes
11 S. Harrison St.
Easton, MD 21601

Dear Ms. Carnes,

Throughout my work history, I have always taken great pride in my meticulous attention to detail and in my ability to provide outstanding customer service to clients. More than 15 years of work experience in sales and account management instilled within me a desire to take care of clients and coworkers with the same kind of respect and efficiency that I would expect from a business. I will bring this sense of dedication to customers, combined with a strong work ethic to your organization.

As a long-time resident of the Maryland Eastern Shore, combined with more than 15 years of management experience in the travel industry, I believe that I have the right combination of travel skills and marketing experience for consideration as your new Tourism Coordinator. My friend, Rebecca Noble, who works in your office, especially encouraged me to apply for this position.

While managing corporate travel accounts, I took great pride in getting to know my clients and learning of their personal preferences, schedules, business needs, and travel interests. They consistently complimented me on my ability to handle the meticulous details of their business trips and vacations. I know that as your new Tourism Coordinator, I can effectively develop and promote marketing and promotion plans that will attract more visitors to Talbot County.

As the last few years of my work have been spent creating and marketing my own business, I have learned how to take an ordinary food, such as pecans, and create a unique trademarked brand that is now marketed on a regional level. In just under four years, I have single-handedly contracted with more than 126 retailers to carry and promote my product. I have increased my sales volume by 125% each year, with 2012 sales projections exceeding $80,000. That dollar figure accounts for more than 8,000 bags of pecans being sold in 2012.

This position appeals to me because I can use the skills and experience that I already possess and work in a team environment where my strengths will be emphasized. I will prove to you that I can quickly adapt to new situations, will take initiative to effectively learn my job, and even offer fresh ideas to improve the services and structure of your business.

Ms. Carnes, I would welcome the opportunity to discuss additional work-related accomplishments with you during a personal interview in the upcoming weeks. We can discuss how my combination of travel management and entrepreneurial experience will be a perfect fit for the Talbot County Office of Tourism.

Thank you for your time and consideration. I look forward to speaking with you soon.

Sincerely,

Candy P. Palate

309

Tourism Coordinator. *Beth Colley, Crownsville, Maryland*

The individual had significant travel industry experience as a travel agent but had spent the last five years creating and maintaining a business. The writer quantifies sales achievements.

MARLENA M. LONG

55555 E. Caspian Place		Home (303) 000-5555
Aurora, CO 80015	marlena6@msn.com	Cell (720) 555-0000

March 31, 20xx

Hiring Manager
Jet Aviation, Inc.
Attn: In-flight Recruiting
5555 Buchtel Avenue
Philadelphia, PA 00000

Dear Jets Aviation Hiring Manager:

If you are looking for an experienced Flight Attendant with excellent abilities to attend to passenger comfort with a personal touch, as well as take care of passengers in emergencies, then I am the professional you are looking for.

I have excelled in my time at Northeast Air. Along the way, I have gained excellent organizational skills, as well as a strong ability to assess and take care of the needs of the passengers. I also have a strong ability to quickly and efficiently prepare for flights.

My flight attendant training has ensured that I can professionally perform effective decision making, skilled passenger handling, passenger-safety briefings, in-flight emergency procedures, post-evacuation considerations, and any type of medical emergency. I have proven these skills several times since completing my training in real emergency situations.

My past employment has given me the ability to "read" passengers and determine how to relate to them and make them feel the most comfortable. I enjoy my work and like to bring a friendly, humorous atmosphere to every flight. I also have a food service background that I frequently use while I work. I am positive that you will come to rely on my knowledge and abilities just as my past employers have.

My experience with Northeast Air has given me strong practical experience as a Flight Attendant. I am now interested in working for a charter flight corporation and show my abilities to provide personalized, first-class service on an individual basis.

The accompanying resume will provide you with the additional details of my accomplishments and skills. I would welcome the opportunity to meet with you and learn how I can make a positive contribution to your corporation.

Thank you for your time and consideration.

Sincerely,

Marlena M. Long

310

Flight Attendant. *Michele Angello, Aurora, Colorado*

The applicant was a commercial flight attendant and wanted to become a charter flight attendant. She learned the name of the hiring manager and personalized the letter before sending it.

TIM CARLETON
5 Ninth Avenue ▸ Winona, MN 55555
555-555-5555 ▸ timcarl@chosen.com

January 5, 20XX

David Sherrill, Regional Director
Mississippi Express
P.O. Box 555
Wabasha, MN 55555

Dear Mr. Sherrill:

I appreciate the time you spent with me yesterday discussing the sales position in the Rochester area and would like to reiterate my interest in the position. Enclosed is a resume reflecting my work history and philosophy.

A manager's and a company's success in the workplace is measured in many ways: productivity of workers ▸ results from managers ▸ job satisfaction ▸ low employee turnover ▸ quality of work, products and services ▸ accountability ▸ respect toward self, company and customers. A rewarding work environment is one in which employees and managers can expand their knowledge, skills and contributions. When an atmosphere of self-pride and company pride prevails, everyone wins—worker, company and customer. Attitudes mean a lot and reflect greatly on the mental image customers carry with them after the sale.

My record has been a good one. I've been able to motivate myself, as well as others, and to generate trust, respect and win-win results. Stability and accomplishment mark my career, as does ongoing learning. Although interviews and references are the preferred methods of learning more about candidates, at least a sketch of past accomplishments can help in forming a mental image of the person. You will see that general business skills complement the people skills—which is my greatest strength and interest. I truly enjoy working with others and have been exploring possibilities in which my biggest contributions can be not only helping a company meet its goals, but also creating an avenue in which I'm enriching in some way the lives of others or the world we leave behind. Social responsibility is a high priority.

I look forward to hearing from you further to discuss the company's direction, needs and concerns. In the next few days, I will contact you to determine your plans for filling this position and to see if you have questions or need additional information.

Sincerely,

Tim Carleton

Enclosure: Resume

311

Thank-You Letter. *Beverley Drake, Hot Springs Village, Arkansas*

After an interview without a resume, the applicant uses this thank-you letter to impress the reader further. The second paragraph expresses the applicant's views on success and a winning work environment.

Thomas Sullivan

555.555.5555
thomassullivan2@xx.com

CONTEXT / EMPATHY / HARMONY / DEVELOPER / ADAPTABILITY

Date

Mr. Dale Wright
Division Manager
ScienceLab Devices

RE: **Together, this is a win-win**

Dear Dale,

I am known to many as a friend, family member, and professional who is driven by the courage of his convictions. I stand strongly dedicated and committed to people and ideas that I believe in.

I have an uncanny and genuine knack for relating to others. Whether in the OR, the doctor's office, or at a neighborhood picnic, this ability is apparent through the rich and sustained relationships I hold. My keen understanding of what good relationships will yield is exactly why I want to express to you that our time together yesterday revealed a twofold opportunity for both of us.

Every step of my education and career so far has been to prepare for enabling the reputation and growth of ScienceLab Devices to excel in market leadership. I feel intuitively that you, as my leader, provide a unique balance. Your expertise and guidance, along with your interpersonal development awareness, are a match in terms of my personality and optimal working style.

What does a sales representative who is optimally motivated by you and the company bring for you personally? Dedication, loyalty, and excellence in acumen and customer service are inherent to how I operate. I assure you that I will truly be playing to my strengths as I commit to my role as Senior Device Sales Representative on your team with a personal fervor that will transcend initiative, teamwork, and overall results you've seen in the past.

Dale, I firmly believe that our meeting yesterday is exactly what I have envisioned in order to leverage my pre- and post-sales expertise and my reputation for technical teaching and coaching. Perhaps most important, I am passionately ready to execute this on behalf of ScienceLab Devices with the true dedication and reliability my clients have come to know as key parts of my brand. Thank you once again for sharing your time with me.

I will call you on Tuesday to follow up.

Sincerely,

Tom Sullivan

StrengthsFinder and ScienceLab Assimilations

CONTEXT.
Known as an active agent for positive change by integrating stories and relevant details.

EMPATHY:
Instinctive ability to understand is powerful; patience and understanding are my hallmarks, and clients deeply value this.

HARMONY:
I don't irritate easily, and seeking common ground comes naturally to me, making everyone around me comfortable in new or stressful situations.

DEVELOPER:
Easily extend myself to others, and others seek me out for help and encouragement.

ADAPTABILITY:
When others get stressed out, I am able to put things in perspective. Proud to be stable yet flexible.

♦ ♦ ♦

312

Thank-You Letter. *Kelly Welch, Raleigh, North Carolina*

This thank-you note showcased the applicant's strengths and used his words in creating a genuine note. The hiring manager considered this letter the best he had seen in 20 years.

Flo Sampson

Fairfield, CT 55555 • 555.555.5555 • fsampson@xx.com • http://www.linked/xx/xxxxxxx

Date

Name
Title
Company
Address
City, State ZIP

Dear Mr. Martin:

As the suggestion of Greg Monroe, Vice President of Sales at Pretelle Corporation, I am contacting you to see if you would be willing to share a few minutes of your time with me. Greg knows me well from our work together at Pretelle where we served on an enterprise-wide marketing task force.

My background as a marketing manager includes 13 years of integrated marketing experience, including online and digital marketing. During the past six years, I have steered the development of highly successful consumer-facing marketing campaigns, media, PR and promotion plans at Tulane Company. We launched a new product onto the national market that drove huge demand—with no budget increase. Sales of this product climbed to more than $158 million within two years.

I am now seeking new challenges where I can continue to contribute and deliver results. Please understand that I don't expect you to have or know of any open positions at this time. However, I would welcome a conversation to discuss my career options and glean any suggestions you can offer. I am researching your industry and would welcome your business insights as I gather information related to my next career move.

May we get together for a brief meeting in the next few weeks?

All the best,

Flo Sampson

P.S. If I can ever help you or someone you know, please let me know. I'd be happy to help.

313

Networking Letter. *Louise Garver, Broad Brook, Connecticut*

The applicant used this networking letter to open doors to conversations with contacts. Through these conversations, she heard about a few openings that led ultimately to interviews and offers.

Jake Aristopoulos _____

555 Campus Drive, Apartment X, Tulsa, OK 55555
(555) 555-5555   jake@xx.net

July 12, 20XX

Mr. Nick DiPrimo, President
XXXX Associates
Enright Building, Suite 00
Route 00 West
Oklahoma City, OK 00000

Dear Mr. DiPrimo:

In a recent conversation with Bob Thompson, a senior manager at XXXX Associates, he mentioned that he will soon need an engineering assistant to work with him on new and existing projects. He urged me to write to you and present my credentials. Having graduated this May from the University of Tulsa with a B.S. in Structural Engineering Technology, I am eager to begin my career and feel, as Bob does, I have the qualifications necessary for success in this field.

Bob has known me all my life and can assure you that I am hardworking, trustworthy, and quick to learn and apply specific principles. Academically, I am well prepared to assume a junior-level position, perhaps in an area where I will able to use my mechanical drawing ability. This fall I will be taking the Engineer-in-Training exam and thereafter plan to continue my graduate studies with the long-range goal of becoming a PE.

Through my association with Bob and another lifelong family friend, Cal Carlson of your Cincinnati office, I have been made well aware of the activities of XXXX Associates and the scope of responsibilities expected of their professional employees. I am ready to accept these challenges and am certain that I will soon become a productive and successful member of your engineering staff.

My resume will give you some details of my internship and senior project. As you will note, I participated in an advanced assignment, planning a shopping mall in a once heavily wooded area. For this endeavor, my team was awarded the highest grade in the class.

I hope to impress you further in a personal interview and would appreciate such an opportunity at your earliest convenience. In the meantime, you may check with Bob and Cal, who will give you an honest appraisal of my character.

Yours truly,

Jake Aristopoulos

cc: Bob Thompson
        Cal Carlson

Enclosure: Resume

314

Networking Follow-Up Letter. *Melanie Noonan, Woodland Park, New Jersey*

The applicant had just graduated with an engineering degree and was applying to a firm where two family friends worked. This letter was sent to the hiring manager and to the friends, who were going to be references.

December 1, 20XX

To: Envirolytic Recruiters

Re: Posting #490 for Sr. Soil Analyst in Richmond, VA

Having just completed an 18-month contract assignment with EarthTech Laboratories as an inorganic chemist, I understand the importance of investigating sources of pollution, particularly those that affect health. During this time, I organized approximately 240 samples per day using appropriate quality control methods, including mercury cold vapor atomic absorption to determine toxicity characteristics of soil, water, and wastewater samples. I have a B.S. in Chemistry and a total of 5 years of lab experience. With my strong theoretical and practical background, I believe I have the qualifications for the Sr. Soil Analyst position recently posted.

In my work at EarthTech Labs, I operated a complex Inductively-Coupled Plasma Mass Spectrometer (ICP/MS) for trace metal detection from bulk samplings and also gained hands-on experience with laboratory equipment/processes, including the centrifuge, fluorometer, pH meter, turbidmeter, polymerase chain reaction (PCR) studies, gram staining, API techniques, and electrophoresis.

In my previous position as a laboratory technician with the Allegheny Water Commission, I ensured quality and safety of drinking water for the southwestern Virginia region by performing various organic and inorganic chemical and microbiological tests to identify and determine the effects of contaminants on water samples.

Your further requirements state that the ideal candidate for the position shall have proficient reasoning skills; knowledge of experimental data analysis; independent problem-solving abilities; and the ability to write technical reports and procedural manuals, work in a team environment, and be productive in an intense work environment. The following illustrates that I have these qualifications:

- Designed tests according to instrument detection limits for various materials, continuously monitoring and troubleshooting to ensure accuracy throughout high production runs.
- Contributed to revamping the quality control program that increased efficiency up to 15%, which was necessary to accommodate additional business growth.
- Wrote standard operating procedure (SOP) for previously undocumented instrument usage to obtain consistent testing results, as mandated by the EPA.
- As part of a laboratory team of 4, I monitored QC, GMP, GLP, OSHA, and ISO 9001 procedures to maintain a safe, aseptic environment for accurate testing.

I will forward my resume under separate cover once you determine from this letter of interest that your client considers me qualified for the position of Sr. Soil Analyst. I am looking forward to a positive decision and continuance of the selection process. Please respond by email to karl@pfeffer.net.

Thank you.

Karl Pfeffer

315

Response to an Online Posting. *Melanie Noonan, Woodland Park, New Jersey*

To prequalify candidates, an environmental lab wanted candidates to submit a letter of interest. Because the employer was not named, the applicant provided only an e-mail address to protect his identity until he could make certain that the job was legitimate.

Denise Gorsky, MS, CCC-SLP
Speech-Language Pathologist
9 Cross Creek Terrace, Peoria, IL 61601
(309) 555-0000
denise@gorsky.net

June 6, 20XX

To those concerned:

It is with great pleasure that I write this recommendation for Ashley Southworth for a teaching assistant position. I have worked with Ashley for the past year and a half at the Communication Disorders Demonstration Program at Illinois Central University. The students attending this program are classified as communication handicapped with varying degrees of autism spectrum disorders. Many have additional physical or emotional factors affecting their ability to comprehend. This program operates under an interdisciplinary model, whereby each staff member is responsible for learning from and teaching the others. Also, because the vast majority of my time is spent in the classroom, I have had ample opportunity to observe and interact with Ashley.

Ashley has been an integral member of this team. She is extremely intuitive and has continually provided valuable insights regarding the children. She readily shares her ideas and her time, and she is always eager to learn and try new ideas or methods. More importantly, Ashley possesses a natural ability to deal with the children regardless of their situation. Her interactions have been flawlessly appropriate, patient, and sensitive to the individual needs of each child. Whether conducting a lesson or supervising on the playground, Ashley is extremely effective, flexible, and creative, but at the same time always aware of the immediate and long-term goals of the children.

I consider myself fortunate to have worked with someone of Ashley's caliber, and have personally and professionally grown from the experience. Ashley would undoubtedly be a valuable asset to the special needs students at any school.

Please feel free to contact me should you need further information.

Sincerely,

Denise Gorsky

316

Employee Recommendation Letter. *Melanie Noonan, Woodland Park, New Jersey*

This letter of recommendation is from a head of a speech therapy program at a university-affiliated clinic for a student who was looking for work in a school for students with special needs.

CAMERON CRAMER

ccramer@earthlink.com

000 Park City Blvd.
Trumbull, CT 00000

Residence: (000) 000-0000
Cell: (000) 000-1111

SPONSORSHIP INFORMATION

"Fear is not an option if you want to win!"

Cameron Cramer competes in what is undoubtedly one of the toughest, exciting, and gripping forms of competition today—Mountain Bike Racing! To face the downhill plunge of hurling over rocks and precipices, rocket down mountainsides, in a blur of flying gravel…that's what it's all about!

Cameron is the 2011 Overall Champion of the Intermountain Cup Mountain Bike Racing Series in the Sport Class. She advanced to the Expert/Pro Division at the end of last season, winning **first place** in her second race in this category by a ripping **6 minutes**! And she podiumed 11 out of 15 races in 2011. Although Cameron has been an all-around athlete her entire life, excelling in soccer and tennis during high school and working as a Ski Pro and Ski Patroller; this is just the beginning of her Mountain Bike Racing career.

What's Next…

11/11 – 3/12:	Preseason Training: Work with Trainer / Coach Donna Allen.
3/12 – 10/12:	On-hill training throughout Utah's Wasatch Front and Back Mountain Range with Concentration in Deer Valley and Park City.
5/12 – 9/12:	Mountain Bike Guide twice a week for Cole Sport with tours throughout the Wasatch Mountain Range.
3/12 – 10/12:	Race Season. Series to include NORBA, Intermountain Cup, Wild Rockies Series, among others.

With participation in all NORBA, Intermountain Cup, and Wild Rockies races for the 2012 season, the **podium potential is very, very high!** Mountain Bike Racing draws substantial media attention, and with Cameron's excellent public-relations skills, strong character, grit, and determination to succeed, the sponsorship bottom line is clear: **expand visual focus and increase brand awareness**. The benefits of advertising exposure and strengthening the company's culture make sponsoring Cameron Cramer cost effective. Sponsorship includes:

- The bike will be detailed with the sponsor's logo.
- The sponsor's logo and name will be on the helmet, shirt, and shorts.
- The sponsor's name and logo will be on all promotional materials—dominant and distinctive.

Enclosed is a resume that is sure to impress you. Past associates, employers, and competitors will confirm a mutual trust and respect that has been developed with Cameron—just check her references. Her aggressive and energetic approach to challenges and strong desire to succeed will make an immediate and significant impact for your company as a sponsor. You can contact Cameron personally at the above numbers or address to discuss your sponsorship needs and how a mutual association could be beneficial.

317

Branding Letter. *Donna Allen, Heber City, Utah*

The applicant was transitioning from a position as a Human Resources Manager to a role as a full-time athlete and was seeking sponsorships. This branding letter positions her as a serious contender in mountain-bike competitions.

P·A·R·T

Best Resume Tips

Best Resume Tips at a Glance

Best Resume Tips

In a passive job search, you rely on your resume to do most of the work for you. An eye-catching resume that stands out above all the others may be your best shot at getting noticed by a prospective employer. If your resume is only average and looks like most of the others in the pile, chances are you won't be noticed and called for an interview. If you want to be singled out because of your resume, it should be somewhere between spectacular and award-winning.

In an active job search, however, your resume complements your efforts at being known to a prospective employer before that person receives it. For this reason, you can rely less on your resume to get someone's attention. Nevertheless, your resume plays an important role in an active job search, which may include the following activities:

- Talking to relatives, friends, and other acquaintances about helping you meet people who can hire you before a job is available

- Researching employers, using Internet and library resources to identify organizations that could use a person with your skills

- Increasing in-person and online networking efforts to directly contact people who are most likely to hire someone with your background and skills

- Using a schedule to keep track of your appointments and callbacks

- Working at least 25 hours a week to search for a job

When you are this active in searching for a job, the quality of your resume confirms the quality of your efforts to get to know the person who might hire you, as well as your worth to the company whose workforce you want to join. An eye-catching resume makes it easier for you to sell yourself directly to a prospective employer. If your resume is mediocre or conspicuously flawed, it will work against you and may undo all your good efforts in searching for a job.

The following list offers ideas for making your resume impressive. Many of the ideas are for making your resume pleasing to the eye, but a number of the ideas are strategies to use for special cases. Other ideas are for eliminating common writing mistakes and stylistic weaknesses.

Best Resume Writing Tips

All resumes contain the same basic types of information, such as a work history and list of skills. But the way in which this information is presented is the difference between a bad resume and a best resume.

Contact Information

Make sure your phone number, e-mail address, and other contact information is clear and easy to find on your resume. Keep the following tips in mind.

■ **Instead of spelling out the name of the state in your address at the top of your resume, consider using the state's postal abbreviation.** The reason is simple: it's an address. Anyone wanting to contact you by mail will probably refer to your name and address on the resume. If they appear there as they should on an envelope, the person can simply copy the information you supply. If you spell out the name of your state in full, the person will have to "translate" the name of the state to its postal abbreviation. Not everyone knows all the postal abbreviations, and some abbreviations are easily confused. For example, those for Alabama (AL), Alaska (AK), American Samoa (AS), Arizona (AZ), and Arkansas (AR) are easy to mix up. You can prevent confusion and delay simply by using the correct postal abbreviation.

If you decide to use postal abbreviations in addresses, make certain that you do not add a period after the abbreviations, even before ZIP codes. This also applies to postal abbreviations in the addresses of references if you provide them.

Do not, however, use the state postal abbreviation when you are indicating only the city and state (not the mailing address) of a school you attended or a business where you worked. In these cases, it makes sense to write out the name of the state.

■ **When listing your phone numbers, adopt a sensible form and use it consistently.** Do this in your resume and in all the documents you use in your job search. Some forms of phone numbers make more sense than others. Compare the following:

123-4567	This form is best for a resume circulated locally, within a region where all the phone numbers have the same area code.
(222) 123-4567	This form is best for a resume circulated in areas with different area codes.
222-123-4567	This form suggests that the area code should be dialed in all cases. But that isn't necessary for prospective employers whose area code is 222. Avoid this form.
222/123-4567	This form is illogical and should be avoided. The slash can mean an alternate option, as in ON/OFF. In a phone number, this meaning of a slash makes little sense.
1 (222) 123-4567	This form is long, and the digit 1 is unnecessary. Almost everyone will know that 1 should be used before the area code to dial a long-distance number.
222.123.4567	This form, resembling Internet addresses, is becoming more popular, particularly with people in computer and design fields.

Note: For resumes directed to prospective employers outside the United States, be sure to include the correct international prefixes in all phone numbers so that you (and your references, if they are listed) can be reached easily by phone.

Professional Profiles and Skills Summaries

The information that immediately follows your name and contact information near the top of the first page is important. If this section fails to grab the reader's attention, he or she may discard your resume without reading further. Try these tips to create a great first impression:

- **To sell yourself near the beginning of the resume, use a Summary of Qualifications, a Profile, or an Areas of Expertise section just after the contact information.** See Resumes 1, 2, and 3.

- **Include a Career Highlights section to draw attention to special accomplishments or achievements.** See Resumes 9 and 10.

- **Spend considerable time determining how to present your skills.** You can present them in various ways, such as Office Skills (Resume 1), Core Strengths (Resume 4), and Key Accomplishments (Resume 7).

- **Display your qualifications, areas of expertise, skills, or strengths in columns to make them easy to alter if your target job or target industry changes.** See Resumes 4, 10, and 11.

- **When your skills and abilities are varied, group them according to categories for easier comprehension.** See Resume 9.

- **When you have letters of recommendation, use quotations from them as testimonials.** Devoting some space (or even a full column) to the positive opinions of "external authorities" helps make a resume convincing as well as impressive. When placed effectively, such quotations can build respect, add credibility, and personalize a resume. See Resumes 4 and 5.

Work Experience

When you write about your work experience in your resumes, consider these tips:

- **State achievements or accomplishments, not just duties or responsibilities.** The reader often already knows the duties and responsibilities for a given position. Achievements, however, can be interesting. The reader probably considers life too short to be bored by lists of duties and responsibilities in a stack of resumes. See Resumes 1 and 7.

- **Consider explaining responsibilities in a paragraph and using bullets to point to achievements, contributions, or awards.** See Resumes 4, 5, 7, 8, and 10.

- **When you indicate achievements, quantify them (Resumes 4 and 6).**

- **Include information that explains lesser-known companies.** See Resumes 4, 6, 7, and 11.

- **Group positions to avoid repetition in a description of duties.** See Resume 6.

Best Resume Design and Layout Tips

Whether your resume is presented on paper or on-screen, it is important that it be inviting and easy-to-read. Otherwise, it might not be read at all!

If you are giving someone your resume in person or sending it as a PDF file, you might consider going beyond simple readability in your design and layout by using a nonstandard format, an unconventional display font, or graphic elements in order to make your resume stand out. Make sure that your resume design choices make sense for your type of job and industry. What is fitting for a resume for an entry-level marketing job, for example, is not always the most appropriate resume strategy for executive positions. Try to match the style of your resume to the target company's "corporate image" if it has one.

Alignment

Misalignment can ruin the appearance of a well-written resume. Avoid this problem by following these tips:

- **Use vertical alignment in tabbed or indented text.** Try to set tabs or indents that control this text throughout a resume instead of having a mix of tab stops in different sections.

- **Try left- or right-aligning dates.** This technique is especially useful in chronological resumes and combination resumes. For several examples of right-aligned dates, look at Resumes 4, 7, and 11.

- **Use centered headings to make them easy to read down a page.** See Resumes 5 and 7.

- **Resist the temptation to use full justification for text** (in which each line goes all the way to the right margin). The price you pay for a straight right margin is uneven word spacing. Words may appear too close together on some lines and too spread out on others. Although the resume might look more uniform, you lose readability.

Bullets and Special Characters

Special characters enhance the look of your resume, and using them correctly demonstrates your attention to detail. (Note that your word processing program may be set up to make some of these changes for you by default.) These tips will help you use bullets and other special characters effectively:

- **Use curly quotation marks (" and ") instead of straight ones (" and ") for a polished look.**

- **Use an em dash (—) instead of two hyphens (--) or a hyphen with a space on either side (-).**

- **To separate dates, use an en dash (a dash the width of the letter *n*) instead of a hyphen, as in 2010–2011.** If you use "to" instead of an en dash in a range of numbers, be sure to use "to" consistently in all ranges in your resume.

- **To call attention to an item in a list, use a bullet (•) or a box (□) instead of a hyphen (-).** Browse through the sample resumes and notice how bullets are used effectively as attention-getters.

- **Try using bullets of a different style, such as diamond bullets (◆), rather than the usual round or square bullets.** For diamond bullets, see Resume 2. For other kinds of bullets, see Resumes 3 (decorative arrow tips), 4 (check marks), and 8 (filled squares).

■ **Make a bullet a little smaller than the lowercase letters that appear after it.** Disregard any ascenders or descenders on the letters. Compare the following bullet sizes:

- Too small   ● Too large   ● Better   • Just right

Fonts

Anyone with a word processing program and an Internet connection has access to a vast array of fonts for resume use. The tips in the section will help you make smart font decisions and avoid common pitfalls:

■ **Consider using unconventional type in headings or for your name to make your resume stand out.**

■ **Beware of becoming "font happy" and turning your resume into a font circus.** Frequent font changes can **distract** the reader, AND SO CAN GAUDY DISPLAY TYPE SUCH AS THIS. Also, if you are e-mailing or submitting your resume online, uncommon fonts may not display correctly if the people receiving your resume don't have that font installed on their machines.

■ **Try to make your resume more visually interesting by offering stronger contrasts between light and dark type.** Some fonts are light; others are dark. Notice the following lines:

A quick brown fox jumps over the lazy dog.

A quick brown fox jumps over the lazy dog.

Most typefaces fall somewhere between these two. With the variables of height, width, thickness, serifs, angles, curves, spacing, ink color, ink density, and boldfacing, you can see that type offers an infinite range of values from light to dark. Browse through the Exhibit of Resumes at the end of this section and notice the differences in light and dark type.

■ **If your resume will be printed, use a serif font for greater readability.** *Serif* fonts have little lines extending from the tops, bottoms, and ends of the characters. These fonts tend to be easier to read than *sans serif* (without serif) fonts, especially in low-light conditions. Compare the following font examples:

Serif	Sans Serif
Century Schoolbook	Gill Sans
Courier	Futura
Times New Roman	Helvetica

Words such as *skill* and *abilities,* which have several thin letters, are more readable in a serif font than in a sans serif font.

■ **If your resume will be read on-screen, consider using a sans serif font, which is the standard for on-screen text.** Sans serif fonts sometimes are used for section headings or your name at the top of the resume.

■ **Avoid using monospaced fonts, such as Courier.** A font is *monospaced* if each character takes up the same amount of space. For example, in a monospaced font, the letter *i* is as wide as the letter *m*. Therefore, in Courier type, iiiii is as wide as mmmmm. Monospaced fonts take up a lot of space, so you can't pack as much information on a page with Courier type as you can with a proportionally spaced font such as Times New Roman.

- **Think twice about underlining words in your resume.** Underlining defeats the purpose of serifs at the bottom of characters by blending with the serifs. In trying to emphasize words, you lose some visual clarity. This is especially true if you use underlining with uppercase letters in centered or side headings.

- **Consider using italic for duties, strengths, achievements, or company descriptions.** Be sure not to use italic too much, however, because italic characters are less readable than normal characters.

- **Use boldfacing to make different job titles more evident (Resumes 1, 3, and 7) or to indicate achievements (Resumes 9 and 10).**

- **Think twice about using all uppercase letters in your resume.** A common misconception is that uppercase letters are easier to read than lowercase letters. Actually, the ascenders and descenders of lowercase letters make them more distinguishable from each other and therefore more recognizable than uppercase letters. As a test, look at a string of uppercase letters and throw them gradually out of focus by squinting. Uppercase letters become a blur sooner than lowercase letters. Professional resume writers, however, may use uppercase letters effectively for emphasis and variety.

Lines, Boxes, and Other Graphics

You can use lines, boxes, and other graphics to enhance your resume in many ways:

- **Use a horizontal line to separate your name (or your name and address) from the rest of the resume.** See Resumes 4 and 8.

- **Use horizontal lines to separate the different sections of the resume.** See Resumes 2, 6, and 9. Resumes 4 and 10 contain shaded bars to distinguish the headings.

- **To call attention to a resume section or certain information, use horizontal lines to enclose it.** Using thicker lines than the rest of the resume will draw more attention to an area.

- **For variety in dividing sections of your resume or in presenting contact information, use partial horizontal lines.** Resume 3 has partial lines that extend from the centered occupation to both the left and right margins.

- **Use a vertical line (or lines) to spice up your resume.**

- **Use a page border to make a page stand out.** See Resumes 1, 4, 5, 6, and 10.

- **Use various kinds of boxes (single line, shadowed, or decorative) to make a page visually more interesting.** See Resumes 4 and 9.

- **For getting attention, make headings white on black if you use software that has this capability.** Resume 10 displays the candidate's name as white letters in a dark box.

- **Consider adding a simple graphic, if appropriate.** See the airplane graphic in Resume 2 for a flight attendant.

- **Visually coordinate the resume and the cover letter with the same font treatment or graphic to catch the reader's attention.** See Resume 1 and Cover Letter 18, Resume 2 and Cover Letter 26, Resume 3 and Cover Letter 82, Resume 8 and Cover Letter 144, and Resume 10 and Cover Letter 171.

Number and Length of Pages

No rule about the number of pages makes sense in all cases. The determining factors are your qualifications and experiences, the job's requirements, and the interviewer's interests and pet peeves. However, these general guidelines are helpful to follow:

- **Use as many pages as you need to portray your qualifications adequately to a specific interviewer for a particular job.** Try to limit your resume to one page, but set the upper limit at four pages. If you know that an interviewer refuses to look at a resume longer than a page, that says it all: You need to deliver a one-page resume if you want to get past the first gate.

- **Make each page a full page.** More important than the number of pages is whether each page is a full page. A partial page suggests deficiency, as if the reason for it is just that information on page one has spilled over onto page two. Then it becomes evident that you don't have enough information to fill two pages. In that situation, try to compress all your information onto the first page. If you have a resume that is almost two pages, make it two full pages. Achieving this look may require that you adjust the character and line spacing settings in your word processing software.

- **Preserve readability.** To avoid a cramped one-page resume that has small print, narrow margins, and reduced line spacing, use a two-page resume instead.

Paper and Printing

If you will be printing your resume instead of sending it electronically, keep the following tips in mind:

- **If you use quality watermarked paper for your resume, be sure to use the right side of the paper.** To know which side is the right side, hold a blank sheet of paper up to a light source. If you can see a watermark and read it, the right side of the paper is facing you. This is the surface for printing. If the watermark is unreadable or if any characters look backward, you are looking at the "underside" of the paper—the side that should be left blank if you use only one side of the sheet.

- **Make certain that characters, lines, and images contrast well with the paper.** Your resume's printed quality depends on the device used to print it. If you use an inkjet or laser printer, check that the characters are sharp and clean, without smudges or traces of extra toner.

Spacing

A sheet of paper with no words on it is impossible to read. Likewise, a sheet of paper with words all over it is impossible to read. These tips will help you make your spacing just right:

- **Have a comfortable mix of white space and words.** If your resume has too many words and not enough white space, it looks cluttered and unfriendly. If it has too much white space and too few words, it looks skimpy and unimportant. Make certain that adequate white space exists between the main sections. For examples that display good use of white space, see Resumes 1 and 3.

- **Make the margins uniform in width and preferably no less than an inch.** If the margins are less than an inch, the page begins to have a "too much to read" look. An enemy of margins is the one-page rule. If you try to fit more than one page of information on a page, the first temptation is to shrink the margins to make room for the extra material. It is better to shrink the material by paring it than to reduce the size of the margins. Decreasing the type's point size is another way to save the margins. Try reducing the size in your resume to 10 points. Then see how your information looks with the font(s) you are using. Different fonts produce different results. In your effort to save the margins, be certain that you don't make the type too small to be readable.

  However, note that margins in resumes for executives, managers, and other administrators tend to be narrower than margins in other resumes. See Resumes 5 and 10. Narrower margins are often used in connection with smaller type to get more information on a one- or two-page resume.

- **Be consistent in your use of line spacing.** How you handle line spacing can tell the reader how attentive you are to details and how consistent you are in your use of them. If, near the beginning of your resume, you insert two line spaces (two hard returns in a word processing program) between two main sections, be sure to put two line spaces between all the main sections in your resume.

- **Be consistent in your use of horizontal spacing.** If you usually put two spaces after a period at the end of a sentence, make certain that you use two spaces consistently. The same is true for colons. If you put two spaces after colons, do so consistently.

  Note that an em dash—a dash the width of the letter *m*—does not require spaces before or after it. Similarly, an en dash, which is a dash the width of the letter *n*, should not have a space before and after it. (An en dash is commonly used between a range of numbers, as in 2008–2012.)

  No space should go between the P and O of P.O. Box. Only one space is needed between a state's postal abbreviation and the ZIP code. You should insert a space between the first and second initials of a person's name, as in I. M. Jobseeker (not I.M. Jobseeker). These conventions have become widely adopted in English and business communications. If, however, you use other conventions, be sure to be consistent. In resumes, as in grammar, consistency is more important than conformity.

Best Resume Writing Style Tips

The following sections provide tips concerning style issues that commonly crop up in resumes. For more detailed information, consult a business writing style guide.

Capitalization

Resumes usually contain many of the following:

- Names of people, companies, organizations, government agencies, awards, and prizes

- Titles of job positions and publications

- References to academic fields (such as chemistry, English, and mathematics)

- Geographic regions (such as the Midwest, the East, northern Florida, and the state of California)

Because of such words, resumes are minefields for the misuse of uppercase letters. These tips address the most common pitfalls:

- **When you don't know whether a word should have an initial capital letter, don't guess.** Consult a dictionary, a handbook on style, or some other authoritative source, such as an official website of the organization or product in question. Often a reference librarian can provide the information you need. If so, you are only a phone call away from an accurate answer.

- **Check that you have used capital letters correctly in computer and technology terms.** If you want to show in a Computer or Technology Experience section that you have used certain hardware, software, or media, you may give the opposite impression if you don't use uppercase letters correctly. Note the correct use of capitals in the following names:

Adobe InDesign	LinkedIn	PowerPoint
AutoCAD	NetWare	QuickBooks
iPad	Microsoft Office	UNIX
JavaScript	Photoshop	Windows

The reason that many computer product names have an internal uppercase letter is for the sake of a trademark. A word with unusual spelling or capitalization is more easily trademarked. When you use the correct forms of these words, you are honoring trademarks and registered trademarks and showing that you are in the know.

- **Use all uppercase letters for most acronyms.** An *acronym* is a pronounceable word or set of letters usually formed from the initial letters of the words in a compound term or sometimes from multiple letters in those words. Note the following examples:

CAD	Computer-Aided Design
OSHA	Occupational Safety and Health Administration

Some acronyms, such as *radar* (*ra*dio *d*etecting *an*d *r*anging) and *scuba* (*s*elf-*c*ontained *u*nderwater *b*reathing *a*pparatus), have become so common that they are no longer all uppercase.

- **Use all uppercase letters without periods for common abbreviations that are pronounced as letters.** Using common abbreviations such as the following can save valuable space:

CEO	Chief Executive Officer
HR	Human Resources

Note: If you think that the person reading your resume might not recognize a certain abbreviation, spell it out the first time you use it in your resume. Also, you should never use abbreviations that represent informal, common phrases, such as FYI, in your resume or cover letter.

- **In headings, follow headline style with upper- and lowercase letters.** That is, capitalize the first word, the last word, and each main word in the heading, but not articles (a, an, and the), conjunctions (and, but, or, nor, for, yet, and so), and short prepositions (for example, at, by, in, and on) within the heading. Capitalize prepositions of five or more letters, such as about.

Hyphenation

Hyphenation is the root of many resume errors. These tips will help you deal with hyphenation issues:

- **Be aware that compounds present special problems for hyphenation.** Writers' handbooks and books on style do not always agree on how compounds (combinations of words) should be hyphenated. Many compounds are evolving from *open* compounds (two different words) to *hyphenated* compounds (two words joined by a hyphen) to *closed* compounds (one word). In different dictionaries, you can find the words *copy-editor, copy editor,* and *copyeditor.* No wonder the issue is confusing! Most style books do agree, however, that in most cases when a compound appears as an adjective before a noun, the compound should be hyphenated. When the same compound appears after a noun, hyphenation is unnecessary. Compare the following two sentences:

  I scheduled well-attended conferences.

  The conferences I scheduled were well attended.

- **Hyphenate so-called *permanent* hyphenated compounds.** Usually, you can find these by looking them up in the dictionary. You can spot them easily because they have a long hyphen (–) for visibility in the dictionary. Hyphenate these words (with a standard hyphen) wherever they appear, before or after a noun. Here are some examples:

all-important	self-employed
day-to-day	step-by-step
full-blown	time-consuming

- **Use the correct form for certain verbs and nouns combined with prepositions.** You may need to consult a dictionary for correct spelling and hyphenation. Compare the following examples:

start up	verb
start-up	noun
start-up	adjective
startup	noun, computer and Internet industry
startup	adjective, computer and Internet industry

- **Avoid hyphenating words with such prefixes as *co-, micro-, mid-, mini-, multi-, non-, pre-, re-,* and *sub-.*** Many people think that words with these prefixes should have a hyphen after the prefix, but most of these words should not. The following words are spelled correctly:

coauthor	midway	nonfunctional
cofounder	minicomputer	prearrange
coworker	multicultural	prequalify
microfiber	multilevel	reenter
midpoint	nondisclosure	subdirectory

Note: If you look in the dictionary for a word with a prefix and you can't find the word, look for just the prefix. You might find a small-print listing of a number of words that begin with that prefix.

For detailed information about hyphenation, see a recent edition of *The Chicago Manual of Style* (the 16th edition is the latest). You should be able to find a copy at your local library.

Parallel Structure and Consistency

Consistency is key to a polished resume:

- **Check that words or phrases in lists are parallel.** For example, notice the bulleted items in the Career Highlights section of Resume 9. All the entries contain verbs in the past tense.

- **Make sure that you use numbers consistently.** Numbers are often used inconsistently with text. Should you present a number as a numeral or spell it out as a word? A useful approach is to spell out numbers one through nine but present numbers 10 and above as numerals. Different approaches are taught in different schools, colleges, and universities. Use the approach you have learned, but be consistent.

Punctuation

These tips address common punctuation pitfalls in resumes:

- **Use (or don't use) the serial comma consistently.** How should you punctuate a series of three or more items? If, for example, you say in your resume that you increased sales by 100 percent, opened two new territories, and trained four new salespersons, the comma before *and* is called the *serial comma*. It is commonly omitted in newspapers, magazine articles, advertisements, and business documents. However, it is often used for precision in technical documents or for stylistic reasons in academic text, particularly in the humanities.

- **Use semicolons correctly.** Semicolons are useful because they help distinguish visually the items in a series when the items themselves contain commas. Suppose that you have the following entry in your resume:

  > Increased sales by 100 percent, opened two new territories, which were in the Midwest, trained four new salespersons, who were from Georgia, and increased sales by 250 percent.

  The extra commas (before *which* and *who*) throw the main items of the series out of focus. By separating the main items with semicolons, you can bring them back into focus:

  > Increased sales by 100 percent; opened two new territories, which were in the Midwest; trained four new salespersons, who were from Georgia; and increased sales by 250 percent.

  Use this kind of high-rise punctuation even if just one item in the series has an internal comma.

- **Avoid using colons after headings.** A colon indicates that something is to follow. A heading indicates that something is to follow. A colon after a heading is therefore redundant.

- **Use dashes correctly.** One of the purposes of a dash (an em dash or two hyphens) is to introduce a comment or afterthought about the preceding information. A colon *anticipates* something to follow, but a dash *looks back* to something already said. Two dashes are sometimes used before and after a related but nonessential remark—such as this—within a sentence. In this case, the dashes are like parentheses, but more formal.

- **Use apostrophes correctly.** They indicate possession (Tom's, Betty's), the omission of letters in contractions (can't, don't), and some plurals (x's and o's), but they can be tricky with words ending in s, possessive plurals, and plural forms of capital letters and numbers. For review or guidance, consult a style guide or a section on style in the dictionary.

- **Know the difference between *its* and *it's*.** The form *its'* does not exist in English, so you need to know only how *it's* differs from *its*. The possessive form *its* is like *his* and *her* and has no apostrophe. The form *it's* is a contraction of *it is*. The trap is to think that *it's* is a possessive form.

Spelling

A resume with just one misspelling is unimpressive and may undermine all the hours you spent putting it together. Worse than that, one misspelling may be what the reader is looking for to screen you out, particularly if you are applying for a position that requires accuracy with words. The cost of that error can be immense if you figure the salary, benefits, and bonuses you *don't* get because of the error but would have gotten without it. Keep the following tips in mind:

- **Remember that your computer's spelling checker can detect a misspelled word but cannot detect when you have used the wrong word** (*to* for *too,* for example).

- **Be wary of letting someone else check your resume.** If the other person is not a good speller, you may not get any real help. The best authority is a good dictionary.

- **For words that have more than one correct spelling, use the preferred form.** This form is the one that appears first in the dictionary. For example, if you see the entry **trav·el·ing** *or* **trav·el·ling,** the first form (with one l) is the preferred spelling. If you make it a practice to use the preferred spelling, you will build consistency in your resumes and cover letters.

- **Avoid British spellings.** These slip into American usage through books and online articles published in Great Britain. Note the following words:

British Spelling	American Spelling
acknowledgement	acknowledgment
centre	center
judgement	judgment
towards	toward

Word Choice

Make the correct word choices to ensure that your resume is clear:

- **Use the right words.** The issue here is correct usage, which often means choosing the right word or phrase from a group of two or more possibilities. The following words and phrases are often used incorrectly:

alternate (adj.)	Refers to an option used every other time. OFF is the alternate option to ON in an ON/OFF switch.
alternative	Refers to an option that can be used at any time. If cake and pie are alternative desserts for dinner, you can have cake three days in a row if you like. The common mistake is to use *alternate* when the correct word is *alternative*.
center around	A common illogical expression. Draw a circle and then try to draw its center around it. You can't. Use *center in* or *center on* as a logical alternative to *center around*.

  For information about the correct usage of words, consult a usage dictionary or the usage section of a writer's handbook, such as Strunk and White's *Elements of Style*.

- **Avoid using shortcut words, such as abbreviations like *thru* or foreign words like *via*.** Spell out *through* and use *by* for *via*.

- **Avoid using the archaic word *upon*.** The common statement "References available upon request" needs to be simplified, updated, or even deleted in resume writing. The word *upon* is one of the finest words of the 13th century, but it's a stuffy word in the 21st century. Usually, *on* will do in place of *upon*. Other possibilities are "References available by request" and "References available." However, because most readers of resumes know that applicants can usually provide several references, this statement is unnecessary. A resume reader who is seriously interested in you will ask about references.

Exhibit of Resumes

This part of the book contains an Exhibit of 11 resumes that accompanied cover letters in the first part of the book. Cross-references let you know readily which cover letter accompanied a particular resume so that you can view the two documents as a package.

Resume writers commonly distinguish between chronological resumes and functional (or skills) resumes. A *chronological resume* is a photo—a snapshot history of what you did and when you did it. A *functional resume* is a painting—an interpretive sketch of what you can do for a future employer. A third kind of resume, known as a *combination resume,* is a mix of recalled history and self assessment. Besides recollecting "the facts," a combination resume contains self-interpretation and is therefore more like dramatic history than news coverage. A combination resume and a functional resume are not always that different; often, all that is needed for a functional resume to qualify as a combination resume is the inclusion of dates for some of the positions held.

Instead of sending the exact same document to many different prospective employers, you should tailor each resume to a specific job target. To do this, emphasize the skills and experience that are important to the specific job and eliminate details that are irrelevant. Also, make sure that you incorporate keywords from the job description in your skills summary and work accomplishments to increase the odds that your resume will be found in an electronic search.

Angela Granato

1234 Pinewood Street
Charleston, SC 00000

(000) 000-0000
agranato@fastmail.com

PROFILE	**Customer service professional,** skilled in problem solving and responsive to needs of clients, coworkers and management. Poised, resourceful and adaptable to any office environment. Organizational ability to handle multiple priorities and meet deadline schedules. Attentive to detail, with sharp awareness of omissions/ inaccuracies, and prompt to take corrective action. A self-starter and quick study, eager to assume increasing levels of responsibility.
OFFICE SKILLS	Professional phone manner; data entry and word processing; updating/ maintenance of files and records; composition of routine correspondence.
EMPLOYMENT HISTORY	

CUSTOMER SERVICE REPRESENTATIVE
Liberty Insurance Corporation, Charleston, SC (2007–2012)

Hired as data entry operator and advanced to customer service position in less than a year. Took over problem desk, which had been inadequately handled by 2 previous employees. Worked closely with underwriters, answering client inquiries by phone or mail. Analyzed complex situations affecting insurance coverage. Recognized opportunities to increase sales and advised clients when coverage was lacking in specific policy areas.

> *Key Accomplishments:* During major restructuring of company resulting in 70% staff reduction, assumed more than triple the normal account responsibility, from 450 to more than 1,500, while still in training. Simultaneously studied for insurance licensing course; passed exam on first try, with score of 95.

APPLICATIONS SCREENER
Marshall & Reiner Insurance Agency, Charlotte, NC (2005–2007)
(Applications processing center for Mutual Surety Corporation)

Screened homeowners' new lines of business applications, verifying coverage against individual state regulations. Filled in whenever needed for switchboard, typing and clerical assignments.

HOMEMAKER/CHILD CARE RESPONSIBILITIES (1998–2005)

CENSUS TAKER
U.S. Census Bureau, Charleston, SC (2000)

Visited individuals who had not filled out census forms properly. Worked in a multiethnic territory, overcoming language barriers and mistrust. Clarified discrepancies and ensured accuracy and completeness of reported information.

SUBROGATION CLERK
Royal Guard Insurance Company, Middleton, SC (1996–1998)

Started as receptionist and promoted shortly thereafter to handle various clerical assignments in Subrogation Department. Prepared paperwork for file with arbitration board. Kept subrogation ledgers up-to-date for auditors' review.

EDUCATION	*Carolina State University*—65 credits in Business Administration (1994–1996) *American Insurance Academy*—Completed 12-week basic course in Property and Casualty, Insurance Law, and Health Insurance (2007)

1

Combination. *Melanie Noonan, Woodland Park, New Jersey*

Bold side headings make it easy to see at a glance the resume's main sections. Italic helps the reader spot employers, schools, and the Key Accomplishments paragraph. See Cover Letter 18 in Part 2.

Melissa O'Brien

XXXX Manchester Court • Valley Center, KS 55555
flygirl@xxx.com • 555-555-0000

PROFILE

❖ More than 11 years of experience providing executive-level customer service in corporate and charter aviation. Additional experience in banking/mortgage industry and retail sales.

❖ Excellent written and oral communication skills complemented by strong interpersonal skills.

❖ Effective organizer and leader who works equally well independently and as part of a team.

❖ Recognized for ability to anticipate the needs of customers.

❖ Professional demeanor and understanding of executive expectations.

❖ Significant travel abroad (Canada, South America, Europe, Middle East, Asia, Southeast Asia); readily adaptable to different cultures and environments.

❖ Experience with wide range of aircraft: Gulfstream (200, 300, 400, 450, 500, 550); Falcon (2000, 900); and Challenger 602.

PROFESSIONAL EXPERIENCE

Midwest Corporate Aviation • Wichita, Kansas   2004–Present
Corporate Aviation Flight Attendant
- Provide comprehensive service to executive passengers and their guests during domestic and international flights. Balance attentiveness with recognition of need for privacy and confidentiality.
- Perform preflight checks of medical and safety equipment. Ensure that equipment is operational.
- Maintain familiarity with and follow mandated Homeland Security guidelines.
- Plan meal and beverage service based on passengers' preferences and allotted budgets. Develop menus, identify caterers, and order food. Complete final food preparations during flights.
- Monitor onboard supplies prior to each flight. Replenish as needed.
- Collaborate with members of the flight crew and ground personnel to ensure passenger satisfaction before, during, and after flights. Act as liaison with partner vendors at destinations as needed.

Deere & Company • Moline, Illinois   2000–2004
Corporate Aviation Chief Flight Attendant
- Trained flight attendants on FAA regulations and the unique demands of corporate flight services.
- Maintained supplies for flight department and ensured appropriate onboard medical equipment.
- Personally staffed flights, stocked aircraft supplies, planned and prepared meals, and served passengers.

RELEVANT TRAINING

❖ Lifesaver First Aid [encompassing First Aid, CPR, and AED] – American Heart Association (recently renewed, valid through 10/19/13)

❖ Corporate Flight Attendant Training [initial and recurrent] – Flight Safety International (annual since 2004; recently renewed 04/30/11)

❖ Corporate Flight Attendant Training [initial and recurrent] – FACTS Training International (2000–2003)

❖ Aircrew Combative training – FACTS Training International (2003)

❖ Medical training – MedAire, Inc. (2000–2003)

❖ National Business Aviation Association conferences (2003 and 2005)

Combination. *Janet L. Beckstrom, Flint, Michigan*

The graphic image of the plane matches that in the cover letter. Distinctive bullets visually link the opening Profile with the closing section on Relevant Training and thus unify the resume. See Cover Letter 26 in Part 2.

35–12 Cottonboll Drive
Selma, AL 00000

Yasheika Ojimobi

Banquet Management Specialist

yasheika@partytime.com

Home: (000) 000-0000
Cell: (000) 000-1111

Areas of Expertise

- Hands-on management in any service area
- Experience with start-up establishments
- Daily opening and closing responsibilities
- Supplier selection/negotiation
- Purchasing of food and paper products

- Inventory maintenance
- Food quality and sanitation issues
- Service staffing and supervision
- Portion/waste/cost control
- Payroll and budgeting

Personal and Professional Qualifications

- Commitment to superior customer service
- Excellent attendance record throughout employment
- Resourceful in dealing with food or staff shortages

- Attentive to special dietary needs
- Maintain high morale and low turnover
- Time management/multitasking ability

Employment

Assistant Banquet Manager

ROYAL INN AND CONFERENCE CENTER, Selma, AL   2002 to Present

A 144 room hotel with professional conference facilities, which include 15 meeting rooms, a grand ballroom with capacity for up to 400, and private meeting and banquet space for up to 250; total banquet seating for 750.

- Report to both banquet manager and general hotel manager. Ensure that all details are attended to in the proper setup for weddings, banquets, meetings, and special events.
- Supervise and schedule staff to service 2–6 daily meetings and 2–3 ongoing banquets evenings and weekends.
- Coordinate bar and kitchen operations, expediting the smooth running of banquet and meeting functions.
- Make arrangements for audiovisual requirements for business meetings.
- Act as the manager on call for problems in other areas of the hotel in absence of regular managers. In this capacity, respond to guest dissatisfaction issues; also intervene in crisis situations that could affect safety and comfort of the guests.
- Take charge of catering functions for hotel employee social events twice a year (average attendance of 350), as well as food/snack service for administrative meetings and recognition luncheons.
- Received Hospitality Award in 2010 for exemplary work to produce happy customers.

Banquet Server

ACE TEMPORARY AGENCY, Selma, AL   2001–2002

- Involved in all phases of service at banquets and private parties contracted through this company.
- Was frequently requested at Royal Inn whenever additional staff was required, then hired permanently.

Counter Person and Back-of-House Worker

ANNIE'S DINER, Selma, AL   1999–2001

- Gained practical experience in every area of running a food-service business.

Education

INTERNATIONAL CORRESPONDENCE SCHOOLS, Scranton, PA
- Certificate course in Hotel Restaurant Management   2002

ROYAL INN CAREER DEVELOPMENT PROGRAM
- Introduction to Computers   2006
- Food Service Sanitation Certification   2005
- Core Skills in Food Service Management   2004

3

Combination. *Melanie Noonan, Woodland Park, New Jersey*

The two-column lists of bulleted items in the Areas of Expertise and Personal and Professional Qualifications sections are easily altered to tailor the resume to each targeted company. See Cover Letter 82 in Part 2.

KAREN L. DUNLOP

Expert at Promoting 100% Client Satisfaction & Loyalty

5555 K Place ♦ McKinney, TX 55555 ♦ (555) 555-5555 ♦ karendunlop@xxx.com
http://www.linkedin.com/xx/xx

CLIENT RELATIONS MANAGEMENT / KEY ACCOUNT MANAGEMENT EXPERT

A highly competitive and results-oriented professional combining polished interpersonal and rapport-building skills to significantly enhance growth, profits, and return on investment (ROI).
8 years of key account management experience in high-visibility, and multitask environments.
Extensive experience working vertically and horizontally with directors, VPs, and C-level executives.
Initiator, quick learner, problem solver, and inspired mentor.

Ability to boost profitability through effective client relations management.

CORE STRENGTHS

- Ability to Leverage Business Relationships
- Extremely Detail-Oriented
- Consultative & Solution Selling Strategies
- Team Development/Excellent Motivator
- Strong Organizational & Multitasking Skills

- Conflict Resolution & Team Dynamics
- Sound Research Skills/Highly Analytical
- Needs Assessment/Excellent Listening Skills
- Presentations/Overcoming Objections
- Streamlining Operations/Process Improvement

Computer Skills: Microsoft Office (Word, Excel, PowerPoint, Publisher), Siebel (CRM database)

VALUE OFFERED

✓ **Recognized for saving top-dollar client account** by getting to the root cause of client's problems and resolving them promptly.

✓ **Recouped $1M revenue and awarded Top Representative for consecutive quarters year after year** for exceeding goals by implementing solutions value-based selling strategies.

✓ **Generated $80K new revenue in first 6 months of employment** by developing new business relationships which resulted in high sales and organic client growth.

✓ **Exceeded accounting software sales goal by 164%.**

> "Karen has exactly what you want in a solid Account Manager. She has the ability to retain clients and revenue and financially expand on these relationships. While doing this, she has built cohesive relationships with her clients, coworkers, and managers."
>
> *Nicole Lampley, Senior Telesales Professional. Intuit*

Ability to integrate insightful business strategy, team synergy and leadership, and technical expertise in pursuit of top- and bottom-line revenue goals.

EMPLOYMENT HISTORY

Marketing Resources Solutions, Inc., Plano, TX ♦ Client Service Manager   02/2011–Present
A professional services agency specializing in finding top-quality candidates in the marketing industry.

✓ **Generated significant new business within 6 months** for staffing services segment of company.

page 1 of 2

4

Combination. *Leeza Byers, Marietta, Georgia*

Because of many visual elements, this two-page resume cannot be read and comprehended in a hurry. Horizontal lines, shaded lines and section headings, shaded text boxes, a variety of bullets,

KAREN L. DUNLOP   karendunlop@xxx.com   page 2 of 2

EMPLOYMENT HISTORY cont'd

VNR-1 Communications, Arlington, TX ◆ Media Sales New Business Development   06/2009–06/2010
A small broadcast public relations company with approximately $1.5 annual revenue.

- ✓ **Generated $80K new business in first 6 months and streamlined all branding messages for company** by creating consistency with all written materials and conducting website updates.

Intuit, Plano, TX ◆ Software Sales Account Manager   10/2004–03/2008
A leading provider of financial software with $3.5B annual revenue.

- ✓ **Increased sales 30%** as part of a new sales team that allowed deeper market penetration to cross-sell other services.
- ✓ **Exceeded upselling goals 30%** by building sustainable relationships with clients, which also resulted in **98% client retention ratings.**
- ✓ **Promoted within 5 months** from At-Risk Team to High-Value Account Management Team.

> **Ability to leverage key performance indicators to improve organizations' effectiveness while maintaining low operating costs.**

Compass Bank, Dallas, TX ◆ Real Estate Banker/Sales Administration   01/2003–02/2004
A leading U.S. banking franchise that ranks among top 20 largest commercial banks.

- ✓ **Increased profitability 25%** by constructing a relationship profitability application with IT design team.
- ✓ **Enhanced productivity considerably** by creating an efficient document-management system for sales team.

American Honda Finance, Irving, TX ◆ Repossession Agent Manager   09/2000–04/2002
A leading wholesale and retail financing company to Honda/Acura automobiles.

- ✓ **Saved company potential loss due to noninsured repossession vendors** by restructuring collections department processes, which resulted in department becoming compliant with company's insurance regulations. **Department able to pass internal audits** because of restructuring conducted.

EDUCATION / PROFESSIONAL DEVELOPMENT & AFFILIATIONS

BS, Marketing ◆ University of Dallas, Dallas, TX   05/2008

- ✓ Graduated magna cum laude.

Toastmasters International ◆ Charter Member, Texas Talkers Club, Plano, TX   10/2005–Present

- ✓ Earned Advanced Communicator Bronze award.
- ✓ Elected VP Membership in 2006 and VP Public Relations in 2007.

Sales Training: Miller-Heiman, How to Get into Your Customer's Head, SPIN (Situation Problem Implications Need—Payoff) Selling, Pro 3 Strategy

italic descriptions of workplaces, and boldfacing of significant information work together to ensure that a reader will pore over this resume before putting it down. See Cover Letter 29 in Part 2.

FINN JOHANSEN, CMA, ICD.D

000 Park City Blvd. • Easton, Oregon 00000
Phone: (000) 000-0000 • E-mail: fjohansen@xxx.com

CHIEF EXECUTIVE OFFICER / CHIEF FINANCIAL OFFICER
Consultant, Developer and Operator of Recreation and Event Sports Venues

"[Johansen] served as an invaluable asset, and our LEED Certified arena project simply would not have come together without his expertise."

Joe Smith, CEO, ABC, Inc.

"Not only were you great to work with, but the other companies and partners you introduced us to have also been a great asset to XYZ Global for ongoing projects."

John Doe, Executive GM, XYZ Global, Inc.

"Finn provided us with critical industry information and insight necessary to develop and roll out the instantly successful ABC Initiative."

Jane Jones, SVP Operations, Spike Sports Centers Worldwide

Seasoned CEO and CFO with a successful history of recognizing and capitalizing on business opportunities. Diverse industry exposure in the real estate development and product development sectors. Analyzes organizational infrastructures, sets realistic priorities, and designs programs that encourage sustainable growth while maintaining project quality and corporate integrity. Recognized for a professional demeanor, innovative approach, and unique willingness to persist despite adversity. A trusted business advisor and board member. Areas of expertise include

START-UPS, TURNAROUNDS, AND ACQUISITIONS • PUBLIC-PRIVATE PARTNERSHIPS

LEED CERTIFICATION PROGRAMS • MULTIUSE VENUES / SPORTS ARENAS • FINANCIAL ENGINEERING

PRODUCT & MARKET EXPANSION • SUSTAINABLE ENERGY PROGRAMS

CAREER HISTORY

ABC WORLDWIDE, INC., Heber City, Utah   2002–Present

CHAIRMAN

Am retained by public and private corporate entities challenged with planning, designing, and building large family-destination recreation and sports event venues. Commence work in the conception phase and spearhead all critical areas of development, including site analysis, forging community and industry partnerships, financial engineering, and designing complexes that incorporate environmental sustainability. Develop comprehensive business plans to include construction schedules, operations management, risk management, and life-cycle analyses. Projects are generally valued between $40M and $200M.

- Projects have included, but are not limited to, the University of Utah's Varsity Center; the City of Redding's LEED Silver Certified Regional Sports and Entertainment Center; the XYZ Corporation Center in New York; the Allen Sports Center in Dubai, UAE; the Luke Street Recreation Complex in Madrid, Spain.
- Retained by Joseph Martin Smithdale, a multidiscipline engineering firm with more than 2,000 professionals, as a specialist in developing sports-based projects.
- Optimized customer service with vertical management of programming, operations, food and beverage services, retail sales, advertising, and sponsorships.
- Over a two-year period, reengineered company financials and established a new banking relationship to protect $500M in assets under administration.

continued

5

Combination. *Donna Allen, Heber City, Utah*

Three significant testimonials appear in the most important location of a resume (here below the contact information and descriptive banner at the top of the first page). A reader of these

FINN JOHANSEN, CMA, ICD.D

WEICHSEL SPORTS MANAGEMENT, INC., Bridgeport, Connecticut   1991–2002

COFOUNDER AND MANAGING DIRECTOR

Developed, as an Owner or Consultant, and operated event arena and recreation projects involving public-private partnerships, as opposed to traditional municipally owned facilities. Hands-on involvement in all aspects of development, including defining business plans, raising seed capital, designing architecture, overseeing construction, and managing facilities. Broke barriers in returning superior customer satisfaction, sales, and earnings by fostering close relationships with stakeholders, such as municipalities, universities, and ski/figure skating organizations.

- Pioneered a user-driven functional design and detailed specifications for design-build construction, which led to projects being completed on time and on budget.
- Retained as Consultant for large, multiuse development projects in the United States, South America, and Europe.
- Developed Weichsel Sports Management, Inc. into a recognized leader in negotiating private-public partnerships. It was sold in 2002 (see partial project portfolio below).

EDUCATION • CERTIFICATIONS • AFFILIATIONS

M.M.H., Cornell University, Ithaca, New York • Degree in Economics

B.A., *with Honours* Royal Military College, Kingston, United Kingdom • Degree in Economics and Commerce

Le College Militaire Royale de Saint-Jean, Paris, France • Concentration in Civil Engineering

ICD.D, DIRECTOR ACCREDITATION — INSTITUTE OF CORPORATE DIRECTORS

CERTIFIED MANAGEMENT ACCOUNTANT (CMA) • *Member:* THE INSTITUTE OF CORPORATE DIRECTORS

PROJECT PORTFOLIO

Projects Designed, Developed, Owned, and Operated

- **The Ski Garden — Park City, Utah**. Developer and owner of a 220,000 sq. ft., six-arena complex.
- **ABC Sports and Entertainment Center — Los Angeles, California**. Owner and operator of a two-pad arena complex with feature rink with 32 suites, 500 club seats, and seating for 6,200.
- **Center for Excellence — Milford, Washington**. Developer of a two-pad, $22M arena with the feature rink having 32 suites, 500 club seats, and seating for 5,000.
- **The Varsity Village — Lancaster, Arizona**. Codeveloped The Varsity Village complex, comprising NHL-sized pads, an extreme sports park, outdoor skating path, ball diamonds, and wall climbing.

Design and Consulting Engagements

- **Trumbull Regional Sports and Entertainment Center — Trumbull, New York**. $52M LEED Silver Certified, 8,000-seat arena complex.
- **Peoa Multiuse Recreation Facility Implementation Plan — Peoa, Wyoming**. Multiuse recreation complex with two arenas, a combined lap pool/leisure pool, fitness center, senior citizen center, multiuse recreation space, and three small community centers.
- **Multipurpose Recreation Center — Zion, Utah**. Feasibility study for the development of a recreation complex comprising a competitive pool, leisure pool, multiuse gym, a fitness club, and a single-rink arena with expansion opportunities.
- **Arena Development Plan — Moab, Utah**. Development plan for the replacement of two existing arenas with a new complex housing three NHL rinks and a fourth training-sized rink.

Full portfolio available upon request

glowing testimonials will want to read further. At the end of this resume is a short Project Portfolio section, which should entice the reader to want to know still more about this individual. See Cover Letter 33 in Part 2.

BRUCE T. MELLON, MBA, CTP

5555 Chester Circle • Los Angeles, CA 00000
BruceTMellon@email.com • 555-555-5555 (C)

SENIOR FINANCE EXECUTIVE

Treasury & Finance Management ♦ Investment Management ♦ Strategic Decision Making

Municipal Finance Officers Association (MFOA) Distinguished Budget Award Winner for 5 Consecutive Years
California Department of Finance and Administration 2005–2006 Budget Award Winner
Laser Solutions Employee Star Award Winner for BPR Leading to 60% Cycle Time Reduction

Highly acclaimed, multilingual **Senior Executive** with a record of excellence in all areas of **finance and treasury management** supported by strength in **sales, marketing, public relations / communications, and business administration. Visionary change agent** who builds and leads motivated teams to drive organizational success within diverse industries and sectors; across domestic, international, and emerging markets; and in the face of challenging economic conditions. Fluent in English; well-versed in Spanish and French. **Online background verification report available for review.**

- Strategic Planning
- Cash Management
- Special Projects
- Entrepreneurship
- Public Relations
- Financial Markets

- Budget Planning & Forecasting
- Performance Management & Measurement
- Generally Accepted Accounting Principles (GAAP)
- Policy & Procedure Development
- Business Process Improvement / Reengineering
- Sales Training and Leadership

- Financial Analysis & Reporting
- Team Building & Motivation
- Revenue Cycle Management
- Cost Control & Reduction
- Variance & Trend Analyses
- Market Share Expansion

PROFESSIONAL EXPERIENCE

COUNTY OF SONOMA – Sonoma, CA   2004–Present
Government agency responsible for administration of public works, law enforcement, public safety, electric, gas, water, and sewer utilities, and related community services, with $60 million in annual revenues and 700 full-time employees.

Senior Budget Analyst (2005–Present)
Management Analyst (2004–2005)
Progressed rapidly to Senior Budget Analyst to manage performance measurement and accountability system across 60 government departments and programs. Conduct budget, revenue, and variance / trend monitoring and analysis of performance and operational results, and provide associated semiannual reports to government officials and the public. Develop annual capital improvement plan, as well as management discussion and analysis (MD&A) for comprehensive annual financial reports. Play key role in development of biennial community citizen survey, attainment of fire department's accreditation, and related functions.

- **Developed and implemented enterprise-wide performance management / measurement system** in 18 months.
- **Effectively secured $3.2 million in grants** despite severe budget constraints.
- **Developed $350 million, 10-year capital improvement plan** with public and municipal input, **$85 million in tax-backed financing, and identification of $40 million in operating impacts** across 15 major construction projects.
- **Provided strategic operational input** including RFP scope of work, vendor selection, and **subsequent $455K professional services agreement.** Played key role in vendor relationship management and development of final project report.

...continued...

6

Combination. *Karen Bartell, Massapequa Park, New York*

Above the Professional Experience section is a place where areas of expertise are listed in three columns. This arrangement is useful for altering the items, if necessary, to match each new

BRUCE T. MELLON, MBA, CTP • Page 2

LASER SOLUTIONS, INC. (Wholly owned subsidiary of Digital Imprints, Ltd.) – Athens, GA   2000–2003
Leading provider of document-management services and printing solutions with $2 billion in annual revenues and locations across the U.S., Canada, and Central America.

Business Analysis Manager

Provided direct oversight of a Market Analysis Manager and a Marketing Business Analyst. Prepared and presented sales, economic, market, competitive, and trends forecasts, analyses, and plans to senior-level executives, directors, sales professionals/trainees, shareholders, and industry analysts, synthesizing data to support improvement recommendations. Collected BI data from industry reports, field reports, and public information. Provided 2 executive teams with support and thought leadership to improve business processes. Represented company as Competitive Analyst at technology tradeshows and showcases.

- Conducted Customer Conversion Campaign analysis that **doubled high-impact, new account unit sales, increasing them by more than 9% in the first year and driving U.S. market share from 3.5% to 4.8%** within 18 months.

- Provided valuable recommendations leading to a **$2.3 million cumulative reduction in 2001 and 2002 corporate marketing budgets.**

- **Quantified market saturation leading to salesforce reduction,** streamlining operations and cutting costs.

- Coauthored a white paper **spearheading the creation of the $75 million Laser Healthcare Sales Organization.**

- Championed an innovative product mix propelling a hardware **sales volume increase of greater than 20%** over an 18-month timeframe.

- Spearheaded the conception and implementation of an **improved unit sales planning and analysis process.**

- **Played key role in development of a profit-building proprietary statistical performance report** measuring territorial sales production against BSC objectives.

● ● ●

*Prior role as **President / CEO** of Columbia Fine Art, Sonoma, CA*

EDUCATION AND CREDENTIALS

M.B.A. in Marketing Management & Management Information Systems (1999)
DeVry University, Keller Graduate School of Management – Columbus, OH
GPA 3.60

B.S. in Diplomacy & Foreign Affairs – Minor in Economics (1991)
Miami University – Oxford, OH

Professional Development	*Licensure*
Program Evaluation & Auditing ◆ Project Management	Certified Treasury Professional
Crystal Reporter, Levels 1 and 2	

Professional Affiliation
Association for Financial Professionals

Technical Proficiencies
Microsoft Office (advanced Excel), BRASS, Cayenta FMS, SAP BusinessObjects

targeted position. As a result of this resume and cover letter (see Cover Letter 108 in Part 2), this applicant secured a position with a 20% salary increase. He then asked the professional writer to prepare a resume and cover letter package for his wife!

CORY J. ERICKSON

5555 5th Avenue North • Little River, MN 55555 • 555-555-5555 • cjerickson@email.com

SENIOR HOTEL MANAGEMENT

Accomplished Certified Hotel Administrator offering more than 19 years of progressive experience in the hospitality industry. Adept at analyzing, planning, and executing strategic solutions. Collaborative team leader with a proven talent for motivating staff to achieve organizational objectives.

Key Strengths

Budget Administration	Financial / Risk Management	Personnel Management
Project Management	Procurement	Training and Team Building
Forecasting / Strategic Planning	Sales, Marketing, and Research	Process Improvement

PROFESSIONAL EXPERIENCE

SMITH MANAGEMENT GROUP, Little River, MN   June 2007–June 2012
Smith Management Group (SMP) provides hospitality development and management services for investment groups. Established in 1988, SMP has partnered to develop and operate more than 30 properties.

Director of Operations
Supervised 4 general managers and directed operations of 4 multiunit hotel properties, including 149-room property with annual revenues of $6.5 million. Collaborated with general managers, management team, and board of managers to oversee strategic planning, financial analysis, forecasting, and budgeting.

- Oversaw detailed logistics of preopening for 2 newly developed hotel properties (management recruitment, FFE procurement and placement, corporate and staff training, and site inspections).
- Conducted sales and marketing training, drawing upon personal experience of successful results.
- Boosted bottom line by conducting post-opening financial analysis, administering changes, and reducing labor costs. Slashed electrical expenses by implementing "green" energy savings programs.
- Identified weaknesses and created a new operations manual that outlined new procedures to enhance operations.

Key Accomplishments

- Oversaw properties that earned corporate awards (top 5% in U.S.) for high employee satisfaction, superior guest satisfaction, and quality control.
- Spearheaded efforts to save time and increase productivity; overcame employee resistance and transformed outdated accounting/payroll procedures into a highly efficient system.
- Implemented a new revenue management program to track and capture revenue opportunities; resulted in outperforming competitors in slow economic times (industry down 17%; SMP down only 5%).
- Succeeded in exceeding profits during sluggish economy by forging cost-containment initiatives (hiring and salary freezes, analysis of restaurant competitors, and menu and price adjustments).

SMITH HOTEL & SUITES, Little River, MN   April 2001–June 2007
Serving guests since 1965, Smith Hotel & Suites offers some of the finest lodging in the Little River area while consistently earning high ratings from guests.

General Manager
Managed a 68-room hotel property with annual revenues of approximately $1 million. Supervised 30 employees (recruiting, interviewing, hiring, training, evaluating performance, and firing). Formulated and maintained a $700,000 budget; analyzed profit and loss statements to ensure a 30 to 35% occupancy rate.

- Succeeded in driving revenue growth from $0 to $1 million through networking, pinpointing business leads, marketing efforts, and thinking creatively to retain and capture new customers.
- Awarded 4 consecutive corporate awards for outstanding service/cleanliness (2002–2005).

continued

Combination. *Connie Hauer, Sartell, Minnesota*

A pair of horizontal lines enclosing a section in a resume draws immediate attention to that section. It is usually the first part of the resume to be seen before any part of it is read. In this resume,

Cory J. Erickson   cjerickson@email.com   Page 2

Smith Hotel & Suites Continued . . .

- Accelerated profits in a highly competitive market by launching a "Stay, Shop, and Play" package, targeting specific markets during seasonal events (accounted for 10% of annual revenues).
- Selected by corporate management to oversee opening procedures and facilitate training at new properties; handpicked to provide interim management for unexpected vacancies.
- Minimized turnover and achieved optimal staff performance by maintaining open lines of communication and leading by example (working side-by-side with staff); achieved 30% staff retention after 4 years.
- Ignited sales by conducting quarterly sales blitzes to corporations.

ANDERSON HOTELS, Little River, MN   December 1993–April 2001
Founded in 1980, Anderson Hotels is a family-owned facility that prides itself on delivering quality accommodations and personalized service.

Front Office Manager (May 1995–April 2001)
Promoted to manage front-office duties for 103-room property, ensuring compliance with corporate standards, policies, and procedures. Supervised up to 20 employees, including hiring, scheduling, and evaluating performance.

- Practiced yield management strategies to ensure optimal profits. Assessed cash-flow shortfalls and instituted strategies to contain costs and drive profits:
  - ➢ Saved approximately $750/week by reducing selected expenses/purchases.
  - ➢ Minimized costs by negotiating new contracts with current vendors, as well as new vendors.
- Introduced a concept for improved service standards, which was approved and adopted by owners.
- Managed all accounts receivables; generated and submitted financial reports to corporate office.

Food and Beverage Supervisor (December 1993–May 1995)
Oversaw the management and execution of banquets and catering events. Supervised 8 employees, including hiring, scheduling, conducting performance reviews, and firing.

- Developed and implemented a training program that motivated employees to optimum performance by tracking goals and establishing incentives to ignite sales.
- Analyzed weekly food and beverage budget and tracked profit and loss; assessed weekly forecasts of labor and revenue to evaluate staffing needs.
- Implemented a customized computer program to streamline procedures and improve tracking of sales.
- Recipient of 2 Employee of the Month awards for exhibiting excellent performance and attitude.

EDUCATION & CREDENTIALS

LITTLE RIVER STATE UNIVERSITY, Little River, MN
   Bachelor of Science, Major: **Management,** Minor: **Travel and Tourism**   1994

CERTIFICATIONS: **Certified Hotel Administrator**   2002

SEMINARS AND TRAINING

Building Business Features • Yield Management Training • Coaching and Team-Building Skills
Sexual Harassment Training • Diversity Seminar • Human Resources Training • General Manager Certificate

PROFESSIONAL AFFILIATIONS

American Hotel and Motel Association • State Innkeeper's Association • Little River Chamber of Commerce
Little River Convention and Visitor's Bureau Board of Directors, Chair of Travel and Tourism Committee

the pair of lines calls attention to the applicant's key strengths listed in three columns. Note in the Professional Experience section the careful use of tabs to make workplaces, positions, key accomplishments, and bulleted items readily seen at a glance. See Cover Letter 134 in Part 2.

María Santaquín

000 Abbot Road ■ Roma, CA 55555 ■ msantaquin@email.com ■ (555) 555-5555

HUMAN RESOURCES DIRECTOR

Human resources leader who improves organizational initiatives through development of successful corporate policies. Direct multifunction, multisite teams to promote organizational mission. Support comprehensive, high-performance human resources roles that promote business excellence. Lead internal policy and procedure development, according to corporate culture. Cut costs on outsourcing with savvy contract negotiations. Streamline processes, eliminating expensive turnover among staff and reducing exposure to litigation. Fully bilingual (speaking, reading, writing) in English and Spanish.

Professional Skill Sets

Human Resources Generalist ■ Recruitment and Retention ■ Policy Development and Implementation
Customer Needs Assessment ■ Project Planning and Project Management ■ Audits ■ Onboarding
Benefits Management ■ Budget Implementation ■ Regulatory Compliance

PROFESSIONAL EXPERIENCE

Human Resources Director / Recruiter   **2007–Present**
Temporary Service Experts, San Diego, CA

Improved corporate business as leader in executive and management-level recruiting for top clients. Simultaneously managed issues concerning candidate placement, ensuring that practice reflected written policies and critical regulations. Monitored business operations of client companies to ensure safe placement of sourced candidates. Revised policies affecting internal operations and candidate placement.

Human Resources Director

- Decreased turnover 25% for candidates placed 90 days temp-to-hire. Instituted skills testing and personality evaluations that ensured job candidates' characteristics aligned with job title sought plus client company requirements and culture.

- Streamlined accounting processes by selecting Akken time clock software, which integrated with QuickBooks software. Eliminated 60 man-hours of work per week.

- Implemented drug screening and background checking for each job search candidate. Verified qualifications of each candidate and ensured that each was trained on company policies.

- Based on background and professional experience in accounting, assisted client companies with tax issues, including helping one select a qualified CPA firm.

- Selected consultant to create affirmative action plan. Ensured that organization complied with all relevant regulations at federal and state levels.

Recruiter

- Placed 20 executive and management candidates per year.

- Filled COO position for pool chemical company, sourcing candidates through a variety of Internet strategies for this extremely particular client, which needed a cost accounting expert. Selected 6 candidates for client interviews; client selected top candidate inside 4 weeks.

...Continued...

Combination. *Amy L. Adler, Salt Lake City Utah*

Distinctive in this resume are bold square bullets that appear on both pages and therefore link them visually. Centered headings enable the reader to look down the center of each page and

María Santaquín msantaquin@email.com **Page 2**

...Continued...

- Placed Information Technology candidate who saved client's company $41K+ by replacing the phone system with advanced technology. Sourced candidate online, interviewing him multiple times in person before sending him to the client.

- Visited client sites for safety checks to ensure each company's compliance with OSHA and other applicable regulations.

Manager, Corporate Accounting and Human Resources | Senior Accountant 2002–2007
LeadPlayer Consultants, San Diego, CA

Led 3 human resources divisional leaders and administrative staff to standardize practices across company. Managed all aspects of human resources leadership, including benefits, unemployment, hiring practices, policy development, and vendor contract negotiations.

- Consolidated human resources functions into corporate office, saving $137K annually.

- Reduced payroll costs 48% by decreasing processing time and creating biweekly payroll schedule.

- Managed annual open enrollment for medical, dental, vision, short-term disability, and life insurance cafeteria plans for 250 enrollees and their families. Ensured that plans and enrollments were in compliance with applicable regulations. Coached employees about their options to assist them in making good decisions about their insurance plans.

- Revised intervention and training processes to prevent losses due to unemployment claims. Worked with expert consultant to manage unemployment hearings and train managers to consistently follow corporate policy. During tenure, company lost only 1 unemployment case.

- Reduced experience modification (X-MOD) levels to 120 over 2 years and reduced workers' compensation losses by 69% and claims by 57%.

- Developed and led safety committee, which included the CFO, corporate controller, plant managers, and plant operations leadership. Instituted safety incentive programs; determined most expensive and most common causes of incidents and addressed those directly with training and new, effective company policies.

- Updated 401(k) plan document, thus improving data collection 50% for discrimination testing.

- Developed policies and procedures with legal counsel to ensure that all were in compliance. Rewrote company handbook in concert with owners and attorneys. Company experienced zero lawsuits during tenure.

- Performed audits on employee files to ensure 100% accuracy and compliance.

- Streamlined expenses related to contracts with temporary staffing agencies.

Prior management experience: Developed significant knowledge of accounting and human resources practices as Staff Accountant (Regular Accounting, San Diego, CA) and Field Auditor Assistant (Tax Action, San Diego, CA) as well as in prior accounting roles.

PROFESSIONAL DEVELOPMENT

Bachelor of Science, Business Administration, Accounting, University of Arizona, Tucson, AZ.

comprehend quickly the resume's overall design. In the Professional Experience section, bullets point to impressive lists of achievements in different positions. See Cover Letter 144 in Part 2.

CARRIE HINKSON

(555) 555-5555 ■ carriehinkson@xxx.com ■ http://www.linkedin.com/xxx/xxxxx

GLOBAL TALENT MANAGEMENT & LEADERSHIP DIRECTOR
SENIOR HUMAN RESOURCES CONSULTANT

Strategy Architect, Change Agent, and HR Business Partner who blends business acumen with distinctive understanding of people and HR systems.

Senior Talent Management Expert with 15+ years of versatile experience leading established domestic and international organizations to highly profitable results.

- Conceptualize, plan, assess, and execute major global talent management projects including recruitment, leadership development, and performance management areas.

- Employ innovative strategies to design user-friendly talent processes, tools, and materials for enhancement of organizational culture collaboration, engagement, and alignment.

- Work vertically and horizontally with directors, VPs, C-level executives, employees across all levels, internal stakeholders, boards of directors, and business partners.

DEMONSTRATED HR VALUE

- Global Talent Management
- Instructional Design
- Organizational Development
- Comprehensive Needs Assessments
- Process Improvement, Six Sigma Green Belt Certified
- Employee Engagement & Relations
- Performance Management

CAREER HIGHLIGHTS

STRATEGY & LEADERSHIP / ORGANIZATIONAL DEVELOPMENT & LEARNING

- **Attained 90% process consistency on key HR processes globally** as the team lead of the US employee relations operations, while driving consistency throughout regional HR teams.
- **Reduced functional readiness time 50% for new managers** by designing and implementing a "New Manager Boot Camp" in the manufacturing sector. Program later rolled out in Networks division.
- **Slashed HR costs 30% and increased efficiency / effectiveness** by creating a new HR service delivery model.
- **Developed skills certification process for manufacturing and technical personnel** and was submitted as a "Best-in-Class Program" by semiconductor company consortium.
- **Led senior leadership team through a thorough review of** global organizational talent, identification of next-generation leaders, and succession planning, including identification of talent gaps, opportunities for development of top talent, and creation of performance improvement plans for low performers.
- **Managed global rotational program for high-potential talent,** including identifying high-potential talent for rotational positions and projects in other organizations; creating position descriptions to fulfill clear development objectives; and establishing robust development plans, goals, and measures.

Page 1 of 2

9

Combination. *Leeza Byers, Marietta, Georgia*

The shaded text box is a plus to ensure that "demonstrated" HR values are seen upfront. The hot zone in a resume—the area from approximately two inches from the top of the first page

CARRIE HINKSON   carriehinkson@xxx.com   Page 2 of 2

PROCESS IMPROVEMENT

- **Recouped more than $600K in funds expended on poor-quality systems** by eliminating process variation, improving data quality, and increasing automation of global HR case management tool.
- **Exceeded process maturity goal 40%** for all critical employee relations processes.
- **Achieved 30% net process quality improvements** by implementing a comprehensive change management plan.
- **Designed and implemented standardized project management methodology for global employee relations** platform to advance critical actions aligned with HR strategies.
- **Served on Performance Management (PM) process steering committee** to direct maintenance, improvement, and deployment of a robust PM process.

CULTURE CHANGE & CHANGE MANAGEMENT

- **Achieved ~10% consistent improvement annually** for annual employee engagement scores because of deployment of "Appreciative Inquiry Methods" used to prioritize employee engagement across various organizations.
- **Designed and executed a comprehensive change management plan and supported cultural infrastructure** to sustain autonomous maintenance and continual improvement.
- **Proposed change for HR transformation plan,** including environmental scan, stakeholder analysis, communication and measurement plan for success, and interventions designed to facilitate its company-wide adoption.

EMPLOYMENT HISTORY

VERIZON WIRELESS, Schaumburg, IL   1990–Present
A global corporation rich in communications and electronics industry innovation, with more than 193K employees worldwide and an annual revenue of more than $40B.

Fast-track promotion through a series of increasingly responsible HR management positions. Promoted rapidly based on consistent success in strategic organizational and leadership development, business process / performance improvement, and team / project leadership in global markets. Positions include:

Leadership Development Consultant	2010–Present
Senior HR Consultant and Program Manager	2008–2010
Employee Relations Operations Manager	2005–2008
Organizational Development Consultant	2003–2005
HR Generalist	2001–2003
Instructional Designer	1999–2001

EARLY PROFESSIONAL CAREER

SEMICONDUCTOR SECTOR, Austin, TX
Total Productive Maintenance Program Manager and Training Specialist

EDUCATION AND CERTIFICATIONS

Six Sigma Green Belt Certification, Verizon Wireless, Schaumburg, IL	2009
M.Ed., Curriculum and Instruction, University of Dallas, Dallas, TX	2002
B.A., English, University of Dallas, Dallas, TX	
Total Productive Management Instructor's Certification, Japan Institute of Plant Maintenance	

down to five inches—is not the start of the race for attention but the finish line. If the reader's interest is not captured here, then a hurried reader may turn away and not even look at the rest of the resume. See Cover Letter 151 in Part 2.

MICHAEL PETERMAN

555 WILTON COURT • NEW YORK, NY 00000
H: 555.555.5555 • C: 555.555.5500
peterman.mike@xmail.net

EXECUTIVE-LEVEL BUSINESS & TECHNOLOGY LEADER

Proven Track Record of Leading Information Technology Development and Operations
Recognized for Leadership of Advanced Technology with 20+ Years of Service Excellence

Accomplished and results-oriented senior executive with expert proficiency in broadband cable IT, wireless services, and business management. Technical talent and analytical expertise in overseeing technology improvement initiatives and aligning information services with business goals. Experience with leading enterprise-wide implementations that streamline operations, optimize productivity, and introduce system efficiencies in a cost-effective manner. Regarded for the ability to drive processes, develop and motivate high-performing teams, and work well under pressure to manage and meet multiple project deadlines on schedule and under budget.

Core Competencies

- ✓ Program & Project Management
- ✓ IT Policy & Procedure Development
- ✓ Strategic Planning & Tactical Execution
- ✓ Business Analysis & Budget Management
- ✓ Enterprise Applications & Network Support
- ✓ High-Profile Management Presentations
- ✓ Operational & Business Support Systems
- ✓ Vendor/Partner Relationships & Negotiations
- ✓ Software Development/Technology Deployment
- ✓ Management Collaboration & Leadership Skills

CAREER HIGHLIGHTS

CHALLENGE: Reorganized 5 major IT operating divisions, including IT integration, network infrastructure, software development, and billing system conversion. Gained buy-in from senior management, developed strategy, and consolidated into a central technology region after merger with ABC Cable.
- **Saved $5.8 million in operating costs; completed project on time and 20% below budget.**

CHALLENGE: Built and led technical team in NYC for a pilot deployment of Wi-Fi for customers as a value-added service. Planned and coordinated hardware installation and network integration with cable network.
- **Completed Phase I deployment and prepared for go-live support of all 1.3 million customers.**

CHALLENGE: Planned and implemented the cable industry's first computerized and automated Wireless Fleet and Work Force Management System. Replaced all handheld telephone devices and 1,400 laptops for the entire region of 2,000 technicians, contractors, and commercial technicians in a 12-week period.
- **Increased productivity, reduced call volume, and produced annual cost savings of $5 million.**

PROFESSIONAL EXPERIENCE

NATIONAL CABLE CORP. (formerly REGIONAL CABLE CO.), New York, NY   1992–Present
Regional Vice President, Information Technology (2009–Present)

Lead the overall strategic and tactical direction of the Regional Information and Technology department for the largest cable operator in the United States. Oversee all day-to-day operational matters related to IT, network operations, and project management. Develop and implement both short- and long-term plans; and policies and procedures. Maintain a $150+ million capital and operating budget; and manage a professional staff of 140 IT employees and consultants.

- **Increased productivity 15% by implementation of green initiative;** provided HP thin clients to all customer contact personnel, which enabled more effective call handling, leading to improved customer service levels.
- **Saved the company about $3.7 million,** projected over 3 years, in IT operating costs with fewer personnel.
- **Produced additional cost savings of more than $1 million** in electricity costs, while reducing greenhouse gas emissions, through removal of 1,500+ desk CPUs, saving on both materials and power consumption.
- **Recognized by colleagues/peers as a valued leader,** received 4.9 out of 5.0 on 360-degree feedback survey.

10

Combination. *Alexander Kofman, San Bruno, California*

The applicant's white-on-black name in a box in the contact information is the distinctive feature of this resume. Stylish too is the use of shading in the text box below the contact information

MICHAEL PETERMAN, Page Two
H: 555.555.5555 • C: 555.555.5500 • peterman.mike@xmail.net

PROFESSIONAL EXPERIENCE – CONTINUED

Senior Vice President, Information Technology (2001–2009)
- **Enhanced systems and improved availability, capacity, and continuity** through design, development, and support of business continuity/disaster recovery solutions.
- **Built team to achieve PCI and Sarbanes-Oxley (SOX) compliance; passed all internal and external audits;** set framework standards and benchmarks which served as examples for all regions in the country.
- **Reduced systems downtime 60%** by providing IT efficiencies across all functional areas of the company.

Vice President, Information Technology (1998–2001)
- **Implemented a Regional Network Operations Center,** reducing mean-time-to-resolution of outages by about 25%, saving the company millions of dollars in operating costs, and dramatically improving customer service.
- **Instituted and refined IT governance model** by convening an executive advisory committee to provide input into decision-making process to ensure technology resources were best utilized to deliver services/products.
- **Virtually eliminated system outages** by implementing a converged regional, high-capacity, wide area network; supported 5,000+ employees on a 24x7 operation, delivering complex voice/data applications.
- **Played instrumental role in the launch and operational support for the Digital TV offering in NYC.**

Director, Information Technology (1992–1998)
- **Designed and implemented installation and integration of a regional Automatic Call Distributor (ACD);** supported 1,500 customer service representatives and 5 million inbound/outbound calls per month.

REGIONAL CABLE CO. (acquired by NATIONAL CABLE CORP.), New York, NY (1989–1992)
Director, Management Information Systems Department

Oversaw department with 55 direct reports. Collaborated with VP of Customer Service, VP of Operations, and VP of Sales and Marketing to devise a total customer support operation.

- **Developed a mainframe database system** that allowed company to sell and support the operation of the first cable system in NYC; grew to 300,000 customers with estimated revenues of about $100 million.
- **Saved more than $80,000 in manual billing costs** by establishing a review committee to create a Request For Proposal (RFP) and selection process for an automated cable billing system.
- **Produced additional 30% savings** in operations over a 5-year period because of contract renewal.

EDUCATION & CREDENTIALS

NEW YORK STATE UNIVERSITY – New York, NY
Master of Science, Management and Information Systems, 2010
Bachelor of Science, Information Systems Management, 2006 (graduated with honors)

ITIL Security Management, 2005
TechKnowledge Training
Certificate in Advanced Internet Technologies, 2000
Internet and Intranet Websites – New York University

AFFILIATIONS & AWARDS

50 Most Influential Hispanic Executives, 2010
Hispanic Information Technology Council (HITEC)
MIT Industry Liaison Program
Society of Information Management
Advisory Council, Accenture Diversity

and with the section headings. With this shading and parallel lines above and below the headings, the overall design of the resume can be seen at a glance. Note the strong use of Challenges in the Career Highlights section. See Cover Letter 171 in Part 2.

SEAN HARRIS

5555 Parksville Avenue, Leesburg, VA 55555 ● (555) 555-5555 ● seanharris@xxxx.com

Qualified for positions as

PATIENT ADVOCATE / DIAGNOSTIC IMAGING SUPPORT SERVICES

*High-performance, results-focused professional with extensive experience in
delivering excellent customer service and patient-centered care.*

Highly reliable self-starter with 5+ years of service experience, recognized for expertise in

✓ Solving problems
✓ Optimizing operations and handling details
✓ Creating synergy among diverse teams
✓ Fulfilling corporate vision through leadership

✓ Maintaining a patient-centric focus
✓ Being nonjudgmental / unbiased
✓ Demonstrating sensitivity and compassion
✓ Communicating orally and in writing

RELATED PROFESSIONAL EXPERIENCE

Inova Loudoun Hospital, Leesburg, VA   08/2008–Present
*A not-for-profit health system rated AA+ by Standard and Poor's Rating Agency, one of the highest
ratings in the healthcare service industry. Managing an operating income of $208M with 15K
employees who serve 700K outpatients with 1,700 licensed hospital beds.*

Patient Advocate – Facilitate patient flow through the radiology department, registration process,
and assist radiology personnel as needed. Ensure fluid and accurate lines of communication between
patients/visitors and staff, while playing an integral role in advocating for the patient according to
the "Patient's Bill of Rights."

Offer value through proactive service and meticulous planning...

- Decreased patients' average wait times 10%–20% by enhancing communication between
  registration and radiology departments.
- Distinguished record in achieving organizational/departmental goals and objectives while
  maintaining a long-term vision of continual improvement.
- Strong interpersonal and communication skills with proficiency to promote comfort in all
  patients.
- Comprehensive insight into and full compliance with Code of Healthcare Practice and
  Privacy Act and sound knowledge of healthcare policies and procedures.

*Employee of the Month award based on high number of compliments received
throughout entire radiology department*

OTHER WORK HISTORY

Potbelly Sandwich Works, Fairfax, VA   04/2006–07/2008
*A fast casual restaurant deemed as one of America's 500 fastest-growing private companies with 200
stores nationwide.*

Assistant Manager – promoted from management trainee program after 6 weeks. Led a team of
25–40 associates to accomplish $25K monthly revenue goal. Trained all new hires.

Integrate insightful business strategy and team leadership ...

- Ranked in top 5 restaurants for highest sales in DC area by conducting extensive outdoor
  marketing (blitzing) to neighboring businesses.
- Maintained sales and labor projections in accordance to budget, resulting in cost savings.
- Set par levels for inventory to ensure minimum product waste, while maintaining high
  quality.

Texas Steakhouse & Saloon, Harrisonburg, VA	**Line Cook**	04/2002–04/2006
Rockingham County Recreation, Harrisonburg, VA	**Referee**	04/2000–04/2004

EDUCATION

Blue Ridge Community College, Weyers Cave, VA   2006
- **Associate of Applied Science in Business Management**

Computer Skills: MS Office (Word, Excel, PowerPoint); Medical Software: Medisoft

Combination. *Leeza Byers, Marietta, Georgia*

In this resume, shading makes the section headings readily visible. Notice the use of center-alignment, boldfacing, and italic to make certain information conspicuous. See Cover Letter 112 in Part 2.

─List of Contributors

The following professional writers contributed the cover letters and resumes in this book. To include here the names of these writers and information about their business is to acknowledge with appreciation their voluntary submissions and their insights about the cover letters and resumes. Cover letter and resume numbers after a writer's contact information are the numbers of the writer's cover letters and resumes included in the Gallery, not page numbers.

Australia

Annemarie Cross, Advanced Employment Concepts
Phone: +61 3 9708 6930
E-mail: success@aresumewriter.net
Website: www.aresumewriter.net
Member: CDI, PARW/CC
Certifications: CEIP, CARW, CPRW, CRW, CCM, CECC, CERW, CWPP
Cover letters: 70, 150

Gayle M. Howard, Top Margin
Phone: +61 3 9020 5601
Toll-free: 1300 726 669
E-mail: getinterviews@topmargin.com
Website: www.topmargin.com
Member: ASA, CDI, PARW/CC
Certifications: MRW, CERW, CRPBS, JLRC, CARW, MCD, CCM, MRWLAA, MCPLAA, CRS-IT, CWPP
Cover letters: 127, 257

Jennifer Rushton, Keraijen
Phone: +61 2 9994 8050
E-mail: info@keraijen.com.au
Website: www.keraijen.com.au
Member: AORCP, CDI
Certifications: CERW, CARW, CEIC, CWPP
Cover letters: 79, 192, 273

Canada

Howard Earle Halpern, MA; Résu-Card
Phone: (416) 410-7247
E-mail: halpern@bell.net
Website: www.NoBlock.com
Member: PARW/CC
Certification: CPRW
Cover letters: 19, 77, 164, 302

Ross Macpherson, MA; Career Quest
Phone: (905) 438-8548
Toll-free: (877) 426-8548
E-mail: ross@yourcareerquest.com
Website: www.yourcareerquest.com
Member: PARW/CC
Certifications: CPRW, CEIP, CJST, Personal Branding Strategist
Cover letters: 3, 17, 158, 190, 202, 235, 266, 300, 308

Tanya Sinclair, Principal Consultant
TNT Human Resources Management
Phone: (416) 887-5819
E-mail: Info@tntresumewriter.com
Website: www.tntresumewriter.com
Member: CDI, CPC
Certifications: MCRS, CHRP
Cover letters: 32, 87, 145, 216

China

Peter Hill, P.H.I Consulting
Phone: +86 137.7448.0436
(For full listing, see Hawaii, United States)

United Kingdom

Sandra Ingemansen, President; Résumé Strategies
E-mail: sandra@resume-strategies.com
Website: www.resume-strategies.com
Member: CDI, NRWA, PARW/CC
Certification: CPRW
Cover letters: 125, 188, 207, 263

United States

Alabama

Don Orlando, MBA; The McLean Group
Phone: (334) 264-2020
E-mail: yourcareercoach@aol.com
Member: CDI, PARW/CC, Phoenix Career Group
Certifications: CPRW, JCTC, CCM, CCMC
Cover letters: 9, 27, 30, 31, 35, 36, 38, 74, 88, 121, 137,
   146, 167, 199, 212, 224, 253, 267, 268, 274

Alexia Scott, Alexia's Desktop
Phone: (334) 201-0045
E-mail: resumes@alexiasdesktop.com
Member: NRWA, PARW/CC
Certification: CPRW
Cover letters: 6, 213

Arkansas

Beverley Drake
Phone: (501) 922-0893
E-mail: bdcprw@aol.com
Member: PARW/CC
Certifications: CPRW, CEIP, JCTC,
Cover letters: 83, 110, 136, 160, 264, 299, 311

California

*Kelly Donovan, Kelly Donovan Professional Resume
   Writing*
Phone: (909) 235-6383
E-mail: admin@kellydonovan.com
Website: www.kellydonovan.com
Member: NRWA, PARW/CC
Certification: CPRW
Cover letter: 126

Alexander Kofman, Resume Pros 4 Less
Phone: (650) 557-1006
E-mail: resume_pros@yahoo.com
Website: www.resumepros4less.com
Member: CDI
Certification: CFRW
Cover letter: 171
Resume: 10

Myriam-Rose Kohn, JEDA Enterprises
Phone: (661) 253-0801
Toll-free: (800) 600-JEDA
E-mail: myriam-rose@jedaenterprises.com
Website: www.jedaenterprises.com
Member: CDI, NRWA, PARW/CC
Certifications: CPRW, CEIP, JCTC, CCM, CCMC, CPBS
Cover letters: 49, 99, 195, 269

Jared Redick, The Resume Studio
Phone: (415) 846-6640
E-mail: jredick@theresumestudio.com
Website: www.theresumestudio.com
Member: CDI, NARW
Cover letters: 53, 282

Vivian VanLier, Advantage Resume & Career Services
Phone: (818) 994-6655
E-mail: vivianvanlier@aol.com
Website: www.careercoach4u.com
Member: CDI
Certifications: CPRW, JCTC, CEIP, CCMC, CPRC, CPBS
Cover letters: 143, 234

Colorado

Michele Angello, Corbel Communications
Phone: (303) 537-3592
Toll-free: (866) 5CORBEL
E-mail: corbelcomm1@aol.com
Website: www.corbelonline.com
Certification: CPRW
Cover letters: 13, 176, 204, 310

Roberta F. Gamza, Career Ink
Phone: (303) 955-3065
E-mail: roberta@careerink.com
Website: www.careerink.com
Member: NRWA
Certifications: CEIP, JCTC, CJST
Cover letters: 5, 135, 156

Melanie Lenci, MAS; Résumé Relief
Phone: (720) 379-6878
Cell: (303) 241-6103
E-mail: ml@resumereliefonline.com
Website: www.resumereliefonline.com
Member: CDI, NRWA, PARW/CC
Certifications: CPRW, CEIP
Cover letters: 78, 250

Ruth Pankratz, MBA; Gabby Communications, LLC
Phone: (970) 310-4153
E-mail: Ruth@GabbyCommunications.com
Website: www.gabbycommunications.com
Member: NRWA, NCHRA (Northern Colorado Human
  Resources Association)
Member: NRWA, PARW/CC
Certifications: NCRW, NCC
Cover letter: 122

Marie Zimenoff, EdM, Counseling and Career Development
  A Strategic Advantage
Phone: (970) 420-8413
Toll-free: (800) 517-2080
E-mail: marie@strategicadvantage.com
Website: www.astrategicadvantage.com
Member: CDI, NRWA
Certifications: NCRW, NCC
Cover letters: 63, 215

Connecticut

Louise Garver, MA; Career Directions, LLC
Phone: (860) 623-9476
E-mail: Louise@careerdirectionsllc.com
Website: www.careerdirectionsllc.com
Member: ACA, ACPI, CPADN, NCDA, CDI, NRWA,
  PARW/CC
Certifications: JCTC, CMP, CPRW, MCDP, CEIP, CPBS,
  CJSS, CCMC, COIS, Certified Career Coach
Cover letters: 20, 47, 57, 92, 98, 101, 102, 133, 159, 194,
  209, 233, 258, 290, 294, 313

Jan Melnik, MA; Absolute Advantage
Phone: (860) 349-0256
E-mail: CompSPJan@aol.com
Website: www.janmelnik.com
Member: NRWA, PARW/CC
Certifications: MRW, CCM, CPRW
Cover letters: 75, 218, 254

Florida

Melanie Denny, MBA; Resume Evolution
Phone: (313) 575-1519
E-mail: melanie@resume-evolution.com
Website: www.resume-evolution.com
Member: PARW/CC
Certification: CPRW
Cover letters: 105, 109, 292

Gail Frank, MA
Frankly Speaking: Resumes That Work!
Phone: (813) 926-1353
E-mail: gailfrank01@tampabay.rr.com
Website: www.callfranklyspeaking.com
Member: NRWA
Certifications: NCRW, CPRW, JCTC, CEIP
Cover letters: 68, 103, 104, 184, 205, 238

Cindy Kraft, Executive Essentials
Phone: (813) 655-0658
E-mail: Cindy@CFO-Coach.com
Website: www.cfo-coach.com
Member: CDI
Certifications: CPBS, COIS, CCMC, CCM, JCTC, CPRW
Cover letters: 1, 73, 96, 256

Debra O'Reilly, A First Impression Resume Service
Phone: (813) 651-0408
E-mail: debra@resumewriter.com
Website: www.resumewriter.com
Member: CDI, NRWA, PARW/CC
Certifications: CPRW, JCTC, CEIP, CFRWC
Cover letter: 271

Haley Richardson, MA; Résumés Done Right
E-mail: resumesdoneright@rocketmail.com
Website: www.resumesdoneright.com
Member: PARW/CC
Certifications: CPRW, JCTC
Cover letters: 139, 184, 219, 223, 305

Edward Turilli, MA; AccuWriter Resume Service
Phone: (239) 298-9514
E-mail: accuwriter@comcast.net
Website: www.resumes4-u.com
Member: PARW/CC, CEW.com
Certifications: CPRW, CRW
Cover letters: 59, 66, 84, 118, 119, 240, 289

Georgia

Leeza Byers; Byers Workforce Solutions, Inc.
Phone: (888) 321-4384
Member: CDI, NRWA, PARW/CC
Certifications: CPRW, GCDF
Cover letters: 29, 112, 151
Resumes: 4, 9, 11

Lea J. Clark, Lea Clark & Associates
Phone: (478) 781-4107
Member: CDI
Certification: CRW
Cover letters: 44, 51, 279

Hawaii

Peter Hill, P H I Consulting
Phone: (808) 384-9461
E-mail: pjhill@phi-yourcareer.com
Website: www.phi.yourcareer.com
Member: CDI, PARW/CC
Certifications: CPRW, CERW
Cover letter: 128

Denette D. Jones, Jones Career Specialties
Phone: (808) 968-7601
E-mail: dj@jonescareerspecialties.com
Website: www.jonescareerspecialties.com
Cover letters: 80, 210, 228

Illinois

Christine L. Dennison, Dennison Career Services
Phone: (847) 405-9775
E-mail: chris@thejobsearchcoach.com
Website: www.thejobsearchcoach.com
Member: PARW/CC, Greater Lincolnshire Chamber of
  Commerce
Certification: CPC
Cover letter: 229

Sandra Ingemansen, President; Résumé Strategies
Phone: (312) 212-3761
(For full listing, see United Kingdom)

Eva Locke
Lake County Health Dept./Workforce Development
Phone: (847) 377-3456
Website: www.lakecountyil.gov/workforcedevelopment
Member: CDI
Cover letters: 111, 239

Steven Provenzano
President, ECS: Executive Career Services & DTP, Inc.
Phone: (630) 289-6222
E-mail: Careers@Execareers.com
Website: www.Execareers.com
Member: PARW/CC, BBB
Certifications: CPRW, CEIP
Cover letters: 12, 154

Michelle P. Swanson, Resume Results
Phone: (618) 307-5589
E-mail: michelle@ResumeResultsOnline.com
Website: www.ResumeResultsOnline.com
Member: NRWA, PARW/CC
Certification: CPRW
Cover letters: 181, 214

Charlotte Weeks; Weeks Career Services, Inc.
Phone: (773) 578-2714
E-mail: charlotte@weekscareerservices.com
Website: www.weekscareerservices.com
Member: CDI, NRWA, PARW/CC
Certifications: NCRW, CCMC, CPRW
Cover letters: 24, 90, 261

Iowa

Billie Sucher, MS
Billie Sucher Career Transition Services
Phone: (515) 276-0061
E-mail: billie@billiesucher.com
Website: www.billiesucher.com
Member: CDI, SHRM
Certifications: CCM, CTMS, CTSB, JCTC
Cover letter: 272

Kansas

James Walker
Phone: (785) 239-2278
E-mail: jwalker8199@yahoo.com
Member: PARW/CC
Cover letters: 221, 225, 304

Kentucky

Sharon Williams, MEd; JobRockit
Phone: (419) 348-2627
E-mail: Sharon@jobrockit.com
Website: www.jobrockit.com
Member: CDI
Certification: CPRW
Cover letter: 50

Maryland

Shauna C. Bryce, JD; Bryce Legal Career Counsel
Phone: (443) 569-3656
E-mail: scbryce@brycelegal.com
Website: www.brycelegal.com
Member: CDI, NRWA, PARW/CC
Certifications: CPRW, CP-OJSRM
Cover letters: 179, 182, 183

Beth Colley, Chesapeake Resume Writing Service
Phone: (410) 533-2457
E-mail: resume@chesres.com
Website: www.chesres.com
Member: NRWA
Certifications: CFJST, CPRW, CERW
Cover letters: 142, 283, 309

Norine Dagliano, ekm Inspirations
Phone: (301) 766-2032
E-mail: norine@ekminspirations.com
Website: www.ekminspirations.com
Member: NRWA
Certifications: NCRW, CPRW, CFRW/CC
Cover letters: 39, 40, 306

Lakeisha Mathews, MS
Assistant Director/Liaison for Graduate Students & Alumni
The Career Center, Loyola University Maryland
Phone: (410) 617-2233, (443) 928-7302
E-mail: lnmathews@loyola.edu, Lakeisha_21244@
 yahoo.com
Website: www.loyola.edu/thecareercenter
Member: PARW/CC
Certifications: CPRW, CPCC
Cover letter: 259

Massachusetts

Jean Cummings, MAT
A Resume For Today
Phone: (978) 254-5492
E-mail: jc@YesResumes.com
Website: www.aresumefortoday.com
Member: CDI, NRWA, PARW/CC
Certifications: CPRW, CPBS, CEIP
Cover letters: 94, 168, 193, 270, 301

Wendy Gelberg, MEd, CAS
Gentle Job Search/Advantage Resumes
Phone: (781) 444-0778
E-mail: wendy@gentlejobsearch.com
Website: www.gentlejobsearch.com
Member: NRWA
Certifications: JCTC, CEIP, CPRW
Cover letters: 11, 116, 149

Jeanne Knight
Phone: (617) 968-7747
E-mail: jeanne@careerdesigns.biz
Website: www.careerdesigns.biz
Member: CDI, NRWA
Certifications: JCTC, CCMC
Cover letter: 72

Joellyn Schwerdlin, Career-Success-Coach.com
Phone: (508) 459-2854
Website: www.career-success-coach.com
Member: CDI
Certifications: CPRW, JCTC
Cover letter: 286

Michigan

Janet L. Beckstrom, Word Crafter
Phone: (810) 232-9257
Toll-free: (800) 351-9818
E-mail: janet@wordcrafter.com
Website: www.wordcrafter.com
Member: PARW/CC
Certifications: ACRW, CPRW
Cover letters: 10, 15, 26, 52, 58, 93, 100, 132, 172, 198,
 211, 220, 241, 252
Resume: 2

Maria E. Hebda; Career Solutions, LLC
Phone: (734) 676-9170
E-mail: maria@writingresumes.com
Websites: www.WritingResumes.com
www.certifiedresumewriters.com
(Resource Guide)
Member: CDI, NRWA, PARW/CC, ICF
Certifications: CCMC, CPRW
Cover letters: 41, 97, 288

Jasmine Marchong, The Right Resume
Phone: (248) 957-8317
E-mail: jmarchong@therightresume.biz
Website: www.therightresume.biz
Member: NRWA
Cover letter: 64

Minnesota

Connie Hauer; CareerPro Services, LLC
Phone: (320) 260-6569
E-mail: chauer@mncareerpro.com
Website: www.mncareerpro.com
Member: NRWA, PARW/CC
Certification: CEIP
Cover letters: 134, 293
Resume: 7

Missouri

Sally McIntosh, Advantage Resumes in St. Louis
Phone: (314) 993-5400
Toll-free (888) 919-9909
E-mail: sally@reswriter.com
Website: www.reswriter.com
Member: CDI, NRWA
Certifications: NCRW, JCTC
Cover letter: 14

Montana

Cheryl Minnick, EdD; Career Counselor/Internship
 Coordinator
The University of Montana (Internship Services)
Phone: (406) 243-4614
E-mail: cminnick@mso.umt.edu
Website: www.umt.edu/internships
Member: NRWA
Certification: NCRW
Cover letters: 22, 76, 85

New Jersey

Carol A. Altomare, World Class Résumés
Phone: (908) 237-1883
E-mail: caa@worldclassresumes.com
Website: www.worldclassresumes.com
Member: CDI, PARW/CC
Certifications: MRW, CPRW, ACRW, CCMC, CJSS
Cover letters: 2, 48

Beverly Baskin, EdS, LPC
Mitchell I. Baskin, MS, PE
BBCS Counseling Services
Toll-free: (800) 300-4079
E-mail: bev@bbcscounseling.com
Websites: www.baskincareer.com and
   www.resumewriternj.com
Member: NCDA, NECA, MACCA, AMHCA, NJCA
Certifications: MA, NCCC, MCC, CPRW, CCHMC
Cover letters: 130, 157, 180, 295, 298

Laurie Berenson; Sterling Career Concepts, LLC
Phone: (201) 573-8282
E-mail: laurie@sterlingcareerconcepts.com
Website: www.sterlingcareerconcepts.com
Member: CDI, PARW/CC
Certification: CPRW
Cover letters: 8, 147, 169

Patricia Duckers; Prism Writing Services, LLC
Phone: (732) 860-8451
E-mail: pduckers@prismwritingservices.com
Website: www.PrismWritingServices.com
Member: CDI, PARW/CC
Certifications: CPRW, CRW, CEIP, CERW, MMRW,
   CFRW, MCD, CEIC, MFCC
Cover letter: 243

Jennifer Fishberg, EdM in Counseling
Career Karma Resume Development
Phone: (732) 421-2554
E-mail: jennifer@careerkarma.net
Website: www.careerkarma.net
Member: CDI, NRWA, PARW/CC
Cover letter: 54

Fran Kelley, MA; The Résumé Works
Phone: (201) 670-9643
E-mail: FranKelley@optonline.net
Website: www.careermuse.com
Member: NRWA, PARW/CC, SHRM
Certifications: CPRW, SPHR, JCTC
Cover letters: 277, 297

Melanie Noonan; Peripheral Pro, LLC
Phone: (973) 785-3011
E-mail: PeriPro1@aol.com
Member: NRWA, PARW/CC
Certification: CPS
Cover letters: 18, 28, 82, 91, 107, 120, 174, 187, 226,
   227, 232, 244, 247, 249, 296, 314, 315, 316
Resumes: 1, 3

Michelle A. Riklan; Riklan Resources, LLC
Phone: (732) 761-9940
Toll-free: (800) 540-3609
E-mail: Michelle@riklanresources.com
Website: www.riklanresources.com
Member: CDI, NRWA, PARW/CC, SHRM, ASTD
Certifications: CPRW, CEIC
Cover letter: 260

Igor Shpudejko, MBA; Career Focus
Phone: (201) 825-2865
E-mail: Ishpudejko@aol.com
Website: www.CareerInFocus.com
Member: PARW/CC
Certifications: CPRW, JCTC, BSIE
Cover letters: 4, 95

Debra Wheatman, Careers Done Write
Phone: (732) 444-2854
E-mail: debra@careersdonewrite.com
Website: www.careersdonewrite.com
Member: PARW/CC
Certifications: CPRW, CPCC
Cover letters: 34, 246

New York

Ann Baehr, Best Resumes of New York
Phone: (631) 224-9300
E-mail: resumesbest@earthlink.net
Website: www.e-bestresumes.com
Member: CDI, NRWA
Certification: CPRW
Cover letters: 71, 140, 175, 217, 262, 287

Karen Bartell, JD; Best-in-Class Résumés
Phone: (631) 704-3220
Toll-free: (800) 234-3569
E-mail: kbartell@bestclassresumes.com
Website: bestclassresumes.com
Member: CDI, PARW/CC
Certification: CPRW
Cover letters: 108, 152, 206
Resume: 6

Arnold G. Boldt, Arnold-Smith Associates
Phone: (585) 383-0350
E-mail: Arnie@ResumeSOS.com
Website: www.NoNonsenseCareers.com
Member: CDI, NRWA, PARW/CC
Certifications: CPRW, JCTC
Cover letters: 165, 237

Kristin M. Coleman, Custom Career Services
Phone: (845) 452-8274
E-mail: kristin@colemancareerservices.com
Cover letters: 62, 81, 231

Deb Dib, Executive Power Brand
Phone: (631) 475-8513
E-mail: DebDib@ExecutivePowerBrand.com
Website: www.executivepowerbrand.com
Member: CDI, NRWA, NAFE
Certifications: CG3C, CPBS, CCMC, NCRW, CPRW,
 CEIP, JCTC, COIS
Cover letters: 21, 60, 148, 189

Donna M. Farrise; Dynamic Resumes of Long Island, Inc.
Phone: (631) 951-4120
E-mail: donna@dynamicresumes.com
Website: www.dynamicresumes.com
Certification: JCTC
Cover letters: 115, 141, 166, 284, 285

John Femia, BS; Custom Résumé & Writing Service
Phone: (518) 357-8181
E-mail: customresume@nycap.rr.com
Website: customresumewriting.com
Member: PARW/CC
Certification: CPRW
Cover letters: 56, 114

Linda Matias, CareerStrides
Phone: (631) 456-5051
E-mail: linda@careerstrides.com
Website: www.careerstrides.com
Member: NRWA
Certifications: NCRW, CIC, JCTC
Cover letter: 65

Barbara Safani, MA; Career Solvers
Phone: (212) 579-7730
E-mail: info@careersolvers.com
Website: www.careersolvers.com
Member: CDI, NRWA
Certifications: CPRW, CERW, CCM
Cover letter: 23

North Carolina

Dayna Feist, Gatehouse Business Services
Phone: (828) 254-7893
E-mail: dayna@bestjobever.com
Website: www.bestjobever.com
Member: CDI, NRWA, PARW/CC
Certifications: CPRW, JCTC, CEIP
Cover letter: 86

Sharon McCormick, MS
Sharon McCormick Expert Career & HR Consulting, LLC
Phone: (919) 424-1244
E-mail: careertreasure@gmail.com
Website: www.careertreasure.com
Certifications: GCDF, CCM, CCMC, CLTMC, DCC,
 CDRCA, CFSESW, MCC, M-BQP, NCCC, NCC, CPRW
Cover letter: 25

Doug Morrison, Career Power
Phone: (704) 365-0773
E-mail: dmpwresume@aol.com
Website: www.CareerPowerResume.com
Member: CDI
Certification: CPRW
Cover letters: 7, 117, 138, 278, 303

Kelly Welch, YES Career Services
Phone: (919) 744-8866
E-mail: kelly@yescareerservices.com
Website: www.yescareerservices.com
Member: CDI
Certifications: MHRM, GPHR, ACC, CPBS, CLTMC,
 CCMC, COIS
Cover letters: 106, 113, 312

Ohio

Melissa L. Kasler, Resume Impressions
Phone: (740) 592-3993
E-mail: resumeimpressions@frontier.net
Website: www.resumeimpressions.com
Member: PARW/CC
Certification: CPRW
Cover letters: 61, 69, 291, 307

Nicole Niemeyer, MBA
Phone: (419) 302-5741
E-mail: Niemeyer_nicole2@yahoo.com
Member: PARW/CCI
Certification: CPRW
Cover letter: 185

Teena Rose, Resume to Referral
Phone: (937) 325-2149
E-mail: admin@resumetoreferral.com
Website: www.resumebycprw.com
Member: CDI
Certifications: CPRW, CEIP, CCM
Cover letters: 162, 281

Janice Worthington (with Jason and Jeremy Worthington)
 Worthington Career Services
Phone: (614) 890-1645
Toll-free: (877) 9RESUME (973-7863)
E-mail: Janice@WorthingtonCareers.com
Website: www.worthingtoncareers.com
Member: CDI, PARW/CC
Certifications: CPRW, JCTC, CEIP
Cover letter: 200

Oregon

Karen Conway, Premier Resumes
Phone: (541) 382-8422
E-mail: premierResume@aol.com
Member: PARW/CC
Certifications: CPRW, CEIP
Cover letters: 67, 124, 129, 191, 230

Pennsylvania

Jane Roqueplot, JaneCo's Sensible Solutions
Phone: (724) 528-1000
Toll-free: (888) JANECOS (526-3267)
E-mail: janeir@janecos.com
Website: www.janecos.com
Member: CDI, NRWA, PARW/CC
Certifications: CPBA, CECC, CWDP
Cover letters: 37, 45, 131, 170, 173, 177, 178, 186, 203, 236, 245, 248, 255, 276

Rhode Island

Edward Turilli, MA; AccuWriter Resume Service
Phone: (401) 268-3020
(For full listing, see Florida)

Texas

Devon Benish, OMG! Resumes
Phone: (210) 599-1913
E-mail: 8seconds@omgresumes.com
Website: omgresumes.com
Member: PARW/CC
Certification: CPRW
Cover letters: 16, 42, 89

Daniel J. Dorotik Jr., 100PercentResumes
Phone: (806) 783-9900
E-mail: dan@100percentresumes.com
Website: www.100percentresumes.com
Member: NRWA
Certification: NCRW
Cover letters: 55, 123, 155, 161, 163, 197, 251, 280

Utah

Amy L. Adler, MBA, MA; Inscribe Express
Phone: (801) 810-JOBS (5627)
E-mail: aadler@inscribeexpress.com
Website: www.inscribeexpress.com
Certification: CARW
Cover letters: 144, 242
Resume: 8

Donna Allen, Resumes by Donna
Phone: (435) 640-1800
E-mail: dallen.heber@gmail.com
Certification: CPRW
Cover letters: 33, 46, 153, 265, 317
Resume: 5

Virginia

Kara Varner, A Platinum Resume
Phone: (719) 339-2659
E-mail: varnervsionmedia@yahoo.com
Website: aplatinumresume.com
Certifications: MAOM, EAPC
Cover letters: 43, 222

Washington

Janice M. Shepherd, Write On Career Keys
Phone: (360) 738-7958
E-mail: janice@writeoncareerkeys.com
Website: www.writeoncareerkeys.com
Certifications: CPRW, JCTC, CEIP
Cover letter: 196

Wisconsin

Susan Guarneri, MS; Guarneri Associates
Phone: (715) 546-4449
Toll-free: (866) 881-4055
E-mail: susan@AssessmentGoddess.com
Website: www.assessmentgoddess.com
Member: CDI, PARW/CC, CTL
Certifications: MRW, CERW, CPRW, JCTC, CEIP, COIS, CMBS, NCC, NCCC, MCC, DCC, CG3C, CCMC
Cover letters: 201, 208, 275

Professional Organizations

If you are interested in working with a professional resume writer, the following organizations can provide more information:

Career Directors International (CDI)
Phone: (321) 752-0442
Toll-free: (888) 867-7972
E-mail: info@careerdirectors.com
Website: www.careerdirectors.com

National Résumé Writers' Association (NRWA)
Toll-free: (877) THE-NRWA or (877) 843-6792
Website: www.thenrwa.com

Professional Association of Résumé Writers & Career Coaches (PARW/CC)
Toll-free: (800) 822-7279
E-mail: PARWhq@aol.com
Website: www.parw.com

Occupation Index

Note: The following entries reflect the positions indicated in the captions for the cover letters. The numbers are cover letter numbers in the Gallery, not page numbers.